Computers and Information Systems: An Introduction

Computers and Information Systems: An Introduction

WILLIAM S. DAVIS
MIAMI UNIVERSITY–OXFORD, OHIO

COURSE
TECHNOLOGY

ONE MAIN STREET, CAMBRIDGE, MA 02142

an International Thomson Publishing company I(T)P®

Cambridge • Albany • Bonn • Boston • Cincinnati • London • Madrid • Melbourne • Mexico City
New York • Paris • San Francisco • Singapore • Tokyo • Toronto • Washington

Computer Information Systems: An Introduction

Copyeditor	Sheryl Rose
Composition	Hespenheide Design
Text Design	Hespenheide Design
Illustration	Miyake Illustration, Hespenheide Design
Cover Image	© Tony Stone Images
Cover Design	Hespenheide Design

Production, Prepress, Printing, and Binding by West Publishing Company

Photo Credits follow the Index

© 1997 by Course Technology—I(T)P®

For more information contact:

Course Technology
One Main Street
Cambridge, MA 02142

ITP Europe
Berkshire House 168-173
High Holborn
London WCIV 7AA
England

Nelson ITP, Australia
102 Dodds Street
South Melbourne, 3205
Victoria, Australia

ITP Nelson Canada
1120 Birchmount Road
Scarborough, Ontario
Canada M1K 5G4

International Thomson Editores
Seneca, 53
Colonia Polanco
11560 Mexico D.F. Mexico

ITP GmbH
Königswinterer Strasse 418
53227 Bonn
Germany

ITP Asia
60 Albert Street, #15-01
Albert Complex
Singapore 189969

ITP Japan
Hirakawacho Kyowa Building, 3F
2-2-1 Hirakawacho
Chiyoda-ku, Tokyo 102
Japan

ISBN 0-314-09724-4

Printed in the United States of America

2 3 4 5 6 7 8 9 01 00 99 98

DEDICATION

TO CATHY

CONTENTS IN BRIEF

CONTENTS

16. APPLICATIONS   359

PREFACE

As the title implies, *Computers and Information Systems: An Introduction* is designed to support an introductory course in information systems. It assumes no prior computer experience and no mathematics beyond high school algebra.

FLEXIBILITY

Like most introductory texts, this book covers all the crucial concepts, but what makes it unique is its flexibility. The material is divided into three sections:

Part I: Introduction	A one-chapter overview of basic computer components.
Part II: Components	Chapters 2 through 10. Each chapter focuses on a single component.
Part III: Systems	Chapters 11 through 16. Each chapter shows how two or more components are combined to form a system.

After the student completes Chapter 1, the Part II chapters can be read in any order; they are written to be independent. Relevant material from Part II (clearly identified at the beginning of each chapter) should be read before the related topics in Part III, but a student need not *complete* Part II before beginning Part III. Except for the link to Part II, the chapters in Part III are independent; they too can be read in any order.

The book also contains five brief (six- to ten-page) *Spotlights* on:

- The Internet, following Chapter 1
- Internet Software Tools, following Chapter 7
- Computers and Privacy, following Chapter 9
- Internet Technology, following Chapter 14
- Computer Crime and System Security, following Chapter 15

Like the chapters, the *Spotlights* are independent and can be read in any order. Separating these topics from the chapter narratives allows the instructor to cover Internet concepts and social issues at any time.

THE INTERNET

Given the Internet's increasing importance, many instructors have added Internet activities to the information systems course. The *Spotlight* following Chapter 1 provides a brief introduction to the Internet. Placing this material with Chapter 1 allows the instructor to overview local Internet access procedures early in the term and assign Internet projects throughout the course.

At the end of each chapter is a set of *Internet Projects* keyed to the chapter material. The projects fall into three categories:

- *News and Notes*   References to product announcements and relevant issues.
- *Topic Searches*   A list of relevant key terms and qualifiers that support Internet searches.
- *Links to Other Sites*   A list of relevant World Wide Web sites and USENET newsgroups.

Once students learn the basics of their local search and navigation tools, they should have little difficulty following these pointers to find interesting information. For example, the *Internet Projects* at the end of Chapter 2 tell the student where to find information on computer-related job opportunities.

One problem with Internet-based projects is currency; simply put, technology (particularly the Internet) changes so quickly that today's state-of-the-art is tomorrow's old news. Consequently, West Educational Publishing maintains a World Wide Web home page. Students and instructors are welcome to access this book's entry on the home page, where more current versions of the Internet projects are listed.

Finally, spread throughout the book are numerous in-chapter entries that link various topics to the Internet. Many of these references appear in the primary narrative; for example, see the Information Superhighway in Chapter 1 and Client/Server Computing in Chapter 14. Other references are presented in feature boxes; for example, see the discussions about Java (Chapter 8), the National Information Infrastructure (Chapter 14), and telecommuting (Chapter 16). Also, Appendix B contains a list of interesting USENET and World Wide Web addresses, a convenient starting point for student browsing.

FEATURES

Looking beyond content and organization, *Computers and Information Systems: An Introduction* contains several features designed to make learning easier:

- *Before you start.* Except for Chapter 1, each chapter begins with a list of key concepts the student should understand before he or she starts reading. These references help to ensure that the student has the necessary background.
- *After you finish.* Each chapter begins with a list of learning objectives designed to help the student focus on the key ideas.
- *Advanced Topics.* These boxes are designed to provide a bit more technical depth on selected topics. Examples include pipelining (Chapter 4), the FAT chain (Chapter 6), inheritance (Chapter 8), and bus standards (Chapter 11).
- *Feature boxes.* Spread throughout each chapter are feature boxes that supplement or illustrate specific chapter topics. There are four types of boxes:

  - *Issues.* The social and ethical implications of computers and information systems. These boxes expose the student to less technical issues and can serve as springboards for class discussion. Examples include downsizing and outsourcing (Chapter 2), software piracy (Chapter 7), and networks and the copyright law (Chapter 14).

- *Notes.* Comments and real-world examples, such as how to read the codes on a check (Chapter 3), surge protection (Chapter 4), caring for your diskettes (Chapter 5), and file backup (Chapter 9). These notes help the student relate the chapter material to the real world.
- *People.* Brief sketches of some of the people who helped to shape modern information technology, including Mauchly and Eckert, the creators of the first electronic digital computer (Chapter 1); Bill Gates and Paul Allen, the founders of Microsoft (Chapter 6); Grace Hopper, the driving force behind the COBOL language (Chapter 8); Steven Jobs and Steve Wozniak, the founders of Apple Corporation (Chapter 11); and computer science pioneer Alan Turing (Chapter 16).
- *The Future.* Where is information technology going? These boxes are designed to give students a sense of how evolving technology will affect them in the near future. Examples include information haves and have-nots (Chapter 2), the Java programming language (Chapter 8), mobile communication (Chapter 13), and the National Information Infrastructure (Chapter 14).

- *Chapter summaries, key term lists,* and *concepts questions.* These three features are designed to provide the student with a thorough review of the chapter material. Note that the concepts questions parallel the chapter learning objectives.
- *Projects.* Suggestions for hands-on and research-oriented activities. Many of the projects are designed to encourage the student to discover that people really do use the technology described in the chapter.
- *Internet Projects.* A set of projects that invite the student to access the Internet for information that supports or expands upon the chapter material. More current Internet activities can be found by accessing West Educational Publishing's World Wide Web site; see the *Spotlight* on The Internet following Chapter 1 for detailed instructions.

SUPPLEMENTS

Additionally, numerous supplements accompany the book, including:

- An *instructor's manual* written by the textbook author and Patricia Roy of Manatee Community College. Both printed and electronic copies are available.
- A *test bank* prepared by the textbook author and Patricia Roy of Manatee Community College. Both printed and electronic copies are available.
- *WESTEST* test-preparation software.
- *Internet updates* available on the World Wide Web at *http://www.westpub.com/Educate*

- A *student study guide* written by Jonathan Trower of Baylor University. The study guide includes a chapter outline, chapter summary, true/false and multiple-choice questions, vocabulary drills, and essay questions. Many students will find the study guide an invaluable aid when preparing for exams.
- A *set of transparency masters* for the book's figures.
- A *PowerPoint presentation* prepared by Anita Steinbacher of Indiana Vocational Technical College. Instructors will find the PowerPoint slides a useful lecture supplement and an additional source of transparency masters.
- *West's Information Systems for Managers Video Series.* Video #1 features a Business Profile on First Bank System's information systems and ten-minute features on Boeing's computer services and American Greeting's information processing control center. Video #2 features four-minute profiles on thirteen Blue Chip companies. Video #3 contains Business Profiles on the information systems of the Minnesota Twins, PriceCosto, and IBAX.
- *Insights: Readings in Information Systems,* a readings book for instructors who wish to supplement text assignments with readings from such sources as *Business Week, FORBES, FORTUNE, BYTE,* and *The Wall Street Journal.*

Contact your West campus representative for additional details.

MICROCOMPUTER APPLICATIONS

Many schools teach microcomputer skills in the context of the introductory information systems course. West's *Understanding and Using Microcomputers* series includes low-cost application manuals that cover the most popular software and Internet tools. Custom versions are available through West's Microcomputer Custom Editions Program. The program offers instructors the flexibility to choose tutorials (available in up to three different module lengths) for a wide range of packages, including Netscape Navigator 3.0, the Internet, Microsoft Windows 95, Microsoft Office for Windows 95, Microsoft Excel for Windows 95, and WordPerfect for Windows. The selected materials are spiral-bound to create an easy-to-use lab manual. See your West campus representative or check West's World Wide Web home page for additional details.

ACKNOWLEDGMENTS

Rick Leyh, my editor, was instrumental in getting this project off the ground, and it was a pleasure to work with Sara Schroeder, my developmental editor. Jayne Lindesmith (production editor), Sheryl Rose (copy editor), and Gary Hespenheide of Hespenheide Design did an excellent job of converting my manuscript into a finished book. Finally, I would like to thank the reviewers listed below for their many valuable insights and suggestions.

William S. Davis
Sarasota, Florida

REVIEWERS

Frank Andera
Central Michigan University

Warren Boe
University of Iowa

Elvin Campbell
Golden West College

Eli Cohen
University of Wollongong

Terry Duke
University of Texas at El Paso

Karen Forcht
James Madison University

James Frost
Idaho State University

Jeff Guan
University of Louisville

Sallyann Hanson
Mercer County Community College

Alanson Hertzberg
Consumnes River College

Herman Hoplin
Syracuse University

Betsy Hoppe
Wake Forest University

Chris House
Southern Union State College

Peter Irwin
Richland Community College

K. Gregory Jin
Western Connecticut State University

Jeffrey Johnson
Utah State University

Willard Korn
University of Wisconsin-Eau Claire

Mary Meredith
University of Southwestern Louisiana

George Novotny
Ferris State University

Elizabeth Pierce
Indiana University of Pennsylvania

Jane Ritter
University of Oregon

Kirk Scott
The College of St. Scholastica

Robert Sindt
Johnson County Community College

Patricia Stans
University of New Mexico

Tim Sylvester
Glendale Community College

John Warns
Albuquerque Technical and Vocational Institute

PART I

INTRODUCTION

Chapter 1 provides you with:

► A brief introduction to the essential concepts you will need to know before you read subsequent chapters.

► A detailed overview of computers and information technology that will help you visualize how the individual components covered in subsequent chapters fit together.

Once you finish Chapter 1, you can read the Part II chapters in any order.

The *Spotlight* following Chapter 1 introduces several important Internet concepts, including Internet addresses, electronic mail, USENET, and the World Wide Web.

What Is a Computer?

When you finish reading this chapter, you should be able to:

▶ Distinguish between data and information.

▶ Define the term *computer* and identify the primary components of a computer.

▶ Distinguish among hardware, software, and data.

▶ Explain the input/process/output cycle.

▶ Explain why secondary storage is necessary.

▶ Distinguish among microcomputers, minicomputers, and mainframes.

▶ Explain what a network is and why networks are valuable.

▶ Briefly discuss the Internet and the evolving information superhighway.

THE INFORMATION AGE

A generation ago, a young college graduate looked forward to a lifelong career with his or her first employer. Times have changed. Today's graduates are likely to face a period of temporary work before launching a career, and they will probably change careers several times before they retire.

One thing is certain, however: Your future will be shaped by technology. You will use a computer, you will access the information superhighway, and those who cannot (or will not) learn how will have difficulty competing. We live in an information age.

The purpose of this book is to help you learn about computers and information technology. It is written for beginners and assumes no prior knowledge. It is designed to make it easy for you to find the specific information you need.

Let's get started.

DATA AND INFORMATION

Imagine a patient with a stomachache visiting a doctor. The problem might be the flu, food poisoning, overeating, an ulcer, appendicitis, or any of dozens of other causes. The wrong treatment can be dangerous, so the doctor's first task is to identify the problem's most likely cause. To do that, he or she collects data about the patient's symptoms and then combines the data to generate information (Figure 1.1).

▲ FIGURE 1.1

Information is derived from data.

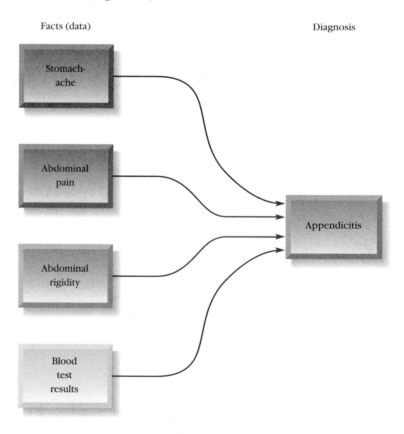

Facts (data)   Diagnosis

5

Evidence and Proof

Most detective stories start with a crime. The police respond by collecting evidence, but the identity of the guilty party remains a mystery. Bit by bit, however, the hero begins to piece together the evidence, recognizing patterns, following leads, and asking probing questions. Then comes the climax—that one last piece of evidence that proves the case.

The evidence (a fingerprint, a hair, a carpet fiber, a footprint, a background noise) consists of facts, or data. By themselves those facts mean very little. The only way to convict the guilty party is to reduce the uncertainty concerning his or her identity by showing the jury exactly what the facts mean "beyond a reasonable doubt." The police collect data. The jury needs information. The detective processes the data, extracts the meaning, and generates the information.

Data are facts, individual observations. **Information** is the meaning that human beings assign to or extract from data. Information is useful to the decision maker because it helps to reduce uncertainty. In the medical example, information increases the probability that the doctor will make the correct diagnosis and thus prescribe the right treatment.

Note that information is *assigned to* or *extracted from* data. Those verbs imply that some action is involved. Information does not simply spring into being by magic. Assigning meaning to and extracting meaning from data takes work.

One way to extract the meaning from data is to process them. **Data processing** involves performing calculations, combining, selecting, filtering, summarizing, and otherwise manipulating data in an attempt to clarify the underlying patterns. Figure 1.2 lists several common data processing operations.

Simply put, a **computer** is a machine that processes data into information. The data are the raw materials. Computers are valuable because they are tools for generating, storing, organizing, analyzing, and disseminating information, and information is valuable.

Data
Facts.
Information
The meaning that human beings assign to or extract from data.

Data processing
Performing calculations, selecting, filtering, summarizing, and otherwise manipulating data in an attempt to clarify underlying patterns.

Computer
An information processing machine.

Collect	Compute	Group, or categorize
Input, or read	Add	Merge
Output, or write	Subtract	Store, or save
Verify	Multiply	Record
Compare	Divide	Retrieve
Count	Sort	Update
Summarize	Select	Reformat
Tabulate		

▲ **FIGURE 1.2**

Some data processing operations.

COMPUTERS

A computer can perform arithmetic and make simple logical decisions. It can manipulate characters, numbers, and images. It can store data and information and retrieve them on demand.

So can you; there is nothing magical about a computer. However, because it is an electronic machine, a computer can perform those functions at incredible speed and with almost perfect accuracy.

The next several pages outline a computer's key components; you will find additional details in Part II.

The User

User
The person who needs data or information.

The **user** is the person who needs the information generated by the computer. Most users directly access a computer, but some do not; for example, a business manager who deals only with printed, computer-generated information is still a user. Some experts prefer to call someone who works *directly* with a computer an end user, but this book will treat user and end user as synonyms.

Hardware

Hardware
A general term for a computer's physical components.
Input device
A hardware component used to input data to a computer.
Output device
A hardware component used to output data and results from a computer.

Hardware is a general term for a computer's *physical* components (Figure 1.3). The hardware is the part of the computer you can see.

PERIPHERALS
Input devices, such as a keyboard and a mouse (Figure 1.3), allow users to enter data to the computer. **Output devices,** such as a display screen, a printer, and a speaker, provide a means for people to get data or information

▲ FIGURE 1.3

The hardware associated with a typical computer.

I S S U E S

Ergonomics

Recently, there has been considerable controversy surrounding the potential health risks associated with video display screens. Some studies suggest that prolonged exposure to the radiation that leaks from these devices can be dangerous, particularly to pregnant women.

There are other concerns, too. Staring at a computer screen can cause eyestrain and headaches. Long periods of typing or using a mouse can lead to carpal tunnel syndrome and similar repetitive stress injuries, and prolonged sitting can be dangerous (again, particularly for pregnant women).

Ergonomics is an applied science that studies and attempts to improve the fit between people, their tools, and their work environments. Over the past several years, various ergonomic studies and the application of ergonomic principles have contributed to the development of screens that offer reduced radiation leakage and a sharper image with less flicker.

Although few schools offer a major in ergonomics, you might be able to find some courses; check with such departments as industrial engineering, psychology, management, human resources, and consumer science. A basic understanding of ergonomics is valuable no matter what your major might be.

from a computer. Secondary storage devices, such as disk drives and CD-ROM drives, hold large amounts of data and information in an electronic form. Because the input and output devices are external to the computer, they are sometimes called **peripherals.**

INSIDE THE COMPUTER

The box just under the display screen in Figure 1.3 is sometimes called the system unit; the computer itself, along with other internal components, is inside that box. You can see the components if you remove the system unit's cover (Figure 1.4).

The basic building blocks of modern computers are tiny integrated circuit **chips** (Figure 1.5). To make the chips easier to handle they are usually mounted on **boards** (Figure 1.6). The boards are then linked electronically to form the computer.

Internally, a computer is a **binary,** or two-state machine that stores and manipulates 1/0 (yes/no, on/off) patterns. For example, picture a light switch. Depending on how the switch is set, the light can be either on (1) or off (0). Each switch holds a single *b*inary dig*it*, or **bit.** The computer works by manipulating bits.

Peripheral
A hardware component that is external to the computer.

Chip
The basic electronic component of a modern computer.

Board
A hardware component that holds numerous related chips.

Binary
A number system that uses two digits, 0 and 1.

Bit
A binary digit.

▲ FIGURE 1.4

Inside the system unit.

▲ FIGURE 1.5

An integrated circuit chip.

▲ FIGURE 1.6

A typical circuit board.

PEOPLE

**John W. Mauchly and
J. Presper Eckert**

The computer age dawned on February 14, 1946, when a computer named the ENIAC was publicly introduced at the University of Pennsylvania. Built by a team of scientists and engineers headed by John W. Mauchly and J. Presper Eckert, the ENIAC weighed thirty tons, stood ten feet tall, and dominated a large room. Today, you may have one of its descendants on your desktop.

After leaving the university, Mauchly and Eckert started a company to manufacture and sell a new computer they called the UNIVAC. During the 1952 presidential election, CBS arranged to have one of the early UNIVAC computers programmed to accept partial voting returns and predict the outcome. The political experts expected a close race, but the UNIVAC projected an Eisenhower landslide. The computer was right and, as a result of that television exposure, computing machines, for the very first time, became a part of popular culture.

When data are input to a computer they are converted to binary form and stored in **memory** (Figure 1.7). A computer's memory consists of a bank of **RAM** (random access memory) chips; in fact, the acronym RAM is sometimes used as a synonym for main memory. A typical computer has enough memory to hold millions of bits.

Once the data are in memory, they can be processed. The **processor** (Figure 1.7) is the component that processes or manipulates the data.

Software

A **program** is a set of **instructions** that tells a computer exactly what to do. Each instruction represents a single operation—add, subtract, compare, and so on. **Software** is a general term for programs.

Hardware is *not* intelligent; it cannot decide independently when to add, or subtract, or request input. Consequently, before a computer can do

Memory
The hardware component on which data and results are held or stored inside a computer.
RAM
Acronym for random access memory.
Processor
The component that manipulates the data.

Program
A set of instructions that guides a computer through a process.
Instruction
One step in a program.
Software
A general term for programs.

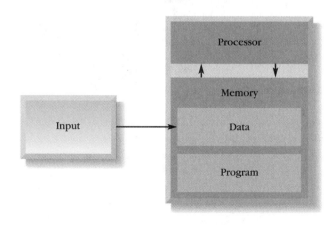

▲ **FIGURE 1.7**

Both the data and the program that controls the processor are stored in memory.

Stored program
A program that is physically stored in the memory of the computer it controls.
Computer
A machine that processes data into information under the control of a stored program.
Application software
Software that performs end-user tasks.

System software
Software that directly controls and manages the computer's hardware.
Windows 95
An operating system developed by Microsoft Corporation that features a graphic user interface.
Operating system
System software that defines a platform or operating environment for writing and executing application programs.

Byte
A group of eight bits that can hold a single character.

anything, a program must first be stored in memory (Figure 1.7). This **stored program** controls the **computer** and allows it to function without human intervention, and that is what distinguishes a computer from a calculator. *A computer is a machine that processes data into information under the control of a stored program.*

Application software allows a user to do something, such as play a game, write a paper, perform a statistical analysis, or create an accounting report. Users typically access a computer through an application program.

System software, in contrast, directly controls and manages the computer's hardware. A good example is **Windows 95,** a popular **operating system** that sits between the application program and the hardware (Figure 1.8) and performs such tasks as loading application programs into memory and controlling peripheral devices. Application programs communicate with the hardware through the operating system.

Data

The other key element of any computer application is data. Hardware processes data. Software controls the hardware. The data are the raw materials. Without data there is nothing to process.

The most elementary unit of data that can be stored in a computer is a single binary digit, or bit. On most computers the bits are grouped to form 8-bit units called **bytes.** When you read an advertisement about a computer, its memory capacity is typically stated in kilobytes (KB, or thousands of

▲ FIGURE 1.8

The operating system sits between the application program and the hardware.

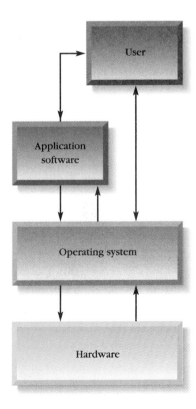

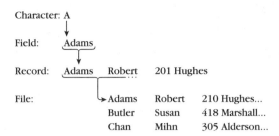

▲ **FIGURE 1.9**

The relationship between characters, fields, records, and files.

bytes), megabytes (MB, or millions of bytes), or even gigabytes (GB, or billions of bytes).

Each byte can hold a single character. Characters are grouped to form logically meaningful units of data called **fields** (Figure 1.9). A set of related fields is called a **record.** A set of related records forms a **file.**

For example, consider a telephone book. Your name, your street address, and your telephone number are all fields. Taken together, those three fields form a single record that holds all the data that pertain to you. The telephone book is a file that holds many similar records, one for each local telephone subscriber.

A **database** is a set of one or more related files. For example, consider the relationship between your school's student, course, and registration files (Figure 1.10). The student file holds data about students. The course file holds data about courses. The registration file links students to courses. Together, those three files can be used to provide a complete set of information on all the courses taken by a given student or on all the students taking a given course.

Field
A group of related characters.
Record
A group of related fields
File
A group of related records.

Database
A set of related files.

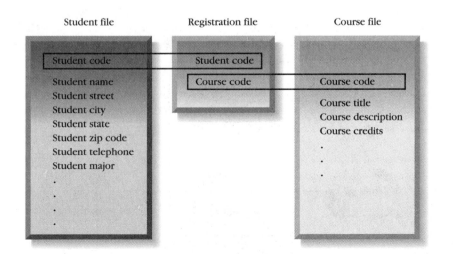

▲ **FIGURE 1.10**

A database is set of related files.

Note that not all data follow the field/record/file/database hierarchy. You will learn about other ways to organize data in subsequent chapters.

The Input/Process/Output Cycle

Picture a program in memory and processing data (Figure 1.11). It cannot process data it does not yet have, so the program's first task is to request data from an input device (1). After the data are read and transferred into memory, subsequent steps in the program tell the processor to manipulate the data (2) and store the results back into memory (3). Finally, the results are sent to an output device (4). That standard **input/process/output cycle** is common to virtually every computer application.

Long-Term Storage

In chemistry, a volatile compound is one that evaporates easily. A computer's memory is considered **volatile** because it loses its contents when power is cut. For example, if you turn off your computer or lose power in an electrical storm, everything stored in memory is lost.

Secondary storage, in contrast, is *not* volatile; it does not lose its contents when power is cut. Consequently, secondary storage serves as the computer's long-term storage. Magnetic **disk** is the most common type of secondary storage.

For example, imagine that you are half finished writing a term paper and for some reason you must interrupt your work. The document is in memory, and if you turn off the computer you will lose that document. Instead, you copy (save) the work from memory to secondary storage (Figure 1.12a). Then you turn off the computer. Later, you copy (load) the partially completed document from secondary storage back into memory (Figure 1.12b) and continue working.

Application programs typically reside on secondary storage and are loaded into memory only when they are being executed. Files and databases also reside on secondary storage, and only the data actually being processed are transferred into memory. Memory holds *active* programs and data. Secondary storage is long-term storage.

Input/process/output cycle
The standard cycle of an application program in which data are input, processed, and the results output.

Volatile
Easily changed.

Secondary storage
A nonvolatile form of supplemental memory.
Disk
The most common type of secondary storage.

▲ FIGURE 1.11

The input/process/output cycle.

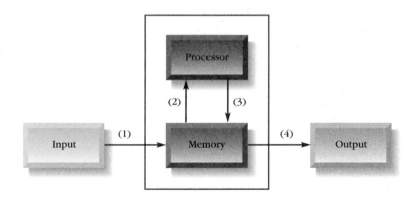

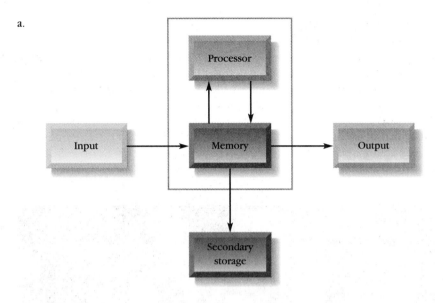

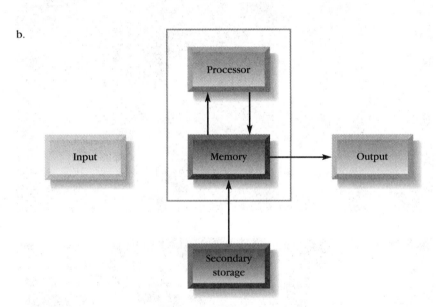

▲ **FIGURE 1.12**

To avoid losing your work:
a. **You save the work to secondary storage.**
b. **Later, you load the work back into memory.**

COMPUTER SYSTEMS

A computer's components cannot function independently; at a minimum you need hardware, software, data, and people (for example, a user) to have a meaningful application. A **system** is a set of components that work together to accomplish an objective.

An **information system** is composed of hardware, software, data, people, and procedures. The purpose of an information system is to deliver the right data and the right information to the right people at the right time. Information systems are discussed in more depth in Part III.

System
A set of components that work together to accomplish an objective.
Information system
A set of hardware, software, data, human, and procedural components intended to provide the right data and information to the right person at the right time.

Classifying Computers

Perhaps you have heard people distinguish among microcomputers, mini-computers, and mainframes. They define different types of computers.

A **microcomputer,** sometimes called a **personal computer,** is a small, relatively inexpensive machine designed to be used by one person at a time. A desktop computer (Figure 1.13), as the name implies, is a personal computer that fits on a desktop. On some powerful microcomputers, the system unit is configured as a tower that (typically) sits alongside or on a desk (Figure 1.14). Laptop and notebook computers (Figure 1.15) are small, light-

Microcomputer
A computer built around a single-chip microprocessor.

Personal computer
A microcomputer system designed to be used by one person at a time.

▲ FIGURE 1.13

A desktop computer.

▲ FIGURE 1.14

A tower computer.

weight, portable machines that can be carried in a briefcase and (literally) used on a laptop, and even smaller hand-held computers called **personal digital assistants** (PDAs) are available (Figure 1.16).

    A **mainframe** (Figure 1.17) is a large, expensive computer that allows multiple users to concurrently access an organization's central database. A

Personal digital assistant (PDA)
A hand-held electronic device that integrates several personal productivity tools.

Mainframe
A large, relatively expensive computer used to support information processing at the corporate level.

▲ **FIGURE 1.15**

A laptop computer.

▲ **FIGURE 1.16**

A personal digital assistant (PDA).

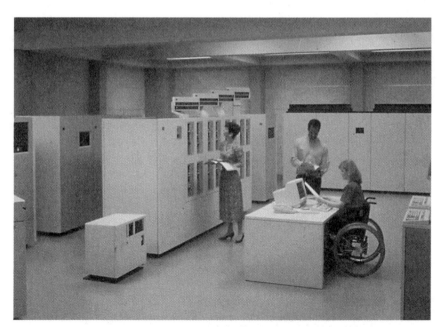

▲ **FIGURE 1.17**

A typical mainframe.

Minicomputer
A mid-size computer that is often used to support the computing needs of a department or an office.

Supercomputer
The most powerful class of computers.

minicomputer (Figure 1.18), as the name implies, is a mid-sized machine that might be used to support a single department or a division of an organization. The most powerful computers, called **supercomputers,** are used to support applications that call for high-speed computation, such as weather forecasting and scientific experimentation.

Technology is constantly changing, and the dividing line between microcomputers, minicomputers, mainframes, and supercomputers is hazy at best. View these terms as guidelines, not absolutes.

▲ **FIGURE 1.18**

Minicomputers support a single department or a division of an organization.

NOTE

Your First Computer

If you do not currently own a personal computer, the odds are very good that you soon will. Unfortunately, with so many choices available, selecting the right computer can be confusing.

Start by listing the tasks you plan to perform with your computer. Next, identify the application software you will need to support those tasks. Every application program is designed to work with a specific operating system, so make sure all your application programs are compatible with the *same* operating system.

Once you have identified your operating system and your applications, their memory, secondary storage, and processor requirements will define a minimum configuration for your computer. Remember that application programs are constantly being updated, and they keep getting bigger. Also, as you become more comfortable with your computer you will discover new applications, so allow room for expansion. The bottom line is: Buy the fastest processor and all the memory and secondary storage you can afford.

Networks

The purpose of an information system is to make data and information available where, when, and to whom they are needed. Often, that means linking computers electronically so they can communicate with each other. A **network** consists of two or more computers linked by communication lines (Figure 1.19).

A **client/server** network makes it easy to share software, hardware, and data. The idea is to implement a key resource (a database, a program, a high-speed printer) on one computer called the **server.** Subsequently, the other computers on the network (the clients) access the resource through the server.

For example, many schools link student microcomputers to a network. Instead of providing each student with a copy of each program, the software is downloaded (or copied) on request to the student (client) machines from the server. Instead of providing an expensive printer for each student computer, the network allows numerous computers to share the server's printer. Instead of providing each student with a list of data to be input, an instructor can store the data on the server and allow the students to access them electronically.

The Internet

The **Internet** is today's best known network. Originally developed to support military and academic research, the Internet is really a network of networks that links colleges, universities, corporations, government agencies,

Network
Two or more computers linked by communication lines.
Client/server computing
A form of computing in which key tasks are assigned to different computers in a network.
Server
A computer that provides a service on a network.

Internet
A well-known, widely accessed, worldwide network of networks.

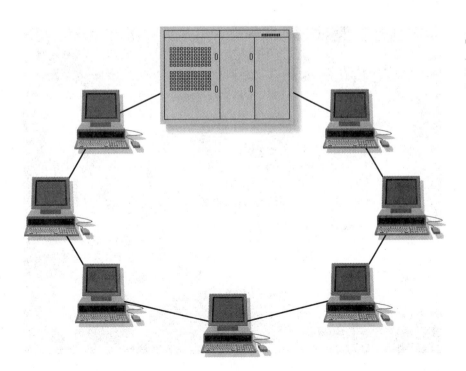

▲ **FIGURE 1.19**

A network consists of two or more computers linked by communication lines.

and research centers throughout the world (Figure 1.20). Recently, companies that provide on-line services have brought Internet access to individual home computers.

See the *Spotlight* section immediately following this chapter for more on the Internet and the World Wide Web. See also the list of newsgroups and World Wide Web home pages in Appendix B.

The Information Superhighway

Information superhighway
A merger of today's computing, television, and communication technologies that promises to dwarf existing information services.

Today's Internet is widely viewed as a prototype for the **information superhighway,** an evolving international network that promises to change the way we live, work, and play. Although much of what you read about the information superhighway is hype, it is coming and you should be prepared. Perhaps the best way to prepare is to learn to use the Internet.

WHAT NEXT?

The purpose of this first chapter was to quickly introduce a number of basic concepts that are essential to understanding computers and information systems. The balance of the book is divided into two sections. Part II, *Components,* introduces an information system's major components, one by one. Part III, *Systems,* shows you how those components are linked to form information systems.

After you complete Chapter 1, you can read the chapters within a section in any order. Relevant material from Part II should be read before related topics in Part III, but you need not *complete* Part II before you begin Part III.

▲ FIGURE 1.20

The Internet is a network of networks.

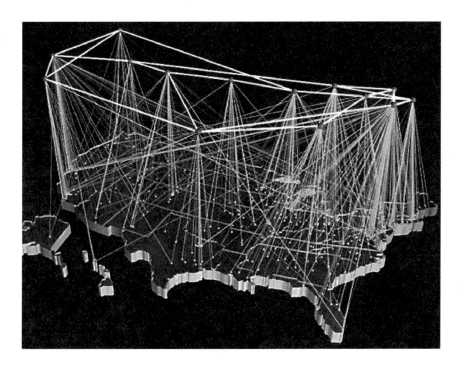

Electronic Textbooks

Imagine using an electronic textbook. Instead of the traditional page layout, you see a narrative displayed in easy-to-read, oversized text with key words highlighted in some way. Clicking on one key term opens a window that displays a relevant photograph or diagram. Clicking on another highlighted term activates a window that holds a video presentation or an animation. Other buttons lead you to interactive exercises, self tests, and additional details about selected topics.

Instead of reading the narrative sequentially, you browse quickly through the material you understand and "drill down" for more coverage as necessary. When you identify passages you consider particularly important, you highlight them and set them aside in your own private file for later review. Those of you who learn conceptually can focus on concepts. Those of you who need real world examples find them, and visually impaired readers have the option of listening to the narrative. In effect, the electronic textbook adjusts itself to the way *you* learn best.

If electronic textbooks are so good, why are you still reading a traditional textbook? The answer is largely economic—the number of students who have convenient access to a personal computer system with a high-quality display screen, a CD-ROM drive (or high-speed access to the information superhighway), and enough power to support an electronic textbook is still too small to justify the expense of developing such products. That is changing, however. Look for electronic textbooks to become widely available in the near future.

SUMMARY

Data are facts. Information is the meaning that human beings assign to or extract from data. Data processing involves manipulating data in an attempt to clarify the underlying patterns. A computer is a machine that processes data into information. The user is the person who needs the information generated by the computer.

Hardware is a general term for a computer's physical components. Input devices allow users to enter data to the computer. Output devices provide a means for people to get data or information from a computer. Secondary storage devices hold large amounts of data and information in an electronic form. Because input and output devices are external to the computer, they are sometimes called peripherals.

The basic building blocks of modern computers are tiny integrated circuit chips. To make the chips easier to handle they are usually mounted on boards. Internally, a computer is a binary, or two-state machine. A single binary digit is called a bit. When data are input to a computer they are converted to binary form and stored in memory (RAM). The processor is the component that processes or manipulates the data.

A program is a set of instructions that tells a computer what to do. Software is a general term for programs. A computer is a machine that processes data into information under the control of a stored program. Application software allows a user to do something. System software, such as the Windows 95 operating system, directly controls and manages computer hardware.

The most elementary unit of data that can be stored on a computer is a single bit. Bits are grouped to form bytes, and each byte can hold a single character. Characters are grouped to form fields, a set of related fields is called a record, and a set of related records forms a file. A database is set of related files.

Most computer applications follow the input/process/output cycle. A system is a set of components that work together to accomplish an objective. An information system is composed of hardware, software, data, people, and procedures, and is intended to provide the right data and information to the right people at the right time.

A computer's memory is considered volatile because it loses its contents when power is cut. Secondary storage (such as magnetic disk) is used as long-term storage because it is not volatile.

A microcomputer, sometimes called a personal computer, is a small, relatively inexpensive machine designed to be used by one person at a time. A personal digital assistant (PDA) is a hand-held computer. A mainframe is a large, multiple-user computer. A minicomputer is a mid-sized machine that might be used to support a single department or a division of an organization. The most powerful computers are called supercomputers.

A network consists of two or more computers linked by communication lines. A client/server network allows client computers to share resources by accessing a server. The Internet is a network of networks that links colleges, universities, corporations, government agencies, and research centers throughout the world. It is widely viewed as a prototype for the evolving information superhighway.

KEY TERMS

Each chapter ends with a list of the key terms that were introduced and defined in the chapter.

application software	information superhighway	personal digital assistant (PDA)
binary	information system	processor
bit	input device	program
board	input/process/ output cycle	RAM (random access memory)
byte	instruction	record
chip	Internet	secondary storage
client/server	mainframe	server
computer	memory	software
data	microcomputer	stored program
data processing	minicomputer	supercomputer
database	network	system
disk	operating system	system software
field	output device	user
file	peripheral	volatile
hardware	personal computer	Windows 95
information		

CONCEPTS

You will find several concepts questions at the end of each chapter. Their purpose is to help you prepare your own summary of the chapter's key points. Note that the questions are keyed to the learning objectives that open the chapter.

1. Why is it so important that you learn about computers and information technology?
2. Distinguish between data and information.
3. What is hardware?
4. Why are input and output devices called peripherals?
5. Distinguish between a computer's memory and its processor.
6. What is a program? What is a stored program? Why is the stored program concept important?
7. Define the term *computer.*
8. Distinguish between application software and system software.
9. Explain the relationship between bits, bytes, characters, fields, records, files, and databases.
10. Describe the input/process/output cycle. Why do most application programs follow that cycle?
11. Why is secondary storage necessary?
12. What is a system? What is an information system?
13. Distinguish among a microcomputer, a minicomputer, and a mainframe.
14. What is a network? Why are networks used?
15. Briefly explain how a client/server network allows numerous users to share resources.

PROJECTS

You will find suggested out-of-class activities at the end of most chapters. Your instructor may choose to assign one or more of them as homework.

1. Attend an orientation session for your school's network and learn about the available student services.
2. Rent and watch a movie in which computers play an important role; suggested titles include *2001: A Space Odyssey, War Games, Short Circuit, Tron, Sneakers,* and *The Net.* How is the computer portrayed? Do you think that portrayal is realistic?

S P O T L I G H T

THE INTERNET

When you finish reading this feature, you should be able to:

▶ Briefly describe today's Internet.
▶ Read and interpret an Internet address.
▶ Explain how e-mail works.
▶ Explain the purpose of newsgroups.
▶ Briefly describe the World Wide Web.

TODAY'S INTERNET

Today's Internet (an acronym for inter-network) is a network of 40 to 50 thousand networks that links 4 to 5 million computers and perhaps as many as 40 million users all over the world. Even more impressive is its growth rate; by some estimates, 100,000 new computers are added to the Internet each *month*.

Internet Access

All you need to access the Internet is a properly equipped computer (see Chapter 13), a telephone, and a valid account. Perhaps you can gain access through your school or your employer. If not, consider joining an on-line service such as America Online, CompuServe, Delphi, GEnie, Prodigy, or the Well. Check your local newspaper, too. Regional Internet providers are springing up all over the country, and any day now Internet access might be available through your cable television company.

Internet Addresses

Domain name
An Internet address.

Before you can effectively use the Internet, you need a basic understanding of Internet addresses. Each computer on the Internet is identified by a unique 32-bit number. Binary numbers are difficult for people to remember, however, so Internet addresses are usually written as plain-English **domain names.**

The easiest way to understand a domain name is to read it from right to left (Figure 1.21). The top-level domain defines the type of organization; for example, schools use *edu* and commercial organizations use *com*. Moving to the left, *location* is the name of a computer that is continuously connected (24 hours per day) to the Internet and *server* is the name of the user's network server. The "at" symbol (@) means, literally, "at." To its left is the user's on-line name or handle. The periods act as separators. Figure 1.22 lists some top-level domains.

22

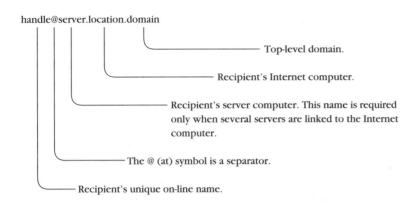

Examples: president@whitehouse.gov
                   davisws@miamiu.muohio.edu

▲ FIGURE 1.21

An Internet address.

For example, consider the path followed by an e-mail message as it moves from your computer to:

elvis@jungle.graceland.com

Read the (imaginary) address as elvis-at-jungle-dot-graceland- dot-com.

To interpret the address, start at the right. The high-level domain is *com,* so the message's first stop is a computer that handles the *com* domain. From there it is routed to an Internet computer named *graceland* which (we'll assume) is located in a well-known Memphis mansion. From *graceland,* the message goes to a server named *jungle* which (we'll assume) is located in a certain room in that mansion. Eventually, someone whose on-line handle is *elvis* logs onto the computer named *jungle* and reads the message.

DOMAIN	SIGNIFIES
com	A commercial organization, such as a corporation.
edu	An educational institution.
gov	A U.S. government agency.
int	An international organization.
mil	The U.S. military.
net	A computer network.
org	A noncommercial organization, such as the Red Cross.
se	Sweden.
uk	The United Kingdom.

▲ FIGURE 1.22

Top-level domains.

SPOTLIGHT

E-mail
Electronic messages input to one computer and transmitted to another computer.

Electronic Mail

Electronic mail, or **e-mail,** is one of the more popular Internet services. An e-mail user begins by typing a message on his or her computer and then transmitting it to the recipient's Internet address. The message is then routed from computer to computer across the Internet and stored on the recipient's server until he or she retrieves it. Because the communication line is in use only for the brief time a message is actually being transmitted, e-mail is quite inexpensive.

The precise procedures for sending or reading e-mail vary considerably with the software you are using, so you will have to learn the specifics of your system. Generally, the first step is to start a mail program. Most respond by displaying a window for composing your message (Figure 1.23). After you enter the recipient's e-mail address and briefly describe the subject of your message, you type the message and send it.

Reading messages is equally straightforward. Generally, after you issue the appropriate command you are presented with a list of the senders and subjects for the messages in your electronic mailbox. You then select a message and either read it, delete it, save it, forward it, or reply to it.

Most e-mail programs offer additional services, too. For example, you may be able to attach a file to a message, simultaneously send the same message to numerous people by citing a mailing list, and use an automatic sorting feature to screen your messages and eliminate electronic junk mail.

An e-mail message lies somewhere between a telephone conversation and a formal letter. Most are short, concise, and to the point. They are typi-

▲ FIGURE 1.23

America Online's mail screen.

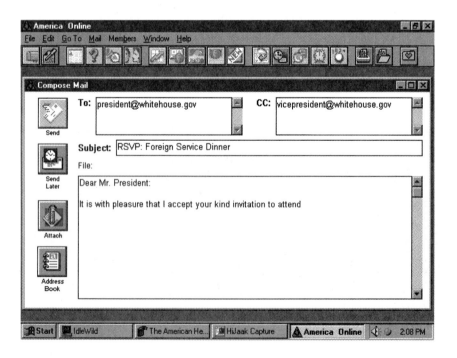

cally composed quickly and sent immediately. The recipient cannot hear you or see you; the words on the screen are all he or she has to interpret your meaning. Consequently, misunderstandings are common, particularly given the Internet tradition of sending aggressively rude messages (called flames) to those who have offended you in some way.

A partial solution is to add simple graphic symbols called emoticons (Figure 1.24) to the text. A joking comment followed by a little smiley face is less likely to give offense than that same remark by itself.

USENET

The Internet also supports an electronic **bulletin board service (BBS)** called **USENET.** The service maintains a collection of thousands of **newsgroups** or discussion groups, each of which is devoted to a single topic. Users post messages called articles to a newsgroup. Other users read those messages and post responses or reply by e-mail. Some newsgroups are moderated; in other words, a central authority (the moderator) decides what is and what is not posted. Other newsgroups are unmoderated, meaning anyone can post a message.

Newsgroup names are read from left to right. For example, *misc.forsale* lists items for sale, *misc.forsale.computers* advertises computers for sale, and *misc.forsale.computers.printers* is a good place to look if you need a printer. Note that periods are used as separators.

Officially sanctioned newsgroups (Figure 1.25) are proposed and voted on by the members of the USENET community. If a newsgroup name starts with *alt.* (alt-dot), it is unapproved, though still supported. Much of the controversy surrounding the Internet's on-line content centers on *alt.* newsgroups, so proceed with caution.

To read news and participate in discussion groups you need an application program called a news reader. Many news readers include a search feature; for example, you might be able to obtain a list of tennis-related newsgroups by searching on the key word *tennis.* Before you begin participating in an on-line discussion group, it is wise to search on the key word *answers* to get the answers to frequently asked questions (FAQs). It might

Bulletin board service (BBS)
A service that allows users to post and read electronic messages.
USENET
The Internet's electronic bulletin board service.
Newsgroup
A USENET discussion group devoted to a single topic.

EMOTICON	MEANING
:-> or :-)	A smile.
;-)	A smile with a wink.
8-)	A goofy smile.
:-(	A frown. Disappointment.
:-&	I am tongue-tied.
:-o	I am shocked.
:-p	I am sticking out my tongue.

▲ **FIGURE 1.24**

Emoticons.
To read them, turn the page sideways.

S P O T L I G H T

answers to get the answers to frequently asked questions (FAQs). It might save you some time.

Figure 1.26 lists a few interesting newsgroups. You will find a longer list in Appendix B.

The World Wide Web

The fastest growing segment of the Internet is the **World Wide Web.** It features a simple, graphic, point-and-click navigational system that allows a user to quickly jump from computer to computer all over the world.

World Wide Web
A segment of the Internet that features a simple, graphic, point-and-click navigational system that allows a user to quickly jump from computer to computer all over the world.

▲ FIGURE 1.25

Official newsgroups.

NEWSGROUP	CONTAINS
alt	Miscellaneous, unapproved topics.
bionet	Biology-related topics.
bit	Miscellaneous topics from the BITNET network.
biz	Business and marketing topics.
clari	Clarion. News and business information.
comp	Computer-related topics.
eunet	Miscellaneous topics from the European network.
k12	Educational topics.
misc	Miscellaneous topics.
news	News about USENET.
rec	Recreational topics.
sci	Scientific topics.
soc	Social issues.
talk	On-line discussions of controversial topics.

▲ FIGURE 1.26

Some interesting USENET newsgroups.

NAME	COMMENTS
alt.angst	For the anxious.
alt.fan.elvis-presley	For Elvis fans.
alt.fan.letterman	Dave, the late-night guy.
alt.mcdonalds	Will you have fries with your burger?
misc.forsale.computers	Computers for sale.
misc.jobs.offered	On-line employment classified ads.
rec.arts.tv.soaps	Your favorite soap opera.
rec.food.cooking	A discussion of cooking-related topics.
rec.humor.funny	The jokes of the day.
rec.travel	Travel-related topics.
rec.sports._____	Topics related to the sport you name.
soc.culture._____	Topics related to the culture of the country or group you name.
talk.politics	A lively discussion of politics.

The starting point for browsing (or surfing) the Web is called a **home page** (Figure 1.27). On the home page are pointers in the form of highlighted words, menu entries, and buttons (or icons). Clicking on a pointer automatically transfers you to the associated home page (usually) on some other computer; for example, Figure 1.28 shows the home page for a tour of the Louvre art museum in Paris.

Home page
The starting point for browsing (or surfing) the World Wide Web. The first page you see when you link to a web site.

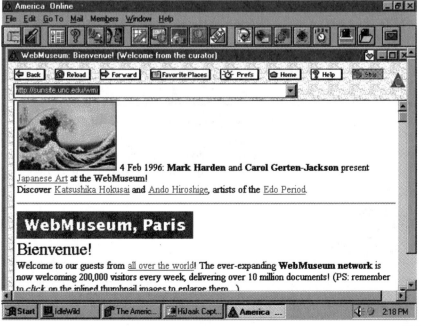

▲ FIGURE 1.27

West Publishing Company's home page.

▲ FIGURE 1.28

This home page marks the start of a virtual tour of the Louvre.

Browser
A program used to navigate the World Wide Web.

S P O T L I G H T

The program you use to navigate the World Wide Web is called a **browser.** The first browser, Mosaic, is a public-domain program that was developed under a grant from the United States government. Netscape is another popular browser, and many on-line services have their own browsing software.

Appendix B lists a number of interesting home pages. See the *Spotlight* feature following Chapter 14 for a detailed explanation of World Wide Web links.

Key Terms

browser	domain name	newsgroup
bulletin board service (BBS)	e-mail	USENET
	home page	World Wide Web

Concepts

1. What is the Internet?
2. You can send an e-mail message to the president of the United States by addressing it to *president@whitehouse.gov.* Interpret that address.
3. Briefly explain how an e-mail message is composed and sent. Briefly explain how to read e-mail messages.
4. What is an electronic bulletin board service?
5. What is USENET? What is a newsgroup?
6. Two newsgroups you might find interesting are *misc.jobs.offered* and *misc.jobs.resumes.* What would you expect to find if you accessed those newsgroups?
7. What is the World Wide Web?
8. Briefly explain the process of browsing (or surfing) the World Wide Web.

Projects

1. Learn how to send and receive an e-mail message using your school's network or a commercial service.
2. Many schools offer short, one- or two-hour classes on how to use the Internet, how to access USENET, and how to navigate the World Wide Web. If you can get into such a class, take advantage of the opportunity.

 ## Internet Projects

1. Given the increasing popularity of the Internet and the World Wide Web, many information system courses incorporate Internet access. To

support such activities, at the end of each subsequent chapter you will find a set of suggested Internet projects in the following categories:

    a. *News and Notes*. Suggested Internet references to product announcements and issues that are relevant to the chapter material.

    b. *Topic Searches*. A list of relevant key terms and qualifiers that might lead to interesting information.

    c. *Links to Other Sites*. A list of relevant World Wide Web sites and newsgroups.

The objective of these Internet projects is to provide on-line activities that are related to the chapter material. Your instructor might choose to assign these projects as starting points for research papers or brief "trip" reports.

2. Because of the incredible variety of Internet and World Wide Web search and navigation tools, explicit directions for using your school's system cannot be economically included in this text. Using a supplemental text, a handout, or other available sources, learn how to access the Internet and the World Wide Web on your school's system.

3. One problem with Internet-based projects is currency; simply put, technology (particularly the Internet) changes so quickly that today's state-of-the-art is tomorrow's old news. Consequently, West Publishing Company maintains a World Wide Web home page that includes more current versions of the Internet projects described in 1. To access the student activities for this book:

    a. Go to *http://www.westpub.com/Educate*

    b. Select *College publications*

    c. Select *What's new?*

    d. Select *The latest news*

    e. Look under *New and Updated Online Supplements,* find the entry for this book, and click on *Student activities*

Once you find the right page, check the *News and Notes, Topic Searches,* and *Links to Other Sites* for Chapter 1. When you finish, write and submit a one-page trip report telling your instructor what you found. Even better, send your instructor an e-mail message outlining your findings.

S P O T L I G H T

29

PART II

COMPONENTS

Each of the chapters in this section focuses on a single information system component. Once you have completed Chapter 1, they can be read in any order.

The *Spotlight* following Chapter 7 examines "Internet Software Tools." Social issues and ethics are reviewed in the *Spotlight* entitled "Computers and Privacy" following Chapter 9.

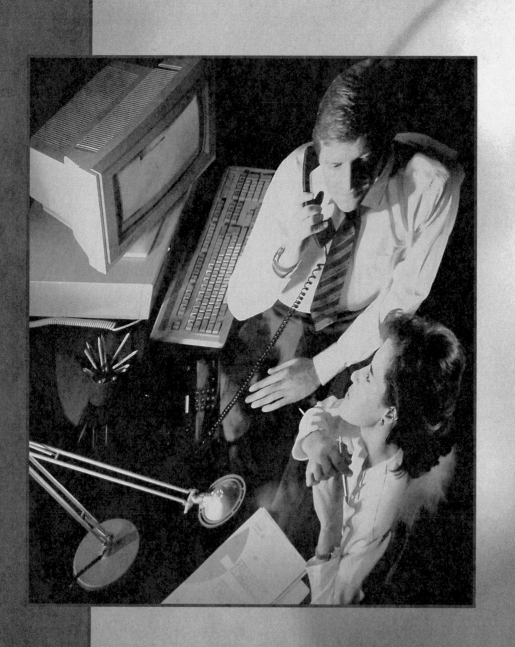

CHAPTER 2

Personnel and Careers

Before you start this chapter, you should be familiar with the following concepts:

- ▶ Computers (p. 6).
- ▶ Hardware (p. 6), software (p. 9), and data (p. 10).
- ▶ Information systems (p. 13).
- ▶ Networks (p. 17) and the Internet (p. 17).

When you finish reading this chapter, you should be able to:

- ▶ Identify the people who create commercial hardware and software.
- ▶ Identify the people who sell and distribute hardware and software.
- ▶ Identify the people who plan and develop information systems.

- ▶ Identify the people who operate and maintain information systems.
- ▶ Sketch a typical information technology management hierarchy.
- ▶ Briefly explain why so much computer-related work is done by consultants.
- ▶ Distinguish among academic programs in computer engineering, computer science, management information systems, and computer information systems.
- ▶ Briefly discuss computer-related job opportunities.
- ▶ Explain why ethics is so important to the computing profession.

THE JOB MARKET

Recently, *Money* magazine's "Forecast 1996" issue published (on p. 21) a list of the "12 best jobs for the next 12 months" (Figure 2.1). Given the aging baby-boomer generation, it is not surprising that six of those jobs are in health care, but three of them (computer engineer, computer systems analyst, and computer programmer) are in the computer field.

Most college students are concerned with starting their professional careers, but midlife career changes are also common these days. An article on p. 1 of the January 1996 issue of the *AARP Bulletin* (a publication of the American Association of Retired Persons) indicated that the demand for computer engineers and systems analysts is likely to grow, making them good candidates for second careers.

Both the *Money* magazine and *AARP Bulletin* articles were based on projections generated by the U.S. Bureau of Labor Statistics. Those projec-

ISSUES

Computers and Employment

The impact of computer-related technology on employment is an emotional issue. Automation (the automatic operation or control of equipment, a process, or a system) often displaces unskilled workers. *Downsizing* is a euphemism for reducing the size of the workforce, and corporate downsizing displaces both skilled *and* unskilled workers. Computers make automation and downsizing possible.

Computers have a positive impact on employment, too, however. Start with the creation of new jobs. Not too many years ago, very few people made a living manufacturing, distributing, selling, installing, programming, or maintaining computer-related products. Today, those jobs are plentiful and the pay (in most cases) is pretty good.

Efficiency is another factor. Simply put, computers make people more efficient and that, in turn, enhances productivity. Historically, increased productivity is the engine that drives economic growth, and (in the long run) economic growth almost always means more jobs.

Do computers create more jobs than they eliminate? Probably, but that question is difficult to answer with any confidence. One thing is certain, however. Computers have changed the nature of most jobs, and people who cannot (or will not) learn how to use them will not do well in the evolving, information-based economy. In other words, prepare yourself.

tions (Figure 2.2) echo the same theme: People trained in most computer-related disciplines are expected to be in demand for the next several years. Although there are no guarantees, you will almost certainly discover that a degree in a computer-related field enhances your job prospects.

▲ **FIGURE 2.1**

Money **magazine's list of the "12 best jobs" for 1996.**

We rank the 12 best jobs for the next 12 months		
Health-care and computer jobs dominate the top 12 occupations for '96—based on the year's prospects for salaries, raises, job demand and long-term growth. High school and special-ed teachers as well as clergy also earned high-ranking spots. University of Minnesota economist Malcolm Cohen, who produces MONEY'S annual job survey, compiled this list.		
Occupation	**Annual Salary[1]**	**Where the jobs are[2]**
1. Physical therapist	$ 50,000	In-home care, pediatrics, neonatal and sports medicine
2. Physician	163,000	Rural managed care, private practice in small cities; surgeons
3. Computer engineer	73,300	Software for safety features in cars and planes; consumer entertainment
4. Computer systems analyst	56,000	Designing networks for businesses and colleges; data processor operations
5. Registered nurse	37,000	Nursing homes, in-home and ambulatory care
6. Radiologic technologist	30,400	High-tech diagnostics such as MRIs and CAT scans
7. Computer programmer	40,000	Setting up computer networks for large and small companies
8. Clergy	28,000	In Midwest and South. Southern Baptist and other evangelical ministries
9. Pharmacist	50,900	National retail chains and managed-care facilities
10. Special-education teacher	35,000	Public school classes for disabled and chronically ill students
11. Psychologist (staff)	34,166	Hospitals and private practice in the fast-growing Southwest
12. High school teacher	37,300	Languages, math, sciences and computer science

Notes: [1]Median income derived from U.S. Bureau of Labor Statistics and industry data. [2]Industry data.

▲ **FIGURE 2.2**

Government projections suggest that there will be job opportunities in most computer-related disciplines.

OCCUPATION	GROWTH (1992–2005)	COMMENTS
Systems analyst	111%	Employment is expected to grow much faster than average. Those with a (computer-related degree) should have good prospects for employment.
Technical manager	32%	Employment is expected to increase faster than average.
Information clerk	32%	Faster than average growth is expected, with many opportunities for part-time work.
Computer programmer	30%	Employment is expected to grow faster than average. Opportunities should be plentiful in data processing services firms, software houses, and computer consulting businesses.
Computer maintenance	30%	Overall employment is expected to grow faster than average.
National average	**22%**	The expected growth rate for all jobs.
Data entry clerk	–4%	Employment is expected to decline. Job prospects will be best for those with a broad knowledge of office technology.
Computer operator	–41%	Employment is expected to decline as data centers become increasingly automated.

Source: *The 1992–2005 Job Outlook in Brief.* Reprinted from the Spring 1994 issue of the *Occupational Outlook Quarterly.* U.S. Department of Labor, Bureau of Labor Statistics.

PERSONNEL

As you may recall from Chapter 1, an information system is composed of hardware, software, data, people, and procedures. This chapter focuses on the people.

There are many ways to organize a discussion of computer-related personnel. Perhaps the most common approach is to start with entry-level positions and then move up the career ladder. The only problem is that there are many different ladders, and they all seem to be missing a few rungs.

Instead, this chapter follows the life cycle of computer hardware, software, and data-related products. Those products must be created, distributed, applied in the context of an information system, operated, and maintained, and the nature of the work varies as you move from stage to stage.

Creating Commercial Hardware and Software

Computer engineer
A technical expert who plans, designs, and builds computer hardware.

Computer scientist
A technical expert who plans, designs, and implements computer hardware and/or software.

CAD/CAM
Acronym for computer-aided design/computer-aided manufacturing.

OEM
Acronym for original equipment manufacturer.

Computer hardware is designed by **computer engineers** and **computer scientists** (Figure 2.3). Much of the integrated circuit manufacturing process is computer controlled, so **CAD/CAM** (computer-aided design/computer-aided manufacturing) software (Figure 2.4) is typically used in the design process. Once a design is complete, the CAD/CAM software automatically generates the programs and the data needed to run the manufacturing process control computers.

To prevent contamination, integrated circuit chips and some circuit boards are manufactured in special clean rooms (Figure 2.5). The finished circuit boards are then assembled to create computers and peripheral devices (Figure 2.6). Both tasks call for production personnel.

The manufacturer of a hardware component is called an **OEM** (original equipment manufacturer). Often, hardware components and subsystems are sold to other companies that incorporate them into commercial products.

▲ FIGURE 2.3

Hardware is designed by computer engineers and computer scientists.

▲ FIGURE 2.4

CAD/CAM.

▲ FIGURE 2.5

A clean room.

For example, Intel processors are found in the computers sold by such firms as AST, Compaq, Dell, Gateway, IBM, Hewlett-Packard, Micron, Packard-Bell, and many others.

Commercial software is created by computer scientists, **software engineers,** software designers, software developers, and **programmers**

Software engineer
A technical expert who plans and designs software, usually system software.

Programmer
A person who writes computer programs.

▲ FIGURE 2.6

A typical assembly plant.

(Figure 2.7). Programming language software might be created by a language design specialist, and the responsibility for writing or enhancing an operating system might be assigned to a system software specialist. Support is provided by such people as librarians, technical writers, technical editors, and documentation specialists (Figure 2.8).

Sales and Distribution

Once the products are created, they must be sold and distributed to customers. Most hardware and software firms employ marketing experts, com-

▲ FIGURE 2.7

Software is written by programmers.

▲ FIGURE 2.8

Documentation must be prepared, too.

On-Line Job Listings

Many currently available computer-related jobs require familiarity with on-line networks, particularly the Internet. One way to ensure that applicants have Internet skills is to post the jobs on the Internet; in effect, those who can find the on-line job listings have already demonstrated their Internet skills. Appendix B lists a number of interesting Internet sites, including several that post job opportunities.

puter sales representatives, and technical sales support personnel to sell expensive mainframes, microcomputer hardware, software, and personal computer systems directly to large customers. Other hardware and software is distributed to retail outlets (Figure 2.9) for eventual sale to individual consumers, and those computer stores employ sales clerks and customer service representatives. Mail-order sales (and mail-order clerks) are also common.

Developing Information Systems

Information systems are planned, designed, and developed by **systems analysts.** The analyst's job is to define the user's needs and translate them into technical specifications (Figure 2.10). Part of that job is selecting the most appropriate hardware and software.

Most systems analysts are technical experts first and application experts second. Some organizations prefer to give the appropriate technical training

Systems analyst
The person who defines the problem, expresses the user's needs in technical terms, and communicates resource requirements to management.

▲ **FIGURE 2.9**

A typical computer superstore.

▲ FIGURE 2.10

Information systems are planned and designed by systems analysts.

Application programmer
A person who writes application software.

System integrator
A business that combines hardware, software, and (often) maintenance services to create a complete package.

Computer operator
A person who operates a computer.

System programmer
A programmer who specializes in installing and maintaining operating system and other system software.

Maintenance programmer
A programmer who maintains existing application software.

to application experts (called business analysts) and then assign to them responsibility for planning information systems.

If the analyst cannot find the right commercial software for an information system, **application programmers** write custom software. An information system's data components are planned and implemented by a database analyst, and networks are designed by telecommunication planners. Additionally, documentation specialists and technical writers are needed to develop the system documentation.

A **system integrator** is a business that combines hardware, software, and (often) maintenance services to create a complete package. For example, a dentist might purchase a dental office management system from a system integrator. In effect, a system integrator does for a class of potential customers what a systems analyst does for a single organization.

Operating and Maintaining an Information System

Once the system is installed, other people operate and maintain it. Mainframe and minicomputer hardware is managed and scheduled by **computer operators** (Figure 2.11). Networks are managed and maintained by network specialists, communication specialists, and network administrators. Service and repair technicians (Figure 2.12) and customer support personnel keep the hardware running, in-house help desk staffers answer the users' software questions, and PC (personal computer) system administrators manage and upgrade both hardware and software.

System software (for example, the operating system) is maintained and fine-tuned by **system programmers.** Application software is maintained by **maintenance programmers.** Information center specialists and microapplications support specialists work directly with the users, maintaining commercial software and answering questions. Many commercial software

A computer operator at work.

providers make a help line, staffed by help line specialists, available to registered owners of their software.

Data are entered into an information system by data entry clerks (Figure
2.13). Once the data are in the system, the responsibility for maintaining
them rests with a **database administrator** or a data librarian.

Computer system auditors, control clerks, and security specialists are
responsible for ensuring that the people who use the system follow the
appropriate procedures. Trainers and instructors are needed to teach users
how to use the system.

Database administrator (DBA)
The person in an organization who is
responsible for the data.

▲ **FIGURE 2.12**

**A computer service technician
at work.**

▲ FIGURE 2.13

Data entry clerks.

Technical Management

Chief Information Officer (CIO)
The person who is responsible for an organization's management information system.

All those people must be managed. Figure 2.14 shows a typical technical management organizational structure.

At the top of the structure is the **CIO,** or **chief information officer.** An information system is composed of hardware, software, and data compo-

▲ FIGURE 2.14

A typical organizational structure for technical management.

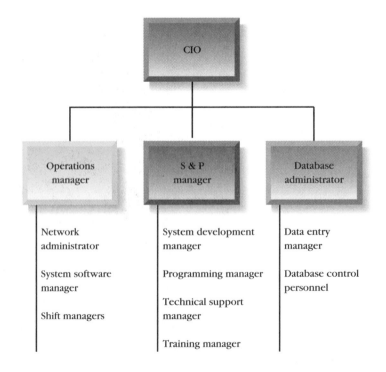

PEOPLE

Ross Perot

Before he became a presidential candidate, Ross Perot was best known as the founder of Electronic Data Systems Corporation, a highly successful information services company. After he graduated from the Naval Academy in 1953 and completed his tour of duty, Perot joined IBM Corporation as a sales associate. A few years later, he left IBM to start EDS. The new company was officially incorporated in 1962 on his birthday, June 27.

One of EDS's first major contracts was with Blue Cross/Blue Shield of Texas. His firm's success in processing Medicare claims led to contracts with several other insurance companies. By the end of the decade, Perot's company was providing information services worldwide to customers in a variety of industries.

EDS was a unique company with an almost military-like camaraderie. Its sense of loyalty to its employees is well documented in *On Wings of Eagles*, a 1983 best-seller by Ken Follett (New York: William Morrow). The book describes an effort to rescue several Iran-based EDS employees following the Iranian revolution, and it resembles a spy thriller. The title is taken from an EDS recruiting slogan: "Eagles don't flock; you have to find them one at a time."

In 1984, Ross Perot sold EDS to General Motors and joined the parent company's board of directors. In 1986, following a series

of public disagreements with management, General Motors paid Perot more than $700 million in exchange for his stock and his resignation. Today, EDS continues to be a leader in the information services field.

nents, so the second management level includes a computer operations or information center manager (responsible for hardware), a systems and programming manager (software), and a database administrator (data).

Reporting to the information center manager are such people as a network administrator, a system software manager, computer center shift managers, and so on. Under the systems and programming manager are the system development, programming, technical support, and training managers. Reporting to the database administrator are the data entry manager and the people responsible for ensuring database quality.

Information systems are planned and developed by short-term project teams that disband when the project is finished. The teams are led by **project leaders** and project managers. Becoming a project leader is often the first step up the technical management ladder.

Project leader
The person in charge of a temporary project team.

Consulting

In all but the largest organizations, technical specialists are needed only occasionally. For example, designing a network might call for the services of several network experts, but once installation is complete a few network administrators are able to keep it running. Consequently, a great deal of in-depth technical work is performed by **consultants** who are hired on a contract basis to do a specific job.

Systems analysts, computer programmers, network experts, trainers, and freelance writers are all available on a consulting basis, and temporary data entry clerks and computer operators can be hired through employment agencies. It is even possible to subcontract responsibility for the operation and maintenance of an organization's entire information system to an information services provider.

Consultant
A person who provides advice and/or expertise on a temporary or project basis.

COMPUTER-RELATED ACADEMIC PROGRAMS

Most professional computer-related jobs require substantial training. Often, the minimum entry-level requirement is a two-year associate degree or a four-year baccalaureate degree in a technical field. In addition to technical training, computer professionals also need good verbal and written communication skills, general problem-solving skills, and an ability to work with other people.

The variety of available degree programs can be confusing, but most fall into one of four broad categories (Figure 2.15):

▶ Computer engineering
▶ Computer science
▶ Management information systems
▶ Computer information systems

Computer Engineering

Computer engineering, as the name implies, is an engineering discipline; at some schools, it is an option in the electrical engineering department. The focus of most computer engineering programs is hardware design. As you might expect, CE majors take numerous science and mathematics courses.

Computer engineering
An academic discipline that trains computer engineers.

DISCIPLINE	FOUNDATION	PROGRAM FOCUS
Computer engineering	Math and science	Hardware design
Computer science	Math and science	System software Hardware Data structures Theory and concepts
MIS	Business core	Application software Information systems Database design Business orientation
CIS	Varies	Application software Hardware concepts Database design Hands-on orientation

▲ FIGURE 2.15

Computer-related academic degree programs.

Computer Science

Many **computer science (CS)** programs are based on a model curriculum recommended by a professional society called the Association for Computing Machinery (ACM). Students typically start by building a strong foundation in mathematics and science and then study the basic principles and theories that underlie computer hardware and software. Depending on the school, students might focus on programming languages, software engineering, system software, data structures, artificial intelligence, hardware design, the theory of computability, applied computation, or any of dozens of other specialties. Computer science programs are typically found in the college of arts and sciences or in the engineering school.

Computer science (CS)
An academic program that studies the basic principles and theories that underlie computer hardware and software.

Management Information Systems

As you might expect, most **management information systems (MIS)** programs are housed in the school of business administration. Many are based on a model curriculum recommended by the Data Processing Management Association (DPMA). (The latest version, IS '95, is just beginning to have an impact.)

MIS students build on a business core that combines a limited exposure to math and science with courses in accounting, economics, management, finance, and other business fields. Theory and principles are taught, but most MIS programs emphasize the application of computers and information technology to business problems.

Management information systems (MIS)
An academic discipline that studies computers and information management in a business environment.

Computer Information Systems

Computer information systems (CIS) programs are more technical than MIS but more applied than computer science. There is a model CIS curriculum (DPMA), but the nature of these programs varies substantially from school to school, so it is difficult to give general guidance on their content.

Computer information systems (CIS)
An academic program that is more technical than MIS but more applied than computer science.

Some CIS programs emphasize hardware, others software, still others systems analysis and design. Check with an advisor for specific information about the CIS curriculum at your school.

None of the Above

Many technical institutes, two-year and community colleges, and quite a few four-year schools offer applied technology programs designed to teach students the specific skills they need to enter the local job market. Some schools of business teach programs that focus on business applications, and you will also find numerous programs that are "none of the above." A complete list of the names of computer-related degree programs would fill several pages.

OPPORTUNITY AND PREPARATION

The fact that there are opportunities in the computer field does not necessarily mean that *all* computer-related positions have a bright future. For

---

THE FUTURE

Information Haves and Have-Nots

In today's information age, the ability to use a computer is essential. Those who know how will be able to participate successfully in the evolving, global, information-based economy. Those who do not will occupy the margins of society.

Computers have the potential to level the playing field. Such things as race, religion, gender, age, and physical handicaps do not matter to a computer. When you are on-line, you are judged by what you can do, not by who you are.

Conversely, computers also have the potential to widen the gap between the information haves and have-nots. The probability that you will have access to a computer depends a great deal on your financial status. Wealthy households have them; poor households do not. Students at expensive private schools take computer access for granted. Students in poor inner-city schools consider themselves lucky if they get to use an obsolete, hand-me-down computer once or twice a week.

Age is a factor, too. Because modern electronic equipment was simply not available when they were young, many people over 40 are uncomfortable with technology in general and computers in particular. Few young people fear computers. Many older people do, and that makes it difficult for them to learn.

Information technology is reshaping society. Not everyone must be a technical expert, of course, but successful people will know how to use computers effectively. Take advantage of every opportunity to ensure that you are among the information "haves."

ISSUES

Downsizing and Outsourcing

When a corporation downsizes, it reduces the number of people it employs. Often, the company *outsources* (or outplaces) work previously done by the displaced personnel because consultants are not paid benefits and can be terminated on short notice.

When a company decides to downsize, those positions that directly add value to the firm's products are usually safe. For example, to stay in business an automobile dealer must order, sell, deliver, and maintain cars, while a software company must plan, write, test, market, and maintain programs. The people who perform those tasks are going to keep their jobs. On the other hand, the automobile dealer is likely to outsource computer programming work, and the software company is likely to outsource the responsibility for maintaining company cars.

If you want a stable job, make sure what you do adds value to your employer's products. Note, however, that the downsizing trend is very good for consultants. One person's problem is another person's opportunity.

example, few experts expect the demand for such nonprofessionals as data entry clerks and assembly personnel to grow. These are relatively low-paying, hourly jobs that require at most a high-school diploma plus job-specific training, and there are few opportunities for advancement.

Computer operators and maintenance technicians have it a bit better, although the number of computer operators is expected to decline. Depending on the employer, these jobs might be hourly or salaried. An associate degree, technical school training, or military training is required for most entry-level positions. There are opportunities for advancement, particularly for those who are willing to continue their educations and earn a baccalaureate degree.

Technical sales positions often pay a salary plus a commission. At the retail level, an understanding of technical terminology might be enough to get you a job, but most nationally known companies require a college degree. The key is the ability to sell, so the degree might be in a nontechnical field; often, the necessary technical training is provided on the job. If the idea of selling computer hardware and software appeals to you, consider a minor in a computer-related discipline.

In most organizations, computer programmers are professional, salaried employees, and the pay is pretty good. Some firms hire entry-level programmers (particularly maintenance programmers) directly from two-year or technical school programs, although most programmer positions require a four-year degree in computer science, management information systems, computer information systems, or a related discipline. A few companies hire entry-level application programmers with a minor in one of those fields. If you want to be a system programmer, the more technical your training, the better.

Until the middle 1980s, most application programs were custom-designed to fit a specific user problem. Since then, commercial software has boomed and the demand for custom software has declined. Consequently, companies (like Microsoft) that market commercial software employ large numbers of application programmers, but user organizations do not. If you want to be an application programmer, look for a company that generates revenue from its software.

Opportunities for systems analysts exist with both user and supplier organizations. Some analysts are hired directly from college, but many firms expect a new hire to work a few years as a programmer before moving up to analysis. At one time it was possible for someone without a college degree to become a systems analyst, but that is relatively rare today. In fact, many analysts have advanced degrees.

Most hardware designers have degrees in such fields as electrical engineering, computer engineering, and computer science, and advanced degrees are common in these professions, too. For obvious reasons, most hardware designers work for firms that make hardware.

A surprising amount of computer-related work is done by consultants and temporary workers. A brief period of high sales might create a short-term need for data entry clerks. Application programmers are often hired on a project basis and dismissed when the work is finished. Such expensive specialists as network analysts, software installers, system maintenance personnel, and system auditors are needed only occasionally, so it makes sense to subcontract such work.

ETHICS

Computers are amoral; they can be used for good or for evil. The choice is ours, and the ability of laws, procedures, and safeguards to guide or direct our choices is, at best, limited. Consequently, ethical standards are particularly important for people who work with computers.

Ethics
The study of the general nature of morals and of the specific moral choices to be made by a person.

Ethics can be defined as the study of the general nature of morals and of the specific moral choices to be made by a person. On an individual level, ethical behavior is defined relative to your own moral code or your own values. Your personal ethics and values might, in turn, be a function of your religious beliefs or your ethnic background. Although there is no single, universally accepted ethical standard, when faced with a choice between doing good and doing bad, a strong sense of ethics is a powerful compass.

Like individuals, organizations have ethical and moral codes. For example, Figure 2.16 reproduces the Data Processing Management Association's Code of Ethics. Codes of ethics help guide the members of a diverse group toward a reasonably consistent sense of right and wrong.

▲ FIGURE 2.16

The DPMA code of ethics.

The DPMA Code of Ethics

I acknowledge:

That I have an obligation to management, therefore, I shall promote the understanding of information processing methods and procedures to management using every resource at my command.

That I have an obligation to my fellow members, therefore, I shall uphold the high ideals of DPMA as outlined in its Association Bylaws. Further, I shall cooperate with my fellow members and treat them with honesty and respect at all times.

That I have an obligation to society and will participate to the best of my ability in the dissemination of knowledge pertaining to the general development and understanding of information processing. Further, I shall not use knowledge of a confidential nature to further my personal interest, nor shall I violate the privacy and confidentiality of information entrusted to me or to which I may gain access.

That I have an obligation to my employer whose trust I hold, therefore, I shall endeavor to discharge this obligation to the best of my ability, to guard my employer's interests, and to advise him or her wisely and honestly.

That I have an obligation to my country, therefore, in my personal, business, and social contacts, I shall uphold my nation and shall honor the chosen way of life of my fellow citizens.

I accept these obligations as a personal responsibility and as a member of this Association, I shall actively discharge these obligations and I dedicate myself to that end.

SUMMARY

The chapter opened with some brief comments on the demand for computer professionals.

Computer hardware is designed by computer engineers and computer scientists, often using CAD/CAM software. The original manufacturer of a hardware component is called an OEM. Commercial software is created by computer scientists, software engineers, and programmers. Some manufacturers directly market their products. Others sell through retail outlets.

Information systems are planned and developed by systems analysts. Application programmers write custom software. A system integrator is a business that combines hardware, software, and (often) maintenance services to create a complete package.

Mainframe and minicomputer hardware is managed and scheduled by computer operators. System software is maintained by system programmers. Application software is maintained by maintenance programmers. The responsibility for the data rests with a database administrator.

The top information system manager is the CIO, or chief information officer. Information systems are planned and developed by short-term project teams led by project leaders. A great deal of in-depth technical work is performed by consultants.

The focus of most computer engineering programs is hardware design. Computer science (CS) students study the basic principles and theories that underlie computer hardware and software. MIS programs emphasize the application of computers and information technology to business problems.

Computer information systems (CIS) programs are more technical than MIS but more applied than computer science. Opportunity is a function of preparation.

Ethics is the study of the general nature of morals and of the specific moral choices to be made by a person. Like individuals, organizations have ethical and moral codes.

KEY TERMS

application programmer
CAD/CAM
CIO (chief information officer)
computer engineer
computer engineering
computer information systems (CIS)
computer operator

computer science
computer scientist
consultant
database administrator
ethics
maintenance programmer
management information systems (MIS)

OEM (original equipment manufacturer)
programmer
project leader
software engineer
system integrator
system programmer
systems analyst

CONCEPTS

1. Identify the people who create commercial hardware.
2. Identify the people who create commercial software.
3. Identify the people who sell and distribute hardware and software.
4. What does a systems analyst do?
5. Distinguish among an application programmer, a system programmer, and a maintenance programmer.
6. Identify the people who operate and maintain information systems.
7. Sketch a typical information management hierarchy.
8. Briefly explain why so much computer-related work is done by consultants.
9. Distinguish among computer engineering, computer science, management information systems, and computer information systems.
10. Identify at least two computer-related jobs that are *not* expected to experience increased demand in the future. Identify at least three computer-related jobs that are open to associate degree holders.
11. Distinguish between commercial software and custom software. Why is that distinction important to future programmers?
12. Why is the study of ethics relevant to computers?

PROJECTS

1. If your school's career planning or placement office publishes job placement data for the previous year's graduating class, obtain a copy. You might find the data useful when you select a major.
2. If you know any graduating seniors, ask them to identify the majors that get the most interviews, the most job offers, and the highest starting salaries.

3. Check the computer-related help wanted advertisements in your local Sunday newspaper and/or on the Internet (see Appendix B) and identify the specific skills being sought. How do those skills compare with the courses and topics being taught by your school's program? Many academic programs do not teach job-specific skills. Why do you suppose that is so?

4. Write a brief summary (a page or two) outlining what you imagine a computer professional does day after day. Then talk to a few computer professionals and compare their descriptions with your assumptions. You might be surprised at the differences.

INTERNET PROJECTS

1. *News and Notes*. You can find information on various government publications starting with the U.S. government's General Services Administration World Wide Web home page at *http://www.gsa.gov*. Follow the links to the Consumer Information Center and look for such publications as:

   Tomorrow's Jobs (2450-1)
   Matching Yourself with the World of Work
   The 1992–2005 Job Outlook in Brief
   Consumer Information Catalog

   Write a brief note or send an e-mail message to your instructor outlining what you find.

2. *Topic Searches*. Check the World Wide Web and/or other Internet resources for information on the following topics:

Key word	Qualifiers
downsizing	a company name
outsourcing	a profession
computer careers	a company name

   Define the key word, identify at least two sources of information on the topic, and briefly summarize the nature of the information you find.

3. *Links to Other Sites*. Appendix B lists several USENET newsgroups and World Wide Web Sites that post employment opportunities. Other useful sites include:

   http://www.careerpath.com
   http://www.espan.com
   http://www.occ.com/occ

   Check at least two of those sites and write a brief note or send an e-mail message to your instructor outlining what you find.

4. Access West Publishing Company's home page and find the Chapter 2 student activities for this book. See Internet Project 3 for the spotlight on *The Internet* following Chapter 1 (page 29) for more detailed instructions on accessing the home page. As appropriate, repeat projects 1, 2, and/or 3 using the more current references you find.

CHAPTER 3

Input and Output

Before you start this chapter, you should be familiar with the following concepts:

▶ Data and information (p. 4).

▶ Hardware (p. 6), peripherals (p. 6), and computer internals (p. 7).

▶ Software (p. 9), data (p. 10), and secondary storage (p. 12).

▶ Computer classifications (p. 14) and networks (p. 17).

When you finish reading this chapter, you should be able to:

▶ Explain the purpose of input and output devices.

▶ Distinguish between data capture and data entry.

▶ Discuss reports, documents, graphic images, multimedia, and other forms of computer data and information.

▶ Identify the input and output devices attached to a typical personal computer system.

▶ Explain how a screen's resolution is measured and how screen resolution affects image quality.

▶ Explain the cursor's significance.

▶ Distinguish between impact and nonimpact printers.

▶ Explain how print quality is measured.

▶ Describe such I/O alternatives as magnetic media, optical media, graphic devices, pen-based computers, terminals, and sound-based media.

▶ Discuss the trend toward using more human-friendly media to communicate with a computer.

DATA AND INFORMATION

A computer is a machine that processes data into information. Unless some human being needs the information, there is no point in processing the data. Without data, there is nothing to process. Input devices and media allow people to provide data to a computer. Output devices and media allow people to obtain data and information from a computer.

Source Data

Transaction
One occurrence of a business activity; for example, a single customer order or a single shipment from a supplier.

Source data
Data that are generated by an event that changes the value of one or more fields. Original data.

Data capture
The process of recording data.

Data entry
The process of converting data to electronic form.

A **transaction** is a single occurrence of an activity, an event, or an object about which data are collected. For example, when you purchase something from a department store, check into a hospital, register for a course, or purchase a ticket to a movie, you are participating in a transaction. The original data that describe each transaction are called **source data.**

Data capture is the process of initially recording the source data. **Data entry** is the process of converting the source data to electronic (or machine readable) form and entering them into a computer. For example, imagine a sales associate in a department store *capturing* the source data that describe a customer order by filling out an invoice form (Figure 3.1). The completed forms (one per order) are then collected and delivered to data entry clerks, who *enter* the data into the computer.

Historically, data capture and data entry were performed as separate steps. Today, however, it is more common to capture and enter the data in a single step through an **on-line** input device that is directly linked to a computer. See Chapter 9 for more on data capture and data entry.

On-line
Directly linked to a computer.

Reports

Report
A listing of data or information.

Detail report
A report that includes one line for each source transaction.

Summary report
A report that shows counts and totals for groups of transactions.

Demand report
A one-time report that summarizes selected data in response to an unscheduled query.

Transaction data are often output in the form of **reports** (Figure 3.2). A **detail report** shows *all* the data, one transaction per line. A **summary report** shows such information as counts and totals for groups of transactions (for example, total sales for the month grouped by store).

Some reports contain only summary data; others combine detailed transactions and summaries. Some are generated periodically; for example, accounting reports appear monthly, quarterly, or annually. **Demand reports,** in contrast, are created on request. Rather than listing or summarizing all the

▲ **FIGURE 3.1**

Data capture and data entry.

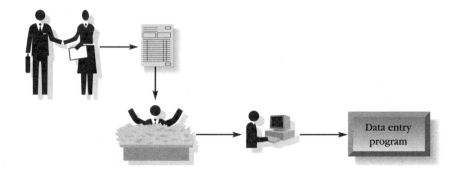

Report
headers

Column
headers

Detail
lines

Summary
line

Report
summary

**Central State University
Student Grade Report**

Student: Pat Smith   Term: Fall, 1996

Course	Description	Hours	Grade	Points
ENG102	English Comp	3	B	9
MTH182	Calculus II	4	B	12
CIS201	Info. Systems	3	A	12
SPN102	Intro Spanish	3	C	6
Totals		13		39

	Term	Cumulative
Hours	13	26
Points	39	81
G.P.A.	3.000	3.115

▲ **FIGURE 3.2**

The structure of a typical report.

data, an **exception report** lists only those transactions or summaries that deviate from a target, such as a budget or a quota.

Exception report
A report that shows only exceptions.

Documents, Images, and Multimedia

Not all source data describe transactions. For example, when you use a computer to write a term paper, the characters you type are a form of source data that collectively form a **document.** Later, you can modify the document, store it on a secondary storage device, retrieve it, and output it.

Document
A logically complete unit of data, such as a term paper, that does not follow the traditional field/record/file data hierarchy.

GIGO

Once, many years ago, an engineer entered a young programmer's office, dropped a notebook on her desk, and announced, "I want this printed on computer paper." The programmer suggested that the computer might be used to perform statistical tests, but the engineer was not interested. He just wanted the contents of his notebook input to a computer and printed, without change. "I know the numbers are right," he said. "If I show people my notebook, they won't believe me. But if I give them the same data printed on computer paper, they will."

Like the people the engineer referred to, some of us are willing to accept anything output by a computer just because it comes from a computer. That can be a mistake. Remember the acronym GIGO; it means *garbage in, garbage out.* The output generated by a computer is no better than the source data input to that computer. It is the content, not the form of the data that really matters.

NOTE

Graphic image
Computer data in such forms as art, a photograph, or an animation.

Multimedia
The combined use of several media, including text, graphics, animation, moving pictures, slides, music, sound, and lighting, in a single application.

Sound patterns, video, and such **graphic images** as art (Figure 3.3), photographs, maps, and animations are other forms of computer data. Like documents, they can be input, stored, retrieved, manipulated, and output. **Multimedia** implies using a computer to merge documents, text, numbers, graphics, sound, video and other media to create an integrated presentation. See Chapter 16 for more on multimedia.

PERSONAL COMPUTER I/O

Input and output devices provide a means for people to enter data to and obtain output from a computer. Because most students have seen (and probably used) a personal computer system, it makes sense to start with the peripherals attached to a typical PC.

Keyboards (Input)

Keyboard
A device for entering input data in character form.

The basic input device on most personal computer systems is a **keyboard** (Figure 3.4). In addition to the standard alphanumeric (alphabetic, numeric, and punctuation) keys, a typical keyboard contains a numeric keypad, a bank

▲ FIGURE 3.3

Graphic images are another form of computer data.

▲ FIGURE 3.4

A typical keyboard.

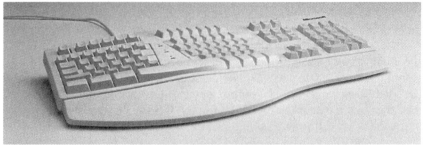

of cursor movement (or cursor control) keys, and a set of function keys. There are many different keyboard configurations, but you will find equivalent keys on most of them.

Display Screens (Output)

As characters are typed through the keyboard, they are input to the computer and stored in memory (Figure 3.5a). From memory, selected characters are output to a **display screen** (Figure 3.5b) so people can view them. In effect, the screen (Figure 3.6), sometimes called a monitor, serves as a window on memory.

Most monitors work by dividing the screen into a grid of **picture elements,** or **pixels.** Each pixel represents a dot or a point (Figure 3.7). Characters or graphic images are formed by selectively turning the points on or off. That on/off pattern is binary, so it can be stored in the computer's memory. An image that is stored as a pattern of pixels or dots is called a **bit-map.**

Display screen
An output device that resembles a television screen.

Picture element
A single dot on a graphic display.
Pixel
A picture element.
Bit-map
An image that is stored as a pattern of pixels or dots.

▲ FIGURE 3.5

A display screen shows selected contents of memory.
a. As characters are typed, they are stored in memory.
b. From memory, they are output to a display screen.

a.

▲ FIGURE 3.6

A display screen or monitor.

b.

A screen displays an image as a pattern of dots called pixels.

Flat-panel display
A thin display screen, such as the screen found on a laptop computer.

Resolution
The level of detail a screen can show, a function of the number of pixels on the screen.

Dot pitch
On a display screen, the space between adjacent pixels.

There are many varieties of computer displays. Both monochrome (single color) and color monitors are available, and the screens come in several sizes. For obvious reasons, a laptop computer requires a **flat-panel display** (Figure 3.8). On a passive matrix display there is one transistor for each row of pixels. On an active matrix display, each pixel has its own transistor, yielding a stronger, sharper image.

RESOLUTION

The quality, or **resolution,** of a screen image is defined by the number of pixels it displays. Early graphic screens had a resolution of 320 × 200 pixels, but higher-resolution 1024 × 768 SVGA (Super Video Graphics Array) screens are common today. As resolution increases, you get more pixels, smaller pixels, a smaller **dot pitch** (the space between adjacent pixels), and the capacity to display finer and finer details.

High resolution has a cost, of course. Since data about each pixel must be stored, high-resolution graphics requires more memory than low-resolution graphics.

▲ **FIGURE 3.8**

A laptop computer with a flat-panel display.

One way to conserve memory and secondary storage space is to **compress** the data. For example, most images contain a significant amount of background white (or solid-color) space. Instead of storing all those pixels, they can be replaced in memory by a code that tells the computer to "insert the appropriate number of white pixels here."

The Cursor

The **cursor** is a marker on the screen that helps you communicate with the computer. Often, the cursor is displayed as a blinking line or a box that marks the spot where the next character you type will appear. On some applications, the cursor is displayed as an arrow, a pointing finger, or a set of crosshairs that can be moved to point to a menu choice, an icon, or a button.

Compression
Conserving memory, secondary storage space, and data transmission time by removing repetitive or unnecessary bits from data.

Cursor
A blinking bar or a small box displayed on the screen that helps you communicate with the computer.

Resolution and Appearance

NOTE

Perhaps you remember playing computer games on an old, low-resolution screen. The little cartoon characters were (at best) crudely drawn, and their arms and legs developed sharp, stair-like breaks as they moved. Drawing horizontal and vertical lines was no problem on such screens, but a 45-degree line had to follow a stepped path because there were no pixels in between those breaks.

Today's displays have much higher resolution. Angled lines still step one pixel to the side and one up or down, but the pixels are so close together that the unaided eye cannot see the break. That is why a graphic image looks so much better on a high-resolution screen.

CONTROLLING THE CURSOR'S POSITION

There are many devices for controlling the cursor's position. Personal computer users can press the keyboard's cursor movement keys or manipulate a **mouse** (Figure 3.9). If you have ever played a video game, you have probably used a joystick. Track balls (Figure 3.10) are common, particularly on laptop computers, and some keyboards have a thumb stick (IBM calls it a Track-Point) near the lower center of the keyboard. With a touch screen or a light pen, you enter a point by touching a spot on the screen.

USING A POINTING DEVICE FOR INPUT

In addition to indicating where the next typed character will appear, the cursor also defines a point on the screen. That fact allows you to input data by pointing and clicking.

For example, one common graphic input technique can be compared to using an electronic Etch-a-Sketch™. Picture the cursor as a pencil point that traces a line on the screen as you move the mouse. Each time you change directions, you click the mouse button to enter the point. Imagine using that technique to input a drawing.

You can also use a pointing device to select a choice from a menu (Figure 3.11). To select a menu option, you move the mouse until the cursor (usually displayed as an arrow or a pointing finger) points to your choice and then click the mouse button. As a result, the cursor's position (which marks your choice) is input. Given that position, the computer knows which option you selected.

Printers (Output)

An electronic image (for example, the image displayed on a screen) is called a soft copy. It is temporary; unless the screen is constantly refreshed, the image fades. By routing the output to a **printer** (Figure 3.12), a permanent copy, called a **hard copy,** is obtained.

Mouse
A pointing device used to select objects or menu choices on a computer screen.

▲ FIGURE 3.9

A mouse.

Printer
An output device that prints data and results on paper.
Hard copy
A printed copy.

▲ FIGURE 3.10

A track ball is built into this laptop computer's case.

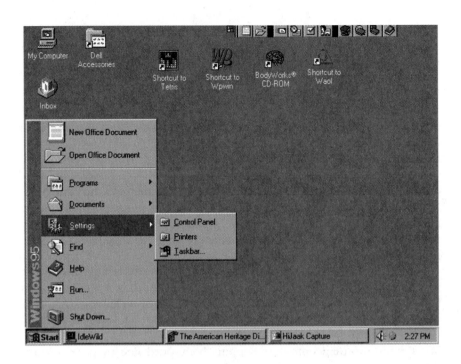

▲ FIGURE 3.11

To select a choice from a menu, you point and click.

IMPACT PRINTERS

Dot-matrix printers form characters and graphic images from patterns of dots at speeds ranging from fifty to several hundred characters per second. They are inexpensive, but the output can be difficult to read.

Letter-quality printers generate complete, solid characters and produce a clean, sharp impression. They are called letter-quality because the type quality matches that of a typewriter.

Dot-matrix printer
A printer that uses pins to form characters and graphic images as patterns of dots.
Letter-quality printer
A printer that forms complete, solid characters and produces a clean, sharp impression with typewriter-like quality.

▲ FIGURE 3.12

A printer.

Impact printer
A printer that forms characters and images by physically striking the paper.

Laser printer
A nonimpact printer that works much like a photocopier.

Ink-jet printer
A printer that forms characters and images by spraying tiny droplets of ink onto the paper.

Nonimpact printer
A printer that forms characters and images without physically striking the paper.

Dot-matrix and letter-quality printers are called **impact printers** because the printing mechanism physically strikes a ribbon and the paper. Consequently, they are good for printing multiple-part forms.

NONIMPACT PRINTERS

A **laser printer** is basically a photocopier. It uses a laser beam to form an electrostatic image of a page on a rotating drum. Toner (the same stuff used in office copiers) is attracted to the image, and the drum transfers (or offsets) the image to a sheet of paper. Personal computer laser printers typically output four to twelve pages per minute. They are relatively expensive, but they produce a very sharp image and can mix text and graphics on the same page.

An **ink-jet printer** literally spits dots of ink onto the page; in fact, some people compare ink-jet printing to (very precise) spray painting. An ink-jet printer offers better quality than a dot-matrix printer, costs less than a laser printer, and supports graphics.

Ink-jet and laser printers are **nonimpact printers** because they work without physically striking the paper. Consequently, they are quieter than impact printers. Most color printers use ink-jet or laser technology.

HIGH-SPEED PRINTERS

Mainframes and minicomputers support high-speed line or page printers (Figure 3.13) that churn out thousands of lines or hundreds of pages per minute. In some applications, to conserve space and save money "printed" output is recorded directly on computer-output microfilm.

PRINT QUALITY

Letter-quality printers produce solid characters. Dot-matrix, laser, and ink-jet printers, in contrast, form characters and images as patterns of dots and measure print quality in **dots-per-inch (DPI).** As a general rule more dots-per-inch means greater dot density, smaller dot size, and a sharper image (Figure 3.14).

Dots-per-inch (DPI)
A common measure of print quality.

▲ FIGURE 3.13

A high-speed printer.

Dot matrix resolution

Twas brillig and the sl

300 dpi resolution

Twas brillig and the sl

600 dpi resolution

Twas brillig and the sl

High resolution

Twas brillig and the sl

Depending on the model, a dot-matrix printer uses 9, 18, or 24 pins to print a pattern of relatively large dots that form crude characters. Many dot-matrix printers can operate in near-letter-quality mode by printing each character twice, with a slight offset. Twice as many dots means greater dot density and a sharper image.

As you can see in Figure 3.14, a laser printer's output (typically, 300 or 600 dots-per-inch) is much sharper than dot-matrix output. Set type, the established quality standard, is printed at 1270 or 2450 dots per inch.

OTHER I/O MEDIA AND DEVICES

Many other input and output media and devices are used with computers, including:

▶ magnetic media
▶ optical media
▶ graphic devices
▶ pen-based devices
▶ terminals
▶ sound and voice media

Magnetic Media

As the category name implies, **magnetic media** rely on magnetic properties. For example, the characters on the bottom of a check (Figure 3.15) are printed with a special magnetic ink called **MICR (magnetic ink character recognition)** that can be read electronically.

Magnetic strip (or stripe) **cards** are a common banking medium. Check your credit card and you will almost certainly see a magnetic strip on the back. The strip holds such data as your account number and credit limit, and it is read much like sound recording tape. Perhaps you have seen a store clerk swipe a credit card through a magnetic reader. Maybe you have done it

Magnetic medium
An input medium that relies on magnetic properties.
Magnetic ink character recognition (MICR)
The magnetic characters printed on the bottom of a check.
Magnetic strip card
A credit-card size card with a strip of magnetic tape on the back. A common banking medium.

NOTE

How to Read the Codes on a Check

Take a look at the numbers preprinted at the bottom of one of your checks. To the left is a string of digits that identifies your bank. Next (usually) comes the check number. Near the center is your account number.

When (or soon after) the check is cashed, the bank number, the check number, the account number, and the amount of the check must be input to the bank's computer. Because the first three values are preprinted in MICR, they are already in machine-readable form. However, the check amount cannot be known until you write it, so that value must be input through a keyboard. Look at a *cancelled* check and you can read the amount at the bottom right.

When you write a check, you record the amount twice, once in digits and once in words. Have you ever made a mistake and written two different values? Have you ever wondered which value the bank will accept?

The answer, in a way, is neither. Ideally, the teller should reject a check containing such an error, but once the check is accepted and an amount is MICR-encoded, what you wrote is irrelevant. As the check works its way through the banking system, the value printed in magnetic ink on the bottom line is the only amount that matters.

When you balance your checkbook against your cancelled checks, pay attention to the bottom line. It shows the amount that was charged to your account. Mistakes are rare, but they do happen.

▲ **FIGURE 3.15**

The MICR characters on the bottom of a check are read magnetically.

JAMES C. MORRISON
1765 SHERIDAN DRIVE
YOUR CITY, STATE 10092

1070

00–6789/0000

_____ 19_____

PAY
TO THE
ORDER OF_____ | $ [   ]

_____ DOLLARS

DELUXE CHECK PRINTERS
YOUR CITY, STATE 12345

NOT NEGOTIABLE
SAMPLE - VOID
DO   NOT   CASH!

FOR_____   _____

⑆000067894⑆ 12345678⑈

yourself; for example, most ATM machines and pay-at-the-pump service stations use magnetic strip readers to capture data from your credit card.

A **smart card** is essentially a credit card with an embedded integrated circuit chip. The chip is used to record data, and the data can be read and updated. Note that smart cards are not accessed magnetically. They are included with magnetic media simply because they resemble credit cards.

Smart card
A credit card with an embedded integrated circuit chip.

In some high-volume applications, source data are entered off-line through a keyboard directly to a magnetic medium such as magnetic tape (key-to-tape) or magnetic disk (key-to-disk). The data are subsequently transferred from the magnetic medium into a computer. A decade ago such applications were common, but they are relatively rare today.

Optical Media

Optical media are read by measuring variations in light intensity. For example, consider standardized test forms (Figure 3.16). Students use a pencil to mark their answers. The white paper reflects light, the black spots reflect much less, and variations in the intensity of the reflected light can be converted to an electronic pattern.

Optical medium
A data medium that is read optically.

OCR (optical character recognition) equipment uses the same principle to read typed or even handwritten material. **Bar codes,** such as the Universal Product Code (UPC) printed on or attached to most retail products, can be read at a checkout station or by a hand-held scanner (Figure 3.17).

Optical character recognition (OCR)
A technique for reading printed characters optically.

Bar code
A code defined by variable-width bars that can be read optically.

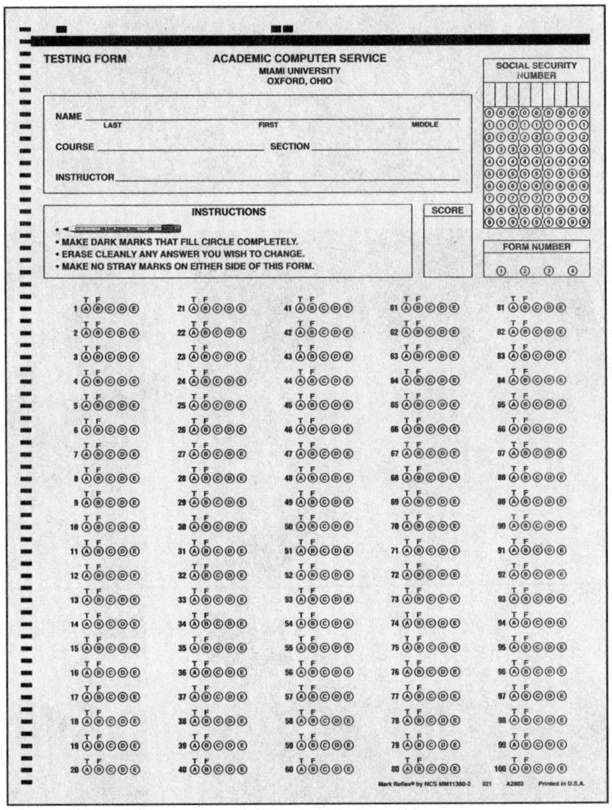
TESTING FORM
ACADEMIC COMPUTER SERVICE
MIAMI UNIVERSITY
OXFORD, OHIO
SOCIAL SECURITY NUMBER
NAME LAST FIRST MIDDLE
COURSE SECTION
INSTRUCTOR
INSTRUCTIONS
SCORE
• MAKE DARK MARKS THAT FILL CIRCLE COMPLETELY.
• ERASE CLEANLY ANY ANSWER YOU WISH TO CHANGE.
• MAKE NO STRAY MARKS ON EITHER SIDE OF THIS FORM.
FORM NUMBER

▲ **FIGURE 3.16**

Standardized test forms are read optically.

Graphic Input and Output

Scanner
A device for electronically capturing data and images from paper.

Plotter
A device for creating hard copy graphic output.

Scanners (Figure 3.18) are used to capture character data, nonalphanumeric data, and graphic images electronically from paper. Most scanners work much like an office copier, converting the image to a grid of dots that can be stored as a bit-map. Later, the bit-map can be sent to an output device and the image reproduced. Another way to capture graphic images is with a digital camera.

Graphic output displayed on a screen is temporary. For a hard copy, the image can be sent to a **plotter** (Figure 3.19) or to a graphics printer.

▲ FIGURE 3.17

The Universal Product Code can be read by a hand-held scanner.

▲ FIGURE 3.18

(below left) Scanners are used to electronically capture data from paper.

▲ FIGURE 3.19

(below right) A plotter.

Characters and Bit-Maps

An OCR reader scans a paper document, identifies individual printed or handwritten characters, and inputs them to a computer, but it cannot accept graphic images. A scanner, in contrast, captures both images and characters. Imagine laying a fine screen on top of a document. Picture each opening in the screen as a black or white dot, and you have a good sense of how a scanner works. Sophisticated scanners record a shade of grey or even a color for each dot, but the principle is the same.

One problem with scanners is that they do not distinguish between characters and images. Instead of capturing individual shapes, they convert the entire document to a bit-map. To a computer, a bit-map is just a string of binary digits that represent dots or pixels. A human being might recognize a particular pattern of dots as the letter M, but the only way a computer can distinguish the characters is to input the bit-map to a pattern recognition program.

Given today's technology, it still makes sense to use OCR devices to read characters and scanners to read images. Eventually, however, pattern recognition software will be good enough (and cheap enough) for general-purpose use, and specialized OCR scanners will gradually fade away.

Pen-Based Computers

Pen-based computers that accept handwritten or hand-marked input are relatively new. Some machines allow the user to "write" directly on the screen using an electronic pen, and data entry tablets (Figure 3.20) are common, too. In addition to allowing the direct input of handwritten characters and hand-drawn graphics, the pen can also be used as a pointing or cursor-control device.

Pen-based computer
A computer that supports handwritten or hand-marked input.

▲ **FIGURE 3.20**

A data entry tablet.

Quality problems with early pen-based systems have slowed acceptance of these devices, but handwriting recognition software is improving. Expect electronic pen-like devices to be a common option on future computer systems.

Terminals

A **terminal** (Figure 3.21) is a input/output device (usually a keyboard and a screen) that is connected to a computer. A **dumb terminal** has no intelligence of its own, and thus can do only what the computer tells it to do. An **intelligent terminal,** in contrast, contains its own computer and thus can perform numerous tasks independently.

Many organizations have replaced their terminals with personal computers linked to a network. Those personal computers, sometimes called **workstations,** can be used both as terminals and as stand-alone microcomputers.

Special-purpose terminals are designed to support specific tasks. For example, an automatic teller machine, or ATM (Figure 3.22) allows a bank customer to perform many common banking transactions; supermarket checkout stations (Figure 3.23) incorporate terminals that read preprinted bar codes; and point-of-sale terminals allow a retail store clerk to capture a sales transaction as it occurs.

Sound and Voice

A relatively new addition to modern personal computer systems is the ability to input, store, and output sound patterns. Typically, a microphone (the input device) is linked to a **sound board** that **digitizes** sound patterns by

Terminal
A keyboard/display unit that allows a user to access a multiple-user computer system or a network.
Dumb terminal
A terminal that contains no processor and thus operates only in response to commands from a computer.
Intelligent terminal
A terminal that contains its own processor and thus can perform certain functions on its own.
Workstation
A microcomputer used to access a network.

Sound board
An integrated circuit board that generates audio input or output.
Digitize
To convert data to a pattern of (often binary) digits.

▲ **FIGURE 3.21**

A terminal.

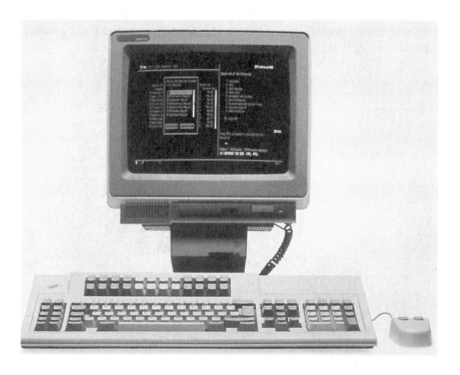

▲ FIGURE 3.22

An automatic teller machine.

▲ FIGURE 3.23

A supermarket checkout station.

NOTE

Punched Cards

From the early 1950s until well into the 1970s, punched cards were by far the most common data input medium. In fact, the warning, *Do not fold, spindle, or mutilate,* printed on many punched cards became a slogan for the depersonalization associated with technology.

Display screens and keyboards were in common use by the middle 1960s, and many people predicted the demise of punched cards, but for years nothing happened. Instead, sometime in the 1970s, they just faded away. Today, if you look hard enough you can still find punched cards in use, but they are no longer a significant data entry medium.

Voice synthesizer
A device that generates spoken output.

Voice input
The act of directly entering spoken data and commands to a computer.

converting them to the computer's internal binary form (Figure 3.24). Later, the digitized sound patterns are sent from memory through the sound board and output to speakers.

Perhaps the most natural way of communicating with a computer is by voice. Many computers use electronic **voice synthesizers** to generate spoken output. For example, when you call directory assistance you initially get a human operator. However, after you identify the party you are trying to reach, the operator switches you to a computer that uses a voice synthesizer to read the number to you.

Voice input, the act of directly entering spoken data to a computer, is much more difficult to achieve. If everyone spoke the same language with the same accent, voice input would already be common, but we do not. (For example, compare English as spoken in Boston to the same language as spoken in southern Georgia.) Add individual variations in speech patterns, and you have a very complex problem.

Voice input is available today in a limited form. Some systems are designed to be used by a handful of individuals who "train" the hardware and the software to recognize certain words as spoken by them. You can also get equipment that recognizes a limited vocabulary as spoken by many different people. Note, however, that today's products limit either the number of speakers, their vocabulary, or both, and systems that break those barriers are quite expensive.

Improvements are coming, however, because everyone recognizes the potential for inexpensive voice input. For example, a general-purpose, dictate-to word processor would have tremendous sales potential for people

▲ FIGURE 3.24

Sound patterns must be digitized before they are input to a computer.

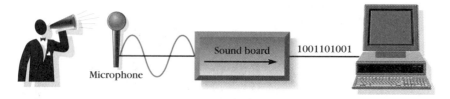

who do not type. That is new business, and every company that sells computer hardware or software would love to be the first to market that product.

LINKING PEOPLE AND COMPUTERS

The purpose of an information system is to deliver the right data and the right information to the right people at the right time. The data, the information, and the people are the keys; the computer is just a tool. Input devices allow people to enter data to a computer. Output devices allow people to obtain data and information from a computer. In other words, input and output devices provide a means for computers and people to communicate with each other.

Imagine a line stretching between a computer and a human being (Figure 3.25). At the computer's end, everything is represented by patterns of 1s and 0s. The human being, in contrast, can see, hear, feel, taste, and smell a variety of objects and other physical phenomena.

To communicate with the first computers, a user or an operator had to input binary data and interpret binary output. Later, punched cards and keyboard/display terminals allowed the user to enter data by pressing the keys on a standard keyboard and read the output in character form. Many of today's personal computers support a less intimidating point-and-click graphic interface, and systems that can recognize handwriting and even spoken words are beginning to enter the market.

Note the trend. Initially, the person had to adjust to the computer but, gradually, the point of interface has moved closer and closer to the human side. Eventually, computers will adjust to us, and we will be able to communicate with them in much the same way we communicate with each other. Perhaps the image of Spock speaking to the computer on board the starship *Enterprise* is not as farfetched as it once seemed.

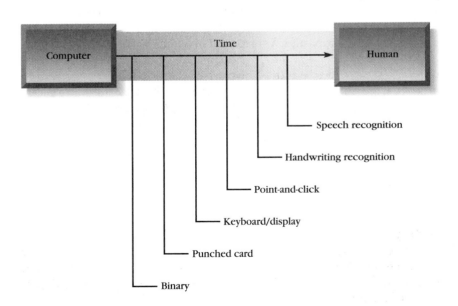

▲ **FIGURE 3.25**

Over the years, communicating with a computer has become more human-like.

SUMMARY

A transaction is a single occurrence of an activity, an event, or an object about which data are collected. The original data that describe each transaction are called source data. Data capture is the process of initially recording the data. Data entry is the process of entering the data to the computer. Sometimes, the data are captured and entered in a single step through an online input device.

Data are often output in the form of reports. A detail report shows one transaction per line. A summary report shows such information as counts and totals for groups of transactions. Some reports are generated periodically. Demand reports are created on request. An exception report lists only those transactions or summaries that deviate from a target.

Documents, sound patterns, video, and graphic images are other forms of computer data. Multimedia implies using a computer to merge documents, text, numbers, graphics, sound, video, and other media to create an integrated presentation.

The basic input device on most personal computer systems is a keyboard. Characters and images are displayed on a display screen. Laptop computers have flat-panel displays. A display works by dividing the screen into a grid of picture elements, or pixels. An image that is stored as a pattern of pixels or dots is called a bit-map. The quality, or resolution, of an image on a screen is a function of the number of pixels displayed. One cost of high resolution is that data must be stored for more pixels. One way to conserve memory and secondary storage space is to compress the data.

The cursor is a marker on the screen that helps you communicate with the computer. You control the cursor's position by pressing the cursor movement keys or by manipulating a mouse or a similar pointing device.

A printer generates a hard copy. Dot-matrix printers and letter-quality printers are called impact printers because the printing mechanism physically strikes a ribbon and the paper. Laser printers and ink-jet printers are nonimpact printers because they work without physically striking the paper. The quality of printed output is measured in dots-per-inch (DPI).

Magnetic media, such as MICR and magnetic strip cards, are read by interpreting magnetic properties. A smart card is a credit card with an embedded chip that allows data to be stored and updated. Optical media, such as OCR documents, bar codes, and the Universal Product Code (UPC) are read by measuring variations in light intensity. Scanners are used to electronically capture images from paper. For hard copy output, a graphic image can be sent to a plotter or to a graphics printer. Pen-based computers accept handwritten or hand-marked input.

A terminal is directly controlled by a computer. A dumb terminal consists of little more than a keyboard and a display screen. An intelligent terminal contains its own computer and can perform numerous tasks on its own. The personal computers that are linked to a network are sometimes called workstations. Special-purpose terminals, such as ATMs and point-of-sale terminals, perform specific tasks.

Sound patterns must be digitized by a sound board before they are input to a computer. Many computers use electronic voice synthesizers to send spoken output to speakers. Voice input is the act of directly entering spoken data into a computer.

To communicate with the first computers, a user or an operator had to input binary data and interpret binary output. Gradually, the point of interface has moved closer and closer to the human side, and that trend continues.

KEY TERMS

bar code	graphic image	optical medium
bit-map	hard copy	pen-based computer
compress, or compression	impact printer	picture element (pixel)
cursor	ink-jet printer	plotter
data capture	intelligent terminal	printer
data entry	keyboard	report
demand report	laser printer	resolution
detail report	letter-quality printer	scanner
digitize	magnetic medium	smart card
display screen	magnetic strip card	sound board
document	MICR	source data
dot-matrix printer	mouse	summary report
dots-per-inch (DPI)	multimedia	terminal
dot pitch	nonimpact printer	transaction
dumb terminal	OCR (optical character	voice input
exception report	recognition)	voice synthesizer
flat-panel display	on-line	workstation

CONCEPTS

1. What is the purpose of a computer's input and output devices?
2. Define the term *transaction*. Define the term *source data*.
3. Distinguish between data capture and data entry. Explain how these two steps can be combined by using an on-line input device.
4. Distinguish among detail, summary, periodic, demand, and exception reports.
5. What is multimedia? What types of data and information might be included in a multimedia presentation?
6. Identify the input and output devices attached to a typical personal computer system.
7. What is a pixel? What is a bit-map?
8. Explain how a screen's resolution is measured. Explain the relationship between a screen's resolution and the quality of the image displayed.
9. Briefly explain how compression can be used to reduce the amount of memory required to hold a bit-map.
10. What is the cursor? Explain how the cursor's position is controlled. Explain how controlling the cursor can be used to provide input to a computer.
11. Distinguish between a soft copy and a hard copy.
12. Distinguish between impact and nonimpact printers, and cite at least two examples of each. Explain how print quality is measured.
13. Relate pixel density, dots-per-inch, and image quality.
14. Identify at least two magnetic media.

15. Identify at least two optical media.
16. What is a terminal? Distinguish among a dumb terminal, an intelligent terminal, and a workstation.
17. Many experts believe that voice recognition and voice response will be significant (perhaps dominant) I/O media once the appropriate technology is perfected. Do you agree? Why or why not?
18. When computers were first developed, people had to communicate with them at the computer's level, but over the years input and output devices have become more human-friendly. Why is that trend significant?

PROJECTS

1. Find out how a check works its way through the banking system.
2. Investigate how a computer-controlled supermarket checkout system works.
3. Find out how your school captures and enters student course registration data.
4. Find out how your school captures and enters end-of-term student grade data and produces student grade reports.?

 ## INTERNET PROJECTS

1. *News and Notes*. Companies often post information about their very latest products on their World Wide Web home pages. Select a company whose products are featured in this chapter's photographs and access its home page. Try the address *http://www.xxx.com;* substitute the company name (for example, *IBM*) for *xxx*. Once you find the home page, look for a button marked *New products* (or something similar) and click on it. Identify and briefly describe at least two new products and submit your findings to your instructor in the form of a brief note or an e-mail message.
2. *Topic Searches.* Check the World Wide Web and/or other Internet resources for information on the following topics:

Key word	Qualifiers
repetitive stress	wrist
injury	elbow
carpal-tunnel syndrome	
resolution	display screen
	laser printer
voice input	application

Define the key word, identify at least two sources of information on the topic, and briefly summarize the nature of the information you find.

3. *Links to Other Sites*. After you access one or more of the following sites, write a brief note or send an e-mail message to your instructor outlining what you find.

    a. Check newsgroup *comp.human-factors* for information on ergonomics.

    b. If you are in the market for computer-related equipment, check newsgroup *misc.forsale.comp.xxx*. Substitute the component you need (for example, *printer*) for *xxx*.

    c. On the World Wide Web, check *http://www.hp.com* for the most current information on Hewlett-Packard printers and other products.

    d. On the World Wide Web, check *http://www.zdnet.com* for current news about computers and computer-related products.

4. Access West Publishing Company's home page and find the Chapter 3 student activities for this book. See Internet Project 3 for the spotlight on *The Internet* following Chapter 1 (page 29) for more detailed instructions on accessing the home page. As appropriate, repeat projects 1, 2, and/or 3 using the more current references you find.

CHAPTER 4

Inside the Computer: Memory and the Processor

Before you start this chapter, you should be familiar with the following concepts:

▶ Hardware (p. 6), software (p. 9), and data (p. 10).

▶ Inside a computer (p. 7).

▶ Systems (p. 13), computer classifications (p. 14), and networks (p. 17).

When you finish reading this chapter, you should be able to:

▶ Distinguish among bits, bytes, and words.

▶ Discuss how data are represented inside a computer and distinguish between numeric and string data.

▶ Explain how memory is addressed.

▶ Distinguish between reading and writing memory.

▶ Distinguish between RAM and ROM. Identify several variations of RAM and ROM. Briefly explain the purpose of cache memory.

▶ Identify the processor's primary components and explain what each of those components does.

▶ Explain how the processor works by describing the steps in a machine cycle.

▶ Distinguish between a computer's instruction set (hardware) and the instructions that make up a program (software).

▶ Distinguish between complex instruction set computers and reduced instruction set computers.

▶ Distinguish among machine-level instructions, microcode, and Boolean logic.

Main Memory

When data enter a computer they are stored in memory (Figure 4.1). From memory, the data are transferred to the processor and manipulated, and the results are stored back in memory. Eventually, those results are sent to an output device.

This chapter focuses on the computer's internal components: memory and the processor. We'll start with memory.

Before a computer can process data, the data must first be stored in memory. Before a computer can execute a program, that program must be stored in memory. To put it another way, a computer's main or primary memory holds the program currently being executed and the data currently being processed. In this book, the term *memory* implies main memory.

Bits, Bytes, and Words

As you learned in Chapter 1, a computer's basic unit of memory is a binary digit, or bit. The amount of information that can be represented by a single 0 or 1 is quite limited, however, so (for the same reason we focus on words and sentences rather than individual letters when we read) the contents of memory are generally envisioned as groups of bits called bytes and words.

A byte contains eight bits, enough to represent a single character. A **word** consists of one or more bytes. Some computers have 8-bit words. Other, more powerful machines work with 16-bit (2-byte), 32-bit (4-byte), and even 64-bit words. Perhaps you have seen advertisements that describe 16-bit and 32-bit computers; those numbers represent word sizes. Generally, a bigger word size means a faster, more powerful computer.

Figure 4.2 outlines a typical memory hierarchy. The basic unit of storage is the bit. Bits are grouped to form bytes, which, in turn, are grouped to form words.

Memory Capacity

In the early 1980s, a typical microcomputer had only 128 **kilobytes,** or **KB** (thousands of bytes) of memory. Over the years, memory capacity has increased steadily. Today, 16-**megabyte** (million bytes, or **MB**) personal computers are common, and computers with **gigabytes** (billions of bytes, or **GB**)

Word
A unit of memory composed of one or more bytes.

Kilobyte (KB)
Approximately 1000 bytes.
Megabyte (MB)
Approximately one million bytes.
Gigabyte (GB)
Approximately one billion bytes.

▲ FIGURE 4.1

The input/process/output cycle.

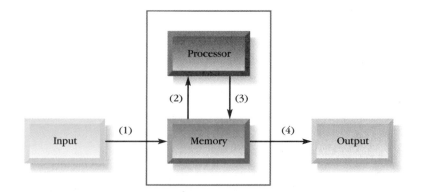

NOTE

The Meaning of "K"

Technically, 1 kilobyte is 1,024 bytes, not 1,000 bytes. Likewise, 1 megabyte is 1,048,576 bytes, not 1,000,000 bytes. Why is that so? As you learned in Chapter 1, a computer is a binary machine, so memory capacity is expressed in binary terms. The number 1,024 is 2^{10}, and 1,048,576 is 2^{20}. Note that both values are integer powers of 2. They are close enough to the decimal numbers 1,000 and 1,000,000 for most purposes, so we talk about thousands of bytes and millions of bytes, but the actual values are just a bit higher.

of memory are a real possibility. As its memory capacity increases, a computer is able to support more sophisticated, more powerful, easier to use software and to process more data.

Memory Contents

The bytes and words that make up a computer's memory store characters, numbers, and program instruction in binary form. As a user, you should know that numeric data and character data are stored differently inside the machine, and that you cannot perform arithmetic on character data. (For example, the result of adding the year of your birth to your zip code is meaningless.) That is why you must distinguish character and numeric values when you use a spreadsheet program or other software that performs arithmetic.

NUMBER SYSTEMS

A number is a set of digits written in relative positions. To compute the value of a number, you multiply each digit by its place or positional value and sum the products. For example, the decimal number 972 is

$$
\begin{array}{rrcr}
+9 \text{ times} & 100 & = & 900 \\
+7 \text{ times} & 10 & = & 70 \\
+2 \text{ times} & 1 & = & \underline{2} \\
& & & 972
\end{array}
$$

Word 0

Byte 0	Byte 1	Byte 2	Byte 3
1011 0011	1010 1101	1010 1001	1011 0100

Bits

▲ FIGURE 4.2

The memory hierarchy.

As you learned in elementary school, the decimal digits are 0, 1, 2, 3, 4, 5, 6, 7, 8, and 9 and the decimal place values are powers of 10 (1, 10, 100, 1000, 10,000, and so on). That is why it is called a decimal or base-10 number system.

BINARY NUMBERS

It is possible to represent numbers using any value as a base. For example, in a binary or base-2 number system, the positional values are powers of 2 (2^0, 2^1, 2^2, 2^3, or 1, 2, 4, 8, and so on), and you need only two digit values, 0 and 1. Figure 4.3 shows the binary equivalents of the decimal numbers 0 through 15. For example, the decimal number 5 is 101 in binary ($1 \times 2^2 = 4$, plus $0 \times 2^1 = 0$, plus $1 \times 2^0 = 1$).

We use decimal numbers because we find them convenient (probably because we have ten fingers). A computer is an electronic machine that represents 0 and 1 as off and on. In other words, a computer uses binary numbers because it finds binary convenient.

See Appendix C for additional information about number systems and computer arithmetic.

NUMERIC DATA

Computers are at their most efficient when working with pure binary **integers** (whole numbers, with no fractional part). For example, the biggest binary value that can be stored in a 32-bit word is

$$01111111111111111111111111111111$$

which is 2^{31} minus 1, or 2,147,483,647 in decimal. The high-order bit is the sign: 0 for plus and 1 for minus.

Scientific notation expresses very large and very small numbers as a decimal value followed by a power of 10; for example, the speed of light in a vacuum is 1.86×10^5 miles per second. The (approximate) binary equivalent of scientific notation is called **floating-point**. Integers are whole numbers without a decimal point. Floating-point numbers are composed of one or more significant digits (the mantissa) and an exponent that specifies decimal point alignment.

Business applications call for precisely rounded decimal numbers, so many computers support (or simulate) a form of decimal data as well. Like

Integer
A whole number with no fractional part.

Floating-point
A type of numeric data that emulates scientific notation on a computer.

▲ FIGURE 4.3

The binary equivalents of the decimal numbers 0 through 15.

DECIMAL	BINARY	DECIMAL	BINARY
0	0000	8	1000
1	0001	9	1001
2	0010	10	1010
3	0011	11	1011
4	0100	12	1100
5	0101	13	1101
6	0110	14	1110
7	0111	15	1111

Business applications call for precisely rounded decimal numbers, so many computers support (or simulate) a form of decimal data as well. Like real numbers, decimal numbers can contain a decimal point.

STRING DATA

Many applications call for such nonnumeric data as names and addresses. Such **string** values are stored as sets of individual coded characters, generally one character per byte. **ASCII** (the American Standard Code for Information Interchange) and **EBCDIC** (the Extended Binary Coded Decimal Interchange Code) are two standard codes (Figure 4.4). For example, the ASCII code for the name SMITH is:

```
1011 0011 1010 1101 1010 1001 1011 0100 1010 1000
```

String
Data values stored as sets of individual coded characters, generally one character per byte.
ASCII
Acronym for American Standard Code for Information Interchange.
EBCDIC
Acronym for Expanded Binary Coded Decimal Interchange Code.

CHARACTER	ASCII	EBCDIC
0	0101 0000	1111 0000
1	0101 0001	1111 0001
2	0101 0010	1111 0010
3	0101 0011	1111 0011
4	0101 0100	1111 0100
5	0101 0101	1111 0101
6	0101 0110	1111 0110
7	0101 0111	1111 0111
8	0101 1000	1111 1000
9	0101 1001	1111 1001
A	1010 0001	1100 0001
B	1010 0010	1100 0010
C	1010 0011	1100 0011
D	1010 0100	1100 0100
E	1010 0101	1100 0101
F	1010 0110	1100 0110
G	1010 0111	1100 0111
H	1010 1000	1100 1000
I	1010 1001	1100 1001
J	1010 1010	1101 0001
K	1010 1011	1101 0010
L	1010 1100	1101 0011
M	1010 1101	1101 0100
N	1010 1110	1101 0101
O	1010 1111	1101 0110
P	1011 0000	1101 0111
Q	1011 0001	1101 1000
R	1011 0010	1101 1001
S	1011 0011	1110 0010
T	1011 0100	1110 0011
U	1011 0101	1110 0100
V	1011 0110	1110 0101
W	1011 0111	1110 0110
X	1011 1000	1100 0111
Y	1011 1001	1110 1000
Z	1011 1010	1110 1001

▲ FIGURE 4.4

The ASCII and EBCDIC codes.

Strings and numbers are different. For example, if you input the digit 1 followed by the digit 2, each character is stored as a code. In ASCII, the digit 1 is represented as 0101 0001 and the digit 2 is represented as 0101 0010, so together those two digits are stored as:

```
0101 0001 0101 0010
```

In contrast, the *number* 12 (stored as a 16-bit binary integer) is

```
0000 0000 0000 1100
```

Compare those two values from left to right. Clearly, they are different.

ADVANCED TOPICS

Parity

On most computers, an extra bit, called a parity bit, is stored with each byte. The purpose of that extra bit is to help the computer identify errors.

With odd parity, the total number of 1 (or on) bits in the 9 bits that make up a byte plus its parity bit must be an odd number. Thus, if a byte holds the ASCII code for the letter A (1010 0001), its parity bit will be set to 0 (yielding a total of three 1 bits), while a byte that holds the letter C (1010 0011) will have a parity bit of 1 (for a total of five 1 bits). With even parity, the total number of 1 bits in a byte plus its parity bit must be an even number. Incorrect parity implies an error that can be detected by the computer's error-detection circuitry.

Addressing Memory

Address
The location of a byte or word in memory.

A typical computer contains well over a million bytes of memory. To identify them, each byte is assigned a unique **address** by numbering the bytes sequentially—0, 1, 2, and so on. A byte is the computer's basic *addressable* unit of memory.

The processor accesses a specific memory location by referencing its address. For example, if the processor needs the data stored in byte 1048, it asks memory for the contents of byte 1048. Since there is only one byte 1048, the processor gets the right data.

Reading and Writing Memory

Read
To extract the contents of one or more bytes or words from memory without changing them.

Write
To record new values in memory, thus destroying the old contents.

When you **read** memory, you extract the contents of one or more bytes or words but you do not change them. For example, imagine that byte number 42 holds the character A. After the processor reads byte 42, the code for the letter A is still there.

When you **write** memory, in contrast, you record new values in the target bytes, and that destroys the old contents. If the processor were to write to byte 42 the code for the character X, the new value would replace the old one, and the A would be lost forever.

Consider the distinction between reading and writing memory from a slightly different perspective. On input, data are read from an input device and written to memory, thus destroying (replacing) any data formerly in the target bytes. On output, data are read from memory and written to an output device, and the contents of the memory bytes are not changed. Note that the term *read* refers to the source of the data, while *write* refers to their destination. A write is a destructive operation; a read is not destructive.

Memory Types

The function of memory is to hold the program being executed and the data being processed. Those tasks seem straightforward, so it might surprise you to learn that there are several different types of memory.

RANDOM ACCESS MEMORY (RAM)

The main or primary memory of most computers is composed of a bank of random access memory (RAM) chips (Figure 4.5). Think of RAM as a scratch pad that holds current programs and current data. A program can read from or write to RAM, for example, requesting the input of new data to replace the data it has already processed. When a program finishes executing, a new program can be loaded into its memory space, enabling the computer to perform a different task.

READ-ONLY MEMORY (ROM)

As you learned in Chapter 1, main memory (more precisely, RAM) is volatile; it loses its contents when power is cut. In contrast, **read-only memory,** or **ROM,** is *not* volatile. As the name implies, ROM is permanent memory that can be read but not written.

ROM is used for a few key program modules and data values; for example, the start-up program that is executed when a computer is first turned on

Read-only memory (ROM)
A type of memory that can be read but not modified.

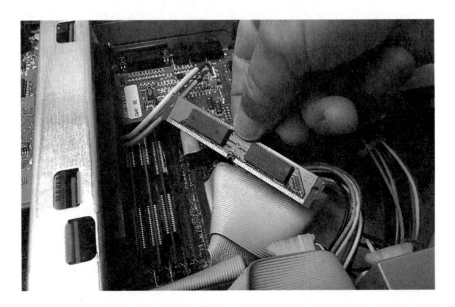

▲ **FIGURE 4.5**

Random access memory (RAM) chips.

Memory Cost

In the 1960s, most computers used magnetic core memory that was manufactured by manually weaving thin, threadlike wires through an array of tiny ferrite rings (called cores). The process was labor intensive and very expensive. In those days, "a buck a byte" was a common rule of thumb for estimating memory cost, and a computer with 256 KB of memory was considered a large machine.

Times have changed. Today, you can add a megabyte of integrated circuit memory to your desktop computer for less than $50. If automobiles had followed the same price curve as computer memory, today's new cars would cost roughly as much as a hamburger (without the cheese), get 500 miles per gallon, go 1,000 miles per hour, and require maintenance at most once a year.

Firmware
Permanent software implemented in ROM.

might be ROM-based. (See "The Boot" in Chapter 6, page 133) A bank of ROM chips that holds a permanent program is sometimes called **firmware** because it exhibits characteristics of both hardware and software.

CHANGING THE CONTENTS OF RAM

Imagine that the computer is preparing a bill for a customer named *SMITH*, and that the last name occupies bytes 1000 through 1004 (Figure 4.6a). One character is stored in each byte, so byte 1000 holds the ASCII code for the letter S, byte 1001 holds the code for the letter M, and so on. Look closely at byte 1002. It contains the binary digits 1010 1001, which, in ASCII code, is the letter I.

Now imagine that a few thousandths of a second have passed and the computer has finished processing Smith's data. As the next input/process/output cycle begins, new data for someone named *PEREZ* are input to memory, so bytes 1000 through 1004 now hold the binary codes for P, E, R, E, and Z (Figure 4.6b). Note that the old contents of bytes 1000 through 1004 are no longer in memory because they have been replaced by new data. Once again, look closely at byte 1002. It now contains the binary digits 1011 0010, which is the ASCII code for the letter R.

OTHER TYPES OF MEMORY

For most users, understanding the distinction between volatile RAM and nonvolatile ROM is adequate, but there are other types of memory.

Dynamic random access memory, or **DRAM,** chips lose their charge unless they are continuously refreshed electronically. In contrast, **static random access memory,** or **SRAM,** retains its contents as long as power is supplied. SRAM is much faster than DRAM, but it is also more expensive, occupies more space, consumes more power, and generates more heat. Consequently, the main memory of most computers is composed of DRAM.

PROM (programmable read-only memory) lies somewhere between ROM and RAM. As the name implies, you can program (or write to) PROM once, but the contents cannot subsequently be changed. **EPROM** (erasable programmable read-only memory), in contrast, can be programmed, erased,

DRAM
Acronym for dynamic random access memory.
SRAM
Acronym for static random access memory.
PROM
Acronym for programmable read-only memory.
EPROM
Acronym for erasable programmable read-only memory.

a.

Address:	1000	1001	1002	1003	1004
Contents: (binary code)	1011 0011	1010 1101	1010 1001	1011 0100	1010 1000
Character:	S	M	I	T	H

b.

Address:	1000	1001	1002	1003	1004
Contents: (binary code)	1011 0000	1010 0101	1011 0010	1010 0101	1011 1010
Character:	P	E	R	E	Z

▲ **FIGURE 4.6**

One coded character can be stored in each byte.
a. **These five bytes hold the ASCII codes for the letters S M I T H.**
b. **After new data are input, the five bytes hold the ASCII codes for the letters P E R E Z.**

and reprogrammed, although the process of erasing memory requires special equipment. **Flash memory** is a type of EPROM that can be erased and reprogrammed by a personal computer without using special equipment. Sometimes called flash RAM, it acts like nonvolatile random access memory.

Flash memory
A type of EPROM that can be erased and reprogrammed by a personal computer without using special equipment.

CACHE MEMORY

One way to increase processing speed is to move program instructions and data from memory to the processor more quickly. For example, using static RAM instead of dynamic RAM can significantly boost processing speed because the processor spends less time waiting for the faster SRAM chips to respond. SRAM is too expensive to use as general-purpose memory, but many computers do contain a block of high-speed SRAM **cache** (pronounced "cash") **memory.**

Think of cache memory as a staging area for the processor (Figure 4.7). The program is stored in standard (DRAM) memory. As the program executes, the active instructions and the active data are transferred to high-speed

Cache memory
High-speed memory that is used as a staging area for the processor.

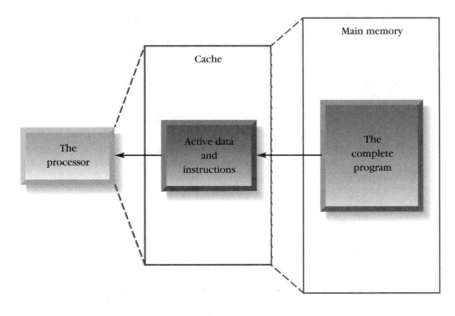

▲ **FIGURE 4.7**

Think of cache memory as a staging area for the processor.

(SRAM) cache memory. From there, individual instructions and the data referenced by those instructions move from cache to the processor. Consequently, the processor waits for high-speed SRAM instead of low-speed DRAM, and that increases processing speed.

ADVANCED TOPICS

Cache Operation

For cache memory to work, instructions and data must be copied from standard memory to high-speed memory *before* the processor requests them. Fortunately, the instructions in most programs are executed in sequence, so if you copy a block of adjacent instructions into cache memory, the "next" instruction will usually be there. (That concept is called *locality of reference.*) Eventually, however, a program will reference an instruction or data not yet in cache. How does the computer deal with that problem?

When data or instructions are copied from main memory into a cache slot, the computer's hardware makes a note of the associated main memory address. When the processor requests data or an instruction (by address), hardware checks to see if the request refers to a region of memory that is already in cache. If it does, the data or instruction goes directly from cache to the processor. If the referenced memory is not yet in cache, the data or a new block of instructions is copied from main memory into cache, where it replaces the least used (least recently referenced) slot. From cache, the requested data or instruction flows to the processor.

One final note: Data and instructions are *copied* into cache; in other words, part of what is stored in main memory is duplicated in cache.

HOW THE PROCESSOR WORKS

Central processing unit (CPU)
Another term for the processor.
Main processor
The central processing unit.

As the name implies, the processor, sometimes called the **central processing unit (CPU)** or **main processor,** is the part of the computer that executes instructions and thus processes data. The processor manipulates data stored in memory under the control of a program stored in memory.

Instructions

A program consists of a series of instructions. Each instruction is a group of bits that tells the computer to perform one of its basic functions. Some instructions are arithmetic: add, subtract, multiply, divide. Some are logical: compare, copy. Others, such as start input or start output, generate control signals from the processor to other system components.

Operation code
The portion of a machine-level instruction that specifies the operation to be performed.
Operand
The portion of a machine-level instruction that specifies the address of data to be processed by the instruction.

Operation Codes and Operands

Each instruction consists of two parts: an **operation code** and one or more **operands** (Figure 4.8). The operation code tells the computer what to do (for example, add, subtract, or compare); think of an operation code as a verb. The operands identify the data to be manipulated by the instruction.

Processor Components

The processor contains four key components (Figure 4.9). The **clock** generates precisely timed pulses of current that synchronize the computer's other components. The **instruction control unit** identifies the next instruction to be executed and retrieves or **fetches** it from memory. The **arithmetic and logic unit** executes most instructions. **Registers** are temporary storage devices that hold control information, current data, and intermediate results.

Machine Cycles

The processor is driven by the clock. When the clock "ticks," it activates the instruction control unit, which fetches an instruction from memory and decodes it. Normally, the arithmetic and logic unit then executes the instruction and stores the result in a register or in memory. On most computers, however, input, output, move, and copy instructions are an exception to that rule because the arithmetic and logic unit is not activated.

One complete fetch/execute sequence defines a single **machine cycle** (Figure 4.10). An instruction is fetched by the instruction control unit during **I-time** or **instruction time** and executed by the arithmetic and logic unit during **E-time** or **execution time.** The clock drives the process, generating pulses of current at precisely timed intervals. That basic machine cycle is repeated again and again until the program is finished.

Note that both the fetch and execute phases call for moving a byte or a word between the processor and memory. Consequently, memory speed limits processor speed.

Clock
A device that drives a processor by emitting carefully timed electronic pulses.

Instruction control unit
The processor component that fetches an instruction from memory.

Fetch
To transfer a copy of an instruction or data from memory to the processor.

Arithmetic and logic unit
The processor component that executes instructions.

Register
A temporary storage device in the processor that holds control information, current data, and intermediate results.

Machine cycle
The process of fetching and executing a single instruction.

Instruction time (I-time)
The phase of a machine cycle during which the instruction control unit fetches and decodes a single instruction.

Execution time (E-time)
The phase of a machine cycle during which a single instruction is executed by the arithmetic and logic unit.

▲ **FIGURE 4.9**

The processor consists of four key components.

▲ **FIGURE 4.8**

An instruction consists of an operation code and one or more operands.

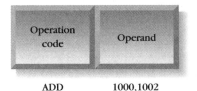

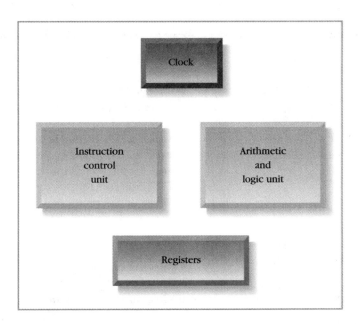

▲ **FIGURE 4.10**

A typical machine cycle.

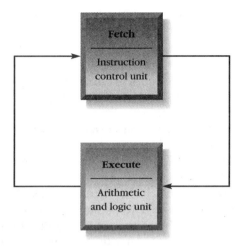

Processor Speed

MegaHertz
One million cycles per second. A common measure of clock speed.

Clock speed is usually measured in **megaHertz (mHz),** or millions of cycles (pulses) per second. In 1980, a typical microcomputer operated in the 10 mHz range, but 150 and even 200 mHz computers are common today and some experts expect 1,000 mHz (gigaHertz) computers by the turn of the century.

A megaHertz processor executes instructions in the microsecond (millionth of a second) range. Experts believe that computers will eventually be able to execute instructions in the nanosecond (billionth of a second) or even picosecond (trillionth of a second) range. Because a standard processor can execute no more than one instruction per machine cycle, a 100 mHz clock speed represents a theoretical limit of 100 million instructions per second, or 100 **MIPS.**

MIPS
An acronym for one million instructions per second. A common measure of processor speed.

NOTE

Surge Protection

Inconsistent power can damage a computer's internal circuitry, so it is wise to install a surge protector between the wall outlet and the machine. A good surge protector will help to shield your computer from electrical spikes caused by lightning, the on/off cycles of heavy equipment (like air conditioners), and other difficult to predict events. Note that power surges can enter a computer through a communication line, so line protection is important, too.

Even better protection is achieved by installing an uninterruptible power source, or UPS, that keeps the system running even if power fails. With an uninterruptible power source, the computer gets its power from a battery, and the battery is constantly recharged from a wall outlet. If the power fails, the battery backup gives the system operator plenty of time to finish active work and conduct a normal system shutdown. Most uninterruptible power sources incorporate surge protectors, too.

PEOPLE

John von Neumann

During World War II, John von Neumann, a Princeton University professor and applied mathematician, worked (like many American scientists of his day) on the atomic bomb project. His mathematical models called for a great deal of computation, and he recognized the value of the ENIAC computer being developed at the University of Pennsylvania at about the same time. Because of his influence, the first significant test application of the ENIAC was a set of calculations performed for the atomic energy laboratory in Los Alamos, New Mexico.

The ENIAC was a very limited machine, and in 1944 work started on a more powerful computer called the EDVAC. John von Neumann worked on the EDVAC project, helping to develop the computer's logical design. His draft version of a paper on the EDVAC design, published in June, 1945, established a base for first-generation computer technology.

One key element of the EDVAC's design was the idea of sequentially fetching and executing instructions from a program stored in the computer's own memory. Although many others contributed to the development of the stored program concept, von Neumann's paper was the first published account, and processors that are driven by a sequential machine cycle are still called von Neumann computers.

Benchmarks

Certain instructions, such as adding the contents of two registers, might be completed in a single machine cycle, but more complex instructions, such as multiplication (repetitive addition) and division (repetitive subtraction), typically consume multiple cycles. Consequently, although a computer's clock speed does set a *theoretical* limit on its processing speed, converting cycles per second directly to instructions per second significantly overstates the truth.

One way to measure a computer's real processing speed is to execute a **benchmark** program, such as estimating pi to multiple decimal positions. The benchmark contains a known number of instructions. If you divide instructions executed by elapsed time you get instructions per second.

Benchmark
A standard program used to estimate a computer's processing speed.

Machine Cycles: An Example

One way to understand how a computer's internal components work is to observe a few machine cycles. Figure 4.11 shows a simplified model of a computer. The processor contains a clock, an instruction control unit, an

▲ FIGURE 4.11

A few machine cycles.
a. **The instruction counter points to the next instruction.**
b. **The instruction control unit fetches the instruction.**

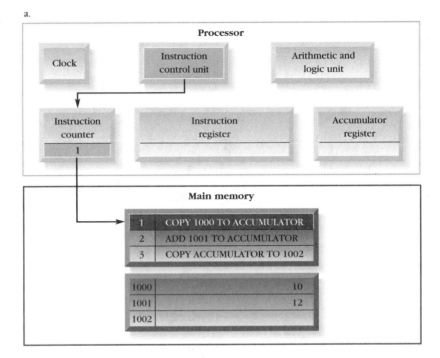

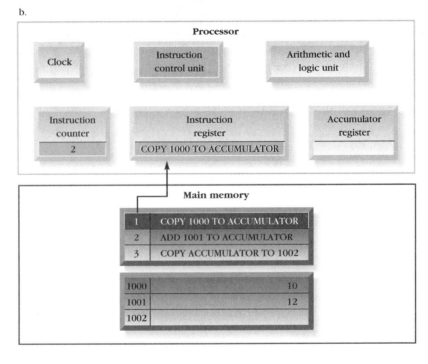

arithmetic and logic unit, and several registers. The computer is controlled by a program; note that the instructions are stored in memory. As the example begins, the data to be processed are also stored in memory.

Three registers are significant in this example. The **instruction counter** points to the next instruction in the program. The **instruction register** holds the actual instruction to be executed. The **accumulator** holds data; as the name implies it is typically used to accumulate (or sum) values.

Processing begins when the clock generates a pulse of current. The instruction control unit responds by checking the instruction counter, which points to the next instruction in memory (Figure 4.11a). The instruction control unit fetches the instruction from memory and copies it into the instruction register (Figure 4.11b). Meanwhile, the instruction control unit increments the instruction counter to point to the "next" instruction (in this example, to instruction number 2).

Once an arithmetic or comparison instruction is fetched, the instruction control unit activates the arithmetic and logic unit. The arithmetic and logic unit, in turn, executes the instruction in the instruction register (Figure 4.11c). As a result (in this example) a data value from memory is added to the accumulator.

The next machine cycle starts when the clock "ticks" again. As before, the instruction control unit checks the instruction counter, fetches the next instruction, copies it into the instruction register (Figure 4.11d), and increments the instruction counter. Then the arithmetic and logic unit executes the instruction (Figure 4.11e).

The process of fetching and executing instructions continues until all the instructions in the program are executed.

Instruction counter
A special register that holds the address of the next instruction to be executed.
Instruction register
A special register that holds the next instruction to be executed.
Accumulator
On many computers, a work register used to add or accumulate values.

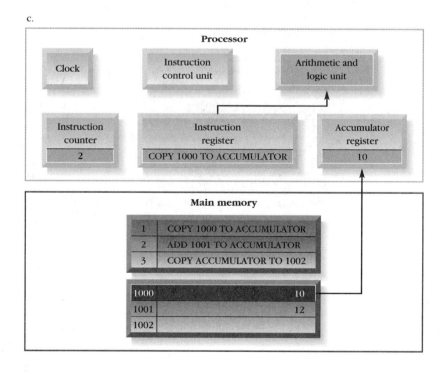

c.

▲ **FIGURE 4.11 (continued)**

c. The arithmetic and logic unit executes the instruction.

▲ FIGURE 4.11 (continued)

d. The instruction control unit fetches the next instruction.

e. The arithmetic and logic unit executes the instruction.

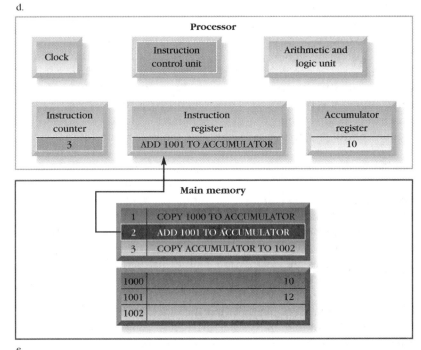

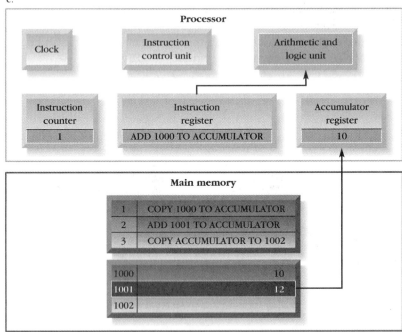

ADVANCED TOPICS

Pipelining

A serial processor is designed to fetch and execute one instruction at a time. In other words, the first instruction is fetched, the first instruction is executed; the second instruction is fetched, the second instruction is executed, and so on.

ADVANCED TOPICS

To gain processing speed, many computers (including some microcomputers) are designed to overlap machine cycle phases, for example, fetching instruction 2 while instruction 1 is executing. On such machines the "next" instruction is ready as soon as the current one finishes executing, so no time is lost fetching instructions.

If you break the machine cycle into additional discrete phases, it is possible to get more than two instructions into the pipeline. For example, during a single machine cycle the processor might: (1) fetch the instruction from memory; (2) locate the first data field; (3) locate the second data field; (4) fetch the first data value from memory; (5) fetch the second data value from memory; and (6) execute the instruction. If you design the processor to overlap all six phases, in theory you can execute six instructions per machine cycle.

Note, however, that a single processor actually *executes* (the final step) only one instruction at a time. Overlapping (or pipelining as it is sometimes called) does not change that basic fact.

PROCESSOR HARDWARE

In Chapter 1 you learned that the basic electronic building blocks of modern computers are tiny integrated circuit chips. A mainframe's processor consists of numerous chips mounted on boards. The **microprocessor** that drives a microcomputer is a complete processor on a single chip. For example, Figure 4.12 shows an Intel Pentium microprocessor chip.

Microprocessor
A complete processor on a single chip.

▲ **FIGURE 4.12**

An Intel Pentium microprocessor chip.

NOTE

The Intel x86 Family

The original IBM PC (announced in 1981) was built around an Intel 8086 microprocessor. A few years later the 8086 was replaced by the Intel 80286. Then came the 80386 and the 80486. Intel's P5, or Pentium (in effect, the 586), is an extension of the same x86 family, as is the recently announced P6, or Pentium Pro.

Focus on the last three digits of those microprocessor numbers. A 286 processor is faster and more powerful than an 086. A 386 is faster and more powerful than a 286, and you can expect a computer with a Pentium processor to be more powerful (and more expensive) than a computer with a 486 processor. That is essentially what the numbers mean.

Incidentally, Intel decided to stop numbering their processors because they could not obtain a trademark on a string of numbers. *Pentium*, in contrast, is trademark protected. Strangely, you can purchase a "586" processor from one of Intel's competitors, AMD, but not from Intel.

The Instruction Set

Instruction set
The complete set of instructions a computer is capable of executing.

The complete set of instructions a computer is capable of executing is called its **instruction set** or instruction repertoire; the set of buttons on a calculator is a good analogy. The electronic circuits that form the instruction set are found in the arithmetic and logic unit.

Complex and Reduced Instruction Set Computers

CISC
Acronym for complex instruction set computer.
RISC
Acronym for reduced instruction set computer.

A **complex instruction set computer,** or CISC, supports a significant number of different instructions, perhaps 100 or more; Intel's x86 processors are examples. A **RISC (reduced instruction set computer),** in contrast, features a processor with a limited number of very efficient instructions; the PowerPC jointly developed by Apple, IBM, and Motorola is an example. For some applications (such as managing a network), RISC machines are faster than complex instruction set computers.

Boolean Logic

Boolean logic
A system of logic based on manipulating true and false conditions, or two states.

A computer performs its arithmetic and logical functions by utilizing **Boolean logic.** The basic rules were developed in the mid-1800s by George Boole. His system is based on manipulating true and false conditions, or two states. A system of logic based on two states is ideal for an electronic machine like a computer because the two states can be represented by on/off switches.

Machine Language and Microcode

Machine level instruction
A program instruction that is actually executed by the computer's hardware.

Programs rarely (if ever) directly reference hardware-level Boolean logic circuits; instead, they are composed of **machine-level instructions.** A processor's machine-level instruction set defines such operations as add, subtract, multiply, divide, compare, and copy. It represents the programmer's closest approach to the hardware.

Typically, a level of **microcode** sits between the machine-level instruction set and the Boolean logic circuits (Figure 4.13). The microcode is a strange hybrid—not quite hardware and not quite software. It translates machine-level instructions into the appropriate Boolean operations.

Carefully distinguish between the instruction set (hardware) and the instructions that make up a program (software). The instruction set defines the elementary operations that are hard-wired into the machine. Each machine-level *program* instruction references one of the hardware instructions. Think of the instruction set as the keys on a piano (potential notes) and the program as a musical score that tells the pianist (the processor) which keys to press and in what order to press them. The instruction set (hardware) never changes. The instructions (software) can be changed by switching to a different program (or a different song).

Although programmers *can* write in machine language, they rarely do. Instead, they write their programs in higher-level languages that are translated to machine level. (See Chapter 8.)

Multiple Processor Configurations

Until recently, most computers contained a single processor and thus could execute only one instruction at a time (serial processing). However, many microcomputers now come with a math **coprocessor** (Figure 4.14) that speeds the execution of certain mathematical operations. Graphic coprocessors are common, too. Additionally, some mainframes and minicomputers are equipped with multiple processors that can function together or independently. Given multiple processors, it is possible to execute two or more instructions simultaneously (parallel processing).

Microcode
A layer of integrated circuits that translate machine-level instructions into the appropriate Boolean operations.

Coprocessor
A second processor that works with the main processor.

▲ **FIGURE 4.13**

A level of microcode sits between the machine-level instruction set and the Boolean logic gates.

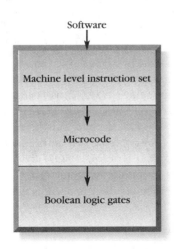

▲ **FIGURE 4.14**

A math coprocessor.

COMPUTER SYSTEMS

The first step in using a computer is to load a program into memory. The processor executes the program by fetching instructions, one by one, from memory. At some point, an input instruction transfers data from an input device into memory. Subsequent instructions move selected data values from memory to the processor, and the results are stored back into memory. Eventually, an output instruction, executed by the processor, sends the results from memory to an output device.

Note how the processor, memory, and the peripheral devices function together. In response to signals from the processor, data flow from an input device into memory and from memory to an output device. Memory holds the active program and the active data. The processor executes the active program, manipulates the active data, and controls the peripherals. Together all the components form a computer system. No one component can function without the others.

You will learn more about computer systems in Chapter 11.

SUMMARY

A byte contains eight bits. Additionally, most computers are able to manipulate a group of bytes called a word. A kilobyte is one thousand bytes, a megabyte is one million bytes, and a gigabyte is one billion bytes.

A computer is a binary machine. Computers are at their most efficient when working with binary integers. The binary equivalent of scientific notation is called floating-point. String values are stored as sets of individual coded characters, generally one character per byte. ASCII and EBCDIC are two standard codes.

To identify them, each byte is assigned a unique address by numbering the bytes sequentially. When the processor reads memory, it extracts the contents of one or more bytes or words but it does not change them. When a processor writes memory, it records new values in the target bytes or words, and that destroys the old contents.

The main or primary memory of most computers is composed of a bank of volatile random access memory (RAM) chips. Read-only memory, or ROM, is permanent memory that can be read but not written. A bank of ROM chips that holds a permanent program is sometimes called firmware because it exhibits characteristics of both hardware and software.

Main memory usually consists of dynamic random access memory (DRAM). Static random access memory (SRAM) is faster, but it is also more expensive, occupies more space, consumes more power, and generates more heat. You can program (write to) PROM once, but the contents cannot subsequently be changed. EPROM, in contrast, can be programmed, erased, and reprogrammed. Flash memory is a type of EPROM that can be erased and reprogrammed by a personal computer without using special equipment. Cache memory is high-speed memory that is used as a staging area for the processor.

The processor, sometimes called the central processing unit (CPU) or main processor, is the part of the computer that executes instructions. A program consists of a series of instructions. Each instruction has two parts: an operation code and one or more operands. The operation code tells the computer what to do. The operands identify the data to be manipulated by the instruction.

The processor contains four key components. The clock generates precisely timed pulses of current that synchronize the computer's other components. The instruction control unit identifies the next instruction to be executed and retrieves or fetches the instruction from memory. The arithmetic and logic unit executes arithmetic and compare instructions. Registers are temporary storage devices that hold control information, current data, and intermediate results.

An instruction is fetched by the instruction control unit during I-time or instruction time and executed by the arithmetic and logic unit during E-time or execution time. One complete fetch/execute sequence defines a single machine cycle. The instruction counter points to the next instruction in the program. The instruction register holds the actual instruction to be executed. The accumulator is typically used to accumulate (or sum) values.

Clock speed is measured in megaHertz (millions of cycles per second). Processor speed is expressed in terms of MIPS (millions of instructions per second). One way to measure a computer's real processing speed is to execute a benchmark program.

A microprocessor is a complete processor on a single chip. The repertoire of instructions a computer is capable of executing is called its instruction set. It is important to distinguish between the instruction set (hardware) and the instructions that make up a program (software). A CISC (complex instruction set computer) features a processor with a large instruction set. A RISC (reduced instruction set computer) features a processor with a limited number of very efficient instructions.

A computer performs its arithmetic and logical functions by utilizing Boolean logic. A processor's machine level instruction set defines such operations as add, subtract, multiply, divide, compare, and copy; it represents the programmer's closest approach to the hardware. Typically, a level of microcode sits between the machine level instruction set and the Boolean logic circuits.

Many microcomputers have a math or graphics coprocessor. A computer with multiple processors can execute two or more instructions simultaneously.

The chapter ended with a brief example that showed how the processor, memory, and the peripheral devices work together to form a system.

KEY TERMS

accumulator
address
arithmetic and logic unit
ASCII code
benchmark

Boolean logic
cache memory
central processing unit (CPU)
clock

CISC (complex instruction set computer)
coprocessor
DRAM (dynamic random access memory)

KEY TERMS (CONTINUED)

EBCDIC code

EPROM (erasable pro-
   grammable read-only
   memory)

execution time (E-time)

fetch

firmware

flash memory

floating-point

gigabyte (GB)

instruction control unit

instruction counter

instruction register

instruction set

instruction time (I-time)

integer

kilobyte (KB)

machine cycle

machine-level instruction

main processor

megabyte (MB)

megaHertz (mHz)

microcode

microprocessor

MIPS

operand

operation code

PROM (programmable
   read-only memory)

read

read-only memory (ROM)

RISC (reduced instruction
   set computer)

SRAM (static random
   access memory)

string

register

word

write

CONCEPTS

1. Distinguish among bits, bytes, and words.

2. What is a number system? Distinguish between digit and place (or posi-
    tional) value. Distinguish between decimal and binary numbers.

3. Briefly distinguish among integer, floating-point, and string data. Why is
    that difference significant?

4. What is a kilobyte? a megabyte? a gigabyte?

5. Explain how a computer's memory is addressed. Why is addressing nec-
    essary?

6. A byte is a computer's basic *addressable* unit of memory. What does
    that mean? Why is it significant?

7. Distinguish between reading and writing memory. Why is that distinc-
    tion important?

8. Distinguish between RAM and ROM. RAM is volatile. What does that
    mean? Why is it significant?

9. Briefly explain how cache memory works. Why is cache memory used?

10. Identify the processor's primary components and explain what each
    component does.

11. Explain what happens during a single machine cycle. Explain how the
    instruction counter and the instruction register are used to support a
    machine cycle.

12. How is the processor's speed measured? What is a benchmark? Why are
    benchmarks useful?

13. Distinguish between the processor's instruction set (hardware) and the
    instructions that make up a program (software).

14. Briefly distinguish between a complex instruction set computer and a
    reduced instruction set computer.

15. A standard processor executes one instruction at a time, but a computer
    with multiple processors can execute two or more instructions in paral-
    lel. Why?

PROJECTS

1. Tour your school's computer center.
2. With the help of someone who knows what he or she is doing, remove the cover from an unplugged microcomputer and identify the internal components.

 INTERNET PROJECTS

1. *News and Notes*. Companies often post information about their very latest products on their World Wide Web home pages. Select a company whose products are featured in this chapter's photographs and access its home page. Try the address *http://www.xxx.com;* substitute the company name (for example, *IBM*) for *xxx*. Once you find the home page, look for a button marked *New products* (or something similar) and click on it. Identify and briefly describe at least two new products and submit your findings to your instructor in the form of a brief note or an e-mail message.
2. *Topic Searches*. Check the World Wide Web and/or other Internet resources for information on the following topics:

Key word	Qualifiers
Pentium processor	200 mHz
SIMM	cost
surge protecton	power surge
UPS	power surge

   Define the key word, identify at least two sources of information on the topic, and briefly summarize the nature of the information you find.
3. *Links to Other Sites*. After you access one or more of the following sites, write a brief note or send an e-mail message to your instructor outlining what you find.

   a. Check newsgroup *alt.folklore.computers* for a discussion of computer folklore.
   b. If you are in the market for computer-related equipment, check newsgroup *misc.forsale.comp.xxx*. Substitute the component you need (for example, *printer*) for *xxx*.
   c. On the World Wide Web, check *http://www.ibm.com* for information on IBM computers and other products.
   d. On the World Wide Web, check *http://www.intel.com* for information on Intel Corporation products.
   e. On the World Wide Web, check *http://www.zdnet.com* for current news about computers and computer-related products.

4. Access West Publishing Company's home page and find the Chapter 4 student activities for this book. See Internet Project 3 for the spotlight on *The Internet* following Chapter 1 (page 29) for more detailed instructions on accessing the home page. As appropriate, repeat projects 1, 2, and/or 3 using the more current references you find.

CHAPTER 5

Secondary Storage

Before you start this chapter, you should be familiar with the following concepts:

► Data and information (p. 4).

► Computers (p. 6), hardware (p. 6), peripherals (p. 6), and inside the computer (p. 7).

► Software (p. 9), data (p. 10), and long-term storage (p. 12).

► Computer classifications (p. 14), networks (p. 17), and the information superhighway (p. 18).

When you finish reading this chapter, you should be able to:

► Explain why secondary storage is necessary.

► Identify and describe several common secondary storage media.

► Define the terms *track* and *sector* and list the components of a disk address.

► Explain why a disk must be formatted before it can be used.

► Explain how a disk drive works and how the data stored on a disk are physically accessed. Define the terms *seek time, rotational delay, latency,* and *data transfer time.*

► Explain how a disk cache or a RAM disk can reduce the time lost to disk access.

► Relate the disk's directory to the process of accessing data on disk.

► Identify the source of a disk's root directory and file allocation table and briefly explain their purpose.

► Discuss write protection and locking and explain why they are necessary.

► Explain why the contents of secondary storage must be backed up.

WHY SECONDARY STORAGE?

As you learned in Chapter 1, main memory is volatile; it loses its contents if power is interrupted for any reason. Secondary storage, in contrast, is non-volatile. Consequently, before you turn off your computer, you copy (save) your work from memory to secondary storage (Figure 5.1a). Later, when you are ready to continue, you copy the work from secondary storage back into memory (Figure 5.1b).

Main memory is relatively expensive and the supply on most machines, though substantial, is limited, so (even ignoring volatility) secondary storage is a better choice for long-term storage. Think of secondary storage as a fast, nonvolatile, high-capacity, long-term supplement to main memory. Because it is inexpensive and nonvolatile, secondary storage is an excellent software and data distribution medium, too.

▲ **FIGURE 5.1**

To avoid losing your work:
a. **You save the work to secondary storage.**
b. **Later, you load the work back into memory.**

a.

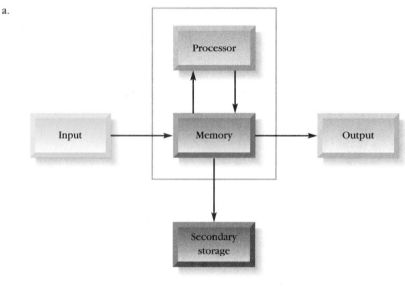

b.

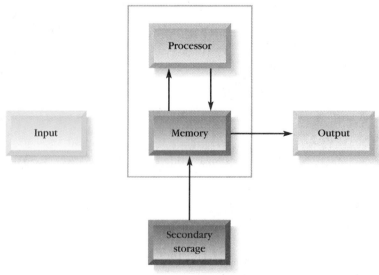

Remember, however, that the processor can directly access only *main* memory, so the *active* program and the *active* data must be in main memory. Typically, your programs and your data files reside on secondary storage and are loaded into memory only when they are being executed or processed.

SECONDARY STORAGE MEDIA

Secondary storage takes many different forms, including:

- ▶ diskette
- ▶ hard disk
- ▶ magnetic tape
- ▶ CD-ROM

Diskette and Hard Disk

Magnetic disk is the most common secondary storage medium. A disk is a circular platter coated with the same magnetic material that covers sound recording tape. You have probably seen **diskettes** (Figure 5.2); both flexible 5.25-inch **floppy disks** and rigid, higher capacity 3.5-inch diskettes are available.

A **hard disk** (Figure 5.3) is faster and has greater storage capacity than a diskette. Most hard disks are found inside the system unit, but portable disk cartridges are available, too. A user might remove a portable hard disk for security reasons or to access the same files and software from both a desktop and a laptop computer.

Diskette
A disk-shaped secondary storage medium that can be inserted into and removed from a disk drive by a user.
Floppy disk
A 5.25-inch diskette.
Hard disk
A high capacity disk that is often located inside the computer cabinet.

▲ **FIGURE 5.2**

A diskette is a form of magnetic disk.

▲ **FIGURE 5.3**

A hard disk.

The first personal computers came with diskette drives that recorded only 180 KB (kilobytes, or thousands of bytes) on a single-sided floppy diskette. Within a few years, those single-sided diskettes had been replaced by double-sided, 360 KB floppy diskettes. By the middle 1980s, microcomputers with 20 MB (megabyte, or million bytes) hard disks were common. Today, most personal computers come with at least one 1.44 megabyte diskette and anything from 500 megabytes to one or more gigabytes (GB, or billion bytes) of hard disk space.

Mainframes and minicomputers access multiple-surface hard disks that consist of several platters stacked on a single drive spindle (Figure 5.4). A multiple-surface disk might hold several gigabytes of data. A mainframe computer system has numerous such disks that hold, in aggregate, terabytes (trillions of bytes).

Figure 5.5 summarizes typical microcomputer diskette and hard disk storage capacities. By the time you read this, the numbers might be even higher.

Magnetic Tape

Magnetic tape
A type of secondary storage that is often used as a backup medium.

Magnetic tape (Figure 5.6), essentially the same stuff used to record sound and video, is fast and inexpensive. A reel of tape or a tape cartridge can store

▲ **FIGURE 5.4**

A multiple-surface hard disk.

▲ **FIGURE 5.5**

Typical diskette and hard disk storage capacities.

MEDIUM	CAPACITY
5.25-inch double-density diskette	360 KB
5.25-inch high-density diskette	1.2 MB
3.5-inch double-density diskette	720 KB
3.5-inch high-density diskette	1.44 MB
Hard disk	500 MB–2 GB

A magnetic tape drive.

roughly as much data as a disk, and digital audio tapes promise even better performance in the near future. Unfortunately, the data stored on a tape can be read or written only in a fixed sequence, and that is unacceptable for many applications. Today, magnetic tape is most often used as a backup medium; you will learn more about backup later in this chapter.

CD-ROM

CD-ROM (Compact-Disk, Read-Only Memory) (Figure 5.7) resembles the compact disks you buy in record stores. Like an audio CD, a CD-ROM is read

CD-ROM
A type of secondary storage that resembles a compact disk.

▲ FIGURE 5.7

CD-ROM.

optically. Because of its storage capacity, CD-ROM is the medium of choice for graphic images, sound patterns, dictionaries, catalogs, and similar reference materials. For example, you can purchase a single CD-ROM that holds a complete set of encyclopedias or an atlas full of detailed maps.

Most of today's CD-ROMs are designed to be read but not written; in other words, you cannot record new data on them. You can, however, purchase **WORM** (write once, read many) optical disks that, as the name implies, allow you to record information once and then access that information over and over again. Optical disks that can be both read and written many times are available, but they have yet to become an important general-purpose secondary storage medium. That might change, however.

Some experts view CD-ROM as a transitional technology, believing that the emerging information superhighway will prove a more efficient channel for distributing information. Time will tell.

RAID

RAID is an acronym for Redundant Array of Inexpensive Disks. The idea is to spread the data over several interconnected hard disks in such a way that the data can be recovered or reconstructed even if one of the disks fails. RAID technology is used when lost data cannot be tolerated.

DISK ACCESS

Given today's technology, magnetic disk is by far the most common secondary storage medium, so this section will focus on how a disk works.

Disk Addresses: Tracks and Sectors

Data are recorded on a disk around a series of concentric circles called **tracks** (Figure 5.8). The outer track is numbered 0; moving inward, subsequent tracks are numbered 1, 2, 3, and so on.

The tracks are subdivided into **sectors.** A sector is the basic unit of disk storage; in other words, data move between the disk's surface and memory one sector at a time. To distinguish the sectors, they are numbered sequentially around the track.

Most disks record data on both sides of the platter, so there is a similar track/sector pattern on the top surface and the bottom surface. (That rule also holds for multiple-surface disks.) A track number, a side (or a surface), and a sector number together define a unique **disk address.**

The Formatting Process

Disks are not manufactured with the tracks and sectors in place. Consequently, before you use a disk you must **format** it. The formatting process (usually performed by the operating system; see p. 127) electronically records the track/sector pattern on the surface. As an alternative to formatting your own disks, you can purchase (for a slight premium) preformatted disks.

WORM
Acronym for write once, read many. A type of CD-ROM.

RAID
An acronym for redundant array of inexpensive disks.

Track
A concentric circle around which data are recorded on a disk surface.
Sector
A sequentially numbered subdivision of a track. Data move between a disk and memory a sector at a time.

Disk address
A track, a side, and a sector.

Format
To prepare a disk for use.

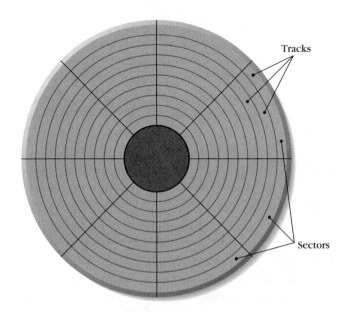

▲ FIGURE 5.8

Data are recorded around a series of concentric circles called tracks. The tracks are subdivided into sectors.

Storage Capacity

The storage capacity of a disk is computed by multiplying bytes per sector, times sectors per track, times tracks per surface, times the number of surfaces.

For example, most personal computer disks store 512 bytes (0.5 KB) per sector. A 3.5-inch diskette has 80 tracks. At 9 sectors per track (double density), that amounts to 720 sectors per side, or 1,440 sectors per disk. Multiply by 0.5 kilobytes per sector, and you get 720 KB. At 18 sectors per track (high density), that amounts to 1,440 sectors per side, or 2,880 sectors per disk. Multiply by 0.5 kilobytes per sector, and you get 1.44 MB.

Disk Drives

A **disk drive** works much like a record turntable. A hard disk spins around its central spindle. The hub opening in the center of a diskette allows the drive to engage and spin it. An **access arm** (or actuator), analogous to a turntable's tone arm, reads and writes the surface.

On a 5.25-inch diskette, access to the surface is through a window near the bottom of the jacket. The hub is on the back of a 3.5-inch diskette; the metal shield near the top moves aside to reveal the recording surface when the disk is inserted into the drive. A two-pronged access arm carries one read/write head for each diskette surface, so one position of the access arm defines a set of two tracks that is sometimes called a **cylinder.**

Each surface of a multiple-surface disk (Figure 5.9) has its own read/write head. The heads are arrayed on a comblike access mechanism, and they all move together. Imagine, for example, that the access mechanism is positioned over track 30. The top read/write head accesses track 30 on surface 0. Moving down, surface by surface, the second head is over track 30 on

Disk drive
A device that reads and writes a disk.

Access arm
The mechanism that carries a disk's read/write heads.

Cylinder
On a disk, one position of the read/write heads that defines a family of tracks, one on each surface.

▲ FIGURE 5.9

A multiple-surface disk has one read/write head per surface.

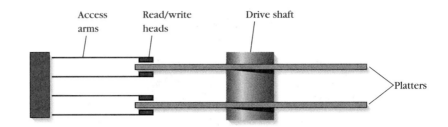

surface 1, the third over track 30 on surface 2, and so on. One position of the access mechanism corresponds to one track on each surface, and that set of tracks forms a cylinder.

Head Clearance

On a diskette drive, the access arm rides directly on the disk's surface. A hard disk spins so rapidly, however, that any physical contact between the disk surface and the read/write head would quickly destroy both. Consequently, a hard disk's access mechanism rides on a cushion of air, a few millionths of an inch above the surface (Figure 5.10). Shaped like an airfoil, it literally flies.

Hard disks are sensitive. Sometimes, because of a manufacturing defect, a hard bump, a rapid temperature change, or a similar cause, the disk drive becomes unbalanced and the head contacts the surface. That event is called a head crash. (If you ever hear one, you will never forget the sound.) A head crash destroys the head, the disk, and everything stored on it.

ADVANCED TOPICS

Bit Density and Head Clearance

Each bit stored on a disk is represented by a tiny magnetic spot on the disk's surface. The storage capacity of a disk is a function of how tightly the bits are packed.

Perhaps you remember an experiment from high school physics in which you laid a sheet of paper on top of a magnet and dumped some metal filings onto the paper. The idea of that experiment was to give you a sense of the shape of the magnetic field. Extend that shape to three dimensions, and you get a cone.

Picture the bits arrayed along the innermost track as a string of cones standing on end. Imagine the access mechanism moving across the tops of those cones. If the read/write head is to distinguish one bit from another, the cones cannot touch. Thus, their circumference at that altitude defines the maximum storage density.

Now imagine dropping the access mechanism a bit closer to the surface. The cones' diameters are not as big at that lower altitude, so the bits can be moved closer together without affecting the ability of the read/write head to distinguish them. Additionally, as the head moves closer to the surface it is able to detect weaker and weaker magnetic fields. A weaker field generates a smaller cone, and that allows the bits to be moved even closer together. The result is increased bit density and greater storage capacity.

There is a limit to that process, of course, but the industry has not yet reached it. Consequently, you can expect disk storage capacity to continue to increase even though the disk's physical size does not.

Disk Timing

A disk's tracks form a pattern of concentric circles around its surface. (Glance back at Figure 5.8 for a visual reference.) Clearly, the outermost tracks define bigger circles than the innermost tracks. Does that mean you can store more data on the outer tracks? The answer is no.

The key to reading data from and writing data to disk is timing, not distance. The disk rotates at a constant speed. Each track has a clearly marked starting point. If there are nine sectors per track, the read/write head is at track 1 at time 0, track 2 at 1/9 of a complete revolution, track 3 at 2/9 of a revolution, and so on.

All tracks hold the same number of bits. A bit on track 1 makes a complete revolution in exactly the same amount of time as a bit on track 80. Like a group of ice skaters playing crack the whip, bits on the outer tracks move faster and bits on the inner tracks are packed more closely together. No matter what track is accessed, however, the same number of bits per second move past the read/write head.

Physical Disk Access

The first step in reading from or writing to a disk is to select the target disk drive. Each drive is assigned a unique drive identifier; for example, your 5.25-inch diskette drive might be named A, your 3.5-inch drive might be B, and your hard disk might be drive C.

Once the correct drive is selected, the computer sends a disk address (consisting of a track number, a side, and a sector number) to the disk's controller. The access arm then moves to the target track (Figure 5.11a), and the

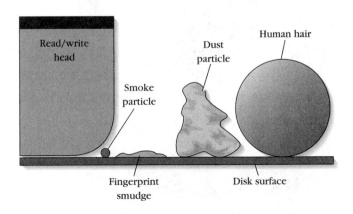

▲ **FIGURE 5.10**

A hard disk's access mechanism rides on a cushion of air.

▲ FIGURE 5.11

Reading or writing a disk.
a. The access arm moves to the target track.
b. The target sector rotates to the read/write head.
c. The target sector is read or written.

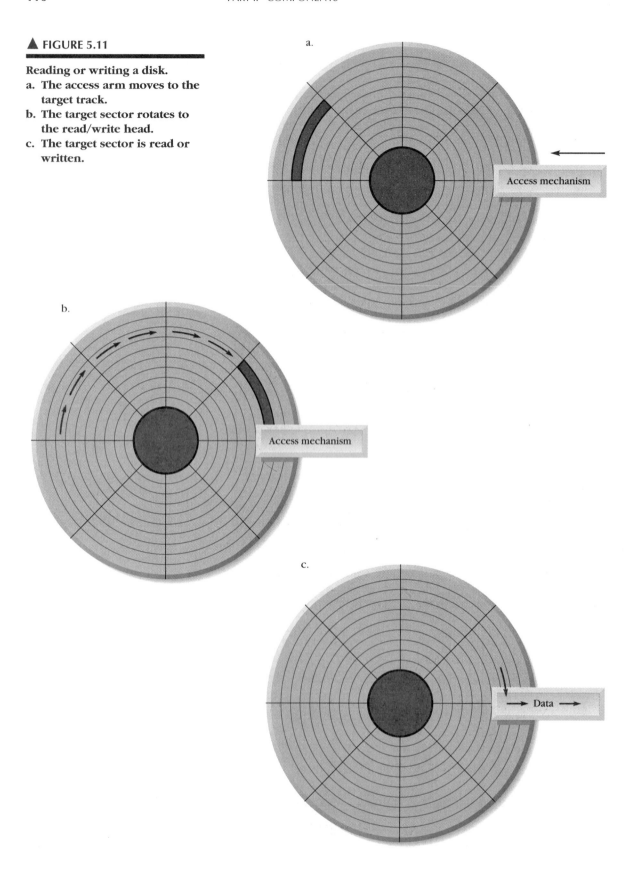

read/write head that accesses the target side is activated. As soon as the target sector rotates to the head (Figure 5.11b), it is read or written (Figure 5.11c).

The time required to bring the drive up to speed and position the access arm is called **seek time.** Remember that data are transferred between the diskette and memory one sector at a time, and the desired sector might be anywhere on the track. The time required for the sector to rotate to the read/write head is called **rotational delay.** Once the target sector is located, **data transfer time** (often expressed as a data transfer rate) is the time required to copy the sector's contents from the disk surface into memory (or from memory to the disk's surface).

Access Time

A diskette spins only when it is being read or written, so the first step in accessing a diskette is to bring it up to operating speed. A hard disk spins constantly, so the access mechanism can be moved immediately. As a result a hard disk's seek time (typically in the 10 microsecond range) is much less than a diskette's.

Rotational delay is a function of rotational speed, perhaps 3,600 revolutions per minute on a modern hard disk. Normally, the disk drive senses the start of sector 1 and then distinguishes the other sectors by timing, so the contents of sector 1 are accessed faster than the contents of sector 18. Because there is no way of predicting which sector will hold the target data, average rotational delay is typically estimated at one-half a revolution. Clearly, one way to reduce rotational delay is to increase rotational speed. That is another reason why a hard disk is faster than a diskette—it rotates faster.

Latency is the time that elapses between the processor's initial request for data and the actual start of data transfer; in effect, it is the sum of seek time and rotational delay. When you read a disk drive's technical specifications, latency is usually expressed as an average that can be less than the maximum seek time, so be careful when you interpret the numbers.

Seek time
On a disk, the time required to position the access mechanism over the target track.

Rotational delay
On a disk, after the access mechanism is positioned over the proper track, the time required for the target sector to rotate to the read/write head.

Data transfer time
Following seek time and rotational delay, the time required to physically transfer data between memory and a disk's surface.

Latency
The time that elapses between the processor's initial request for data and the actual start of data transfer. The sum of seek time and rotational delay.

THE FUTURE

Nonvolatile RAM

Secondary storage devices move. Disks and CD-ROMs rotate, and the access arm moves in and out. Magnetic tape drives pull tape from one reel to another.

Movement implies wear, so a device that moves is much more likely to fail than a device that does not. Contrast disk and CD-ROM to integrated circuit memory chips. RAM does not move. That is one reason why your personal computer system's disk drive is likely to fail long before its memory.

Today we use disk and CD-ROM because nonvolatile RAM, though available, is very expensive. The cost is dropping, however. Perhaps someday, rotating secondary storage media will be made obsolete by massive banks of low-cost, high-speed, nonvolatile RAM.

Disk Cache

Accessing secondary storage is slower than accessing main memory. On some applications, the time delays associated with frequent disk access can be a problem, so a portion of main memory called a **disk cache** (pronounced "disk cash") is set aside to simulate a disk. The main memory of most computers is composed of random access memory (RAM) chips so the disk cache is sometimes called a **RAM disk.** (See p. 83 for a more complete discussion of RAM.)

When a disk cache is used, the relevant data are loaded from disk into memory. As the program runs, the data are accessed and modified in memory at internal speeds. When processing is finished (or at key intermediate points), the contents of the disk cache are copied back to the hard disk as appropriate. To the user, the disk cache behaves just like a real disk, only faster.

Note that a disk cache is implemented in memory (hardware) but controlled by software. In contrast, cache memory (p. 85) is implemented in hardware and controlled by hardware.

The Directory

Given its storage capacity, a disk can hold many different programs and the data for numerous applications. To help the computer keep track of a disk's contents, the location of every program and every data file stored on the disk is noted in the disk's **directory** (Figure 5.12).

Disk cache
Pronounced "disk cash." A portion of main memory set aside to simulate a disk.
RAM disk
A disk cache.

Directory
A list of the addresses of every program and every set of data stored on a disk.

▲ FIGURE 5.12

A disk's directory is its table of contents.

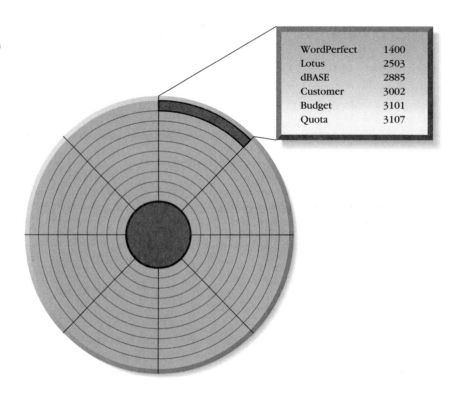

WordPerfect	1400
Lotus	2503
dBASE	2885
Customer	3002
Budget	3101
Quota	3107

Long and Short File Names

When personal computers were first introduced, the early operating systems imposed limits on the length of file names. A common structure was *filename.ext,* which limited the *filename* to no more than eight characters followed by an optional one- to three-character extension that identified the type of file. Today's system software supports long file names. Why the change?

A good file name clearly indicates the file's contents; for example, *payroll* is a better name for a file of payroll data than *filex.* The problem with eight-character file names is that they often force you to invent cryptic abbreviations that do not adequately identify the file. *AR* is a reasonable name for an accounts receivable file, but *accounts receivable* is better. *MISa1bud* is not nearly as descriptive as *MIS101 assignment 1 budget spreadsheet.* Clear file names make it much easier to find the specific file you need.

When a program or a data file is first stored on a disk, the user assigns it a **file name.** That name, along with the file's disk address, is recorded in the directory.

Later, to access the disk you give the computer the desired file's name. The system (more accurately, the operating system or some other system software routine) then checks the directory and discovers exactly where on the disk's surface the target file can be found. In effect, the directory serves as a table of contents for the disk.

File name
A logical name assigned by a user to a file.

The Root Directory and the FAT

When you format a disk, several things happen. First, the format command writes the electronic markers that divide the disk's surface into tracks and sectors. Next, it creates a boot record (see Chapter 6), a **root directory,** and a **file allocation table (FAT)** (Figure 5.13) for the disk. The root directory is the disk's primary directory. The file allocation table is an index to the disk's sectors; the operating system uses it to keep track of which sectors are allocated to which files. Also, any defective sectors are marked in the file allocation table so they will not be used to store data.

Root directory
A disk's primary directory.
File allocation table (FAT)
An index to the disk's sectors used by the operating system to keep track of which sectors are allocated to which files.

Partitioning

On large disks, it sometimes makes sense to divide or **partition** the disk into sections called **logical drives;** for example, a 1.6 gigabyte hard drive might be divided into four 400 megabyte partitions. To the programmer or the user, each logical drive appears to be a different disk drive. Partitioning allows you to physically group related files, and that can make disk access both easier and more efficient.

Partition
A subdivision of a hard drive that appears to the programmer or the user to be a different disk drive. Also known as a logical drive.
Logical drive (or Logical disk)
A partition on a hard disk that appears to the programmer or the user to be a different disk drive.

The format command establishes the track/sector pattern and creates a root directory and a file allocation table.

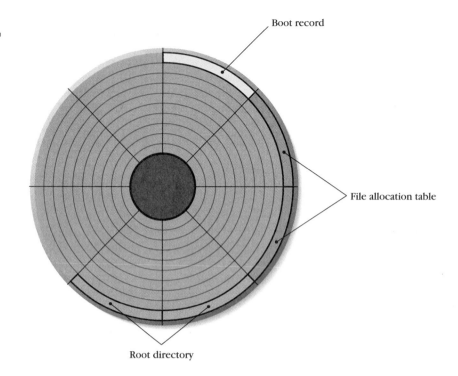

Boot record

File allocation table

Root directory

PROTECTING YOUR DATA

The fact that you store your data on a disk does not necessarily guarantee that they are safe. Secondary storage media are nonvolatile, but if you tell a computer (intentionally or accidentally) to erase, modify, or replace the data stored on a disk, the old data are lost. There are other ways to lose your data, too; see the *Note* entitled "Caring for Your Diskettes."

Given the amount of data that can be stored on a disk, losing one can be disastrous. It is important that you protect your data.

Write Protection and Locking

Write-protect
To set a disk so that data can be read from but not written to it.

Lock
To make a file or record unavailable for use.

One way to prevent lost data is to **write-protect** a diskette by covering the slot on a 5.25-inch diskette or by opening the sliding notch on the back of a 3.5-inch diskette. You cannot accidentally erase, modify, or replace the data on a write-protected diskette. On a hard disk, it is possible to designate certain data as read-only or to limit access to certain users by electronically **locking** a file or even selected records and fields. Locking implies denying access to all but authorized users.

Backup

Back up
To copy the contents of a secondary storage device to another secondary medium.

No matter how careful you are with your data, accidents do happen, so it is wise to regularly **back up** your disks. A diskette can be backed up by copying it to another diskette. A hard disk can be copied to multiple diskettes, to

Caring for Your Diskettes

Today's diskettes are rugged and reliable, but they are not indestructible. Following a few simple rules can greatly reduce the risk of lost data, however.

Avoid bending a 5.25-inch floppy disk, and always keep the disk in its protective jacket when not in use. Do not touch the disk surface; if you must handle a disk, pick it up by a corner. Do not attach fasteners (such as paper clips) to the disk. Prepare a handwritten label at your desk and *then* attach it to the disk. If you must change the label, use a felt-tip pen, not a ballpoint pen or a pencil.

A 3.5-inch disk's hard plastic cover solves many of the problems described in the previous paragraph, but others remain. If you slide to the left the metal cover near the top of a 3.5-inch disk, you can see the disk surface; do not touch it. A disk (any size) is a magnetic medium, so avoid magnetic fields; for example, do not leave your disks on top of an audio speaker. Avoid temperature extremes; for example, do not leave a disk in your car on a hot, sunny day. Avoid spilled liquids, too; a few drops of your favorite soft drink can render a disk unreadable. Finally, if you physically break its plastic cover, a 3.5-inch diskette is useless.

Incidentally, if you ever have to take a computer disk on an airplane, do not carry it with you through airport security. The security door uses a magnetic field to determine if you are carrying any metal, and magnetism can damage the contents of a disk. Instead, ask the guard to hand check the disk.

another hard disk, or to a magnetic tape reel or cartridge. Should the original data be lost or damaged, the backup copy allows you to restore the data.

Large computer centers maintain multiple backup copies of crucial files. For example, a bank might copy its customer checking account file from disk

Make Backup a Habit

Get into the habit of backing up your data. For example, when you write a paper or create a spreadsheet on the computer, you almost certainly save your work to disk before you quit. Add one more step to the process. Slip a diskette (or another diskette) into the drive and save your work again, so you have two copies. That way, if anything happens to your hard disk or your primary diskette, you can always access your work from the backup copy.

If you are typical you will ignore that advice; after all, saving the same thing twice seems like a waste of time. Eventually, however, you *will* lose your work and be forced to reconstruct it from scratch. (The only question is when, not if.) When it happens to you, you will understand why backup is so important.

to magnetic tape every day at midnight and keep the backup tapes for three days. Today's tape is called the son, yesterday's tape is called the father, and the tape from two days ago is called the grandfather. Combined with the appropriate transaction data (for example, daily records of deposits and withdrawals), the backup tapes can be used to recreate the file.

Because such disasters as fires, floods, hurricanes, and explosions can destroy an entire computer center, many organizations keep their backup tapes and disks off-site. That way, should disaster strike the data can be restored on another computer.

Summary

Secondary storage is a fast, inexpensive, nonvolatile, high-capacity, long-term supplement to main memory. Typically, programs and data files reside on secondary storage and are loaded into memory only when they are being executed or processed.

Magnetic disk is the most common secondary storage medium. Diskette is a type of magnetic disk; both flexible 5.25-inch floppy disks and rigid, higher capacity 3.5-inch diskettes are available. A hard disk is faster and has greater storage capacity than a diskette. Many large computers access multiple-surface disks that consist of several platters stacked on a single drive spindle.

Magnetic tape is fast, with data transfer rates comparable to disk. CD-ROM (Compact-Disk, Read-Only Memory) resembles the compact disks you buy in record stores. On a WORM (write once, read many) optical disk you can record information once and then access that information over and over again. RAID is an acronym for Redundant Array of Inexpensive Disks. The idea is to spread the data over several interconnected hard disks in such a way that the data can be recovered or reconstructed even if one of the disks fails.

Data are recorded on a disk around a series of concentric circles called tracks. The tracks are subdivided into sectors. A track number, a side, and a sector number together define a unique disk address. The formatting process electronically records the track/sector pattern on the disk's surface. The storage capacity of a disk can be computed by multiplying bytes per sector, times sectors per track, times tracks per surface, times the number of surfaces.

A disk drive works much like a record turntable. An access arm, analogous to the tone arm, reads and writes the surface. The access arm carries one read/write head for each surface. One position of the access arm defines a set of tracks called a cylinder. A diskette drive's access arm rides directly on the disk's surface. A hard disk's access mechanism rides on a cushion of air, a few millionths of an inch above the surface. The key to reading data from and writing data to disk is timing, not distance. No matter what track is accessed, the same number of bits per second move past the read/write head.

The time required to bring the drive up to speed and position the access arm is called seek time. The time required for the sector to rotate to the read/write head is called rotational delay. Once the target sector is located, data transfer time is the time required to copy the sector's contents from the disk surface into memory. Latency is seek time plus rotational delay. On some applications, the time delays associated with frequent disk access can be a problem, so a portion of main memory called a disk cache or a RAM disk is set aside to simulate a disk.

The location of every program and every data file stored on a disk is noted in the disk's directory. When a program or a data file is first stored, the user assigns it a file name. That name, along with the file's disk address, is recorded in the directory.

In addition to writing the electronic markers that divide the disk's surface into tracks and sectors, the formatting process creates a root directory and a file allocation table (FAT) for the disk. It sometimes makes sense to divide or partition a large disk into smaller logical disks To the programmer or the user, each logical disk appears to be a different disk drive.

One way to prevent lost data is to write-protect a diskette. On a hard disk, it is possible to designate certain data as read-only or to limit access to certain users by locking a file, selected records, or even selected fields. No matter how careful you are with your data, accidents do happen, so it is wise to regularly back up your data.

KEY TERMS

access arm	file allocation table (FAT)	RAID
backup	file name	RAM disk
CD-ROM	floppy disk	root directory
cylinder	format	rotational delay
data transfer time	hard disk	sector
directory	latency	seek time
disk address	lock, or locking	track
disk cache	logical drive	write-protect
disk drive	magnetic tape	WORM
diskette	partition	

CONCEPTS

1. Why is secondary storage necessary?
2. Briefly, compare and contrast diskette, hard disk, magnetic tape, and CD-ROM.
3. Define the terms *track*, *sector*, and *cylinder*.
4. Outline the components of a disk address.
5. A disk must be formatted before it can be used. Why? What happens during the formatting process? Explain the purpose of a disk's root directory and file allocation table.
6. Explain how bytes per sector, sectors per track, and tracks per surface determine a disk's storage capacity.
7. Explain how data stored on a disk are physically accessed.
8. Finding a specific sector on a track is a function of timing, not distance. Explain that statement.
9. Relate the terms *seek time, rotational delay, data transfer time,* and *latency*.
10. Explain how a disk cache (or RAM disk) works. Why is disk cache used?
11. What is a disk's directory? Why is the directory necessary? How does the directory relate to the process of accessing data on a disk.

12. What is partitioning? What is a logical disk? Why is partitioning valuable?

13. How do you write-protect a disk? What does it mean to lock a file or a record? Why are such things as write protection and locking necessary?

14. Why is it so important that you back up the contents of a disk or other secondary storage medium?

PROJECTS

1. Investigate the difference between 2x, 4x, and 6x CD-ROM drives and explain why that difference is significant.

2. Schools and computer centers sometimes keep a few damaged disk drives to use as teaching aids. If you have access to such a damaged drive, take it apart and examine the components.

 ## INTERNET PROJECTS

1. *News and Notes*. Companies often post information about their very latest products on their World Wide Web home pages. Select a company whose products are featured in this chapter's photographs and access its home page. Try the address *http://www.xxx.com;* substitute the company name (for example, *IBM*) for *xxx*. Once you find the home page, look for a button marked *New products* (or something similar) and click on it. Identify and briefly describe at least two new products and submit your findings to your instructor in the form of a brief note or an e-mail message.

2. *Topic Searches*. Check the World Wide Web and/or other Internet resources for information on the following topics:

Key word	*Qualifiers*
long file name	Windows 95
backup	magnetic tape
file recovery	utility program
disaster planning	network

Define the key word, identify at least two sources of information on the topic, and briefly summarize the nature of the information you find.

3. *Links to Other Sites*. After you access one or more of the following sites, write a brief note or send an e-mail message to your instructor outlining what you find.

a. If you are in the market for computer-related equipment, check newsgroup *misc.forsale.comp.xxx*. Substitute the component you need (for example, *disk*) for *xxx*.

b. On the World Wide Web, check *http://www.seagate.com* for information on Seagate products.

c. On the World Wide Web, check *http://www.zdnet.com* for current news about computers and computer-related products.

4. Access West Publishing Company's home page and find the Chapter 5 student activities for this book. See Internet Project 3 for the spotlight on *The Internet* following Chapter 1 (page 29) for more detailed instructions on accessing the home page. As appropriate, repeat projects 1, 2, and/or 3 using the more current references you find.

CHAPTER 6

System Software

Before you start this chapter, you should be familiar with the following concepts:

▶ The user (p. 6).

▶ Hardware (p. 6), peripherals (p. 6), and inside the computer (p. 7).

▶ Software (p. 9) and data (p. 10).

▶ Long-term storage (p. 12).

▶ Information systems (p. 13), computer classifications (p. 14), and the Internet (p. 17).

When you finish reading this chapter, you should be able to:

▶ Identify the functions performed by a microcomputer operating system.

▶ Explain how the command processor (or shell) makes it possible for a user to communicate with the operating system.

▶ Explain the purpose of the file system. Discuss files, file names, and directories, and briefly explain directory structures.

▶ Briefly discuss how the operating system manages disk space.

▶ Distinguish between open and close. Explain why it is necessary to open and close a file.

▶ Describe how the operating system converts the programmer's logical I/O requests to physical primitive commands.

▶ Distinguish between resident and transient routines, and explain why many operating systems are designed around a kernel.

▶ Describe the boot process and explain why it is necessary. Distinguish between the boot process and initial program load.

▶ Discuss the tasks performed by utility programs.

▶ Identify several microcomputer operating systems and interpret a software version number.

▶ Identify the primary components of MS-DOS, and briefly explain how Windows 95 changes the way a Windows user communicates with hardware.

THE OPERATING SYSTEM

As you learned in Chapter 1, application software performs tasks that people want to do, while system software manages the computer's resources. One example of system software is the operating system that bridges the gap between hardware and application software (Figure 6.1). The user accesses the application program, the application program communicates with the operating system, and the operating system deals directly with the hardware. Consequently, the user and the application programmer can ignore the hardware details, and that makes the computer much easier to use.

The computers marketed by different manufacturers are often incompatible; a program written for one brand of computer will not necessarily run on another. All communication with the hardware goes through the operating system, so a common operating system solves that problem (Figure 6.2). Because application software is written for the operating system, not for the hardware, a given application program can run on any computer that supports its operating system. In effect, the operating system defines a **platform** or **operating environment** for writing and executing application software.

This chapter focuses on microcomputer operating systems, such as MS-DOS and Windows 95. Mainframe and multiple-user operating systems are the subject of Chapter 12.

Platform
A particular operating system running on a particular computer. Also known as an operating environment.
Operating environment
Another name for a platform.

OPERATING SYSTEM FUNCTIONS

A microcomputer operating system performs numerous support functions. Specifically, it:

▲ **FIGURE 6.1**

The operating system bridges the gap between hardware and application software.

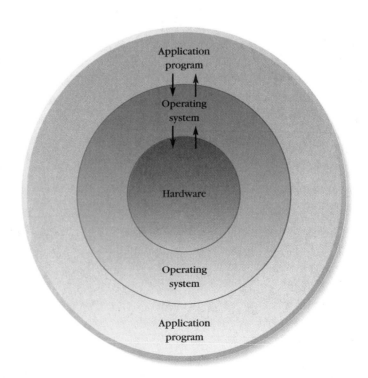

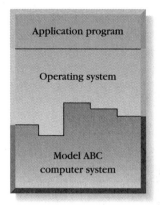 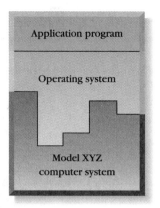

▲ FIGURE 6.2

The operating system defines an operating environment.

► provides an interface for communicating with the system,
► allows users and application programs to manage files,
► manages the work flow through the system's hardware.

Those functions are common to virtually all applications, and it would make little sense to duplicate them in every program. A better option is to implement the necessary logic once, in the operating system, and then let all the application programs access the common routines.

COMMUNICATING WITH THE OPERATING SYSTEM

Before an operating system can do anything, someone must tell it what to do. A user issues orders, or **commands**, each of which tells the operating system to perform a specific task, such as copy a file or prepare a disk for use. The operating system module that accepts, interprets, and carries out commands is called the **command processor** (Figure 6.3).

Command
A cryptic message, usually typed on a single line, that tells the system to carry out a specific task.
Command processor
The operating system module that accepts, interprets, and carries out commands.

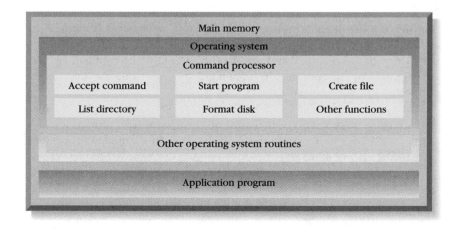

▲ FIGURE 6.3

The command processor is composed of several software routines, each of which performs a single task.

PEOPLE

Bill Gates, Paul Allen, and MS-DOS

In 1974, while Bill Gates was attending Harvard University, he and Paul Allen developed some software for the first personal computer, the MITS Altair 8800. In those days, microcomputers were of interest primarily to hobbyists and hackers, but Gates saw their mass market potential. After he left Harvard, he and Paul founded Microsoft Corporation to market their software.

Their big break came when IBM asked Microsoft to develop a new operating system for the soon-to-be announced IBM PC. Following its release in 1982, IBM's PC was an immediate hit, and MS-DOS quickly became the new microcomputer operating system standard.

Today, Bill Gates runs Microsoft and, through his company, dominates the lucrative microcomputer software business. Paul Allen left Microsoft several years ago. He currently owns the Portland Trail Blazers professional basketball team, and remains active in the field of state-of-the-art information technology.

The Command Language

Command language
A programming language for issuing commands to an operating system.

The rules for issuing commands are defined in a **command language** that has its own syntax, style, and punctuation. Generally, the user types a command through the keyboard and presses the enter key. The command processor responds by interpreting the command and activating the instructions that perform the requested task.

Prompt
A message from the operating system that tells the user that the command processor is ready to accept a command.

For example, consider the task of copying a file. As the process begins, a **prompt** (for example, C>) is displayed on the screen. The prompt is a message from the operating system that tells the user the command processor is ready to accept a command.

In response to the prompt, the user types a command and presses the enter key (Figure 6.4). The command processor responds to a COPY command by copying a file. After the operation is completed, the command processor displays another prompt and waits for the next command.

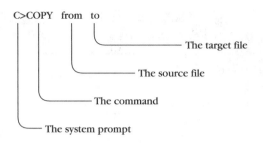

The Shell

The command processor is sometimes called the **shell.** It represents the user's primary interface with the system; in effect, the user accesses the computer through the shell.

The simplest shell is the command-line interface illustrated in Figure 6.4. A command interface is often the quickest, most efficient way for experienced people to access a computer, but many beginners find cryptic commands confusing.

One option is to let the user select a command from a **menu** (Figure 6.5). A menu is, essentially, a list of commands. Rather than typing the command, you select the one you want by pointing to it and clicking a mouse or by pressing a key. Menus are easy for beginners to use, but negotiating several levels of menus can slow an experienced user.

Some shells incorporate a **graphic user interface,** or **GUI** (pronounced GOO-ee) (Figure 6.6). In addition to menus, a graphic user interface

Shell
Another name for the command processor.

Menu
A list of available commands or other options.

Graphic user interface (GUI)
An interface that utilizes windows, boxes, icons, and other graphical elements to provide the user with visual cues.

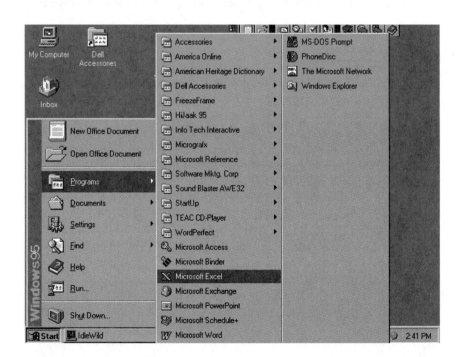

▲ **FIGURE 6.5**

A typical menu.

▲ **FIGURE 6.6**

A graphic user interface.

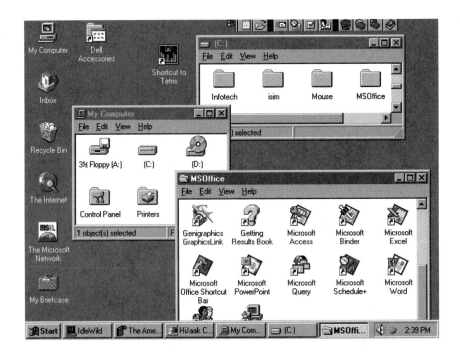

utilizes windows, boxes, icons, and other elements to provide the user with visual cues to the available support functions. Users typically issue a command by pointing to the desired icon or menu choice and clicking with a mouse.

A graphic user interface is sometimes called a WIMP interface. The acronym WIMP stands for Windows, Icons, Menus, and Pointers. Contrary to the usual meaning associated with the word, a WIMP interface is very powerful.

FILE MANAGEMENT

File system
An operating system routine that helps the user keep track of files.

A disk can hold hundreds of different files. The operating system's **file system** helps the user keep track of them.

Files and File Names

File name
A logical name assigned by a user to a file.

Most operating systems allow a user to assign a logically meaningful name to each file. Figure 6.7 summarizes the rules for defining MS-DOS file names. A **file name** is a string of characters that uniquely identifies the file; for example, *RESUME* might be a good name for the file that holds your résumé.

In the past, only brief, cryptic file names could be used (eight characters was a typical limit), but many current operating systems support long file names (often up to 255 characters). A long file name can more clearly indicate the contents of the file.

Extension
A three-character addition to a DOS file name.

A file can hold a program or data. A data file might hold traditional records, a graphic image, a sound pattern, a video clip, or any other information that can be stored electronically. To distinguish file types, some operating systems add an **extension** to the file name.

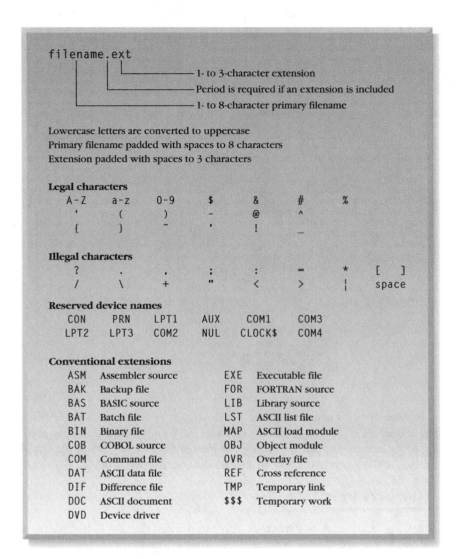

MS-DOS file names and extensions.

Formatting a Disk

Before you can store a file on a disk, you must first **format** the disk. Format is an operating system command that writes the electronic markers that divide the disk's surface into tracks and sectors (p. 106) and prepares the disk for use.

Format
To prepare a disk for use.

Directories

The data and program files stored on a disk are listed in the disk's **directory** (Figure 6.8). The directory is essentially a table of contents for the disk. It is the key to accessing files by name.

When a file is first written to disk, its file name and its location are recorded in the directory. To retrieve the data, the directory is read and searched by file name, the file's location is extracted, and the necessary input or output commands are issued. When a file is deleted, its entry is removed from the directory. The file system manages the directory.

Directory
A list of the addresses of every program and every set of data stored on a disk.

▲ FIGURE 6.8

The files stored on a disk are listed in the disk's directory.

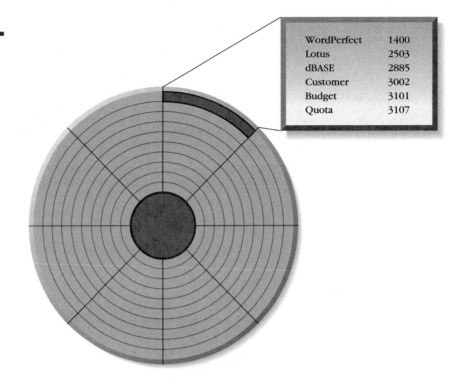

WordPerfect	1400
Lotus	2503
dBASE	2885
Customer	3002
Budget	3101
Quota	3107

Folder
A directory.

Some operating systems refer to directories as **folders.** Often, icons of file folders are displayed on the screen and the user selects a folder by pointing to its icon and clicking a mouse. Inside the folder is a table of file names or a set of file icons that allow you to access the individual files.

Directory Trees

Root directory
A disk's primary directory.

A disk's primary or **root directory** is created when the disk is first prepared for use, or formatted (pp. 106 and 113). The root directory is the disk's primary directory.

Subdirectory
A directory that is stored as a file in another directory.

Tree structure
A directory structure that resembles a tree growing from the root.

On most systems it is possible to create special files called **subdirectories** to hold additional file names and disk addresses (Figure 6.9). The directory structure is sometimes called a **tree structure** because it resembles a tree growing from the root.

The main reason for using subdirectories is to organize your files and your program library. For example, when this book was written, each chapter was assigned a file name and all the chapter files were grouped on a subdi-

▲ FIGURE 6.9

A typical directory structure.

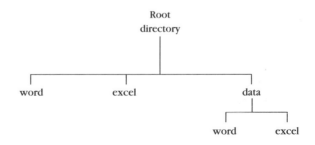

rectory named *cis.* Consequently, a reference to directory *cis* yielded a list of all the book's chapters and excluded other files that had nothing to do with this project.

Disk Space Management

The file system is also responsible for allocating disk space. Data are stored on a disk around a series of concentric circles called tracks (Figure 6.10), and the tracks are subdivided into sectors (p. 106). The file system assigns space to files in allocation units called **clusters.** A cluster contains (depending on the type of disk) one or more sectors. For example, on a 3.5-inch, 1.44 megabyte diskette, each cluster represents two sectors.

    The key to space management is an index to the disk's clusters called the **file allocation table,** or **FAT.** Like the root directory, the file allocation table is created when the disk is formatted. Any defective clusters are marked in the table so the file system does not attempt to use them to store data.

Cluster
The file system's basic disk space allocation unit.

File allocation table (FAT)
An index to the disk's sectors used by the operating system to keep track of which sectors are allocated to which files.

The FAT Chain

ADVANCED TOPICS

Disk space is allocated to files in clusters, and the file allocation table (FAT) contains an entry for each cluster on the disk. When a file is initially stored, the number of its first cluster is recorded in the directory. Consequently, the directory entry points to the beginning of the file.

    If the file subsequently needs more space, the number of its second cluster is recorded in the first cluster's FAT entry, the number of its third cluster is recorded in the second cluster's FAT entry, and so on. (Note that the clusters need not be physically adjacent.) Thus, given the number of the file's first cluster (from the directory), the operating system can follow a chain of pointers through the file allocation table to find all its clusters.

▲ **FIGURE 6.10**

Data are stored on disk around a series of concentric circles called tracks.

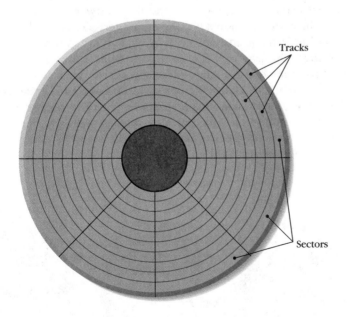

Tracks

Sectors

PEOPLE

Ken Thompson, Dennis Ritchie, and UNIX

Back in the 1960s, the term "user friendly" was rarely (if ever) applied to an operating system. In those days, the operating system's primary purpose was to ensure the efficient utilization of expensive computer hardware, and if the user was inconvenienced, so be it.

Ken Thompson and Dennis Ritchie (of AT&T's Bell Laboratories in Murray Hill, New Jersey) decided to do something about that state of affairs. Starting in 1969, and working on a little-used Digital Equipment Corporation PDP-7 minicomputer, they set out to create an application development environment that they liked. The result, an operating system christened UNIX, was developed between 1969 and 1973, and was widely available by 1975.

Although (given today's standards) no one would consider UNIX user friendly, it has proven to be extremely popular, particularly in academic environments. One reason for its popularity is AT&T's decision to offer UNIX to universities at minimal cost. In addition to AT&T's UNIX System V, other popular versions of this operating system include the Berkeley Software Distribution (BSD) of UNIX, XENIX, POSIX, and AIX.

HARDWARE MANAGEMENT

The operating system also manages the flow of work through the system's hardware.

The Input/Output Control System

Few users care about where or how their data are physically stored. Instead, most users simply want the data, and the hardware details associated with finding them are (or should be) the computer's concern. The operating system's **input/output control system,** or **IOCS** (Figure 6.11), is the routine that bridges the gap between the user's request for data and the specific hardware operations needed to physically access them.

One potentially confusing point is the difference between the file system and the input/output control system. Generally, the input/output control system is the module that communicates *directly* with peripheral devices. The file system, in contrast, performs such logical functions as managing directories and allocating disk space.

Input/output control system (IOCS) The operating system routine that bridges the gap between the user's request for data and the specific hardware operations needed to physically access them.

▲ FIGURE 6.11

The input/output control system bridges the gap between the user's request for data and the hardware operations needed to physically access them.

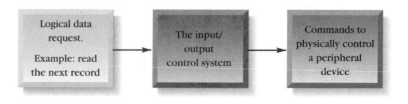

OPEN AND CLOSE

To access a file, you **open** it. The input/output control system responds to an open request by reading the directory, searching the directory for the file name, and retrieving the file's disk location.

When you are finished with a file, you **close** it. Closing a file deletes the program's link to it, thus minimizing the risk that the data will be accidentally modified or destroyed.

Once you open a file, you can read or write its individual records. Once you read a record, you can process its fields. Files are opened and closed. Records are read and written. Fields are processed.

Open
To prepare a file for use.

Close
To break the link between a program and a data file. To make a data file unavailable for use.

PRIMITIVE COMMANDS

On the surface, the task of transferring data between a peripheral device and memory appears simple, but it can be surprisingly complex. For example, data are stored on a disk around a series of concentric circles called tracks (Figure 6.10). The tracks are subdivided into sectors, and it is the contents of a sector that move between the disk's surface and the computer's memory (p. 109).

Assume you have already opened a disk file and you want to access one of its records. A disk drive can perform a very limited number of operations, including:

▶ move the access mechanism to the target track (seek),
▶ read a selected sector from that track,
▶ write a selected sector to that track.

Consequently, the only way to read data from a disk into memory is to send the disk drive a series of **primitive commands,** each of which tells the drive to perform one of its basic operations. For example, to read the contents of a sector takes two commands: one to move the access mechanism to the target track (seek) and a second to read the sector that holds the desired data.

Note that the disk drive must be told exactly where to position the access mechanism and exactly which sector to read. If you work at a primitive level, it is your responsibility to remember which sector holds which data, and if you forget you might never see your data again.

This example was based on accessing a disk. The input/output control system is responsible for communicating with the system's other peripherals (including input and output devices), too. Each physical device is controlled by its own unique set of primitive commands. Application programs issue logical requests to start input or to start output. The input/output control system accepts those logical requests and generates the primitive commands needed to physically control a specific peripheral device.

Primitive command
A command that tells a peripheral device to perform one of its basic operations.

PROTOCOLS

Establishing communication with a peripheral device involves more than just generating primitive commands, however. For example, before two hardware components (such as a computer and a disk drive) can communicate, they must be carefully synchronized by exchanging a predetermined set of signals called a **protocol.** Starting and checking protocol signals is a tedious process usually assigned to the operating system.

Protocol
A set of rules that governs communication between two devices.

DEVICE DRIVERS

Primitive commands and protocols can vary significantly from device to device. One way to deal with such diversity is to group the instructions that are unique to a given device in a routine called a **device driver.** For example, when you send data to a printer, the input/output control system takes care of such general tasks as counting the number of bytes transmitted, while the device driver handles such device-specific tasks as moving the print head or skipping a line. Note that only the device drivers for the peripherals that are actually attached to a computer must be loaded into memory.

Memory Management

As programs run, their memory requirements change, and it is the operating system that keeps track of how memory is being used. A map of memory (Figure 6.12) generally starts with space to hold the key data the operating system needs to monitor system status. Next come the input/output control system, the file system, and the command processor. The remaining memory is called the **transient area.** This is where application programs and less essential operating system routines are loaded.

Some operating system modules directly support application programs as they run. Those routines are **resident;** in other words, they remain in memory as long as the operating system is running. Others, such as the routine that formats disks, are used only occasionally. These **transient** modules (more accurately, programs) are stored on disk and read into memory when needed. The resident part of the operating system is sometimes called the executive.

The Kernel

The computers made by different manufacturers are often incompatible at the hardware level. If an operating system is to define a common platform or operating environment for developing application software, it must incorporate instructions that deal with each machine's unique features while still presenting users and application programs with a consistent interface.

Device driver
A routine that holds the control instructions that are unique to a given peripheral device.

Transient area
A region of memory where application programs and less essential operating system routines are loaded.
Resident
A routine that stays in memory as long as the computer is running.
Transient
A program that is stored on disk and read into memory when needed.

▲ FIGURE 6.12

A memory map for a typical microcomputer operating system.

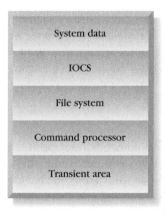

System data
IOCS
File system
Command processor
Transient area

One way to do that is to isolate the instructions that deal directly with the hardware into a **kernel** (Figure 6.13). The other operating system components communicate with the hardware through the kernel. Ideally, two versions of an operating system that run on different computers will differ only in their kernels.

Kernel
An operating system routine that holds the instructions that deal directly with the hardware.

LOADING THE OPERATING SYSTEM

Application programs are loaded and started by the operating system, so the operating system must be in memory before any application program can run. On some systems, the operating system is stored in permanent (read-only) memory, but the main memory of most computers is composed of volatile RAM. Consequently, the first step in using a computer is to load the operating system.

The Boot

Usually, the operating system is stored on disk and loaded into memory by a special program called the **boot.** When the computer is first activated, hardware automatically reads the boot program into memory (Figure 6.14a). Once it is in memory, the boot loads the rest of the operating system (Figure 6.14b). Once the operating system is in memory, you can load and execute application programs. This process is called booting the system.

Boot
A program that loads the operating system into memory.

AUTOEXEC.BAT

ADVANCED TOPICS

Perhaps you have wondered about the cryptic information that scrolls rapidly across the screen when you boot your computer. What you are seeing is a series of commands that initialize key system variables, load various routines, and sometimes start an application program. Those commands are part of a file that is automatically executed as soon as the boot process is finished. Under MS-DOS, that file is called AUTOEXEC.BAT.

▲ **FIGURE 6.13**

The kernel holds the operating system routines that deal directly with the hardware.

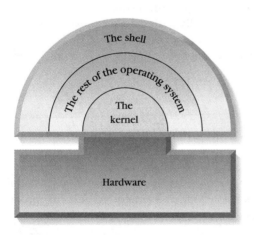

▲ FIGURE 6.14

The boot process.
a. **Hardware reads the boot program into memory.**
b. **The boot loads the rest of the operating system.**

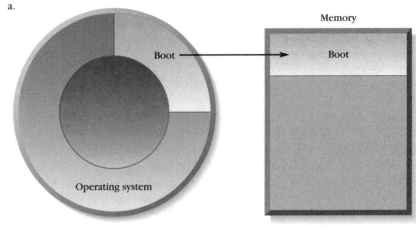

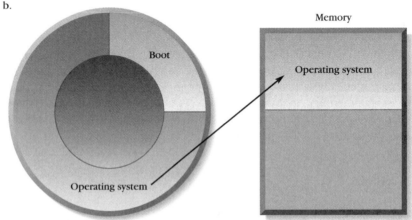

Initial Program Load (IPL)

Initial program load (IPL)
The process of starting a mainframe computer.

The boot process transfers a microcomputer's operating system from disk into memory, but the task of starting a mainframe is considerably more complex. Mainframes are usually initialized by a professional computer operator who follows a set of **initial program load,** or **IPL,** procedures that might include a boot routine. Microcomputers are booted. Mainframes are IPLed.

UTILITIES

Utility program
A program that performs a single system function.

Most operating systems include **utility programs** that allow you to format your diskettes, backup your files, optimize your directories, copy files, and perform similar tasks. You can also purchase independent utility routines to supplement the operating system. Some of the tasks commonly performed by utility programs include implementing security procedures, managing program and data libraries, monitoring and enhancing system performance, making backup copies of data and programs, recovering the contents of a file after a system failure, and so on.

MICROCOMPUTER OPERATING SYSTEMS

Initially released in 1981, Microsoft's Disk Operating System, better known as **MS-DOS,** was for years the microcomputer standard. In 1984, Apple's Macintosh computers introduced a graphic user interface that was clearly superior to the DOS command interface, so Microsoft countered by creating a graphic DOS shell called **Windows.** Following the release of version 3 in 1990, Microsoft Windows became a de facto microcomputer standard. Windows 95 (the version released in 1995) is a full-featured operating system that runs without MS-DOS. In effect, the shell swallowed the operating system.

Apple's **System 7** operating system runs on Macintosh computers. **OS/2** was created to support IBM's PS/2 computer series; it can run virtually all MS-DOS and Windows programs. Originally developed by AT&T, **UNIX** has become the de facto Internet standard.

Version Numbers

Operating systems change constantly as errors are corrected and new features are added. The **version number** tells you when a particular copy of an operating system was released and what features it contains.

The version number is usually shown as a whole number, a decimal point, and a decimal fraction. The whole number represents a major release; for example, version 6 is a significant upgrade from version 5. The decimal fraction represents a minor release, often to correct errors in the previous release. For example, version 6.2 is much like version 6.1.

That version numbering standard is widely, but not universally accepted. For example, the latest release of Microsoft Windows is called Windows 95, not Windows 4.0. The 95 indicates the year it was released. One reason for the change is that Windows 95 is a new operating system, not just an upgrade.

New software releases typically support upward compatibility but not downward compatibility. For example, software and files created under version 5 will almost certainly work without change under version 6, but files and programs created under version 6 might not work with version 5.

DISK OPERATING SYSTEM (DOS)

MS-DOS is composed of three primary modules (Figure 6.15). **COMMAND.COM** is the command processor. The functions of the input/output control system and the file system are divided between two routines, MSDOS.SYS and IO.SYS. **MSDOS.SYS** performs logical, hardware-independent tasks such as managing directories. **IO.SYS**, on the other hand, communicates directly with the hardware and contains device-dependent code. (In fact, on the original IBM PC, major parts of IO.SYS were implemented in hardware on a chip called the BIOS, or basic input/output system.) Versions of

MS-DOS
A popular microcomputer operating system developed by Microsoft Corporation.
Windows
A popular microcomputer operating environment developed by Microsoft Corporation.

System 7
The Macintosh operating system.
OS/2
A microcomputer operating system developed by IBM Corporation.
UNIX
An operating system developed by AT&T. The de facto Internet standard operating system.

Version number
A number that tells you when a particular copy of an operating system or an application program was released and what features it contains.

COMMAND.COM
The MS-DOS command processor.
MSDOS.SYS
The MS-DOS routine that deals with logical input and output operations.
IO.SYS
The MS-DOS routine that communicates directly with hardware.

▲ FIGURE 6.15

MS-DOS is composed of three primary modules.

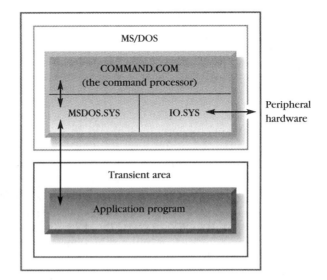

MS-DOS written for different computers should differ only in their IO.SYS logic.

When MS-DOS is booted, COMMAND.COM, MSDOS.SYS, and IO.SYS are copied into memory (Figure 6.15). The transient area consists of memory not assigned to the operating system. Application programs, system utilities, transient routines, and data are loaded into the transient area as needed.

ADVANCED TOPICS

Memory Levels

The original versions of MS-DOS were designed to support up to 640 KB of conventional memory plus a maximum 384 KB upper memory area. Data and program instructions were restricted to conventional memory. The upper memory area was used to manage system hardware, such as the monitor.

In the early 1980s, 640 KB was a substantial amount of memory, but today it represents a significant limitation. One solution is to add *extended* memory over and above the 1024 KB (1 MB) nominal limit. Programs that are specifically designed to work with extended memory can store and access instructions and data in the extra space.

Another option is to add *expanded* memory. Programs do not directly access expanded memory. Instead, the expanded memory space is divided into pages. When a program needs information stored in expanded memory, the appropriate page is copied into the conventional memory area where the program can access it.

Windows and Windows 95

Microsoft's Windows was initially released as a graphic user interface shell that ran under DOS (Figure 6.16). The user communicated directly with DOS, with the shell, or with an application program. Windows, in turn, communicated with the hardware through DOS.

Windows 95 is an operating system in its own right (Figure 6.17). The user still accesses the system through the Windows shell or an application program, but Windows 95 communicates directly with the hardware. Removing DOS from the chain makes Windows 95 more stable and better able to deal with today's increasingly complex operating environments.

▲ **FIGURE 6.16**

Windows was initially a shell.

▲ **FIGURE 6.17**

Windows 95 is an operating system.

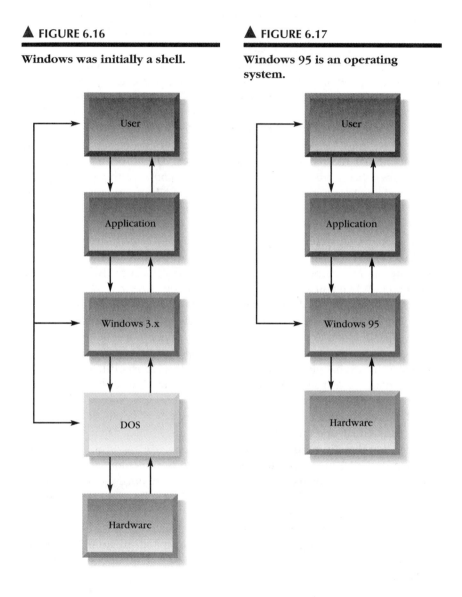

SUMMARY

The operating system serves as an interface, bridging the gap between hardware and application software. The operating system defines a platform or operating environment for writing and executing application software. A microcomputer operating system provides an interface for communicating with the system, allows users and application programs to manage files, and manages the work flow through the system's hardware.

A user issues orders, or commands, that tell the operating system to perform a specific function, such as copy a file or format a disk. The operating system module that accepts, interprets, and carries out commands is called the command processor. The rules for issuing commands are defined in a command language that has its own syntax, style, and punctuation. The system indicates it is ready to accept a command by displaying a prompt. The command processor is sometimes called the shell. Some shells let the user select a command from a menu, essentially, a list of commands. Some shells incorporate a graphic user interface, or GUI.

The operating system's file system helps the user keep track of files. A file name (plus the optional extension) is a string of characters that uniquely identifies the file. All the files stored on a disk are listed in the disk's directory. Some operating systems refer to directories as folders.

A disk's primary or root directory is created when the disk is formatted. On most systems it is possible to create special files called subdirectories to hold additional file names and disk addresses. The directory structure is sometimes called a tree structure because it resembles a tree growing from the root. The file system assigns space to files in allocation units called clusters. The key to space management is an index to the disk's clusters called the file allocation table, or FAT.

The operating system's input/output control system, or IOCS, is the routine that bridges the gap between the user's request for data and the specific hardware operations needed to physically access the data. To access a file, you open it. When you are finished with a file, you close it.

To read data from disk into memory, the operating system's input/output control system sends the disk drive a series of primitive commands, each of which tells the drive to perform one of its basic operations. Before two hardware components can communicate, their electronic signals must be synchronized by exchanging a predetermined set of signals called a protocol. The instructions that are unique to a given device are found in a routine called a device driver.

The transient area is the region of memory where application programs and less essential operating system routines are loaded. Operating system modules that directly support application programs as they run are resident. Transient modules are stored on disk and read into memory when needed. The instructions that deal directly with the hardware form the operating system's kernel.

The operating system is stored on disk and loaded into memory by a special program called the boot. Mainframes are usually initialized by a professional computer operator who follows a set of initial program load, or IPL procedures that might include a boot routine. Most operating systems include utility programs.

Popular microcomputer operating systems include MS-DOS, Microsoft's Windows 95, Apple's System 7, IBM's OS/2, and UNIX. The version number tells you when a particular copy of an operating system was released and what features it contains.

MS-DOS is composed of three primary modules: COMMAND.COM, MSDOS.SYS, and IO.SYS. Microsoft's Windows was initially released as a graphic user interface shell that ran under DOS, but Windows 95 is an operating system in its own right.

KEY TERMS

boot
close
cluster
command
COMMAND.COM
command language
command processor
device driver
directory
extension (file name)
file allocation table (FAT)
file name
file system
folder
format

graphic user interface
  (GUI)
initial program load (IPL)
input/output control
  system (IOCS)
IO.SYS
kernel
menu
MS-DOS
MSDOS.SYS
open
operating environment
OS/2
platform
primitive command

prompt
protocol
resident
root directory
shell
subdirectory
System 7
transient
transient area
tree structure
UNIX
utility program
version number
Windows

CONCEPTS

1. Identify the functions performed by a microcomputer operating system.
2. What are commands? What is a command language? Why is something like a command language necessary?
3. What is a shell? Distinguish among a command shell, a menu interface, and a graphic user interface. What are the advantages and disadvantages associated with each?
4. Explain how a file name uniquely identifies a file. Who is responsible for assigning file names? Why?
5. What is a directory? Why are directories necessary? Briefly explain directories, subdirectories, and directory structures. Why does it make sense to organize directories and subdirectories to form a directory structure? This last part of the question is not explicitly answered in the book, so think about it.
6. Briefly discuss how the operating system manages disk space.
7. Briefly explain what an operating system's input/output control system does.
8. Distinguish between open and close. Why is it necessary to open and close a file? What does the operating system do when an application program opens a file?
9. Describe how the operating system converts the programmer's logical I/O requests to physical primitive commands. Why is that conversion necessary? Briefly explain the purpose of protocols and device drivers.
10. Distinguish between resident and transient routines. Explain why many operating systems are designed around a kernel.

11. Describe the boot process and explain why it is necessary. What is initial program load? How does it resemble the boot process? How is it different?
12. What are utility programs?
13. Identify several popular microcomputer operating systems.
14. Assume you are comparing MS-DOS release 5.1 to MS-DOS release 6.0. What do those numbers mean?
15. Sketch a diagram showing the primary components of MS-DOS and briefly explain what each routine does.
16. In its earlier releases, Microsoft Windows was a shell, but Windows 95 is an operating system in its own right. Briefly explain how that change affects the way a user communicates with the hardware.

PROJECTS

1. Identify the operating systems that are used on the computers at your school. Note that there may be several.
2. Print out a directory tree for a computer's hard disk drive and identify the directories and files.

 INTERNET PROJECTS

1. *News and Notes*. Companies often post information about their very latest products on their World Wide Web home pages. Select a company whose products are mentioned in this chapter and access its home page. Try the address *http://www.xxx.com;* substitute the company name (for example, *microsoft*) for *xxx*. Once you find the home page, look for a button marked *New products* (or something similar) and click on it. Identify and briefly describe at least two new products and submit your findings to your instructor in the form of a brief note or an e-mail message.
2. *Topic Searches.* Check the World Wide Web and/or other Internet resources for information on the following topics:

Key word	Qualifiers
Bill Gates	Internet
plug and play	Windows 95
OS/2	Windows 95

Define the key word, identify at least two sources of information on the topic, and briefly summarize the nature of the information you find.

3. *Links to Other Sites.* After you access one or more of the following sites, write a brief note or send an e-mail message to your instructor outlining what you find.

   a. On the World Wide Web, check *http://www.ibm.com* for information on IBM software.

b. On the World Wide Web, check *http://www.microsoft.com* for infor-
    mation on Microsoft products.
c. On the World Wide Web, check *http://www.zdnet.com* for current
    news about computers and computer-related products.

4. Access West Publishing Company's home page and find the Chapter 6
    student activities for this book. See Internet Project 3 for the spotlight
    on *The Internet* following Chapter 1 (page 29) for more detailed
    instructions on accessing the home page. As appropriate, repeat
    projects 1, 2, and/or 3 using the more current references you find.

CHAPTER 7

Application Software

Before you start this chapter, you should be familiar with the following concepts:

▶ Computers (p. 6), the user (p. 6), software (p. 9), data (p. 10), and long-term storage (p. 12).

▶ Classifying computers (p. 14), networks (p. 17), and the Internet (p. 17).

When you finish reading this chapter, you should be able to:

▶ Briefly describe several common user interfaces.

▶ Briefly explain software licenses and site licenses.

▶ Identify the basic functions of word processing and desktop publishing software. Discuss document creation, editing, formatting, printing, document management, and mail merge.

▶ Identify the basic functions of an electronic spreadsheet program and list several spreadsheet applications. Describe several common spreadsheet features and outline basic spreadsheet design principles.

▶ Identify the basic functions of database software, including queries and report generation. Discuss database creation, indexes, and relationships.

▶ Identify the basic functions of graphics software.

▶ Identify several other types of commercial software.

▶ Briefly discuss software suites and integrated software.

▶ Define object linking and embedding and dynamic data exchange.

▶ Identify two techniques for customizing commercial software.

▶ Briefly discuss public domain software and shareware.

WHAT IS APPLICATION SOFTWARE?

As you learned in Chapter 1, application software solves user problems or meets user needs. For example, if there were no computer you would find some other way to play a game, write a paper, perform a statistical analysis, or create an accounting report. We use computers because they allow us to perform application tasks more efficiently.

THE USER INTERFACE

A user accesses a computer through a set of hardware and software elements that form the **user interface.** *Physical* access (the hardware) is discussed in Chapter 3. The screens, commands, and operations that together support logical access are implemented through software.

Most modern user interfaces are interactive. The software presents the user with a set of choices, the user makes a choice, and the software carries out the appropriate operations. The software then presents the user with a new set of choices, and a new cycle begins. The exchange of information between the user and the program is called a **dialogue.**

The user issues commands to a **command interface** (Figure 7.1) by pressing a function key or by typing a cryptic, single-line message in response to a prompt displayed by the program. Each command tells the system to carry out a specific task. A command interface is often the quickest, most efficient way for experienced people to access a computer, but beginners typically find command line syntax confusing (and a bit intimidating).

A prompted interface is a form of command interface. The system starts the process by displaying a prompt that requests a piece of information or poses a question. The user responds, and based on the content of the response the system displays the next prompt.

A **menu** interface presents the user with a list of commands (Figure 7.2). Rather than typing the command, you select the one you want by pointing to it and then clicking a mouse or pressing a key.

Many of today's applications incorporate a **graphic user interface,** or **GUI** (pronounced GOO-ee) (Figure 7.3). A graphic user interface utilizes **windows** (screen boxes that hold messages or menus), **icons** (pictures or symbols that represent programs or files), and other elements to provide the user with visual cues. Users issue commands by pointing to the desired icon

User interface
A set of hardware and software components that define how a user accesses the system.

Dialogue
A set of screens and the rules for using them that together allow the computer and the user to exchange information.

Command interface
A user interface that allows the user to communicate with the computer by issuing commands.

Menu
A list of available commands or other options.

Graphic user interface (GUI)
An interface that utilizes windows, boxes, icons, and other graphical elements to provide the user with visual cues.

Windows
A popular microcomputer operating environment developed by Microsoft Corporation.

Icon
A picture or symbol that represents a program or a file.

▲ FIGURE 7.1

A typical command interface.

```
C:\>DIR B:
    Volume in drive B has no label
    Volume Serial Number is 165C-50B0
    Directory of B:\

COMMAND  COM    47845 04-09-91    5:00a
    1 file(s)         47845 bytes
                     610304 bytes free


C:\>
```

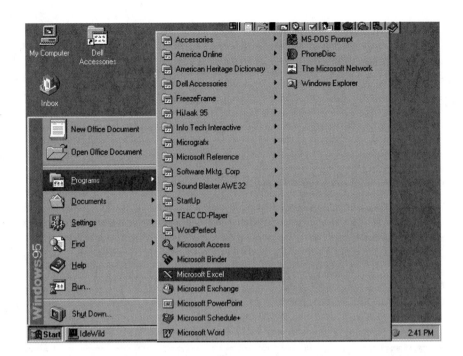

▲ FIGURE 7.2

A menu is, essentially, a list of commands.

or menu choice and clicking a mouse. Menu interfaces and graphic user interfaces support a "point and select" mode of operation that is particularly convenient when the system is equipped with a mouse. Microsoft Windows and Apple's Macintosh environment are the best known graphic user interfaces.

The trend is toward increasing ease of use. For example, many graphic user interfaces are designed around a desktop metaphor that allows the user to visualize manipulating objects and tools on a desktop. A well-executed

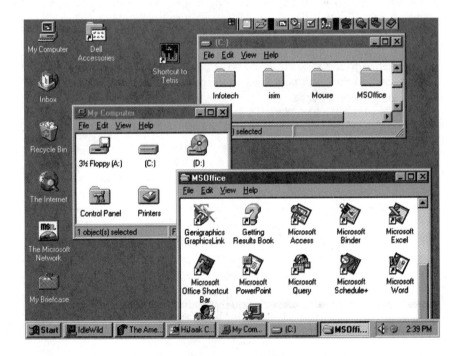

▲ FIGURE 7.3

A typical graphic user interface.

metaphor presents a consistent interface that allows the user, given minimal training, to rely on his or her prior understanding (in this case, of a desktop) to make reasonable, intuitive, and usually accurate assumptions about how the interface works.

The primary form of person-to-person communication is verbal. Given the trend toward increasing ease of use, you can expect a voice interface to be a common option in the near future.

COMMERCIAL SOFTWARE

A few decades ago, most large organizations employed a staff of professional programmers, and virtually all application programs were custom written to solve a specific problem or perform a specific task. Commercial software, in contrast, is software that is prewritten to perform a common task, such as preparing a payroll or playing a computer game. For many applications, commercial software is more cost effective than writing custom software that (in effect) reinvents the wheel.

I S S U E S

Software Piracy

Software piracy, the illegal copying and/or distribution of software, is a serious problem that costs the software industry millions of dollars per year. Part of the problem is that many people (including some students) see nothing wrong with "borrowing" a program from a friend. Unauthorized software copying is a violation of federal copyright law, and the fact that what is stolen is a pattern of bits rather than some physical entity does not change that reality.

Most commercial software is sold with a licensing agreement that gives the user the right to install the program on a single computer and to make one backup copy. If you own a desktop computer and a laptop that you use when you travel, few software distributors would challenge your right to install the program on both machines, but the legality of the second copy is questionable.

Pirated software comes without manuals or vendor support; in other words, if you encounter a problem, you are on your own. Additionally, pirated software is a common agent for spreading computer viruses. Think twice before you accept free software. It might cost more than you can imagine.

The personal computer revolution created a huge market for commercial software, and today you can purchase programs to perform almost any information processing task you can imagine. The software development process is the subject of Chapter 8. This chapter focuses on commercial software.

Commercial software can be purchased through a retail outlet, via mail order, or directly from the developer or distributor. Technically, however, what you buy is a **software license** that gives you the right to use the program on a single computer. Often, large organizations purchase a **site license** that allows them to distribute numerous copies of the program (on disk or over a network) for a fixed fee.

Games and Entertainment

Games were among the very first commercially successful personal computer programs. Perhaps you remember spending hours, joystick in hand, playing Pong, Space Invaders, or Pac Man. Those games seem crude by today's standards, but they were a start.

Today we have action games like Tetris (Figure 7.4), Missile Command, DOOM, and Wolfenstein; sophisticated simulations like SimCity, X-Wing, and Flight Simulator; adventure games like King's Quest and MYST (Figure 7.5); children's games like Grandma and Me (Figure 7.6); and electronic versions of virtually every sport you can imagine. You can even use a computer to learn how to play chess, cards, or your favorite casino game.

The trend is toward better graphics and greater realism. Over the years game and entertainment programs have exhibited the state of the art in computer graphics.

Software license
A legal agreement that gives a user the right to use a given program on a single computer.
Site license
A legal agreement that allows an organization to distribute numerous copies of the program (on disk or over a network) for a fixed fee.

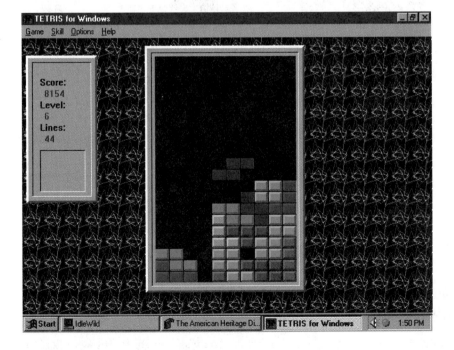

▲ **FIGURE 7.4**

Tetris.

▲ **FIGURE 7.5**

MYST is a popular adventure game.

▲ **FIGURE 7.6**

Grandma and Me is a popular children's game.

Word Processing

Word processing
Application software that supports writing text.

Word processing software simplifies the task of creating, editing, formatting, and printing documents (Figure 7.7). In a business environment, documents are often prepared as group projects, so modern word processors incorporate features that support work groups. Major competitors include Microsoft Word, WordPro (formerly Ami Pro), WordPerfect, DeScribe, and many others. The manuscript for this book was prepared using WordPerfect.

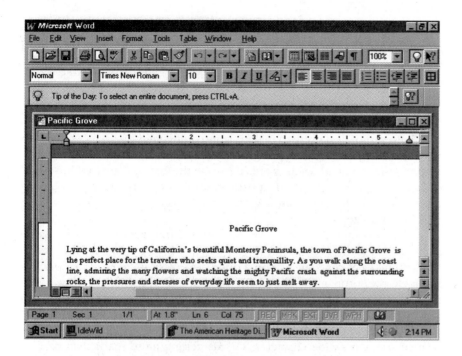

A word processing document.

CREATING AND EDITING DOCUMENTS

A word processing program includes numerous features that simplify the task of creating a document. For example, **word wrap** senses when the text has moved beyond the right margin and automatically advances to the next line, thus eliminating the need to press the return key at the end of each line. Other features make it easy to navigate the document and scroll quickly from screen to screen. Some word processors even check your spelling as you type.

The secret to quality writing is to revise and rewrite material several times, so word processing software includes extensive editing facilities that allow the user to justify, delete, insert, cut, copy, paste, and move words, sentences, paragraphs, and even large blocks of text.

Word wrap
A word processing feature that senses when the text has moved beyond the right margin and automatically advances to the next line, thus eliminating the need to press the return key at the end of each line.

Version Numbers

NOTE

Software changes constantly as errors are corrected and new features are added. The version number tells you when a particular copy of a commercial software product was released and what features it contains.

The version number is usually shown as a whole number followed by a decimal point and a decimal fraction. The whole number represents a major release; for example, version 6 is a significant upgrade from version 5. The decimal portion designates a minor release; for example, little changes as you move from version 6.1 to version 6.2.

Spelling checker
A common word processing feature that checks spelling.

Thesaurus
An electronic version of a book of synonyms.

Grammar checker
A common word processing feature that checks a document's syntax, punctuation, and so on.

Font
A complete set of characters in one typeface and size.

Typeface
A complete set of characters in a particular design or style.

Point size
The size of a character measured in points. A point is roughly $1/72$ of an inch.

Monospacing
In a printed or displayed document, assigning the same amount of space to each character without regard for the character's size.

Pitch
The number of characters printed or displayed per inch.

Proportional spacing
Allocating space to characters in proportion to character size.

Kerning
On a printed or displayed document, considering the relationship between adjacent characters to yield optically even letter spacing.

Most word processors include a **spelling checker** and a **thesaurus,** and some incorporate **grammar checkers.** Other features allow the user to search a document for a specific character string, replace that string with a different one, keep track of footnotes and endnotes, and count words.

FORMATTING DOCUMENTS

Once a document is created, other features allow the user to specify its format. For example, one way to make a printed document more effective is to vary **fonts** (Figure 7.8). A **typeface** is a complete set of characters in a particular design or style. Each typeface can be printed or displayed in several different weights (light, **bold**), **point sizes** (a point is roughly $1/72$ of an inch), and slants (roman, *italic*). A font is a complete set of characters in one typeface and size.

Spacing is another variable (Figure 7.9). **Monospacing** assigns the same amount of space to each character (both M and i, for example). **Pitch** refers to the number of characters printed or displayed per inch. Note that pitch is inversely proportional to point size; for example, the characters on a line printed at 10 pitch (10 characters per inch) will be bigger than the characters on a line printed at 12 pitch (12 characters per inch).

Proportional spacing varies the space allocated to a letter to reflect its relative size, with wide characters (W, M) getting more space than narrow characters (i). With **kerning,** the relationship between adjacent characters is taken into account to yield optically even letter spacing.

Other formatting options allow a user to define columns and tables, create lists, add page headers and footers to a document, number pages, insert graphics (Figure 7.10), justify text, set margins, and add lines, borders, and shading.

A few years ago, most word processing programs implemented document formatting by inserting hidden codes within the narrative, and all too often the appearance of the printed output was a surprise. Today's full-featured word processors show the document on the screen exactly as it will appear

▲ FIGURE 7.8

Most word processing programs support a variety of type fonts.

TYPEFACES & STYLES different typefaces and styles: bold, underline, and italics	**Chicago** **Chicago Bold**	Helvetica Helvetica Underlined	Times Roman *Times Roman Italicized*

POINT SIZES

different point sizes can be used to make type larger or smaller

6 point   8 point   10 point   12 point   14 point   20 point

30 point   50 point

Monospacing:	`The quick brown fox . . .`
Proportional spacing:	The quick brown fox. . .
Kerning:	The quick brown fox . . .

▲ **FIGURE 7.9**

Proper spacing can improve readability.

on the printer, an approach called **WYSIWYG** (pronounced WIZ-e-wig, for what-you-see-is-what-you-get).

WYSIWYG
Acronym for what-you-see-is-what-you-get.

PRINTING DOCUMENTS

Finished documents are typically printed. Many (non-WYSIWYG) word processors include a **print preview** feature that allows the user to see exactly how the pages will look before they are sent to the printer. Other options allow you to control paper orientation (portrait or landscape), print selected pages, specify the number of copies, specify print quality (draft, medium, high), and so on.

Print preview
A feature of many application programs that allows the user to see a document on the screen exactly as it will appear when printed.

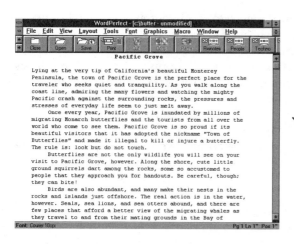

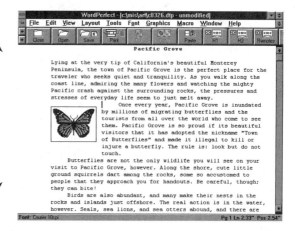

▲ **FIGURE 7.10**

Graphic images can be inserted into a document.

NOTE

GIGO

Sometimes, people do things just because they can. Modern word processors support multiple type fonts and graphics, so people spend hours "creating" visually stimulating memoranda that say absolutely nothing. Spreadsheet programs generate sophisticated three-dimensional charts, so we get beautiful plots of meaningless data. The fact that you can does not necessarily mean that you should.

The tendency to misuse software is important because people tend to assign extra significance to almost anything output by a computer. Plot the data and you can hide errors or suggest nonexistent relationships just as easily as you illuminate meaning. Make a document look good and you can direct the reader away from the weak points in your presentation.

Remember the acronym GIGO. It means "garbage in, garbage out." The output generated by a computer is only as good as the input data.

Page description language
A programming language that defines text, graphic images, fonts, and other elements in a form that makes sense to the printer.

Many laser printers are designed to accept output formatted in a device-independent page description language such as Postscript, Interpress, or DDL. The **page description language** defines the text, graphic images, fonts, and other elements on the page in a form that makes sense to the printer. Most word processing programs have the ability to generate output in a page description language.

DOCUMENT MANAGEMENT

Although its significance may not be obvious, word processing software also helps with document management. An organization creates an incredible number of documents, and the ability to store, manage, and retrieve them efficiently is valuable.

Generally, each document is treated as a separate file, and that allows the word processing software to take advantage of the file management facilities provided by the operating system. Other features allow you to copy, move (rename), and delete a file, assign a password to a file, and search (by key word or file name) for a file. You can also translate file formats; for example, a WordPerfect file can be converted to Microsoft Word format, and vice versa. Some word processors can even convert a file into Internet or World Wide Web format.

MAIL MERGE

Mail merge
A software routine used to prepare letters by merging the data from a name and address file with a template.

Efficient **mail merge** routines are another common word processing feature. The mail merge application allows a user to send personalized copies of a form letter to all the people whose names and addresses are stored in a file. The program starts with a template (for example, a letter with codes to show where variable data are to be inserted) and then adds the data from one name and address record (Figure 7.11). Then it reads the second record, creates a second personalized document, and so on.

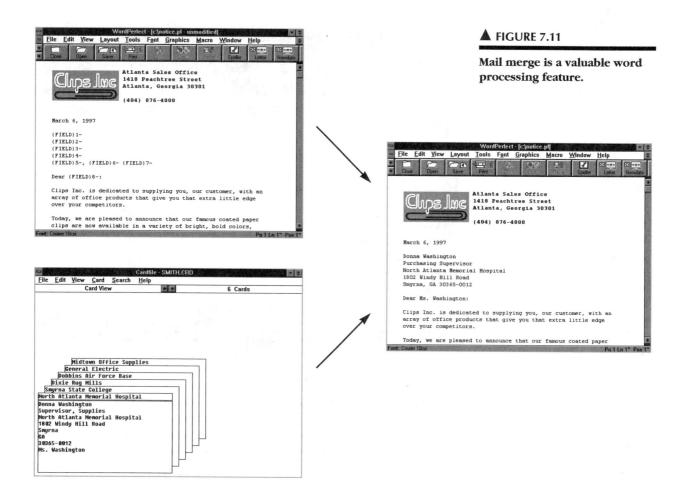

Desktop Publishing

Desktop publishing programs, such as Microsoft Publisher, PageMaker, Ventura Publisher, and QuarkXPress allow you to lay out (or compose) a page that combines the text created on a word processor, the images created by a graphics program, and other elements such as lines, borders, shading, and so on. Modern word processors support a limited form of desktop publishing that is good enough for many applications, but creators of newsletters, advertising copy, periodicals, and books need the extra power of a true desktop publishing program.

Spreadsheets

Accountants use **spreadsheets** (sheets of paper divided into tables made up of horizontal rows and vertical columns) to prepare budgets and analyze financial data. An **electronic spreadsheet** program simulates a spreadsheet on a computer screen (Figure 7.12) and simplifies the task of preparing one. Today's best-known electronic spreadsheet programs include Excel, Lotus 1-2-3, and Quattro Pro.

Desktop publishing
Application software that allows you to lay out a page that combines text and graphic images.

Spreadsheet
A sheet of paper (or a screen) divided into horizontal rows and vertical columns.

Electronic spreadsheet
An application program that simulates a spreadsheet on the screen.

▲ FIGURE 7.12

▲ FIGURE 7.12

An electronic spreadsheet program simulates a spreadsheet on a computer screen.

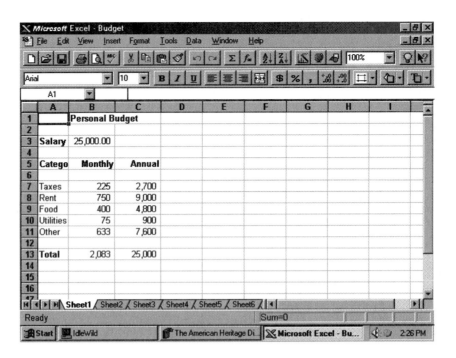

SPREADSHEET APPLICATIONS

Any time you see data organized as a table, you are looking at a possible spreadsheet application; your checkbook register is a good example. Spreadsheets are used to perform such tasks as preparing budgets, tracking expenses, analyzing data, organizing statistics, tracking personal financial data, maintaining inventory, and many others. The spreadsheet data can be used to quickly create visually appealing bar charts, pie charts, and graphs (Figure 7.13) and you can even plot demographic data on maps.

In the business world, **what-if analysis** is an important application. The idea is to define a spreadsheet and then change the values of key variables to see how those changes affect the outcome. For example, a manager might use this technique to compute the likely outcomes of all possible alternatives before making a decision.

SPREADSHEET FEATURES

Figures 7.12 and 7.14 show two different versions of a personal budget spreadsheet. The numbers down the left side of the screen represent **rows;** the letters across the top identify **columns.** The intersection of a row and a column is called a **cell.** A cell can hold a **label** (a string of characters) or a **value** (a number). Note that cell A3 holds the word *Salary* (a label), while cell C7 holds the value *2,700.*

An electronic spreadsheet user can specify a **formula** (a special type of value defined as an algebra-like expression) for a given cell and have the computer find the value. That reduces computational errors.

If you define formulas to link key cells, you can change a single value and have the program recompute all the linked cells. For example, if the salary in Figure 7.12 is increased to $30,000, a new spreadsheet (Figure 7.14) can be generated by changing only cell B3. This feature is called automatic recalculation.

What-if analysis
A form of numerical analysis in which you determine the likely outcomes of each alternative and select the option that yields the best outcome.

Row
A horizontal set of cells in a spreadsheet or a table.
Column
A vertical set of cells in a spreadsheet or a table.
Cell
The intersection of a row and a column.
Label
A character (non-numeric) value in a spreadsheet cell.
Value
A number in a spreadsheet cell.
Formula
In a spreadsheet, an algebra-like expression for computing the value of a cell.

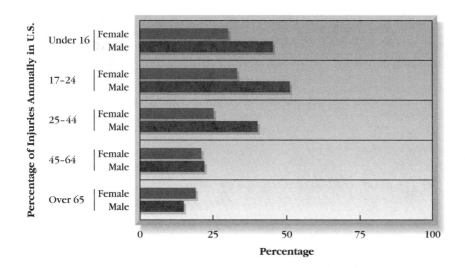

▲ FIGURE 7.13

The spreadsheet data can be used to create charts and graphs.

Once a spreadsheet is created, the user can modify it by moving and copying data and formulas, inserting and deleting rows and columns, and performing numerous other editing tasks. Additionally, built-in functions can be used to perform sophisticated mathematical and statistical analyses, and charts and graphs can be generated to help clarify or communicate the meaning of the data.

SPREADSHEET DESIGN

Although the structure of a spreadsheet can vary significantly with the application and the user, there are a few generally accepted principles of spreadsheet design.

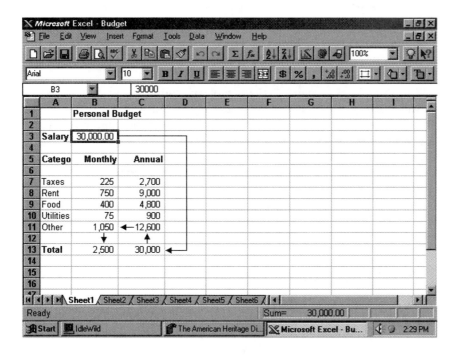

▲ FIGURE 7.14

Formulas are used to link key cells.

PEOPLE

VisiCalc and Lotus 1-2-3

The first commercially successful spreadsheet program, VisiCalc, was written for the Apple II computer by two college students named Dan Bricklin and Bob Frankston. Before VisiCalc, most microcomputer users were hobbyists, but the ability to create and manipulate spreadsheets gave business people a reason to purchase a microcomputer. Some experts believe that it was the *combination* of the Apple computer and VisiCalc that triggered the personal computer revolution.

By the early 1980s, Lotus 1-2-3 had replaced VisiCalc as the best selling spreadsheet program. It was written primarily by Jonathan Sachs. As a result of marketing problems, legal disagreements, and competitive pressures, VisiCalc is no longer available, but Lotus 1-2-3 continues to be a top seller. One reason for the continued success of Lotus 1-2-3 was the support and stability provided by

Lotus Development Corporation, the company founded by Jonathan Sachs and Mitch Kapor. Recently, Lotus was purchased by IBM Corporation.

The body of the spreadsheet contains the data to be displayed or manipulated (Figure 7.15). A well-designed spreadsheet also includes a documentation block that clearly identifies the spreadsheet and distinguishes it from similar spreadsheets.

The third block in Figure 7.15 is a table of **assumptions.** An assumption is a value that is treated as a constant on this spreadsheet but that might be assigned a different value on a subsequent version of the same spreadsheet. As a general rule, assumptions should be listed in a table rather than buried in various formulas because: (1) the assumptions table is a valuable source of documentation, and (2) using an assumptions table simplifies spreadsheet maintenance.

A template is a predefined spreadsheet that allows a user to (literally) just add data. Templates are available for a variety of business and statistical applications.

Database Software

Assumption
A number that is treated as a constant but that might subsequently be assigned a different value.

Database software
Application software that allows a user to create, access, manage, and maintain a database.

Database software is concerned with the efficient storage and retrieval of data. Key competitors include Access, dBase, Paradox, Filemaker Pro, Approach, 4th Dimension, Alpha Four, Oracle, and many others.

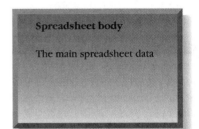

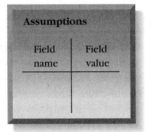

▲ **FIGURE 7.15**

A well-designed spreadsheet contains a body, a documentation block, and a table of assumptions.

Most database programs include routines for creating and maintaining a database. Other features help users retrieve the data selectively, often in response to a **query.** The word *query* is a synonym for *question* or *inquiry.* In effect, the user extracts information from the database by posing inquiries, such as: *List all customer names for overdue balance > 0.* Many database programs include a **query-by-example** feature that allows a user to define a query by, essentially, outlining an example of the desired output.

Report writers are another common feature of database software. Typically, a user can define the structure of a report (Figure 7.16) by simply listing the fields it is to contain.

DATABASE CREATION

In Chapter 1, you learned that a database is a set of related files, a file is a set of related records, and a record is a set of related fields. Database software

Query
A question. Usually, a request for data or information.

Query-by-example
A common database feature that allows a user to define a query by, essentially, outlining an example of the desired output.

Report writer
A common database feature that allows a user to quickly generate a report by specifying the contents.

▲ **FIGURE 7.16**

A typical report.

Report headers —

Column headers —

Detail lines —

Summary line —

Report summary —

```
Central State University
Student Grade Report

Student: Pat Smith        Term: Fall, 1996

Course  Description    Hours   Grade   Points
ENG102  English Comp    3        B        9
MTH182  Calculus II     4        B       12
CIS201  Info. Systems   3        A       12
SPN102  Intro Spanish   3        C        6

Totals                 13                39
              Term      Cumulative
Hours          13           26
Points         39           81
G.P.A.      3.000        3.115
```

ISSUES

Reverse Engineering

Reverse engineering is the process of studying an existing product or process by defining precisely what it does and then using that information to design a new product that performs the same functions. For example, an automobile manufacturer might reverse engineer its own cars as a means of improving them or reverse engineer a competitor's products in an attempt to determine what must be done to match the competition.

Software can be reverse engineered, too. For example, Microsoft might reverse engineer its Access database program to produce equivalent versions to run on different computers. Programmers have been reverse engineering software almost as long as computers have existed.

Reverse engineering can be controversial, however. For example, imagine that the ABC Software Company has just released a new program. Rather than starting from scratch, their competitor, XYZ Software, purchases a copy of ABC's product, reverse engineers it, and quickly brings out a lower-priced version.

Is that legal? Yes, it probably is. Software is protected by copyright laws, and as long as you do not duplicate the code or precisely reproduce any screens, you probably do not violate those laws.

Is such reverse engineering ethical, however? What do you think? If you knew the XYZ product was a clone of the ABC product, which one would you buy? If the XYZ version was 20 percent less expensive, would that influence your decision?

---

begins with routines for defining fields, records, files, and databases. Data are typically entered (and later displayed) in tabular (spreadsheet) form (Figure 7.17) or one record at a time (Figure 7.18).

INDEXES AND RELATIONSHIPS

An important feature of most database software is the ability to **index** the data. An index is a table that relates the values of **key** fields to the records that hold those values. A key field is a field that uniquely identifies a record. For example, if you have all the records in a file indexed by last name, it is possible to search the file and extract data by last name.

As you learned in Chapter 1, a database is set of related files. The **relationships**, or links, between files are typically defined through

Index
A list of the keys and locations of each record in a file.

Key
A field that uniquely defines a single occurrence of an entity.

Relationship
A logical link between two files.

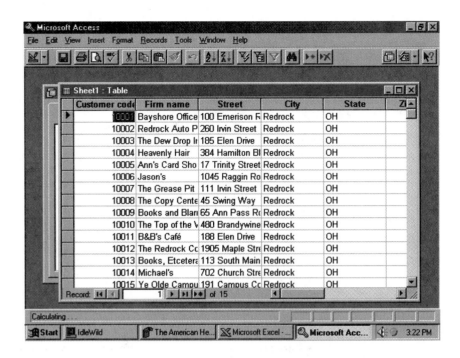

▲ FIGURE 7.17

The data in a database can be displayed as a table.

indexes. For example, a student file and a course file might be linked by a registration file that pairs student codes and course codes (Figure 7.19). In this example, you can use the relationships to generate a list of all the courses taken by a given student or a list of all the students taking a given course.

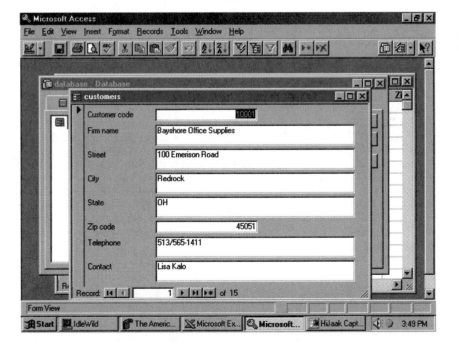

▲ FIGURE 7.18

The data can also be displayed one record at a time.

▲ FIGURE 7.19

A database is set of related files.

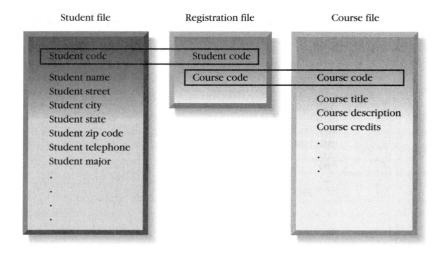

Student file   Registration file   Course file

▲ FIGURE 7.19

A database is set of related files.

Presentation graphics
Application software that allows a user to create graphic images.

Graphics Software

Presentation graphics software allows you to create effective business presentations on the computer. Most are designed around a slide show metaphor, with each screen equivalent to one slide (Figure 7.20). Examples of presentation graphics software include Harvard Graphics, PowerPoint, Freelance, Astound, Adobe Persuasion, Macromedia Action, and Presentations.

Many presentation graphics programs incorporate an outliner to help you plan your presentation. A variety of slide types are available, including titles, bulleted lists, tables, organization charts, pie charts, bar charts, and so on.

▲ FIGURE 7.20

Presentation graphics software allows you to create business presentations.

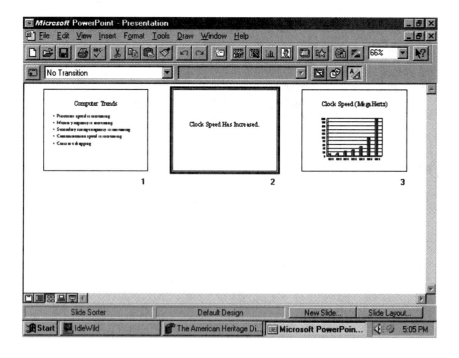

Once a slide is created, you can use various editing features to modify, copy, move, size, and rotate elements as desired. Some programs include professionally designed backgrounds, templates, and **clip art** (predrawn electronic images) to make your presentations more visually appealing. Various playback options are available, and many programs allow you to add sound, animation, and video to a presentation.

Presentation graphics is primarily a communication tool. Other graphics tools are used to create images. Drawing programs such as CorelDRAW serve as electronic sketch pads (Figure 7.21). CorelFLOW, Visio, and ABC Flowcharter are charting tools, and AutoCAD is a de facto standard for preparing engineering drawings. If you need a form for recording data, try PerForm or FormTool Gold. If you have to work with electronic images of photographs, try Adobe Photoshop. The list seems endless.

Other Software

As the name implies, **accounting software** is used to support such business applications as accounts payable, accounts receivable, payroll, billing, and general ledger. Peachtree Accounting, DacEasy Accounting, and Intuit Quickbooks are three well-known packages.

If you plan to send and receive facsimile (fax) images or e-mail, transfer files between computers, access the Internet, or perform other data communication tasks, you will need **communication software.** Netscape, Qmodem Pro, Lotus Notes, Lotus cc: Mail, and WinComm Pro are some well-known titles. Many users get their communication software from America Online, CompuServe, The Microsoft Network, Prodigy, or some other on-line service.

Clip art
Predrawn electronic images that can be inserted into a document.

Accounting software
Application programs that perform such accounting tasks as accounts payable, accounts receivable, general ledger, and payroll.

Communication software
Application programs that support data communication.

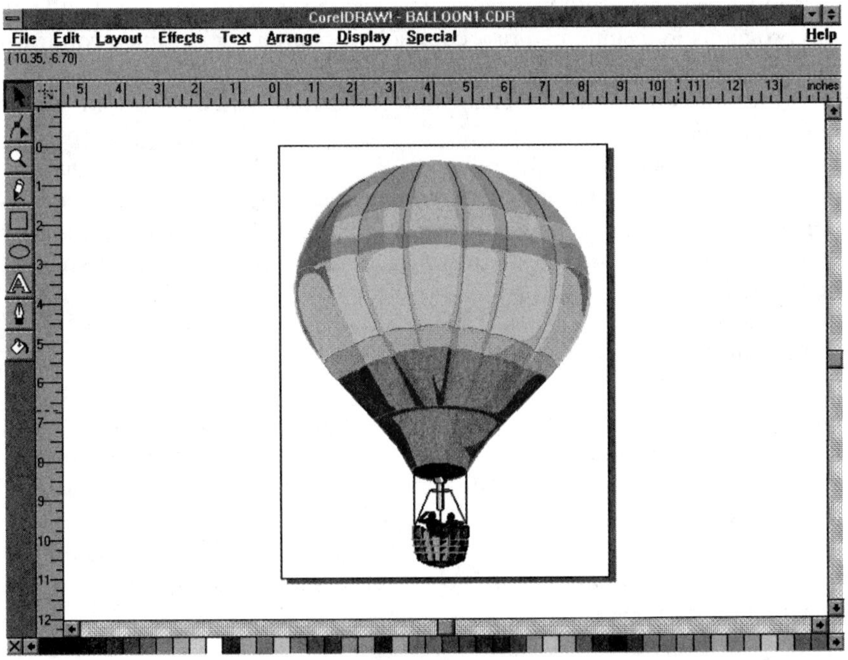

▲ **FIGURE 7.21**

Drawing tools allow you to create graphic images.

162   PART II COMPONENTS

Personal finance software
Application programs that perform such tasks as managing a checking account, tracking a stock portfolio, or computing income tax.

Personal information management software (PIM)
Such software as an electronic calendar, a note pad, and a card file that supports an individual's daily activities.

Project management software
Application software for organizing and managing a project team.

Statistical package
A set of application programs that allow a user to perform statistical analysis.

Suite, software
A set of application programs that are designed to work together.

Integrated program
A program that incorporates several applications, for example, word processing, spreadsheet, database, and presentation graphics.

Object linking and embedding (OLE)
A technique for combining in a single document information created by several different applications.
Dynamic data exchange (DDE)
A technique for combining in a single document information created by several different applications.

Personal finance software has the potential to become a major application. Programs such as Kiplinger's Simply Money, Managing Your Money, Microsoft Money, and Quicken are used to track investments, manage debt, monitor a budget, pay bills, write checks, and perform financial analyses. TurboTax, TaxCut, and Tax Edge can help you prepare your income tax.

Personal information management (PIM) software is designed to help busy people manage their time. A typical package might include an appointment calendar, a notepad, an address and telephone number book, a contact manager, fax and e-mail support, automatic dialing, and many other features. Examples include Janna Contact, Microsoft Scheduler+, Goldmine, SideKick, Lotus Organizer, PackRat, and many others.

Project management software is used by managers. These packages support the project planning process, generate project schedules, and allow the manager to graphically compare actual results to the plan. Examples include Microsoft Project, Timeline, and CA-SuperProject.

Statistical packages, such as SAS, Minitab, and SPSS, are also popular. They are used to perform sophisticated, highly analytical statistical computations.

There are thousands of other programs that fit none of these categories, and new software is released on a daily basis. There is simply no way to compile a complete list of available commercial software. Check one of the popular personal computer magazines, such as *PC World* or *Macworld,* for more current information.

Suites and Integrated Software

A **suite** is a set of integrated application programs that are designed to work together. There are two primary arguments for purchasing a suite. The first one is cost; the selling price is far less than that of the aggregate cost of the individual programs sold separately. The second is ease of use; generally, all the programs in a suite feature a common user interface, so once you learn one program you are well on your way to knowing them all. Figure 7.22 outlines the contents of three popular suites; Microsoft Office is the clear leader in this market.

Not all users need the full power of the standard commercial programs. An option is to purchase a low-cost **integrated program** that incorporates limited word processing, spreadsheet, database, and presentation graphics facilities in a single package. Microsoft Works and Claris Works are two good examples.

OLE and DDE

Object linking and embedding (OLE) and **dynamic data exchange (DDE)** are two techniques for combining in a single document information (text, charts, graphic images, sound clips, spreadsheets) created by several different applications. With OLE, you can activate the program you used to create the imported object and edit the object from within the target document. With DDE, you must switch to the source application before you can edit an imported object.

SUITE NAME	PROGRAMS	APPLICATIONS
Microsoft Office	Excel	Spreadsheet
	Word	Word processing
	PowerPoint	Presentation graphics
	Schedule+	PIM
	Access	Database
Lotus SmartSuite	WordPro	Word processing
	Freelance	Presentation graphics
	Approach	Database
	Lotus 1-2-3	Spreadsheet
	Organizer	PIM
	Notes	Communication
Corel Wordperfect Suite	WordPerfect	Word processing
	Quattro Pro	Spreadsheet
	Presentations	Presentation graphics
	Envoy	Electronic publishing
	Paradox	Database
	Corel Flow	Charting
	Sidekick	PIM

▲ FIGURE 7.22

Three popular suites.

CUSTOMIZING COMMERCIAL SOFTWARE

Writing custom software is expensive and time consuming. That is one reason why commercial software has replaced custom software for many applications. There are, however, ways to customize commercial software to make it better fit a given application.

Macros

Many commercial programs allow the user to write **macros** to perform application-specific tasks. A macro is an executable routine that is written as part of an application; for example, an Excel user might use Excel's macro language to write a macro to plot a bar chart for a selected set of data values.

Most macro languages work by capturing keystrokes or commands and then repeating them when the user references the macro name. For example, printing a logo, your return address, and the current date at the top of a business letter calls for several word processing commands. Imagine creating a macro by running through the process once, capturing the keystrokes, and then saving the macro in a file. Once you write the macro, you can add all those elements to your future business letters by simply referencing the macro name or clicking on an icon.

Macro
A routine, often written by a user, that performs an application-specific task in the context of a more general program.

Bridges

Another way to customize commercial software is to write a **bridge routine** to convert an organization's existing data to the format required by the purchased program (Figure 7.23). In other cases, the bridge routine might

Bridge routine
A program that provides a link to a commercial software routine.

Commercial software can be customized by writing bridge routines.

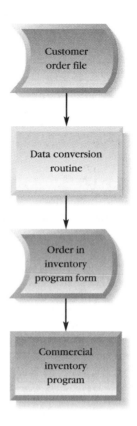

convert the output generated by a commercial program to the organization's existing data format.

Often, bridge routines are written in a programming language (such as Visual BASIC) that has "hooks" to the commercial program; for example, both the programming language and the software might support object linking and embedding (OLE). Customizing commercial software can be far less expensive than developing an equivalent custom program.

PUBLIC DOMAIN SOFTWARE AND SHAREWARE

Public domain software
Software that is available free to anyone who wants to use it.
Shareware
A copyright protected program you can try free of charge.

Public domain software is available free to anyone who wants to use it. The government and universities are common sources. **Shareware** programs are copyright protected but you can try them free of charge. If you decide to keep a shareware program, you are expected to register your copy and pay a small fee.

SUMMARY

Application software solves user problems or meets user needs. A user accesses an application program through the user interface. The exchange of information between the user and the program is called a dialogue.

The most basic user interface is a command interface. A menu interface presents the user with a list of commands; a command is selected by pointing to it and then clicking a mouse or pressing a key. A graphic user interface utilizes windows, icons, and other elements to provide the user with visual cues. Many graphic user interfaces are designed around a desktop metaphor. Expect a voice interface to be common in the near future.

A software license gives you the right to use a program on a single computer. A site license allows an organization to use numerous copies of the program for a fixed fee. Games were among the first commercially successful personal computer programs.

Word processing software simplifies the task of creating, editing, formatting, and printing documents. On word processing software, word wrap senses when the text has moved beyond the right margin and automatically advances to the next line. Most word processors include a spelling checker and a thesaurus, and some incorporate grammar checkers.

A typeface is a complete set of characters in a particular design or style. A font is a complete set of characters in one typeface and point size. Characters can be monospaced; pitch refers to the number of characters per inch. Proportional spacing varies the space allocated to a letter to reflect its relative size. With kerning, the relationship between adjacent characters is taken into account to yield optically-even letter spacing. Modern word processors implement WYSIWYG.

Many word processors include a print preview feature that allows the user to see exactly how the pages will look before they are sent to the printer. A page description language defines the text, graphic images, fonts, and other elements on the page in a form that makes sense to the printer. Document management and mail merge are important word processing features. Desktop publishing programs allow you to lay out (or compose) a page that combines text, graphics and other elements such as lines, borders, and shading.

An electronic spreadsheet simulates a spreadsheet on a computer screen; business people use spreadsheets to perform what-if analysis. A spreadsheet is divided into horizontal rows and vertical columns. The intersection of a row and a column is called a cell. A cell can hold a label or a value. A formula is a special type of value defined as an algebra-like expression. An assumption is a value that is treated as a constant but that might be assigned a different value on a subsequent version of the spreadsheet.

Database software is concerned with the efficient storage and retrieval of data. Many database programs include a query-by-example feature that allows a user to define a query by, essentially, outlining an example of the desired output. A report writer allows a user to define the structure of a report by listing the fields it is to contain.

Data are added to and displayed from a database in table or single-record mode. An index is a table that relates the values of key fields to the records that hold those values. A database is set of related files. The relationships, or links between files are defined through indexes.

Presentation graphics software allows you to create effective business presentations. Some programs include predrawn electronic images called clip art. Other graphics tools allow a user to create flowcharts, forms, organization charts, floor plans, and art on a computer screen.

Accounting software is used to support such business applications as accounts payable, accounts receivable, payroll, billing, and general ledger. Communication software supports such tasks as e-mail, facsimile (FAX) transmission, and Internet access. Personal finance software is used to track investments, manage debt, monitor a budget, pay bills, write checks, perform financial analyses, and pay taxes. Personal information management (PIM) software helps busy people manage their time. Project management software is used by managers. Statistical packages support sophisticated, analytical statistical analysis.

A suite is a set of integrated application programs that are designed to work together. An integrated program incorporates limited word processing, spreadsheet, presentation graphics, and database facilities in a single package.

OLE and DDE are two techniques for linking objects created by one application to a document created by another application. Often, customizing commercial software is a better option than writing a custom program. A macro is a series of keystrokes or commands that are captured, stored, and later repeated. Another way to customize commercial software is to write a bridge routine.

Public domain software is available free to anyone who wants to use it. Shareware is copyright protected but you can try it free of charge.

KEY TERMS

accounting software	kerning	query
assumption	key	query-by-example
bridge routine	label	relationship
cell	macro	report writer
clip art	mail merge	row
column	menu	shareware
command interface	monospacing	site license
communication software	object linking and embedding (OLE)	software license
database software		spelling checker
desktop publishing	page description language	spreadsheet
dialogue	personal finance software	statistical package
dynamic data exchange (DDE)	personal information management (PIM) software	suite
electronic spreadsheet		thesaurus
font	presentation graphics	typeface
formula	pitch	user interface
grammar checker	point size	value
graphic user interface (GUI)	print preview	what-if analysis
icon	project management	window
index	proportional spacing	word processing
integrated program	public domain software	word wrap
		WYSIWYG

Concepts

1. Distinguish among a command interface, a menu interface, and a graphic user interface. What is a metaphor? Why are user interfaces designed around metaphors?
2. What is a software license? What is a site license?
3. What is the purpose of a word processing program? List three popular word processing programs. Briefly explain how a word processing program supports document creation, editing, formatting, and printing.
4. Distinguish between point size and pitch. Distinguish between a typeface and a font. Why is document management such an important word processing feature? What is mail merge? Why is mail merge important?
5. What is the purpose of a desktop publishing program?
6. What is the purpose of an electronic spreadsheet? List three popular spreadsheet programs, and identify several spreadsheet applications. Distinguish among spreadsheet rows, columns, and cells. Distinguish among labels, values, and formulas.
7. What is the difference between a constant and an assumption?
8. What is the purpose of database software? List three popular database programs. What is a query? What is query-by-example? What is the purpose of a database report writer?
9. A database is a set of related files. What is a relationship? How are relationships defined?
10. What is the purpose of a presentation graphics program? List three popular presentation graphics programs.
11. Cite examples of at least four types of commercial software other than word processing, spreadsheet, database, and presentation graphics.
12. What is a software suite? Why are software suites popular? What is an integrated program? Why are integrated programs popular? Cite two examples.
13. Define object linking and embedding (OLE). Define dynamic data exchange (DDE).
14. What is a macro? How are macros created? Why are they used? What is the purpose of a bridge routine?
15. What is public domain software? What is shareware?

Projects

1. The only way to effectively learn about an application program is to use it. Many introductory computer courses include hands-on training in one or more applications. An alternative is to teach yourself. Most application programs come with excellent on-line, self-paced tutorials (check the *Help* menu), and you will find numerous self-teaching books in the library and on the computer shelf at almost any bookstore.
2. Application software changes so rapidly that published information is (almost by definition) outdated before you can read it. The World Wide Web is a good place to find the most current information about software. Access the home page for a company like Microsoft, Corel, or

IBM and read through the current software postings and press releases; see Appendix B (Corporations) for some addresses to help you get started.

INTERNET PROJECTS

1. *News and Notes.* Companies often post information about their very latest products on their World Wide Web home pages. Select a company whose products are mentioned in this chapter and access its home page. Try the address *http://www.xxx.com;* substitute the company name (for example, *microsoft*) for *xxx.* Once you find the home page, look for a button marked *New products* (or something similar) and click on it. Identify and briefly describe at least two new products and submit your findings to your instructor in the form of a brief note or an e-mail message.

2. *Topic Searches.* Check the World Wide Web and/or other Internet resources for information on the following topics:

Key word	*Qualifiers*
software piracy	international copyright
reverse engineering	software
software suite	Microsoft
	Corel

Define the key word, identify at least two sources of information on the topic, and briefly summarize the nature of the information you find.

3. *Links to Other Sites.* After you access one or more of the following sites, write a brief note or send an e-mail message to your instructor outlining what you find.

   a. On the World Wide Web, check *http://www.ibm.com* for information on IBM software.
   b. On the World Wide Web, check *http://www.microsoft.com* for information on Microsoft products.
   c. On the World Wide Web, check *http://www.corel.com* for information on Corel products.
   d. On the World Wide Web, check *http://www.zdnet.com* for current news about computers and computer-related products.

4. Access West Publishing Company's home page and find the Chapter 7 student activities for this book. See Internet Project 3 for the spotlight on *The Internet* following Chapter 1 (page 29) for more detailed instructions on accessing the home page. As appropriate, repeat projects 1, 2, and/or 3 using the more current references you find.

INTERNET SOFTWARE TOOLS

Before you start this feature, you should be familiar with the following concepts:

- ▶ The Internet (p. 17).
- ▶ Today's Internet (p. 22) and the World Wide Web (p. 26).

When you finish reading this feature, you should be able to:

- ▶ Identify the functions performed by Archie, a gopher, Veronica, WAIS, and a World Wide Web browser.
- ▶ Briefly explain hypertext and hypermedia.

GOPHERS AND BROWSERS

The amount of information available on the Internet is so overwhelming that finding what you need is a bit like trying to drink from a fire hose. Fortunately, there are several search tools that can help.

A program named **Archie** allows you to access and search an index of files that reside on roughly 1,500 host computers around the world. The files are listed by file name, and the index can be searched by a key word (or a character string) in the file name. Once you find the target file or files, you log off Archie and use a file transfer routine to copy the files to your computer.

A document delivery tool called a **gopher**, initially developed at the University of Minnesota (the Golden Gophers), is essentially an improved, menu-based version of Archie. Once you locate a file, the gopher can transfer a copy to your computer, so there is no need to log off and activate a file copy program.

Veronica is another program that builds on the Archie legacy. It searches (by key word) menus at gopher sites around the world, in effect giving you access to numerous gophers. Officially, Veronica is an acronym for Very Easy Rodent-Oriented Netwide Index to Computerized Archives, an interesting example of net humor.

. One problem with Archie, gopher, and Veronica is that they search on file names, not file contents. **WAIS** (pronounced *ways,* for Wide-Area Information Servers) is a service that allows a user to search the contents of files based on search criteria that are defined by asking natural language questions.

As you learned in Spotlight: The Internet (p. 26), the program you use to navigate the World Wide Web is called a browser. A gopher searches through a list of files stored on a remote computer and copies selected files to your computer. A browser, in contrast, allows you to execute programs on a remote computer. In effect, the browser logs you onto the remote computer and your computer temporarily becomes a terminal (an input/output device).

Archie
An Internet program that allows a user to access and search (by file name) an index of files that reside on roughly 1,500 host computers around the world.

Gopher
An improved, menu-based version of Archie that allows a user to locate a file and transfer a copy to his or her computer.

Veronica
An Internet program that searches (by key word) menus at gopher sites around the world, in effect giving the user access to numerous gophers.

WAIS
Acronym for Wide-Area Information Servers. An Internet service that allows a user to search the contents of files based on search criteria that are defined by asking natural language questions.

HYPERTEXT AND HYPERMEDIA

Although technically not Internet features, hypertext and hypermedia are important elements in many Internet and World Wide Web applications. **Hypertext** is a method for defining pointers that link one text passage to another (Figure 7.24). **Hypermedia** (the multimedia version of hypertext) links text, graphics, sound, video, and so on. On the Internet, a hypertext or hypermedia link might reference data, information, or even software that is physically stored on a different computer.

Hypertext simulates the associative links that tie together pieces of our memories. For example, when you think of the word *automobile,* you trigger a flood of memories that might include sights, smells, colors, speed, an accident, an encounter with a police officer, an old friend, places you have been, and so on. If you have ever "surfed" an encyclopedia by reading one entry, picking out an interesting term, looking it up, and reading its entry, you have done something very much like what hypertext allows you to do electronically.

The basic unit of hyper-information is called a **node**; think of each node as a single index card. A given node can hold text, a graphic image, a video clip, a sound clip, a window, the name of a program on a remote computer, and so on.

Given a set of nodes, you can define **associative links** to connect the nodes to each other. Those links can be embedded in the text and highlighted in some way; for example, in Figure 7.24 the word *hardware* might be displayed in blue or reverse video. Links can also be represented as buttons or icons. Clicking on a link in one node activates the linked node.

On the Internet, home pages and hypertext/hypermedia links are created and maintained using a programming language called **hypertext markup language (html)**. Often, a preliminary version of the document is

Hypertext
A method for defining logical pointers that link one text passage to another.

Hypermedia
The multimedia version of hypertext that links text, graphics, sounds, videos, and so on.

Node
The basic unit of hyper-information.

Associative link
A hypertext or hypermedia link that connects two nodes.

Hypertext markup language (html)
A programming language for creating and maintaining home pages and hypertext/hypermedia links.

▲ FIGURE 7.24

Hypertext and hypermedia links.

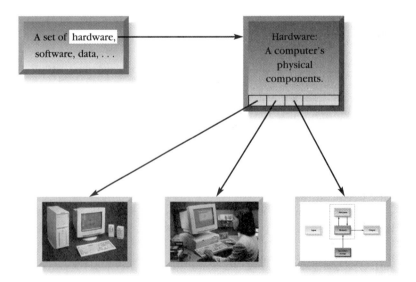

prepared using a word processor or some other tool and then converted to html so the necessary screen format codes, hyperlinks, and references to graphic images can be added.

KEY TERMS

Archie	hypertext	Veronica
associative link	hypertext markup	WAIS
gopher	language (html)	
hypermedia	node	

CONCEPTS

1. Archie, gophers, and Veronica are different tools for performing the same function. What is that function? How do those three tools differ?
2. What is WAIS? How does WAIS differ from Archie, gopher, and Veronica?
3. What is the purpose of a World Wide Web browser? How does a browser differ from Archie and WAIS?
4. What is hypertext? What is hypermedia?
5. Hypertext simulates the associative links that tie together pieces of our memories. Briefly explain that statement.
6. Briefly, what is hypertext markup language?

PROJECT

1. Use Archie or a gopher to search for files that hold information about the most recent U.S. census. Then conduct a search on a topic of interest to you.

SPOTLIGHT

CHAPTER 8

Software Development

Before you start this chapter, you should be familiar with the following concepts:

▶ Data and information (p. 4).

▶ Computers (p. 6), the user (p. 6), hardware (p. 6), peripherals (p. 6), and inside the computer (p. 7).

▶ Software (p. 9), data (p. 10), and the input/process/output cycle (p. 12).

▶ Classifying computers (p. 14).

▶ The Internet (p. 17) and the information superhighway (p. 18).

When you finish reading this chapter, you should be able to:

▶ Explain why a program must be physically stored on a computer in binary, machine-language form.

▶ Distinguish among an assembler, a compiler, an interpreter, and a fourth-generation language.

▶ Distinguish between source code and object code.

▶ Discuss the evolution of programming languages.

▶ Outline the steps in the program development process and explain what happens during each step.

▶ Identify several tools that are used to plan the flow of logic through a program.

▶ Describe the three basic logic blocks: sequence, selection, and iteration.

▶ Identify the objectives of structured programming.

▶ Briefly describe the object-oriented approach to software development.

▶ Define the terms *object*, *method*, and *signal*, *encapsulation*, and *object class*.

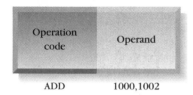

ADD   1000,1002

A machine language instruction consists of an operation code and one or more operands.

Machine language
The binary instructions that are stored in memory and actually control a computer.
Operation code
The portion of a machine-level instruction that specifies the operation to be performed.
Operand
The portion of a machine-level instruction that specifies the address of data to be processed by the instruction.

PROGRAMMING LANGUAGES

A program is a set of instructions that guides a computer through a process. Programs are written in a programming language by people called programmers.

Machine Language

In Chapter 1, you learned that a computer is controlled by a program stored in its own memory. You also learned that a computer is a binary machine.

A stored program in memory consists of a set of binary **machine language** instructions. Each of those instructions tells the hardware to perform one of its basic operations (add, subtract, multiply, divide, compare, copy, . . .). The processor executes the program by fetching the instructions, one by one, from memory.

A machine language instruction consists of two parts: an **operation code** and one or more **operands** (Figure 8.1). The operation code tells the computer what to do (add, subtract, compare, . . .); think of the operation code as a verb. The operands identify the data to be manipulated by the instruction. For example, the four machine language instructions in Figure 8.2 tell a particular computer (an IBM mainframe) to add two numbers.

The very first computers were programmed in binary (first-generation) machine language. If we still had to program computers in machine language, there would be very few programmers. Fortunately, there are alternatives.

Assembly Language

During the 1950s, **assembly languages** (sometimes called second-generation languages) were developed. An assembly language programmer writes one statement for each machine-level instruction, but uses mnemonic (memory-aiding) codes (such as A, for add) instead of binary codes. An **assembler** program translates those statements to machine language (Figure 8.3).

SYMBOLIC ADDRESSING
The first instruction in Figure 8.3 reads

```
L 3,STOCK
```

It tells the computer to load the contents of a memory location named STOCK into a special storage location in the processor known as register 3.

Assembly language
A programming language in which the programmer writes one source statement for each machine-language instruction.
Assembler
A program that translates assembly language instruction to machine level.

Four machine language instructions.

```
0101100000110000110000000000000000
0101100001000000110000000000000100
0001101000110100
0101000000110000110000000000001000
```

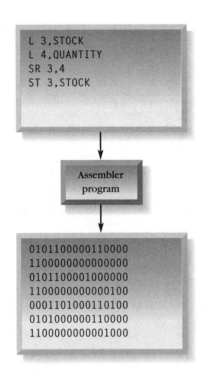

```
L 3,STOCK
L 4,QUANTITY
SR 3,4
ST 3,STOCK
```

Assembler
program

```
0101100000110000
1100000000000000
0101100001000000
1100000000000100
0001101000110100
0101000000110000
1100000000001000
```

▲ FIGURE 8.3

An assembler program converts mnemonic statements to machine language.

STOCK is an example of a **symbolic address.** While writing a program, the programmer assigns variable-like symbolic addresses to significant memory locations. The assembler program keeps track of the symbolic addresses and converts them to the binary memory addresses the processor needs.

MACRO INSTRUCTIONS

Generally, each assembly language instruction is converted to a single machine-language instruction. That one-to-one relationship can become tedious when the same basic operations appear over and over again, however. Consequently, most assembly languages allow the programmer to define **macro instructions** that generate more than one machine-level instruction.

The programmer creates a macro by writing the appropriate assembly language instructions and then assigning that set of instructions a name. In the future, when the assembler encounters the macro name in a program, it replaces the reference with the set of precoded instructions. Using macros saves the programmer the trouble of writing the same instructions over and over again.

Source Code and Object Code

Note that using an assembly language to create a computer program is a two-step process. The programmer writes **source code** using mnemonic codes to represent instructions, but the computer's hardware cannot understand those source instructions. The assembler program reads the source statements, translates them to machine language, and creates a binary **object module** that can be loaded into memory and executed.

Symbolic address
A variable-like source code reference that is later converted by a compiler or an assembler into a specific memory location.

Macro instruction
An assembly language instruction that generates more than one machine-level instruction.

Source code
Instructions written by the programmer in an assembler or a compiler language.
Object module
A binary, machine-language translation of a set of source code that can be loaded into memory and executed.

PEOPLE

Grace Hopper

In the 1950s, most programs were written in assembly language, and many programmers still did much of their work in binary. One problem with assembly and machine languages is that they are machine dependent; in other words, an assembly language program written for one manufacturer's equipment will not run on any other brand of computer.

That bothered Grace Hopper, a career naval officer and a computer pioneer who started working with computing devices in the 1940s. To "Amazing Grace," the act of writing programs to fit specific machines seemed terribly inefficient. In the early 1950s, she developed a series of compilers named A-0, B-0, and Flow-matic for UNIVAC Corporation. Her ideas eventually led to the creation (in 1959) of the COBOL programming language. The fact that COBOL is still an important programming language almost a half century later is clear evidence of the power of Grace Hopper's vision.

Compilers

An assembly language programmer must, literally, think like a computer, and that is difficult for most people to do. Thus, as computers became more common, third-generation, high-level programming languages that allowed programmers to express logic in a more human-like form began to be developed.

For example, one way to view addition is as an algebraic expression: $C = A + B$. Why not allow a programmer to write something like algebraic expressions, read those statements into a translator program, and have the translator program generate the necessary machine-level code? That is exactly what happens with a **compiler** (Figure 8.4). A compiler is a program that reads statements written in a human-like form, translates them into machine language, and generates an object module.

Compiler
A program that reads source code written in a human-like language, translates those instructions to machine language, and produces an object module.

▲ FIGURE 8.4

A compiler reads high-level statements and translates them to machine language.

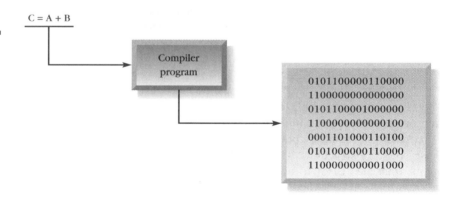

The difference between an assembler and a compiler is subtle, so be careful. Each assembly language statement is translated to a *single* machine language instruction. Each compiler statement generates *several* machine language instructions. Consequently, the high-level programmer writes fewer statements to accomplish the same task. On the other hand, because assembly language instructions correspond directly to machine language, the assembly language programmer has greater control over what the computer actually does and thus can write programs that run faster and require less memory.

There are many different compiler (or third-generation) languages (Figure 8.5). Some, such as FORTRAN, BASIC, Pascal, and PL/1, are algebraically based. Statements in the most popular business-oriented language, COBOL, resemble English sentences. Ada is the required language for U.S. government military projects. Visual BASIC, Visual C, and other visual languages incorporate tools that simplify writing programs in a Microsoft Windows environment. Simula, Smalltalk, HyperCard, Eifel, Common LISP Object System (CLOS), and C++ are object-oriented languages, and object-oriented versions of several other languages are either available or under development. You will learn more about object-oriented software later in this chapter.

Interpreters

An assembler or a compiler translates a complete source program into a complete object module that is (typically) stored on a disk and subsequently loaded into memory and executed. An **interpreter,** in contrast, reads a *single* source statement, translates it to machine-level, executes the resulting instructions, and then moves on to the next source statement.

Interpreters are useful during program development, but because each line of code must be translated before it can be executed, interpreters tend to be quite slow. With a compiler, the complete machine language program can be created, captured electronically, and then executed over and over again, without further translation.

Interpreter
A program that reads a single source statement, translates it to machine-level, executes the resulting instructions, and then moves on to the next source statement.

Fourth-Generation Languages

Assembly and high-level languages are considered **procedural languages** because the programmer must write a step-by-step procedure to tell the computer exactly how to perform a logical operation. With a **nonprocedural language** (sometimes called a fourth-generation, declarative, or problem-oriented language), the programmer defines the logical operation and then lets the language translator decide how to perform it. Examples of nonprocedural languages include Prolog, Focus, Lotus 1-2-3, dBASE, SQL, ORACLE, Ingress, and many others.

Procedural language
A programming language that requires the programmer to write a step-by-step procedure to tell the computer exactly how to perform a logical operation.
Nonprocedural language
A programming language that allows the programmer to simply define the logical operation and let the language translator decide how to perform it.

▲ **FIGURE 8.5**

There are many different compiler languages.

LANGUAGE	SOURCE STATEMENT
BASIC	LET STOCK = STOCK - QUANTITY
C	stock = stock - quantity;
COBOL	SUBTRACT QUANTITY FROM STOCK.
FORTRAN	STOCK = STOCK - QUANTITY
Pascal	STOCK = STOCK - QUANTITY;

Program Generators

A **program generator,** sometimes called an application generator, is a translator program that accepts input in graphical, narrative, list, or some other logical form and outputs the appropriate source code. For example, instead of writing the instructions to define a menu, a programmer can lay out the desired menu on the screen and let a menu generator create the source code. Similarly, a screen painter can convert the prompts, field names, and other information on a dummy input or output screen to the equivalent source code.

The Evolution of Programming Languages

Note how the nature of programming languages has changed over time (Figure 8.6). At first, people communicated with the computer in binary. Next came assembly languages that allowed programmers to write machine-level statements as codes rather than bit strings. Using a compiler, a programmer can write instructions that resemble algebraic statements. Fourth-generation languages and program generators allow the user to ask a question or describe an example of the desired solution.

Each development moves the interface further away from the computer and closer to the human being. Some day, it may be possible to program a computer in a natural (human) fifth-generation language. Perhaps the image of Spock talking to the computer on the starship *Enterprise* is not quite as farfetched as it once seemed.

THE PROGRAM DEVELOPMENT PROCESS

The act of writing a program demands a unique combination of creativity and precision. Different programmers go about the task differently, but the process generally includes the following five steps:

▲ FIGURE 8.6

The nature of programming languages has changed over time.

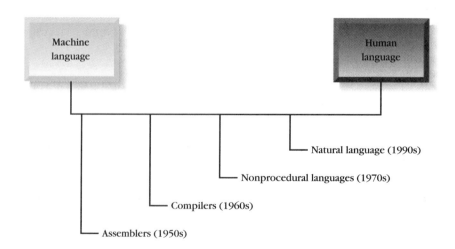

Java

To the software developer, the Internet represents both opportunity and challenge. On the one hand, the incredible number of projected users defines a massive market for software and services. On the other hand, the Internet's mix of micros, minis, mainframes, and supercomputers controlled by many different operating systems forms the most complex operating environment imaginable.

Enter Java, a programming language developed by Sun Microsystems specifically for multiple platform environments like the Internet. Using Java, a programmer writes source code that is compiled into machine-independent "bytecode" instructions. The bytecode can subsequently be executed on any computer that has a Java interpreter. Interpreting bytecode is much faster than interpreting source code. In those cases where high performance is essential, the bytecode can be translated to machine language.

Java is designed to create the robust, highly reliable, portable, secure, tamper-free applications that will be essential on tomorrow's information superhighway. It just may be the programming language of the future.

- ▶ planning
- ▶ coding
- ▶ debugging
- ▶ testing
- ▶ documentation

Planning the Program

The first step in creating a program is planning the logic. In Chapter 1, you learned about the input/process/output cycle (Figure 8.7). Because it is common to virtually every computer application, that cycle provides a structure for planning.

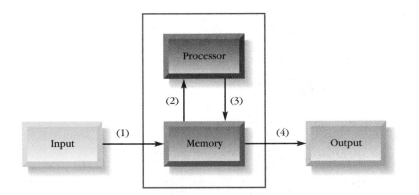

▲ **FIGURE 8.7**

The input/process/output cycle.

Every application begins with a user who needs information. The desired information is the program's output. Obtaining the output is the reason for writing the program, so it makes sense to start there.

Any information output by a program must either be input to or generated by the program. Thus, the next step is to define the **algorithms** needed to generate the output. An algorithm is a set of rules for arriving at an answer in a finite number of steps; an algebraic expression is a good example.

Algorithms require input data; for example, before you can solve the expression $C = A + B$ you must have values for A and B. Thus, the final step in the planning process is to identify the necessary input data.

Given the inputs, the algorithms, and the desired output, the programmer knows exactly what the program must do. Given a plan, the programmer can begin to translate the data descriptions and the algorithms into programming language instructions.

PLANNING THE LOGIC

There are several tools for planning a program's logic. Some programmers write a preliminary draft of the program using **structured English** (a tight, highly constrained version of English) or **pseudocode** (a rough approximation of a programming language that ignores many syntax details). Figure 8.8 shows how a program to compute an arithmetic average might be written in pseudocode.

A **process flowchart** (Figure 8.9) is another useful planning tool. A flowchart is a diagram that graphically shows the flow of logic, control, and data through the program. Figure 8.10 is a flowchart for a program to compute an arithmetic average. Compare the flowchart to the pseudocode version of the program.

Coding

Once the program's logic is planned, the programmer begins writing or **coding** the actual program instructions. For example, Figure 8.11 shows how an arithmetic average program might be coded in BASIC.

Each programming language has its own spelling, syntax, and punctuation rules. Beginners often become bogged down in the mechanics of writing the code, but the real key to programming is logic, not mechanics. (Think of syntax as grammar and logic as content and organization.) A good pro-

Algorithm
A rule for arriving at an answer in a finite number of steps.

Structured English
A tight, highly constrained version of English used to plan program logic.
Pseudocode
A rough approximation of a programming language that ignores many syntax details. Used to plan program logic.
Process flowchart
A graphic depiction of the flow of logic through a process.

Coding
The phase during which the programmer writes the source statements in a programming language.

▲ **FIGURE 8.8**

A pseudocode version of a program to compute an average.

```
count = 0
sum = 0
INPUT x

WHILE x >= 0
        count = count + 1
        sum = sum + x
        INPUT x
ENDWHILE

average = sum / count
DISPLAY count, sum, average

END
```

▲ FIGURE 8.9

Common flowcharting symbols.

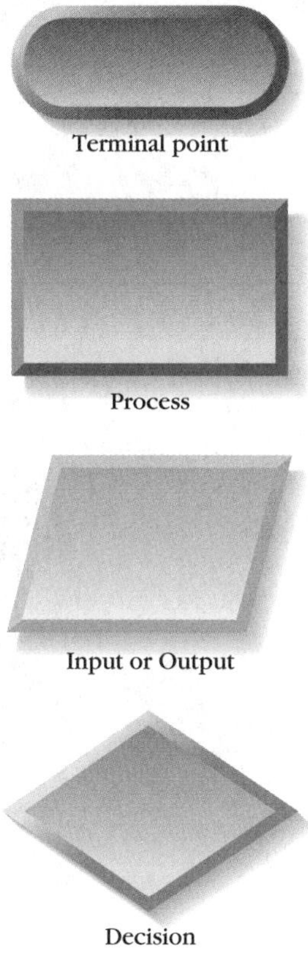

Terminal point

Process

Input or Output

Decision

▲ FIGURE 8.10

A flowchart.

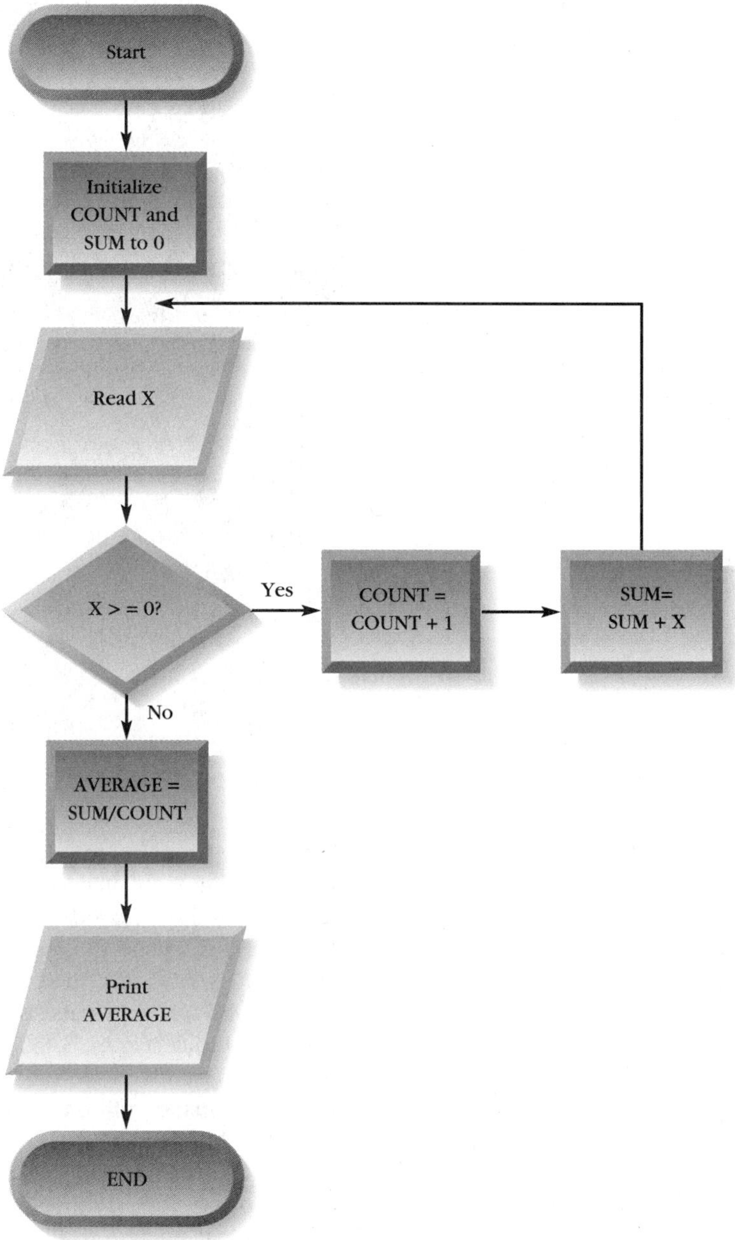

Start

Initialize COUNT and SUM to 0

Read X

X > = 0?

Yes

COUNT = COUNT + 1

SUM= SUM + X

No

AVERAGE = SUM/COUNT

Print AVERAGE

END

of syntax as grammar and logic as content and organization.) A good program is composed of the right instructions written in the right order.

SEQUENCE, SELECTION, AND ITERATION

There are three standard instruction patterns that serve as basic building blocks for coding virtually all programs: sequence, selection, and iteration.

▲ FIGURE 8.11

A BASIC program to compute an
arithmetic average. The lines
that begin with single quote
marks are comments that
explain the code.

```
' Initialize count and sum to zero.
      COUNT = 0
      SUM = 0
' Read first data value.
      PRINT "This program computes and prints an arithmetic"
      PRINT "average. Enter the numbers to be averaged one"
      PRINT "by one. Enter a negative value after all the"
      PRINT "numbers have been input."
      PRINT
      PRINT "Enter a number: ";

      INPUT VALUE
' Accumulate and count positive and zero values.
' The loop ends when a negative value is input.
      DO WHILE VALUE >= 0

            COUNT = COUNT + 1
            SUM = SUM + VALUE

            PRINT "Enter another number: ";
            INPUT VALUE
      LOOP
' Compute and print average.
      AVERAGE = SUM / COUNT

      PRINT "You entered "; COUNT; "numbers."
      PRINT "The sum of the numbers you entered is "; SUM

      PRINT "The average of those numbers is "; AVERAGE
      END
```

Sequence
A block of program logic in which the
instructions are executed in a fixed
order.
Selection
A block of program logic in which the
instructions to be executed depend on a
condition that cannot be known until
execution time.
If-then-else
Another name for a selection block.
Case structure
A form of selection block that provides
more than two logical paths.
Iteration
A logic block in which the instructions
are executed repetitively as long as an
initial condition holds (DO WHILE) or
until a terminal condition is met (DO
UNTIL).
Loop
Another name for an iteration block.

In a **sequence** block (Figure 8.12), the instructions are executed in a
fixed order, from first to last, without exception. In a **selection** block (Figure
8.13), sometimes called an **if-then-else** block, the instructions to be executed depend on a condition that cannot be known until execution time. If
the condition is true, the instructions in the THEN block are executed. If the
condition is false, the ELSE block is executed. Another form of selection
block, called a **case structure,** provides more than two logical paths. In an
iteration block (Figure 8.14), sometimes called a **loop,** the instructions are
executed repetitively as long as an initial condition holds (DO WHILE) or
until a terminal condition is met (DO UNTIL).

Note that each block has a single entry point and a single exit; in other
words, once the program enters a block it completes *all* the block's relevant
instructions before it moves on to the next block. Each block represents a
single logical operation. Programmers code instructions to build blocks of
logic and then combine those blocks to form a program.

Debugging and Testing

Syntax errors are mistakes in spelling, punctuation, and grammar. They are
easy to correct because the compiler flags them. Logical errors, valid instructions that tell the computer to do the wrong thing, are much more difficult to
find and to fix.

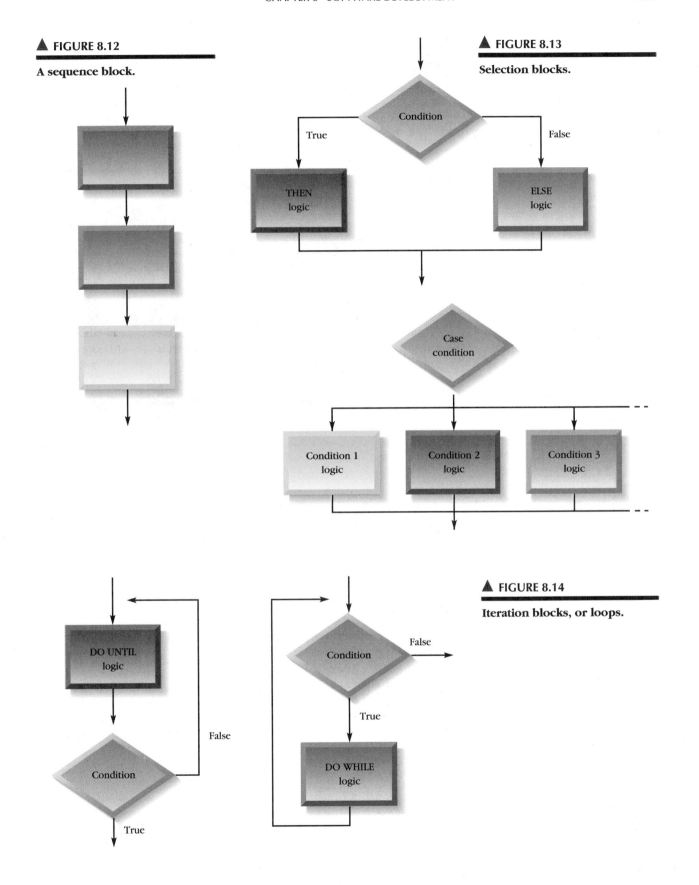

▲ FIGURE 8.13

Selection blocks.

▲ FIGURE 8.14

Iteration blocks, or loops.

ISSUES

Programming and Gender

Perhaps because the young women of that era sensed the computer field was more accessible than most, roughly half the majors in many late 1970s and early 1980s university-level computer-related degree programs were females. Those young women did very well. Their academic performance was every bit as good as that of their male counterparts, and a significant percentage of today's programmers are female.

That could change, however. Over the past decade the number of young women choosing to major in computer science and (to a lesser degree) management information systems has declined steadily, and most computer-related majors are now male dominated. Although many people have opinions, no one has offered a compelling explanation for this phenomenon. What do you think?

Bug
A logical error in a program.

Debug
To remove errors from program code.

Black box testing
A technique for identifying bugs.

Walkthrough
A peer review.

A logical error in a program is called a **bug.** The term was coined in 1947 by Grace Hopper when she and her colleagues, after hours of careful study, discovered that the cause of the Mark II computer's failure was a moth that had apparently flown into the machine and short-circuited two wires (Figure 8.15). Ever since that day, the process of removing errors from the code has been called **debugging.**

The first step in debugging a program is to recognize that an error has occurred. Bugs are identified through **black box testing** (Figure 8.16). Before the program is tested, a set of test data and the expected results are generated. The code is then executed and the actual results are captured. If the actual output does not match the expected output, something is wrong.

Once a bug is identified, the next task is to find the instructions that produced the wrong result. One approach is to desk check the logic by reading through the program, instruction by instruction, and reproducing the results by hand. Many modern programming languages include an interactive debugging feature that allows the programmer to step through the logic, instruction by instruction, on the computer.

Some bugs are tough to spot simply because it is difficult to debug your own code. For example, a programmer who adds two values instead of subtracting them might never spot that error because he or she *meant* to code a subtraction operation. To another programmer, such errors are obvious, so the debugging process often includes peer reviews, or **walkthroughs,** of the code.

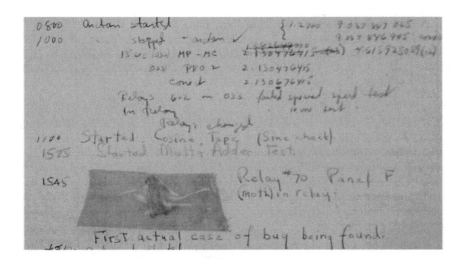

▲ **FIGURE 8.15**

The first bug.

BETA TESTING

The technical experts who design and write a program can become so familiar with their work that it is difficult for them to debug it fully. Because they know exactly how the program works, they sometimes find it impossible to anticipate the errors and problems that a real user might encounter.

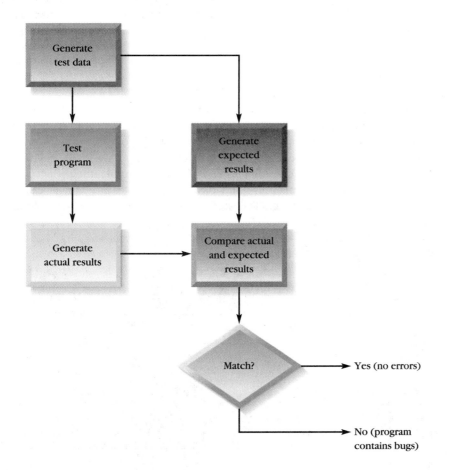

▲ **FIGURE 8.16**

Black box testing.

Beta test
A software test in which real users who are unfamiliar with the technical details exercise a preliminary, prerelease version of the software.
Beta version
A preliminary, prerelease version of a program used in a beta test.

Documentation
Flow diagrams, charts, comments, and other materials that explain a program's logic.

Comment
A brief written note in a program that explains the code.

The purpose of a **beta test** is to allow real users who are unfamiliar with the technical details to exercise a preliminary, prerelease **beta version** of the software. The beta testers work with the program, identify its strengths and weaknesses, describe any errors they find, and report their impressions back to the developers.

Beta testers are usually experienced users of a previous or competitive version of the software being tested. Some work for the company that developed the software, but most are independent. Some beta testers are paid for their work, some receive a free copy of the finished version, and some actually pay for the privilege.

Documentation

In addition to writing and debugging the software, the programmer also prepares diagrams, comments, and other **documentation** to clarify and explain the code. The documentation is an important aid to debugging and to program maintenance.

Documentation begins with program design. A well-designed, well-written program is almost self-documenting (at least to another programmer).

Comments, brief written notes that explain the code, help, too. For example, Figure 8.17 shows two versions of a section of a program written in generic COBOL. The three lines in the documented code that begin with asterisks are comments. A careful review of the code reveals that the two versions contain identical instructions, but the documented code is much easier to follow because of the comments and the descriptive file and field names.

STRUCTURED PROGRAMMING

Earlier in this chapter, you learned that a programmer plans a program's logic by defining its outputs, algorithms, and inputs and then using such tools as flowcharts, structured English, and pseudocode to lay out the flow of logic through the program. Those steps are probably enough for a small program, but large, complex programs demand considerably more planning.

One technique for planning and designing a large program is called **structured programming.** The key to this approach is **functional**

▲ **FIGURE 8.17**

Documented code is easier to follow.

```
Undocumented Code

READ FILE_1.
READ FILE_2
SUBTRACT X FROM Y.
REWRITE FILE_2.
```

```
Documented Code

*      This routine updated the inventory
*      file to reflect customer purchases.
*
READ CUSTOMER_ORDER.
READ INVENTORY_RECORD.
SUBTRACT QUANTITY_PURCHASED FROM STOCK_ON_HAND.
REWRITE INVENTORY_RECORD
```

One technique for planning and designing a large program is called **structured programming.** The key to this approach is **functional decomposition.** The basic idea is to break down (or decompose) the program into small, independent units called modules based on the processes or tasks they perform.

Cohesion and Coupling

The terms **module** and **routine** are often used as synonyms, but their meanings are subtly different. A routine is a set of instructions that performs a specific, limited task. A module is a portion of a larger program that performs a specific task. Thus all modules are routines, but a stand-alone routine is not a module.

A good module is **cohesive,** or complete. Every statement in the module should relate to the same function, and all of that function's logic should reside in the same module. When a module becomes large enough to decompose, each submodule should perform a cohesive subfunction.

Coupling is a measure of a module's independence. Perfect independence is impossible because each module accepts data from and passes data to other modules, but the less data a module shares with the others, the more independent it is. A good module is loosely coupled to the rest of the program.

The Control Structure

A well-structured program consists of a set of cohesive, loosely coupled modules linked by a **control structure** that resembles an organization chart (Figure 8.18). At the top is a main control module that calls secondary control structures. At the bottom are the computational modules, each of which implements a single algorithm.

A well-designed control structure balances two conflicting objectives: depth and breadth. Depth is the number of levels in the control structure,

Structured programming
An approach to programming that calls for decomposing the program into small, independent units called modules based on the processes or tasks they perform.
Functional decomposition
To break down (or decompose) a program into small, independent units called modules based on the processes or tasks they perform.
Module
A portion of a larger program that performs a specific task.
Routine
A set of instructions that performs a specific, limited task.
Cohesion
A measure of a module's completeness.
Coupling
A measure of a module's independence.

Control structure
Program logic that determines the order in which the computational modules are executed.

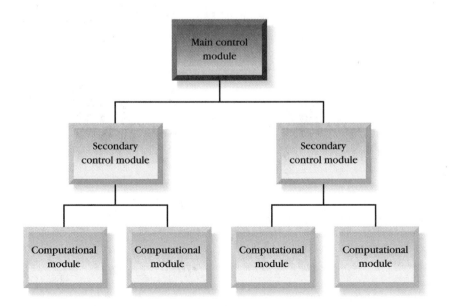

▲ **FIGURE 8.18**

A well-designed program consists of a set of cohesive, loosely coupled modules linked by a control structure.

and shallow structures tend to be better than deep structures. Breadth, or span of control, is a measure of the number of modules directly controlled by a higher-level routine. Too many subordinates adds to complexity, so narrow structures tend to be better than broad structures.

Top-Down Testing

After each of the modules has been independently tested, they are assembled and the program is tested from the top down. An initial test might be performed on the program's control structure with dummy computational routines that do little more than return a constant value (Figure 8.19). Assuming the control structure is correct, the first real computational module replaces the equivalent dummy routine (Figure 8.20), and the program is tested again. Then a second computational routine is added, the program is retested, and so on until all the computational routines are in place.

Following each test, the actual results are compared to the expected results. If they match, the just-added module is probably correct. If they do not match, then something is wrong with the program, and the error is probably in the most recently added module. **Top-down testing** simplifies debugging because it highlights the likely source of the error.

OBJECT-ORIENTED SOFTWARE

Every year, it seems that applications become more and more complex. Today, we build highly integrated, user-friendly programs that hide their sophistication beneath layers of complex software.

The **object-oriented** approach to software development is one way to deal with such complexity. The basic idea is to design and write the software as a set of independent objects linked by signals, but several of the terms in that definition require further explanation.

Top-down testing
A software testing technique in which modules are added to a control structure one by one and then tested.

Object-oriented
An approach to programming that focuses on objects.

▲ FIGURE 8.19

Testing a program's control structure.

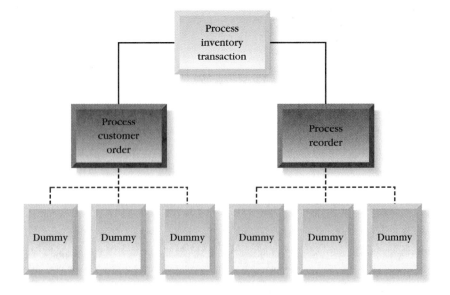

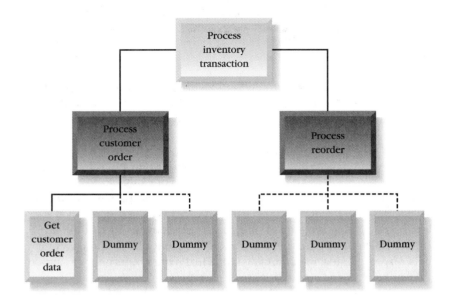

▲ **FIGURE 8.20**

The computational modules are added one by one.

Objects and Methods

An **object** is a thing about which data are stored and manipulated. Objects really exist. Look around your classroom and you can identify such objects as students, a faculty member, textbooks, an overhead projector, and so on. The fact that the term *object* means essentially what you think it means is one of the strengths of the object-oriented approach.

In software terms, an object contains both data and **methods** (Figure 8.21). For example, each student attending your school is an object described by such data as Social Security number, name, address, major, and so on. A method is a process that accesses and manipulates the object's data; methods are the routines that change the data when a student is admitted, changes majors, moves, graduates, and so on. The data define the object's state; the methods define its behavior.

One goal of the object-oriented approach is generating reusable code. Microsoft Windows provides a good example. Because the objects (data and methods) that support pointing and clicking already exist, a Windows programmer developing a new application can reuse those objects instead of writing new ones. That saves time and, because pointing and clicking have been so thoroughly tested, reusing them generally means fewer errors in the new program.

Signals and Operations

Objects communicate by transmitting and responding to **signals.** The signals are sent and received by entities called **operations** (Figure 8.21, near the left). An operation is an external view of the object that can be accessed by other objects. The methods are hidden inside the object, so they are private. Operations, in contrast, are public.

Object
A thing about which data are stored and manipulated.

Method
A procedure associated with an object.

Signal
The means by which two objects communicate.
Operation
An external view of an object that can be accessed by other objects.

BLOBs

Such difficult-to-classify entities as blocks of text, graphic images, and sound patterns have one thing in common: They can all be stored on a computer as binary patterns. In the object-oriented world, they are treated as binary large objects, or BLOBs.

Inside a BLOB, the rules imposed by a word processor or a graphics program might govern how the content is manipulated, but other applications treat the BLOB as an independent object. For example, if you use a word processor to prepare text, a graphics program to prepare illustrations, and a spreadsheet program to prepare tables, you can subsequently use a desktop publishing program to integrate those elements by treating the text, the illustrations, and the tables as independent BLOBs and positioning them on a page. Imagine arranging individual pieces of furniture in a room, and you have a good visualization of the process.

Advantages

Objects really exist. People naturally describe objects in terms of their attributes (data) and the things they do (methods), so the object-oriented approach makes sense to most users. Because the objects are so independent, object-oriented software is easier to maintain than structured software. Given those advantages, it is not surprising that many new applications are being developed using the object-oriented approach.

Encapsulation

Figure 8.21 pictures a generic object. The data form the core of the object. Surrounding it are methods that allow a user to create, maintain, delete, update, and perform a number of other operations on the data. The only way other objects can obtain the object's data is through one of its methods. That makes the object highly independent. Hiding implementation details in this way is called **encapsulation.**

Object Classes

Encapsulation
Hiding implementation details by enclosing data and methods inside an object.

In biology you distinguish among mammals, birds, reptiles, and insects. In politics, you distinguish among Republicans, Democrats, and Independents. Instead of separately tracking each item in an appliance store's inventory, the warehouse manager counts refrigerators, ranges, and television sets. Classifying or grouping objects with similar objects to form **classes** or **object types** makes it easier to keep track of them.

Class or Object type
A set of similar objects.

For example, Figure 8.22 shows how an office products store might classify its inventory. At the bottom are such discrete, physical objects as a box of copier paper and a pen (the smallest unit sold). That box of copier paper is but one instance of a more general class—copier paper. Moving up

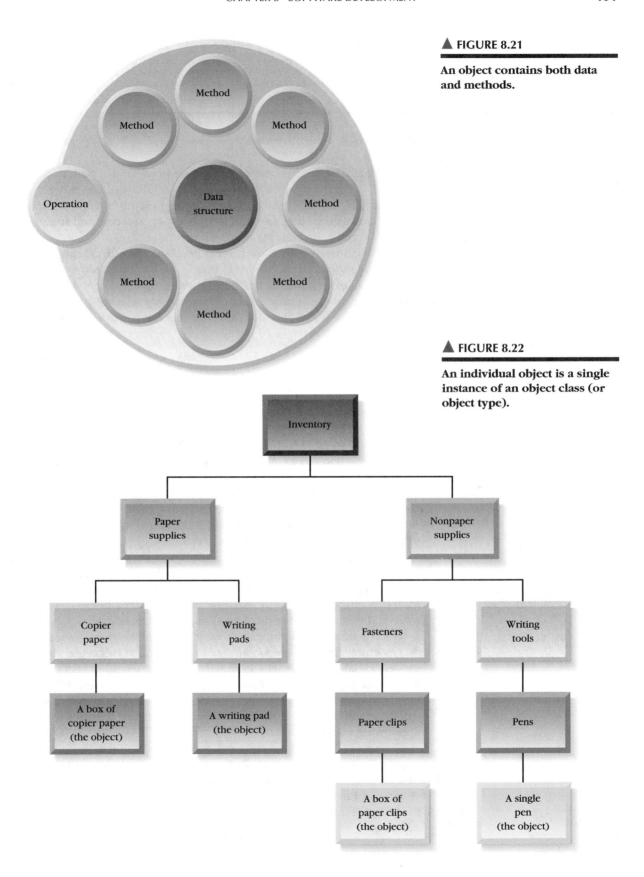

▲ FIGURE 8.21

An object contains both data and methods.

▲ FIGURE 8.22

An individual object is a single instance of an object class (or object type).

the classification hierarchy, the store might distinguish between paper supplies and nonpaper supplies. Note that an individual object is a single instance of an object class (or object type).

ADVANCED TOPICS

Inheritance

A Mazda Miata can be described as a small, two-seat, sporty automobile. Because it is a type (subclass) of automobile, you can ignore all the attributes the Miata shares with other automobiles (four wheels, an engine, a cooling system, methods for propulsion, steering, and stopping) and focus on the attributes that make it unique.

Moving down another level, a specific Miata (an object) can be described in terms of the attributes that make it unique (red, convertible top, serial number), and the attributes it shares with other Miatas (small, two seats, sporty) can be assumed. In effect, each subclass borrows (or inherits) attributes and methods from its superclass. This concept is called inheritance.

SUMMARY

Programs are physically stored in memory in binary form. Each machine language instruction has an operation code and one or more operands. A program written in assembly language is made up of one mnemonic statement for each machine-level instruction. The assembler program keeps track of the programmer's symbolic addresses and converts them to real addresses. Instead of repetitively writing the same assembly language statements, programmers sometimes write macro instructions.

The programmer writes source code. The assembler program translates the source statements to machine language and creates a binary object module. A compiler reads statements written in a human-like form and translates each of them to one or more machine language instructions. An interpreter reads a *single* source statement, translates it to machine level, executes the resulting instructions, and then moves on to the next source statement.

Assembly and high-level languages are procedural languages. With a nonprocedural language (sometimes called a fourth-generation or declarative language), the programmer defines the logical operation and lets the language translator decide how to perform it. A program generator starts with information in graphical, narrative, list, or some other logical form and outputs the appropriate source code.

The steps in the program development process include planning, coding, debugging, testing, and documentation. The first step in the planning process is to define the program's output data, algorithms, and input data. Structured English and pseudocode are program planning tools. A process flowchart graphically shows the flow of logic, control, and data through a program.

Once the logic is planned, the programmer codes the actual program instructions. In a sequence block the instructions are executed in a fixed order. In a selection block, sometimes called an if-then-else block, the flow of logic depends on a condition that cannot be known until execution time. A case structure is a selection block with several alternative logical paths. In an iteration block (or loop), the instructions are executed repetitively as long as an initial condition holds or until a terminal condition is met.

Syntax errors are easy to find because the compiler flags them. A logical error in a program is called a bug. The process of removing logical errors is called debugging. Bugs are identified through black box testing and removed by desk checking or interactive debugging. The debugging process often includes walkthroughs of the code. The purpose of a beta test is to allow real users to exercise a prerelease beta version of the software, identify its strengths and weaknesses, describe any errors they find, and report their impressions back to the developers.

In addition to writing and debugging the software, the programmer also prepares documentation. Comments are brief written notes that explain the code.

One technique for planning and designing a large program is called structured programming. The key to this approach is functional decomposition. A routine is a set of instructions that performs a specific, limited task. A module is a portion of a larger program that performs a specific task. A well-designed program consists of a set of independent single function modules linked by a control structure. Structured programs are tested from the top down.

The basic idea of the object-oriented approach to software development is to design and write the software as a set of independent objects linked by signals. An object is a thing about which data are stored and manipulated. A method is a process that accesses an object; the object incorporates both data and methods. An operation is an external view of an object.

In an object-oriented program, each object's data and methods are bundled so that the only way to access the data is through the object's own methods. Hiding implementation details in this way is called encapsulation. To simplify tracking them, objects are grouped with similar objects to form classes or object types.

KEY TERMS

algorithm	compiler	macro instruction
assembler	control structure	method
assembly language	coupling	module
beta test	debugging	nonprocedural language
beta version	documentation	object
black box testing	encapsulation	object module
bug	functional decomposition	object-oriented
case structure	if-then-else	object type
class	interpreter	operation
coding	iteration	operation code
cohesion	loop	operand
comment	machine language	procedural language

KEY TERMS (CONTINUED)

process flowchart	sequence	symbolic address
program generator	signal	top-down testing
pseudocode	source code	walkthrough
routine	structured English	
selection	structured programming	

CONCEPTS

1. The program that actually controls a computer must be stored in memory in binary, machine-language form. Why?
2. What does an assembler program do? Briefly, what is a symbolic address? What is a macro instruction? Why do programmers use macros?
3. Distinguish between source code and object code.
4. Distinguish among an assembler, a compiler, and an interpreter.
5. What is a nonprocedural (fourth-generation) language? How does a nonprocedural language differ from assembly and high-level languages?
6. Discuss the evolution of programming languages.
7. Outline the steps in the program development process and explain what happens during each step.
8. Program planning begins with identifying the desired output data, the necessary algorithms, and the input data. Explain why.
9. Identify several tools that are used to plan the flow of logic through a program. Describe (or sketch) the flow of logic through a sequence block, a selection block, and an iteration block.
10. What is the basic objective of structured programming?
11. What is cohesion? What is coupling? A good module is cohesive and loosely coupled. Why?
12. A well-structured program consists of a set of independent modules linked by a control structure. What does that mean?
13. Briefly describe the top-down approach to program testing.
14. Briefly describe the object-oriented approach to software development. What is a beta test?
15. What is an object? What does an object contain? What is encapsulation? Why is encapsulation important? Briefly explain object classes.

PROJECTS

1. Talk to a programmer and find out what he or she does during a typical work day.
2. To get a sense of how outstanding programmers think, read a book like Susan Lammers's *Programmers at Work* (Redmond, WA: Tempus Books of Microsoft Press, 1989).

INTERNET PROJECTS

1. *News and Notes*. Companies often post information about their very latest products on their World Wide Web home pages. Select a company such as Microsoft, IBM, or Sun Microsystems (Sun) that markets software development tools and access its home page. Try the address *http://www.xxx.com;* substitute the company name (for example, *microsoft*) for *xxx*. Once you find the home page, look for a button marked *New products*, or *Software development*, or something similar and click on it. Identify and briefly describe at least two new products and submit your findings to your instructor in the form of a brief note or an e-mail message.

2. *Topic Searches*. Check the World Wide Web and/or other Internet resources for information on the following topics:

Key word	Qualifiers
Java	Sun Microsystems
	application
object-oriented	software development
application generator	

   Define the key word, identify at least two sources of information on the topic, and briefly summarize the nature of the information you find.

3. *Links to Other Sites*. After you access one or more of the following sites, write a brief note or send an e-mail message to your instructor outlining what you find.

   a. On the World Wide Web, check *http://www.ibm.com* for information on IBM products.

   b. On the World Wide Web, check *http://www.microsoft.com* for information on Microsoft products.

   c. On the World Wide Web, check *http://www.sun.com* for information on Sun Microsystems products.

   d. On the World Wide Web, check *http://www.zdnet.com* for current news about computers and computer-related products.

4. Access West Publishing Company's home page and find the Chapter 8 student activities for this book. See Internet Project 3 for the spotlight on *The Internet* following Chapter 1 (page 29) for more detailed instructions on accessing the home page. As appropriate, repeat projects 1, 2, and/or 3 using the more current references you find.

CHAPTER 9

Data Management

Before you start this chapter, you should be familiar with the following concepts:

- Data and information (p. 4).
- Computers (p. 6), hardware (p. 6), and peripherals (p. 6).
- Software (p. 9), data (p. 10), and long-term storage (p. 12).
- Systems (p. 13) and classifying computers (p. 14).

When you finish reading this chapter, you should be able to:

- Explain the purpose of data management.
- Define source data. Distinguish between data capture and data entry.
- Describe the standard field/record/file data structure.
- Define the term *object*. Identify several objects that do not fit the standard field/record/file hierarchy.
- Distinguish among master, transaction, backup, and history files.
- Identify and explain the three basic data maintenance operations.
- Explain why data integrity is so important.
- Explain how and why files are opened and closed.
- Distinguish between sequential and direct access.
- Distinguish between logical and physical I/O and explain how the relative record concept is used to bridge the gap between logical and physical I/O.
- Distinguish between logical and physical records. Describe blocked and spanned records.

WHY DATA MANAGEMENT?

Imagine that you have just registered for the next academic term. Think about what happens to the data on your registration form.

First (obviously), those data are used to generate your class schedule (Figure 9.1). The same data are used by the finance office to prepare your bill, and a few weeks later the bursar's office will check your registration data to verify your payment. Later, the registrar's office will add your current courses to your academic record.

You are not the only person registering for classes, of course; every student attending your school submits a similar registration form every academic term. The data from all those forms are used to compile class lists for your instructors. At the end of the term, the registration data are used to generate final grade reporting forms.

The point is that in the real world data are not simply input, processed, and forgotten. Instead, the data are used over and over again to support numerous, interrelated applications.

▲ FIGURE 9.1

The same data are used over and over again.

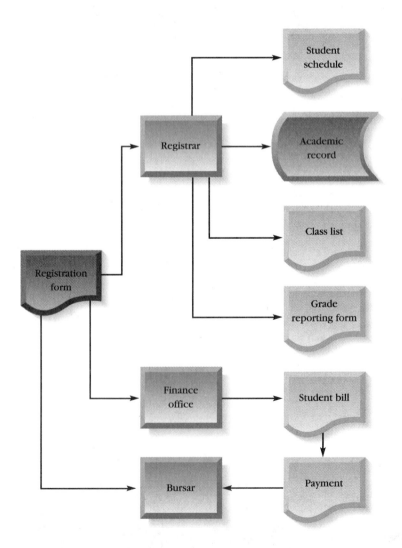

Further complicating matters is data volume. One registration form per student represents a sizable pile of forms, and it makes no sense to input the same data over and over again. Instead, the data are typically input once, stored on disk, and retrieved on demand. **Data management** is concerned with capturing, entering, storing, maintaining, and retrieving a system's data.

SOURCE DATA

A **transaction** is a single occurrence of an activity, an event, or an object about which data are collected. For example, when you purchase something from a department store, visit a hospital emergency room, register for a course, or purchase a ticket to a movie, you are participating in a transaction. The data that describe each transaction are called **source data.**

Data Capture and Data Entry

Data capture is the process of initially recording the source data. **Data entry** is the process of converting the source data to electronic (or machine readable) form and entering them to the computer.

BATCH DATA ENTRY

The distinction between data capture and data entry is best illustrated through an example. Imagine a sales associate in a retail store *capturing* the source data that describe a customer order by filling out an invoice form. The completed forms (one per order) are then collected and delivered to data entry clerks, who *enter* the data through a keyboard (Figure 9.2). The act of collecting a batch of source data forms and subsequently entering them at a later time is called **batch data entry.**

SOURCE DATA AUTOMATION

Batch data entry is relatively rare today. Instead, data are typically captured electronically (by swiping a credit card through a scanner, for example) and

Data management
Capturing, entering, storing, maintaining, and retrieving data.

Transaction
One occurrence of a business activity; for example, a single customer order or a single shipment from a supplier.

Source data
The data that describe each transaction.

Data capture
The process of recording data.
Data entry
The process of converting data to electronic form.

Batch data entry
Entering source data in a batch.

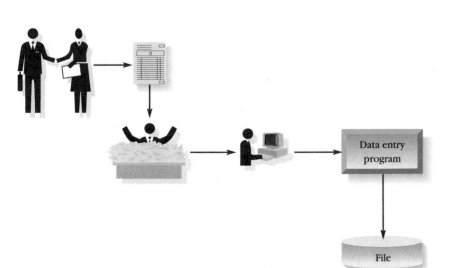

▲ **FIGURE 9.2**

Batch data entry.

Turnaround Time

Turnaround time is a measure of the elapsed time between submitting a job to a computer and getting the results back. Given the technology available in the 1960s, 24-hour turnaround was considered normal, so the delays inherent in batch data entry were acceptable. Today, however, we access our personal computers interactively and expect them to respond in a fraction of a second, and the very idea of waiting 24 hours to get the data we need seems absurd. In many ways, the definition of "timely" is relative to what we expect.

Source data automation
Capturing data electronically and entering them immediately to a computer.

entered immediately to a computer. The process, called **source data automation,** reduces the tedium of data capture and data entry, cuts errors by eliminating manual procedures, and makes the data available for processing much more quickly.

Ensuring Data Accuracy

The best time to catch bad data is before they enter the system. For example, instead of having their sales clerks enter the price of each item digit by digit, some fast-food outlets use cash register terminals equipped with buttons that picture the menu items (Figure 9.3). Pressing a picture of a hamburger (or a button marked *Hamburger*) is faster and less error prone than typing the digits 1.89.

ERROR DETECTION SOFTWARE

Some errors can be detected by the computer. For example, if the standard work week is 40 hours and a clerk enters 90 hours for one employee, the data entry program can request confirmation before accepting that value. Other tests can flag clearly incorrect data, such as an employee's sex entered as anything but M or F, or a zip code that contains alphabetic characters.

Any time a human being enters data through a keyboard, transposition errors (123 instead of 132) are particularly common. One way to catch such errors is to use a check digit. For example, many systems add a tenth digit to a Social Security number. The extra digit is actually computed from the first nine. If the tenth digit as computed and the tenth digit as entered match, the Social Security number is probably correct. If not, the data entry clerk probably made a transposition error.

Note, however, that the computer cannot *guarantee* correct input data. If an employee actually worked 20 hours last week but the data entry clerk types 40 hours, the computer will probably accept the incorrect value because it seems reasonable. If a clerk enters Arnold Schwarzenegger's sex as female, incorrect data will enter the system. Granted, the idea of a female Arnold Schwarzenegger is absurd, but a computer has no sense of the absurd.

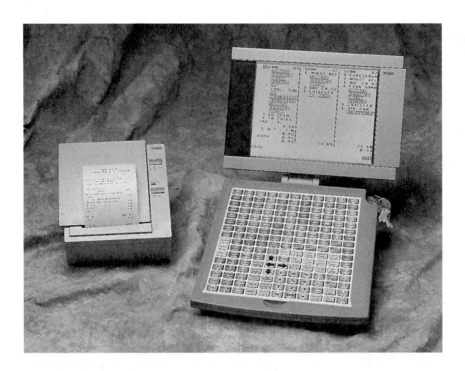

▲ **FIGURE 9.3**

These cash register buttons
describe the menu items.

VERIFICATION

Verification is a powerful tool for ensuring data accuracy. The idea is to get the same data from two different sources, at two different times, or in two different forms and then compare them. If the values match, the data are probably correct. If the values do not match, you have an opportunity to correct an error. Verification is perhaps the best way to detect and correct transcription errors that occur when the data as entered do not match the data as recorded.

For example, many magazines access their subscriber records by zip code and name. If you call the customer service department to change your mailing address, the representative will ask for your zip code, enter it, ask for your name, enter it, and then read your old street address to you. If the address is correct, then the data you gave the representative matches the data stored on the computer, thus verifying that the correct customer entry has been found. If the address is unfamiliar, either you provided the wrong data or the representative made a mistake.

Verification
Obtaining the same data from two different sources, at two different times, or in two different forms and then comparing them.

DATA STRUCTURES

The point of capturing and entering source data is to make those data available for subsequent processing. Before you can process the data, you must be able to distinguish the fields (more accurately, the individual data items). A **data structure** is a rule (or a set of rules) for organizing data. If the fields are stored according to a well-defined data structure, it is possible to distinguish them by remembering that structure.

Data structure
A rule (or set of rules) for organizing data. A set of data elements that are stored, manipulated, or moved together.

NOTE

Manual Data Entry and Accuracy

A few decades ago, most data were recorded on source documents and then submitted to a keypunch operator who used a typewriter-like keyboard to copy the data to punched cards. To improve the accuracy of the data, the cards were then loaded into another machine called a verifier, and the original source data were rekeyed. If the data entered by the keypunch operator and the verifier operator did not match, the offending card was marked and corrected.

In those days, the standard for keypunching accuracy was 95 percent. Verification increased the accuracy rate to 99 percent, meaning that 99 of every 100 keypunched and verified cards matched the source document. If the source data were wrong the associated card was wrong, of course, but that did not count as an error.

Imagine a keypunch operator preparing labor cards that will be used to compute your weekly pay. If you work for a small company that employs 100 people, five checks will be wrong every week. Add verification, and you still get one bad check per week. That is unacceptable. Numbers like 95 percent and 99 percent suggest very high accuracy until you consider the consequences. We must do better. That is yet another reason for capturing data electronically.

Fields, Records, and Files

You learned about fields, records, and files in Chapter 1 (Figure 9.4). A field is a group of characters that forms a logically meaningful unit of data; a subscriber's name in a telephone book is a good example. A set of related fields (a single subscriber's name, address, and telephone number) forms a record, and a set of related records (the entire telephone book) forms a file.

Lists and Arrays

List
The most basic data structure.

A **list** is the most basic data structure. For example, Figure 9.5 pictures a list of four-digit numbers separated by commas. (Spaces, semicolons, and slashes

▲ FIGURE 9.4

Fields, records, and files.

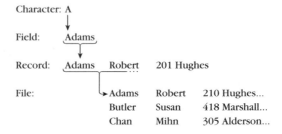

are other common separators.) The last number in the list, -1, is a sentinel value that marks the end of the list; negative numbers and "impossible" values are popular sentinels. (Typically, the program processes the data until it reaches the sentinel value.) Lists are common in statistical and computational applications.

A matrix or **array** (Figure 9.6) resembles a table. The intersection of a row and a column is called a cell, and each cell holds one data value (or one field). The combination of the row identifier and the column identifier gives each cell a unique address and allows you to access its contents.

Objects

Programs, documents, graphic images, spreadsheets, and several other entities are all stored in files, but they do not fit the standard field/record/file hierarchy. For example, consider a word processing document. Characters are characters, and a complete document might be a file, but there is no way to map words, paragraphs, blocks, sections, and chapters to fields and records. Graphic images present an even greater challenge. Is there any part of the image pictured in Figure 9.7 that you can treat as a field or a record?

Some applications start with a very different basic unit called an **object.** An object is a thing about which data are stored. For example, look around your classroom. Each student is an object. The professor is an object. The room itself, your textbook, and each of the chairs are all objects. (Surprisingly, the word *object* means pretty much what you think it does.)

Technically, an object consists of a set of data and the software routines (called methods) that manipulate or access the data. For example, a student object (you) holds the data that describe a particular student (name, address, major, grade-point average, . . .) and a set of routines to perform such tasks as changing an address or computing a new GPA.

Array
A data structure that resembles a table or a spreadsheet.

```
1714, 0374, 3447, 9945,
9586, 2617, 7893, -1
```

▲ **FIGURE 9.5**

A list.

Object
A thing about which data are stored.

	A	B	C	D	E	F	G
1							
2							
3							
4							
5							
6							
7							
8							
9							
10							
11							
12							
13							
14							

▲ **FIGURE 9.6**

A two-dimensional array, or matrix.

▲ FIGURE 9.7

Graphic images do not fit the traditional field/record/file structure.

Desktop publishing provides a good example of object processing (Figure 9.8). Assume that the text was prepared using a word processing program and the graphic image was created by a graphics program. Now imagine using a pair of scissors to cut a printed version of the text into small blocks and then arranging the blocks of text and the graphic image on a blank sheet of paper. That is essentially what a desktop publishing program does electronically. Note that the software can rearrange the objects, but it cannot change their contents.

Blocks of text and graphic images are examples of objects. So are spreadsheets, sound patterns, menus, icons, animations, photographs, video sequences, files, and virtually any other thing you can imagine.

DATA MAINTENANCE

Once the source data have been captured, entered, and stored on a file, they must be maintained.

File Types

Master file
A permanent data file.

A **master file** is a permanent file. For example, most businesses maintain master files on their employees, their customers, the items in inventory, pending orders, bills, and so on.

Transaction file
A file of records that describe current transactions.

A **transaction file** holds records that describe current transactions, such as name and address changes, customer purchases, and incoming shipments. The records in a master file are used over an extended period of time. The records in a transaction file are typically needed only until the appropriate master file is updated.

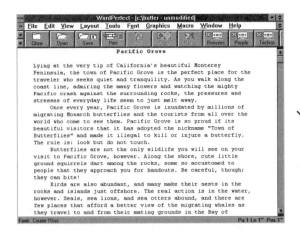

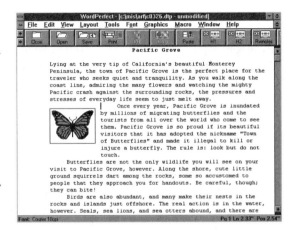

▲ **FIGURE 9.8**

Processing objects.

A **backup file** is a copy of a master file or a transaction file that is used to recover data if disaster strikes. A **history file,** sometimes called an archive file, holds already processed transactions that might someday be needed (perhaps by auditing or by the legal department). History files can also be used to help reconstruct a damaged master file.

On some systems, the data in a master file are updated interactively. Although technically such systems have no need for transaction files, any transaction that changes a master file record is typically logged to a difficult-to-change medium such as magnetic tape. The transaction log serves as a backup file, and can also be used as evidence in the event of a security breach.

Add, Delete, and Update

After the transaction data are captured and entered, they are used to maintain one or more master files. Over time, records must be added to the appropriate master file to reflect new customers, new products, and new employees. Customers defect to competitors, employees resign, and products are discontinued, so it must be possible to delete records from a master file. A change in a customer's or employee's address or a product's price calls for

Backup file
A copy of a master file or a transaction file that is used to recover data if disaster strikes.
History file
A file of already processed transactions.

modifying or updating a master file record. **Add, delete,** and **update** are the three basic data maintenance operations.

Data Integrity

There is more to data maintenance than just adding, deleting, and updating records, however. The fact that you can economically capture, enter, store, and retrieve data means little if you cannot protect those data against loss or contamination, because people will not use data they do not trust. To ensure **data integrity,** access to the data must be carefully controlled and managed from the time they first enter the system until they are of no further use.

The legal concept of a chain of evidence is a good way to visualize data integrity. Unless you can prove that no one tampered with the evidence between the time it was collected and the time it is presented in court, that evidence is inadmissible. Similarly, the data cannot be trusted unless you can prove that (1) the data came from an approved source, (2) only sanctioned changes were made to the data, and (3) those changes were made according to approved procedures.

One key to ensuring data integrity is to clearly assign responsibility for the data. Many organizations divide the management information system function into three groups (Figure 9.9). Operations works with the hardware, systems and programming creates and maintains the software, and the **database administrator** (or **DBA**) is responsible for the data.

Auditing is another key to ensuring data integrity. The point of auditing is not to detect or correct errors, but to ensure that the established procedures and controls are followed. For example, a well-conducted audit might not catch an incorrect value input by a data entry clerk, but it should flag an attempt by an unauthorized person to change that value. The idea is to ensure that a particular unit of data was captured, entered, stored, processed, and maintained properly.

Security

Information system **security** involves procedures and other safeguards designed to protect the hardware, software, data, and other system resources from unauthorized access, use, modification, and theft. Once a system's security is breached, the data are particularly vulnerable because they are so easy

▲ **FIGURE 9.9**

The database administrator is responsible for the data.

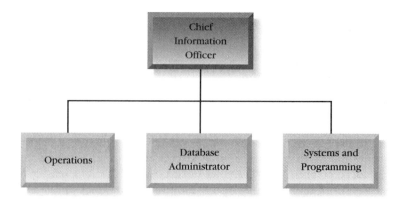

Why Back Up?

Any time you use a computer to create a spreadsheet, a document, or some other data, take the time to back up your work. Computers do fail, and disks and diskettes can be damaged or partially erased. The question is not *if* you lose your data, it is *when*. The few seconds it takes to make an extra copy are insignificant when you compare them to the trauma of redoing lost work.

Backup is even more crucial to a large organization. Imagine, for example, what might happen if your automobile insurance company were to lose its policy records or your school were to lose the academic records of all its current students. The inconvenience to you would be minor compared to the effort required to recreate such massive amounts of data. Think of backup as inexpensive data insurance.

to copy or to change. It is impossible to ensure data integrity if unauthorized people can access the data.

Backup and Recovery

Disk drives can fail. Files can be accidentally deleted. Fires, floods, hurricanes, tornadoes, earthquakes, and other disasters can destroy an information system. To protect against lost data, files must be backed up regularly.

To **back up** a file, you copy all the data to some other medium; for example, a disk file can be backed up by copying it to magnetic tape. Should a disaster occur, **recovery** procedures are used to recreate the data from the backup copy. Effective backup and recovery procedures are an important part of data maintenance.

Back up
To copy the contents of a secondary storage device to another secondary medium.
Recovery
Restoring a computer system and/or a set of data files after a disaster.

ACCESSING FILES

The first step in processing data is to find the file that holds the data. A computer system might have hundreds or even thousands of different files in secondary storage. How does the computer find the right file?

Directories

The key to finding a specific file on disk is the disk's directory (Figure 9.10) The directory lists the file name and disk address of every file stored on the disk. Think of the directory as the disk's table of contents.

Open and Close

When a program is ready to access a file, it asks the operating system to **open** the file. The operating system responds by searching the disk's directory, determining exactly where the file is stored, and passing the file's location

Open
To prepare a file for use.

The directory is the disk's table of contents.

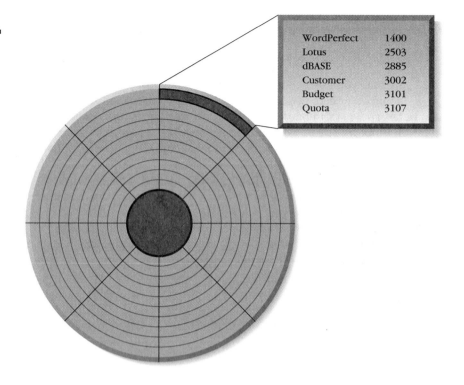

WordPerfect	1400
Lotus	2503
dBASE	2885
Customer	3002
Budget	3101
Quota	3107

Close
To break the link between a program and a data file. To make a data file unavailable for use.

Sequential access
A data access technique in which a series of records is processed in sequence.

back to the application program. Given the file's location, the application program can read and write its records. Once a given record is in memory, the program can manipulate or process the individual fields.

When processing is finished, the application program asks the operating system to **close** the file. The operating system responds by deleting the file's location from memory so the application program can no longer find it. (Note that once a file is closed, the program cannot accidentally modify the data.)

ACCESSING RECORDS

Once a file is opened, the process of accessing its records can begin. When a program needs input data, it reads a record; when it is ready to output results, it writes a record. Note that the read and write operations deal with selected *records,* not with the entire file. Files are opened and closed. Records are read and written. Fields are processed.

When a program needs a record, it needs a *specific* record; for example, if you want a copy of your transcript, some other student's academic history will not do. One way to simplify finding the right record is to organize the file. The idea is to store the records according to a well-defined set of rules and then retrieve the records by using those same rules.

Sequential Access

Sequential access means that the records in a file are read and written in a fixed order. For example, imagine preparing meeting announcements for a club. You need a set of mailing labels, and each member's name and address is recorded on an index card. The easiest way to generate the labels is to copy the data from the first card, turn to the second card and copy its data, and so on. Note that the records are processed sequentially, from the beginning of the file to the end.

Magazine publishers face the same problem with each new issue, but they need labels for tens of thousands of subscribers. Rather than using index cards, they store customer data on disk or magnetic tape, one record per subscriber. The easiest way to ensure that all the labels are generated is to process the records in order, proceeding sequentially from the first record in the file to the last one.

Activity is a measure of the percentage of a file's records that are accessed each time the relevant application program is run. Sequential processing is an excellent choice when the level of activity is high. Preparing weekly paychecks, monthly bills, quarterly accounting reports, and address labels for a weekly magazine are sequential applications. So is backing up a file.

The Key Field

Each record in a file has a **key** field that uniquely identifies it; note that no two records can have the same key. Your Social Security number is a good key because the government does not issue duplicate Social Security numbers. If anyone else has your Social Security number, either somebody made a mistake or one of you obtained the number illegally.

Often, the records in a sequential file are sorted and stored in key order. For example, if a magazine publisher stores subscriber records in zip code order, a sequential list of the records in that file will generate address labels in zip code order, and that means a discounted postal rate.

Direct Access

Sequential processing is an excellent choice when the level of activity is high, but many applications call for accessing and processing a single record. When the level of activity is low, direct access is a better choice. **Direct,** or **random access** implies that a specific record can be read or written without first going through all the records that precede it on the file.

For example, when a subscriber moves, his or her address must be changed. Searching sequentially for a single record is like looking for a telephone number by reading the phone book line by line. You would not even consider conducting a sequential search for a telephone number. Instead, you take advantage of the fact that the telephone book is in alphabetical order, reference the names printed at the top of each page, find the right page, and quickly locate the right number. The way you use a telephone book is a good example of direct access.

Indexing

One way to implement direct access is to **index** the records. An index is a table of key field values paired with the associated records' locations on disk.

For example, picture a student data file indexed by student identification number. As each student's record is added to the student file, the student ID

Activity
A measure of the percentage of a file's records that are accessed each time the relevant application program is run.

Key
A field that uniquely identifies a given record.

Direct access
Selecting a specific record from the database.
Random access
Selecting a specific record from the database.

Index
A list of the keys and locations of each record in a file.

(the key) and the disk address where that record is stored are recorded in an index (Figure 9.11). The index is itself stored on the disk.

Once the index is created, it can be used to find individual records. To access a particular student's record, the computer reads the index into memory, searches it for the target student identification number, extracts the disk address where that student's record is stored, and retrieves the record. Note that searching an index in memory is *much* faster than searching through a series of records on disk.

Indexed Sequential Files

Indexed sequential file
A file in which the records are physically stored in sequential order and indexed. Consequently, the records can be accessed sequentially or directly.

As the name implies, an **indexed sequential file** is a sequential file with an index. Because the records are physically stored in sequence, they can be read and written sequentially. Because the records are indexed, they can be accessed directly.

LOGICAL AND PHYSICAL I/O

Logical I/O
The input or output of a logical record.

Physical I/O
The physical transfer of data between memory and a peripheral device.

A programmer thinks in terms of **logical I/O,** requesting the next record or the name and address for a particular customer without regard for where the data are physically stored. Hardware, in contrast, "thinks" in terms of the specific **physical I/O** operations that are needed to transfer data between the computer's memory and a particular peripheral device. Before an input or output operation can take place, the programmer's logical request must be translated into physical terms.

The Relative Record Concept

Relative record
A record's location relative to the beginning of a file.

One key to physically accessing data on disk is the **relative record** concept. The basic idea is to assign to each record a number that indicates its relative position in the file, and then to use that number to compute the record's physical disk address.

For example, imagine a string of 100 records. Number the first one 0, the second 1, the third 2, and so on. The numbers indicate a given record's posi-

▲ **FIGURE 9.11**

An index can be used to support direct access.

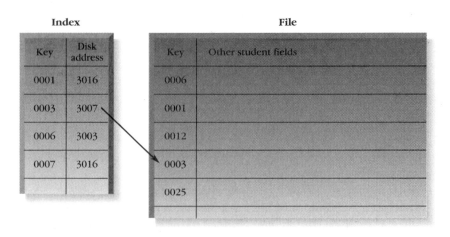

Index			File	
Key	Disk address		Key	Other student fields
0001	3016		0006	
0003	3007		0001	
0006	3003		0012	
0007	3016		0003	
			0025	

tion relative to the beginning of the file. The file's first record (relative record 0) is at "start of file plus 0," the second record is at "start of file plus 1," and so on.

Data on disk are stored around a series of concentric circles called tracks (Figure 9.12). The tracks are subdivided into sectors, the basic units of disk storage. Data move between the disk and memory one sector at a time.

Imagine that each sector holds one record. Number the sectors relative to the start of the file—0, 1, 2, and so on (Figure 9.13). Note that the relative record number, a logical concept, and the relative sector number, a physical address, are identical. Given a relative record number, it is possible to compute a relative sector number. If you add the relative sector number to the file's start address (from the directory), you get the record's physical disk address.

Some systems address data by relative bytes or characters rather than by relative records. The basic concept, however, is the same. The location of any given data element or group of elements can be computed by counting bytes, words, records, or other units of storage from the beginning of the file and adding the result to the file's start address (from the directory).

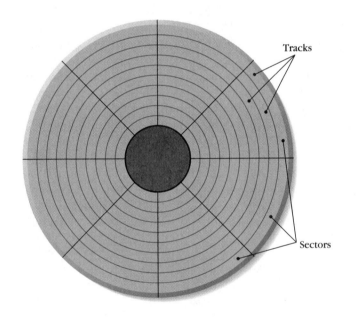

▲ **FIGURE 9.12**

Tracks and sectors.

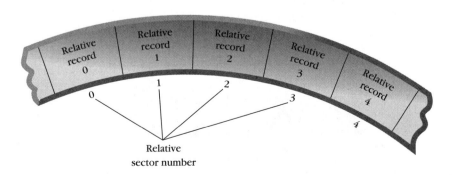

▲ **FIGURE 9.13**

The relative record number can be used to compute a physical address.

ADVANCED TOPICS

Hashing

Maintaining an index is not the only way to implement direct access. One alternative, called hashing, relies on an algorithm to convert a record's logical key directly to a relative record number.

The division/remainder method is one common hashing technique. The idea is to divide the key (a Social Security number, for example) by a prime number that is relatively close to the number of records in the file. The remainder of that division operation will be a number no less than 0 and no greater than the divisor. If the divisor is roughly equal to the number of records in the file, then the remainder can be used as a relative record number. Note that the remainder generated by a given key will always be the same, so the hashing algorithm will yield the same relative record number when you create the record and, later, when you retrieve it.

Blocks and Spanned Records

Data move between a disk and memory one sector at a time. A sector is a fixed-length unit of storage; 512 bytes is common.

Imagine an application in which the records are exactly 100 bytes in length. Storing one record per sector would be terribly inefficient because each sector would hold 412 bytes of unused space. A better solution is to combine five records to form a 500-byte **block** and store one block per sector (Figure 9.14).

The sector represents a **physical record,** the unit of data that moves between memory and the peripheral device in response to a *physical* input or output operation. A **logical record** is the set of data the programmer expects each time he or she issues a *logical* input or output operation. A block is a set of logical records that are physically stored together. Programmers think in terms of logical I/O. Hardware performs physical I/O.

Note in Figure 9.14 that 12 of the sector's 512 bytes are unused. One way to use those bytes is to store the first part of logical record 6 in one sector and the rest in the next sector (Figure 9.15), creating a **spanned record.**

When a logical record spans two sectors, reading or writing that record requires two physical I/O operations. For example, when the program reads logical record 6, hardware responds by physically transferring *both* sectors into memory. Software (the operating system) then extracts the relevant bytes from the two sectors, combines them to form the requested logical record, and passes the logical record back to the application program.

Block
A set of logical records that are physically stored together.
Physical record
The set of related fields that are physically stored together in the same file.
Logical record
The set of related fields needed to complete one input, process, output cycle of a program.

Spanned record
A logical record on a disk that is physically stored in two or more sectors.

▲ **FIGURE 9.14**

Blocking.

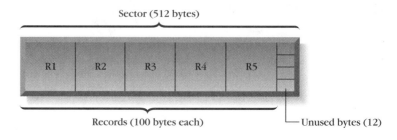

Sector (512 bytes)

| R1 | R2 | R3 | R4 | R5 | |

Records (100 bytes each)   └─ Unused bytes (12)

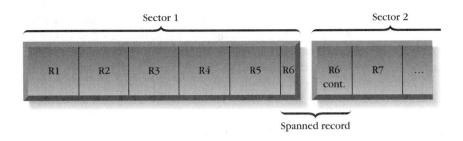

Sector 1   Sector 2

| R1 | R2 | R3 | R4 | R5 | R6 | | R6 cont. | R7 | ... |

Spanned record

▲ **FIGURE 9.15**

A spanned record.

The ability to define blocked and spanned records gives the user or the programmer a great deal of flexibility, but it comes with a cost. Simply put, a complex data structure requires a complex (and hence more expensive) operating system. Such technological trade-offs are common.

SUMMARY

Data management is concerned with capturing, entering, storing, maintaining, and retrieving a system's data.

A transaction is a single occurrence of an activity, an event, or an object about which data are collected. The data that describe each transaction are called source data. Data capture is the process of recording the source data. Data entry is the process of converting the source data to electronic form. The act of collecting a batch of source data for later entry is called batch data entry. Capturing data electronically and entering them immediately is called source data automation. Verification is a powerful tool for ensuring data accuracy.

A data structure is a rule (or a set of rules) for organizing data; the field/record/file hierarchy is a good example. A list is a string of values separated by commas (or some other separator) and terminated by a sentinel value. A matrix or array is a data structure that resembles a table. An object is a thing about which data are stored.

A master file is a permanent file. A transaction file holds records that describe current transactions. A backup file is a copy of a master file or a transaction file that is used to recover data if disaster strikes. A history file holds already processed transactions that might be needed someday.

Add, delete, and update are the three basic data maintenance operations. To ensure data integrity, access to the data must be carefully controlled and managed from the time they first enter the system until they are of no further use. The database administrator is responsible for the data. Auditing is concerned with ensuring that proper data management procedures are followed. Information system security is designed to protect the system's resources from unauthorized access, use, modification, and theft. To back up a file, you copy all the data to some other medium. Should a disaster occur, recovery procedures are used to recreate the data from the backup copy.

A disk's directory is its table of contents. When a program is ready to access a file, it opens the file. When processing is finished, the file is closed.

Sequential access means that the records in a file are read and written in a fixed order. Sequential processing is an excellent choice when the level of activity is high. Each record has a key field that uniquely identifies the record. Direct, or random access implies that a specific record can be read or written without first going through all the records that precede it. One way to implement direct access is to index the records. An indexed sequential file can be accessed sequentially or directly.

A programmer thinks in terms of logical I/O. Hardware "thinks" in terms of the specific physical I/O operations that are needed to transfer data between the computer's memory and a peripheral device. One key to physically accessing data on disk is the relative record concept. A physical record is the unit of data that moves between memory and a peripheral device. A logical record is the set of data the programmer expects each time he or she issues a *logical* input or output operation. A block is a set of records that are physically stored together. A spanned record is split over two or more sectors.

KEY TERMS

activity	database administrator	physical I/O
add (record)	(DBA)	physical record
array	delete (record)	random access
auditing	direct access	recovery
back up	history file	relative record
backup file	index	security
batch data entry	indexed sequential file	sequential access
block	key	source data
close	list	source data automation
data capture	logical I/O	spanned record
data entry	logical record	transaction
data integrity	master file	transaction file
data management	object	update (record)
data structure	open	verification

CONCEPTS

1. What is the purpose of data management?
2. What are source data?
3. Distinguish between data capture and data entry. Distinguish between batch data entry and source data automation.
4. Describe the standard field/record/file data structure.
5. What is a list? What is a sentinel value? What is an array?
6. What is an object? Identify several objects that do not fit the standard field/record/file hierarchy.
7. Distinguish between a master file and a transaction file.
8. What is a backup file? Why are backup files used? What is a history file? Why are history files used?
9. Identify and explain the three basic data maintenance operations.
10. Why is data integrity so important? List several steps that can be taken to help ensure data integrity. What is the purpose of backup and recovery?
11. Explain how and why files are opened and closed.

12. Distinguish between sequential and direct access.
13. Distinguish between logical and physical I/O. Explain how the relative record concept is used to bridge the gap between logical and physical I/O.
14. What is a logical record? What is a physical record? How are they related?
15. Records are sometimes stored as a block. Why? What is a spanned record?

PROJECT

1. Compile a list of files that you know hold data about you. (You should be able to find several at your school.) Request copies of your data. See if you can find any errors.

 ## INTERNET PROJECTS

1. *News and Notes*. Check into the on-line data available from the U.S. Census Bureau at *http://www.census.gov* on the World Wide Web. Find the most recent data on the population of the United States of America and your state and submit your findings to your instructor in the form of a brief note or an e-mail message.
2. *Topic Searches*. Check the World Wide Web and/or other Internet resources for information on the following topics:

Key word	*Qualifiers*
data compression	disk
disaster planning	computer center
backup and recovery	data

   Define the key word, identify at least two sources of information on the topic, and briefly summarize the nature of the information you find.
3. *Links to Other Sites.* After you access one or more of the following sites, write a brief note or send an e-mail message to your instructor outlining what you find.

   a. Check newsgroup *alt.missing-kids* for current pictures and descriptions of missing children.
   b. On the World Wide Web, check *http://thomas.loc.gov* for U.S. Congressional news.
   c. On the World Wide Web, check *http://www.nytimes.com* for current news. Several other newspapers are available on-line, too, so try your favorite.

4. Access West Publishing Company's home page and find the Chapter 9 student activities for this book. See Internet Project 3 for the spotlight on *The Internet* following Chapter 1 (page 29) for more detailed instructions on accessing the home page. As appropriate, repeat projects 1, 2, and/or 3 using the more current references you find.

SPOTLIGHT

COMPUTERS AND PRIVACY

Before you start this feature, you should be familiar with the following concepts:

► Data capture and data entry (p. 199).
► Data accuracy (p. 200) and data integrity (p. 206).

When you finish reading this feature, you should be able to:

► Explain how computers simplify data access.
► Explain why maintaining data integrity is so important.
► Identify several privacy laws.
► Discuss e-mail privacy.
► Briefly discuss the issue of censorship versus free speech on the Internet.

PRIVACY IN THE INFORMATION AGE

There was a time when collecting, processing, storing, and disseminating information on large numbers of individuals was simply impractical, but the computer has changed the rules. As a result, personal **privacy** is an important issue in our evolving information age.

Privacy
The state of being free from unsanctioned intrusion.

Data Access

You might be amazed to discover the amount of data available on-line about you. Start with your school. When you apply for admission, all the data on your application form are entered into a computer. If you apply for financial aid, details about your parents' financial status are also input. During your years in school, data are collected about the courses you take, the clubs you join, the student jobs you hold, any disciplinary actions recorded against you, and many other things.

Once you get a job, your employer maintains personal data, salary data, and supervisory evaluations. Your bank has data about your checking account, your savings account, and your credit card balance. Marriages, divorces, births, deaths, address changes, job changes, automobile registrations, driver's licenses, and utility payments are but a few examples of events that generate data that are stored electronically on computers.

There is good reason for collecting and storing virtually all those data. The real concern is that computers make access so easy. Just knowing that someone equipped with little more than your Social Security number can (literally at the push of a button) compile an impressive dossier on the details of your life is disquieting.

Ensuring Data Integrity

You may not be aware that financial data about you appear in one or more credit bureau databases and that your credit rating will be a major factor in determining whether or not you get an automobile loan, a credit card, a mortgage, an insurance policy, or perhaps even a job. What if the data are wrong? What if an agent accidentally codes your Social Security number on someone else's bad credit report? What if a data entry clerk makes a mistake and enters the wrong code? What if a someone breaks into the credit bureau system and maliciously changes your credit data? All of those things have happened, and the results can be disastrous for the person whose record is corrupted.

Data management and auditing procedures can help to minimize the risk, and most credit bureaus do a good job of ensuring data integrity, but problems do occur. You have a right to review your credit report and request that incorrect entries be changed. If you are ever turned down for a loan, insist on exercising that right.

Privacy Laws

In the United States, each citizen's right to privacy is a serious concern. Figure 9.16 lists several privacy laws, but technology changes so quickly that the laws are not always effective. Privacy is, at heart, an ethical issue.

DATE	LAW	PURPOSE
1970	Fair Credit Reporting Act	Gives consumers the right to review their credit reports.
1974	Family Educational Rights and Privacy Act	Prohibits the release of student records to unauthorized people.
1974	Privacy Act	Prohibits federal agencies from using information for anything but the intended purpose.
1978	Right to Financial Privacy Act	Limits federal government access to bank customer data.
1984	Computer Fraud and Abuse Act	Prohibits unauthorized access of government computers.
1986	Electronic Communications Privacy Act	Extends privacy laws pertaining to the postal service and the telephone company to e-mail and other electronic media.
1991	Telephone Consumer Protection Act	Regulates telemarketers.
1994	Computer Abuse Amendments Act	Amends 1984 act to prohibit the transfer of harmful computer code, such as viruses.

▲ FIGURE 9.16

A brief summary of selected U.S. privacy laws.

PRIVACY AND FREE SPEECH ON THE INTERNET

The Internet is evolving so rapidly that it is almost impossible for laws and operating procedures to keep pace. Two recent cases involving electronic mail and free speech help to illustrate the complexity of the problem.

E-mail and Privacy

Have you ever sent a highly personal e-mail message? If you have, you probably assumed that the contents were private. You were wrong.

E-mail is electronic. When a message is sent, the sending computer retains a copy so it can be retransmitted if the entire message fails to get through. Additionally, on many systems all messages are logged and retained for a time. If a message is retained, it can be read by someone other than the intended recipient.

Recently, the issue of e-mail privacy entered the courts when an employee was fired based on information his employer discovered by monitoring his e-mail. The employee claimed that his e-mail messages were private and that the employer had no right to monitor them, but the courts disagreed. The computers and the network were the employer's property, and the employer had every right to monitor them. The employee lost the case and his job.

Remember that next time you are tempted to fire off a nasty note or a much too personal e-mail message. Someone might be reading over your (electronic) shoulder.

Censorship on the Internet

Recently, free speech became a controversial issue on the Internet when one of the major on-line services temporarily blocked its subscribers' access to selected newsgroups in response to a ruling by a German court concerning alleged pornography and other illegal on-line activities. Reacting to the same perceived problems, the U.S. Congress has debated bills for regulating content on the information superhighway. Activists counter by calling such laws censorship and arguing that any attempt to control what can and cannot be communicated over the Internet will have a chilling effect.

Should the information superhighway be a free and open medium for the unfettered exchange of information? Or do governments have the responsibility to regulate content and restrict such activities as child pornography? The issue is highly controversial and far from decided.

KEY TERM

privacy

CONCEPTS

1. Why do computers add to concerns about privacy?
2. Identify at least three important privacy laws and briefly describe the purpose of those laws.
3. Why is it so difficult to define meaningful privacy laws in our modern information age?
4. Do you believe that your personal e-mail should be private? Why, or why not? Do you believe that it *is* private?
5. Do you believe that the Internet should be free of censorship? Why, or why not?

PROJECTS

1. Compile a list of files and databases that hold data about you. Start with your school. What files are maintained on students? Then check your wallet; your driver's license, credit cards, Social Security card, club membership cards, and other documents probably all signify an entry in a database somewhere. You might be surprised at the length of the list.
2. Check with your instructor or your school's network manager and find out how (or if) your e-mail messages can be accessed by someone other than you or the addressee. Disregard procedures, guidelines, and rules prohibiting such access. Instead, ask if such access is *physically* possible.
3. Do some research into privacy issues as they relate to public databases. For example, what rights do you have to control or review your own credit history data?

S P O T L I G H T

219

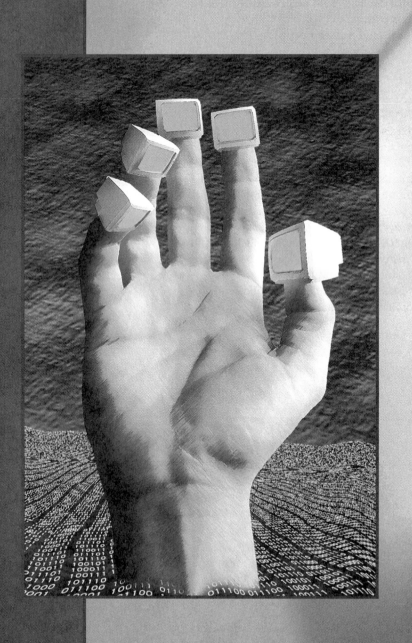

CHAPTER 10

Databases

Before you start this chapter, you should be familiar with the following concepts:

- ▶ Data and information (p. 4).
- ▶ Computers (p. 6), the user (p. 6), and inside the computer (p. 7).
- ▶ Software (p. 9), data (p. 10), and long-term storage (p. 12).
- ▶ Classifying computers (p. 14).

When you finish reading this chapter, you should be able to:

- ▶ Define the terms *data redundancy* and *data dependency* and explain why they are problems.
- ▶ Define the terms *entity, occurrence, attribute, key,* and *relationship.*
- ▶ Explain the purpose of a data dictionary, entity-relationship models, and data normalization.
- ▶ Explain what a database management system does.

- ▶ Distinguish between physical and logical records in a database.
- ▶ Distinguish between schema and subschema.
- ▶ Distinguish among the flat-file, hierarchical, network, and relational database models.
- ▶ Identify the root, parent, and child records in a hierarchical database. Identify the owner and member records in a network database.
- ▶ Relate the terms *relation, tuple, attribute,* and *domain* to traditional fields, records, and files.
- ▶ Define the relational operators: join, select, and project.
- ▶ Briefly discuss object-oriented databases.
- ▶ Distinguish among a data definition language, a data manipulation language, and a data control language.

TRADITIONAL DATA MANAGEMENT

Payroll was one of the very first computerized business applications. Running payroll on a computer significantly reduced the need for payroll clerks, making the application easy to cost justify.

Once payroll was installed, other applications soon followed. Running a billing program was less expensive than hiring billing clerks, so a billing application was developed. Tracking inventory by computer was cheaper than hiring inventory clerks, so an inventory application was installed. Maintaining accounting records on a computer was more efficient than keeping books by hand, so general ledger, accounts receivable, and accounts payable systems soon followed.

Note that each of those applications evolved independently. Payroll, billing, inventory, and accounting were (and still are) separate departments, so the organizational structure supported independent applications. Additionally, the early computers did not have the memory or the computing power to implement integrated applications. Thus, the payroll program accessed a set of payroll files, the billing program accessed a set of billing files, and so on (Figure 10.1), and all those files were independent.

Data Redundancy

The problem with independent files is that the data are not really independent. For example, customers purchase products from sales associates. Consequently, you would expect to find the customer's name and address both in the customer file and on one or more sales orders (Figure 10.2). Similarly, sales associate data are found in both the sales order file and the employee file, and product data are common to both the sales order file and the product file.

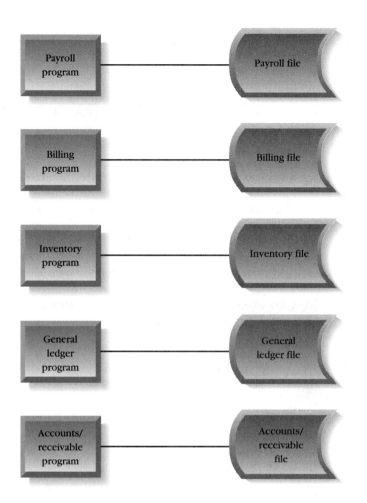

▲ FIGURE 10.1

Traditionally, each application has its own independent data files.

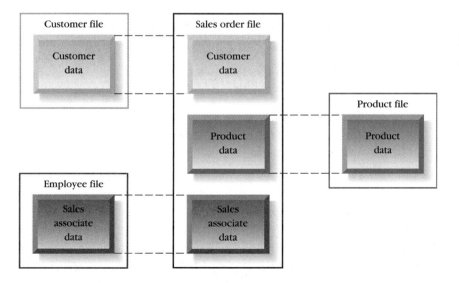

▲ FIGURE 10.2

The data are not really independent.

The Year 2000

Many business organizations "age" their customer accounts. A customer whose account is 30 days overdue might be sent a reminder. Customers who fall 60 days behind might be issued a warning. If an account is 90 days in arrears, the customer's credit might be terminated.

A billing program ages an account by comparing the purchase date to the billing date. If the difference is less than 30 days, the account is current; if the difference falls between 30 and 60 days, you have a 30-day account, and so on. Billing is not the only program that relies on comparing dates; similar logic is found in numerous applications.

As the year 2000 approaches, that is a source of concern. In an effort to save disk space, many systems were designed to save a two-digit year; for example, 97 instead of 1997. For years that shortcut has worked well—12/31/96 clearly comes before 1/1/97. What happens on January 1, 2000, however? Is 1/1/00 one day greater than or 100 years less than 12/31/99?

You know the correct answer to that question, but to a program written to process two-digit years, 00 is clearly less than 99. In other words, on January 1, 2000, any program written to compare two-digit years will no longer work correctly. Fixing all those programs will keep quite a few programmers busy.

Redundant
Stored repetitively in two or more places.

When the same data appear in two or more different files, those data are **redundant,** and redundant data are difficult to maintain. If a customer's address is stored in the customer file and the sales order file, and the customer moves, the contents of *both* files must be changed. If the data are corrected in one file but not the other, then the two files will list different addresses for the same customer, and one of those addresses will be wrong.

Data Dependency

Data dependency
The state of a program whose logic is so tightly linked to the data that changing the structure of the data will almost certainly require changing the program.

Data dependency is a more subtle problem. A programmer can make a given program run more efficiently by custom-designing the software to fit the data. When that happens, the program's logic becomes linked to the data, and changing the structure of the data will almost certainly require changing the program. As a result, programs that use traditional, independent files can be difficult to maintain.

THE DATABASE APPROACH

The solution to both the data redundancy and data dependency problems is organizing the data as a single, integrated database.

Entities, Occurrences, and Attributes

As you learned in Chapter 1, a database is a set of related files. There are a few key terms you should know before you begin investigating databases, however.

An **entity** is a person, place, activity, or thing about which data are stored. For example, a business collects data about customers, sales associates, sales orders, the products in inventory, and so on. An **occurrence** of an entity is a single instance of that entity; for example, you are an occurrence of the entity *student* and your instructor is an occurrence of the entity *faculty member*.

An **attribute** is a single fact that describes, qualifies, or is otherwise associated with an entity. For example, each student has a name, a street (or dormitory) address, a city, a state, a zip code, and so on.

Attributes are sometimes called **data elements** because they are the smallest units of data that have logical meaning. J, O, and N are just characters; they mean nothing until they are combined with other characters. JONES, in contrast, is someone's last name. The number 2 is just a digit, but 404/555-1212 is a telephone number.

Attributes are generally stored as fields. A set of related attributes (or fields) comprises a single occurrence of the entity and is usually stored as a record. A file is a set of occurrences of the same entity, so each file holds data for one and only one entity. A database is a set of related files.

Keys and Relationships

Figure 10.3 pictures a portion of a customer sales order screen. As part of the sales process, there are at least four entities about which data are collected: the customer, the sales associate, the products to be purchased, and the sales

Entity
A person, place, activity, or thing about which data are stored.
Occurrence
A single instance of an entity.

Attribute
A single fact that describes, qualifies, or is otherwise associated with an entity.

Data element
The smallest unit of data that has logical meaning. A unit of data that cannot be logically subdivided.

▲ **FIGURE 10.3**

A sales order screen.

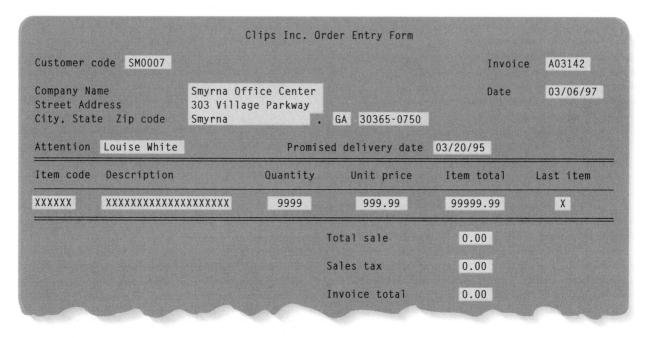

order itself (Figure 10.4). Each entity is described by certain attributes; for example, each customer has a customer code, a name, an address, a telephone number, and so on. A complete set of attributes for a single occurrence of the entity (a single customer, for example) forms a record.

To allow the system to distinguish the records, one (or more) of the attributes serves as a **key** that uniquely identifies a single occurrence of the entity (a single record). For example, a customer might be identified by a customer code, an employee might be identified by a Social Security number, and so on. Note that no two customers can have the same customer code and no two employees can have the same employee code; in other words, the key must *uniquely* identify a single occurrence of the entity. The key fields are highlighted in Figure 10.4.

Files are often indexed by key. The **index** holds one entry for each record in the file. A given record's index entry might consist of the record's key and information that tells the system where the record is physically stored. Once a file is indexed, it is possible to access the individual records by referencing their keys.

Given a set of indexed files, you can define **relationships,** or links, between the files that reflect how the entities interact. The relationships between files are usually defined by storing the key for one file in the other file. For example, a sales order record might include a customer code (the key to the customer file), an employee code (the key to the employee file), and a product code (the key to the product file).

Given those relationships, a billing program could read a sales invoice and then get the necessary customer data from the customer file, the employee data from the employee file, and the product data from the product file (Figure 10.5). That set of related files forms a database.

Key
A field that uniquely defines a single occurrence of an entity.

Index
A list of the keys and locations of each record in a file.

Relationship
A logical link between two files.

▲ FIGURE 10.4

The sales invoice holds data about the customer, the sales associate, the products purchased, and the sales order. The key fields are highlighted.

CUSTOMER	SALES ASSOCIATE
customer code	*employee code*
customer name	name
address	address
telephone	home telephone
	salary
	date of hire

PRODUCT	SALES ORDER
product code	*invoice number*
product description	invoice date
unit selling price	customer code
stock on hand	total sale
reorder point	

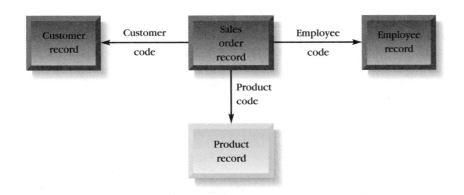

▲ **FIGURE 10.5**

A set of related files forms a database.

Planning a Database

The task of planning a database is part of the systems development process, the subject of Chapter 15.

THE DATA DICTIONARY

The first step in planning a database is to identify the entities about which data will be stored. Next, you list the attributes and select a key field for each of those entities.

The attributes and the keys are documented in the **data dictionary** (Figure 10.6), a collection of data about the system's data. The idea is to name and rigorously define each and every data element. Often, the process of defining the data reveals redundant, inconsistent, and even superfluous data elements.

Data dictionary
A collection of data about a system's data.

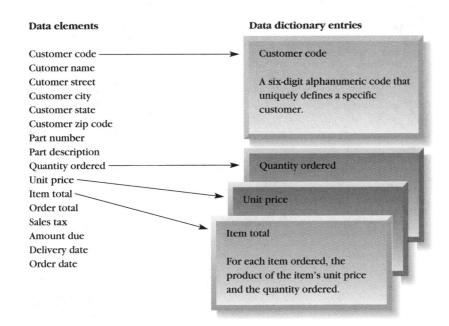

▲ **FIGURE 10.6**

The data are documented in the data dictionary.

ENTITY-RELATIONSHIP DIAGRAMS

The data entities are linked by relationships that can usually be stated as short sentences (Figure 10.7); for example, the *customer* (one entity) *places* (the relationship) a *customer order* (another entity). One way to visualize the relationships between entities is to prepare an **entity-relationship diagram,** a data model that shows visually how the data are related (Figure 10.8).

Entity-relationship diagram
A logical model of the relationships between the system's primary data entities.

▲ FIGURE 10.7

Relationships can be stated in the form of short sentences.

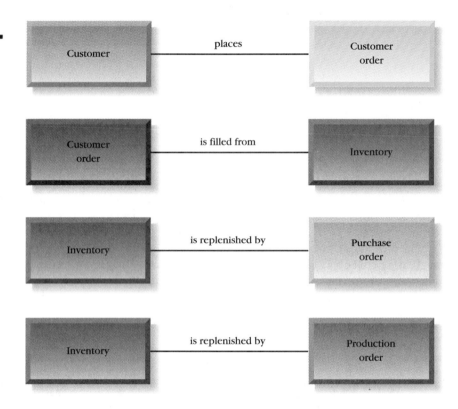

▲ FIGURE 10.8

An entity-relationship diagram.

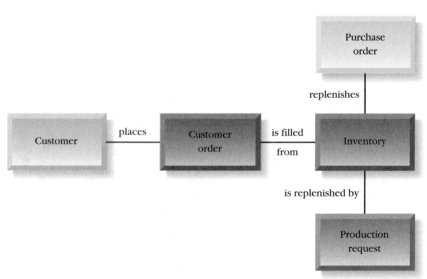

Cardinality

The strength and stability of the relationship between two data entities is a function of cardinality, a measure of their relative numbers of occurrences. For example, consider an examination. Each student submits one answer sheet and each answer sheet is associated with one student, so the relationship between students and answer sheets is one-to-one. At the end of the term, each student has several exams, but each discrete exam is associated with only one student, so the relationship between students and exams is one-to-many. You might be enrolled in several courses, and each of those courses enrolls numerous students, so the relationship between students and courses is many-to-many.

For a variety of reasons, one-to-many relationships tend to be the most stable and the easiest to maintain, so analysts often prepare an entity-relationship model to help them document the cardinality of each relationship and to test alternative ways of converting one-to-one and many-to-many relationships into one-to-many relationships. Should you ever take a formal course in data management, you will learn how to prepare entity-relationship models.

DATA NORMALIZATION

Data normalization is a formal technique for organizing entities and attributes into efficient, easy to maintain fields, records, and files. The idea is to make sure that each attribute in a file is a function of the file's key. Attributes that depend on some other key or on only part of the key are moved to another file, and a relationship is established between the two files.

Data normalization
A formal technique for organizing entities and attributes into efficient, easy to maintain fields, records, and files.

THE DATABASE MANAGEMENT SYSTEM

The **database management system,** or **DBMS,** is a set of software routines that define the rules for creating, accessing, and maintaining a database. The idea is to create one file for each entity and then specify the relationships that link those files.

Once the database and its relationships are defined, there is little need for redundant data. For example, any application that requires customer data can use the customer code to access the customer file. Consequently, the customer's name and address are stored only in the customer file, and if a customer moves, the address must be changed only once because there is only one copy. (Granted, selected keys, such as the customer code, might be stored redundantly in several different files, but that is much better than duplicating the entire record.)

Application programs access the database through the database management system (Figure 10.9). Since the responsibility for physically accessing the data rests with the database management system, the programmer can ignore the physical details of how the data are stored. As a result, programs tend to be much less dependent on their data, and that makes them much easier to maintain.

Database management system (DBMS)
A system software routine that defines the rules for accessing the database.

▲ FIGURE 10.9

Application programs access the database through the database management system.

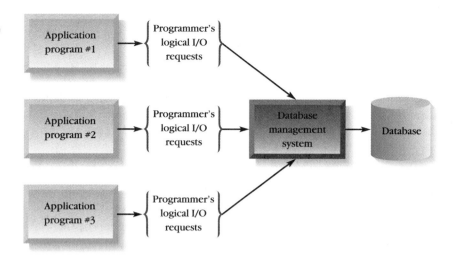

Physical and Logical Records

Picture a billing program. To prepare each customer's bill, the program needs such data as the customer's name and address, the sales date, the order number, and the unit price and quantity for each item purchased. The program will accept a set of data for the first customer, do any necessary processing, output the bill, and then accept the data for the next customer.

The problem is that the data are physically stored on several different files. The name and address are on the customer file. The sales date, the order number, and a list of items purchased are on the sales order file. The unit price is on the product file.

Physical record
The set of related fields that are physically stored together in the same file.
Logical record
The set of related fields needed to complete one input, process, output cycle of a program.

The set of related fields that are physically stored together form a **physical record.** The set of related fields needed to complete one input/process/output cycle of a program is called a **logical record.** The physical record reflects the way the data are actually stored. The logical record reflects the user's view of the data.

Fortunately, users and application programmers can ignore the difference between physical and logical records because the database management system takes care of those details. When the application program requests a logical record (Figure 10.10a), the database management system reads the necessary physical records (Figure 10.10b), creates the logical record by assembling the requested data (Figure 10.10c), and then returns the logical record to the application program (Figure 10.10d). The process is transparent. As far as the application program is concerned, it asked for a logical record and received the requested data.

Schemas and Subschemas

Schema
A general description of the entire database that shows all the record types and their relationships.

If the database management system is to bridge the gap between physical and logical records, it must know exactly what the database contains. The database contents are defined in a **schema,** a general description of the entire database that shows all the record types and their relationships.

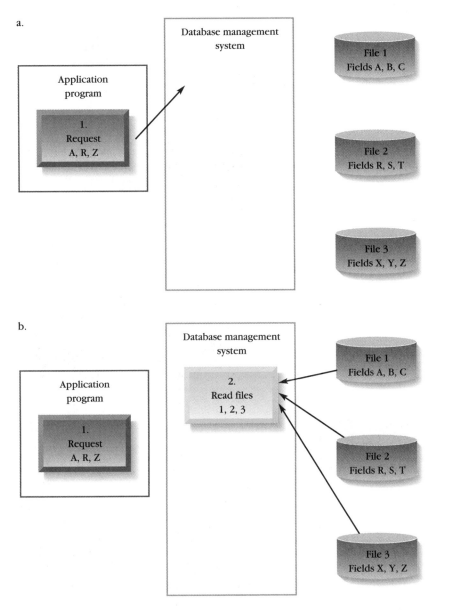

a.

b.

▲ FIGURE 10.10

Reading a logical database record.
a. **The application program requests a logical record.**
b. **The database management system reads the physical records.**

A large mainframe database might link scores of files, but most users will access only a few of those files. To minimize the risk of a user accidentally accessing confidential data or changing data in an unneeded file, custom **subschemas** that include only those records and relationships needed by a particular user or class of users can be defined.

Maintaining Database Integrity

To ensure **data integrity,** access to the data must be carefully controlled and managed from the time they first enter the system until they are of no further use. In other words, the data must come from an approved source and only sanctioned changes are permitted.

Subschema
A partial schema that includes only those records and relationships needed by a particular user or class of users.

Data integrity
The state of a database that is protected against loss or contamination.

▲ FIGURE 10.10 (continued)

c. **The database management system creates the logical record.**
d. **The logical record is returned to the application program.**

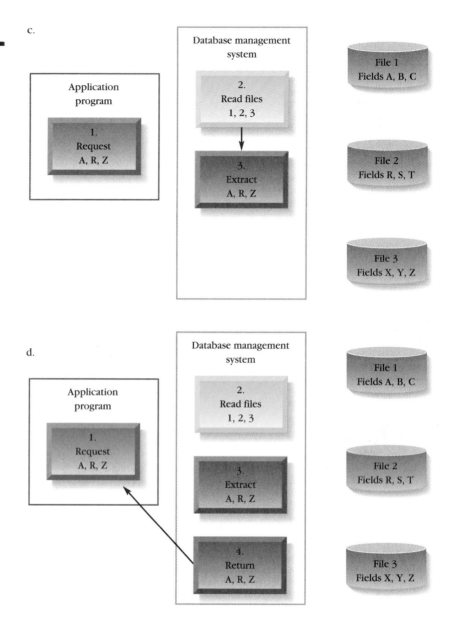

Maintaining data integrity is particularly difficult when several files are linked and a record on one of those files is updated or deleted. For example, if a student drops out of school and that student's record is deleted from the database, all references to that student must be deleted from all other files or they will point to a nonexistent record. Note, however, that it is much easier to correct such inconsistencies on a database than in traditional files.

DATABASE MODELS

There are several different types of databases, including:

- ► flat-file
- ► hierarchical
- ► network
- ► relational
- ► object-oriented

Flat-File Databases

The simplest model (technically, not a database) is called a **flat-file database.** All the data in a flat-file database are stored in a single, spreadsheet-like table that is not linked with any other files. The advantage is simplicity. Although flat files share most of the disadvantages of traditional independent files, they are fine for many personal computer applications.

Flat-file database
A single, spreadsheet-like table that is not linked with any other files.

Hierarchical Databases

In a **hierarchical database,** the files are linked to form a hierarchy (Figure 10.11). Database access starts at the top of the hierarchy and flows downward, so, in this example, it is possible to access a customer record by starting from a sales order, but not vice versa.

Hierarchical database
A database in which the files are linked to form a hierarchy.

ROOT, PARENT, AND CHILD RECORDS

The top record in a hierarchical database is called the **root record.** Database access flows from the top down, from a **parent** record to a **child** record. In Figure 10.11, the sales order record (the root) is the parent and the customer, product, and employee records are its children. Note that the relationship runs from the parent record to the child record, and that a child can have only one parent.

Root record
The top record in a hierarchical database.
Parent
A high-level record in a hierarchical database.
Child
A lower-level record in a hierarchical database.

Network Databases

The relationships between files can flow in any direction in a **network database** (Figure 10.12). For example, if each sales order holds the customer code for the associated customer record and each customer record contains

Network database
A database in which links or pointers can be defined to describe relationships between any two files in any direction.

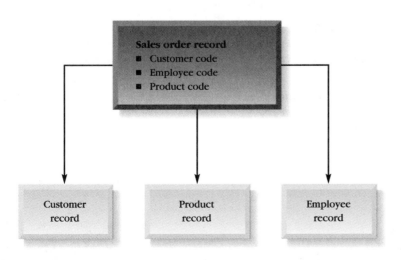

▲ **FIGURE 10.11**

A hierarchical database.

the invoice number or numbers for all that customer's active sales orders, a complete set of data for a given sales order can be prepared starting with *either* file.

OWNERS AND MEMBERS

Owner
A parent record in a network database.
Member
A child record in a network database.

In a network database, a parent record is called an **owner** and a child record is called a **member;** in other words, the relationship runs from the owner to the member. Note, however, that relationships can run in both directions, so a single record can be both an owner and a member. Note also that a member can have more than one owner and an owner can have more than one member.

For example, consider the sales order record in Figure 10.12. It is an owner, and because it has relationships that point to the customer, product, and employee records, they are all its members. Shift to the customer record. The relationship that flows from it to the sales order means that the customer is the owner and the sales order is the member. Note also that the sales order has three owners: the customer, product, and employee.

Relational Databases

Relational database
A database in which the files can be visualized as two-dimensional tables or spreadsheets.

The files that form a **relational database** (Figure 10.13) can be visualized as spreadsheet-like, two-dimensional tables (flat-files), with each row holding a single record and each column holding values of a single field. For example, the first row in a customer file might hold values for the first customer's name, address, and other attributes, while the second row holds values of the same fields for the second customer, and so on.

A relational database's files are linked by inserting a common attribute in both of them. For example, if the customer code is stored as one field in the sales order file, that key value can be used to find the appropriate customer's data in the customer file (Figure 10.13).

Using today's technology, a hierarchical or network database can access data more quickly than an equivalent relational database. The hierarchical and network models require less storage space, too, so they tend to dominate mainframe environments. Relational databases are easier to use, however, and efficiency is less vital on a microcomputer, so the relational model has emerged as the de facto microcomputer standard.

▲ FIGURE 10.12

A network database.

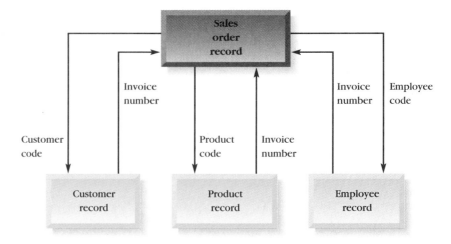

Sales order file

Invoice number	Invoice date	Customer code		
0001				
0002		Customer B		
0003				
0004		Customer F		
0005				
0006				
.				
.				
.				

Customer file

Customer code	Customer name	Customer street		
A				
B				
C				
D				
E				
F				
.				
.				
.				

▲ **FIGURE 10.13**

A relational database can be visualized as a set of two-dimensional tables.

RELATIONS, TUPLES, ATTRIBUTES, AND DOMAINS

The ideas that underlie the relational database model are derived from mathematical set theory. The data are organized to form tables called **relations.** Each row in a table is called a **tuple,** and each cell (each column) holds a single attribute. In more traditional terminology, relations are files, tuples are records, and attributes are fields. A **domain** is the range of values that can be assigned to a given attribute.

RELATIONAL OPERATORS

The data in a relational database are accessed by using three basic relational operators: join, select, and project. **Join** merges or combines data from two or more relations (tables, or files). **Select** extracts specific tuples (rows, or records) from a relation. **Project** extracts the requested attributes from the selected tuples.

For example, assume you need a list of the professors who teach the courses being taken by the players on the basketball team. You might start by selecting the players' records from the student file. The next step is to join the selected student records with the appropriate course records from the course file and professor records from the professor file. Finally, you project

Relation
A table (analogous to a file) in a relational database.
Tuple
One row in a relational database table (or relation). Analogous to a record.
Domain
The range of values that can be assigned to a given attribute.

Join
To merge or combine data from two or more relations (tables or files).
Select
To extract specific tuples (rows, or records) from a relation.
Project
To extract the requested attributes from a set of selected tuples.

the student names, course names, professor names, and other relevant attributes to create the desired list.

Object-Oriented Databases

Object
A thing about which data are stored and manipulated.
Method
A procedure associated with an object.
Object-oriented database
A database of objects.

An **object** is a thing about which data are stored and manipulated. Objects contain both data and processes, called **methods,** that access the data (Figure 10.14). The data define the object's state. The methods define its behavior. As the name implies, an **object-oriented database** holds objects and defines the links or relationships between them.

DATABASE SOFTWARE

You can purchase many different software packages to create, maintain, and access a database. Access, Paradox, dBase, Filemaker Pro, Approach, 4th Dimension, and Alpha Four are popular microcomputer database programs. Examples of mainframe database software include DB2, IDMS, and ORACLE.

The Data Definition Language

Data Definition Language (DDL)
A database language that is used to specify file structures, relationships, schema, and subschema.

Most database management systems include a **data definition language (DDL)** for specifying file structures, relationships, schemas, and subschemas. For example, Figure 10.15 shows a Microsoft Access screen that defines the structure of a customer file.

The Data Manipulation Language

Data Manipulation Language (DML)
A database language that is used to access and maintain the database.

Once the database is created, its contents are accessed and maintained using a **data manipulation language (DML).** Typically, authorized users can

PEOPLE

C. Wayne Ratliff

The original version of Borland's dBASE software, dBASE II, was written in the early 1980s by C. Wayne Ratliff. He learned to program as an employee of Martin Marietta Corporation where, as a member of NASA's Viking Flight Team, he wrote a data management system called MFILE. In 1976, the Viking spacecraft landed on Mars, making Ratliff one of the few programmers who can claim interplanetary distribution of his software.

In the late 1970s, Ratliff wrote a database program called Vulcan because he wanted to analyze some statistics to improve his chances of winning a football pool. He saw the commercial possibilities of his program and tried to market it himself for a few years. Finally, in 1980 he signed a marketing agreement with Ashton-Tate, renamed the program dBASE II, and joined Ashton-Tate as their vice president for new technology. Database software has improved dramatically since dBASE II, but you can still find Ratliff's influence in today's best-selling products.

▲ **FIGURE 10.14**

An object contains both data and methods.

issue DML commands to update a database by inserting, deleting, or replacing records. The contents of a database can be displayed as individual records or in table form (Figure 10.16). The user can control the order in which the data are displayed by sorting or indexing the records on a key field.

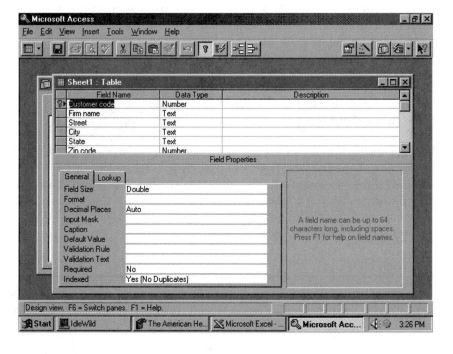

▲ **FIGURE 10.15**

This screen defines the structure of the customer file.

▲ FIGURE 10.16

A data list in table form.

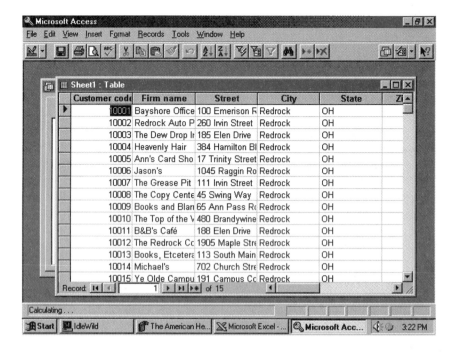

Query language
A language for specifying queries.

Structured Query Language (SQL)
A data manipulation language that is common to many database management systems.

View
A subset of a database that includes only selected fields from the records that meet a set of conditions defined in a logical filter.

Filter
A set of logical conditions defined in a database query.

Query-by-example (QBE)
A common database feature that allows a user to define a query by, essentially, outlining an example of the desired output.

Report writer
A common database feature that allows a user to quickly generate a report by specifying the contents.

Data Control Language (DCL)
A database tool used to perform such activities as backing up files, keeping track of user names and passwords, and monitoring system performance.

Most database management systems incorporate a **query language** that makes it easy for even nontechnical personnel to access the data. **Structured Query Language,** or **SQL** (pronounced sequel), is a standard query language that is common to many database management systems.

A query defines a **view** (or subset) of the database that includes only selected fields from the records that meet a set of conditions defined in a logical **filter.** For example, it is possible to define a query that displays only the names and telephone numbers of the students currently taking Professor Smith's sections of CIS 101. Many query languages support a **query-by-example (QBE)** facility that allows a user to define a query by, essentially, laying out an example on the screen.

Report writers are another common data manipulation language feature. As the name implies, a report writer allows a user to lay out the contents of a printed (or displayed report) by listing the fields to be included, specifying filters to select the records to be included, and defining the appropriate summary fields.

The Data Control Language

The database system manager uses the **data control language (DCL)** to perform such activities as backing up files, keeping track of user names and passwords, and monitoring system performance.

SUMMARY

In the early days of electronic computing, each application had its own independent files. That led to data redundancy and data dependency. The solution to both problems was to create a database.

An entity is a person, place, activity, or thing about which data are stored. An occurrence of an entity is a single instance of that entity. An attribute, or data element is a single fact that describes, qualifies, or is otherwise associated with an entity. Each record has a key that uniquely identifies a single occurrence of the entity. Files are often indexed by key. Given a set of indexed files, you can define relationships, or links, between the files that reflect how the entities interact.

Planning a database is part of the systems development process. The data dictionary is a collection of data about the data. An entity-relationship diagram is a model that shows visually how the data are related. The strength and stability of the relationship between the data entities is a function of cardinality. Data normalization is a formal technique for organizing entities and attributes into efficient, easy to maintain fields, records, and files.

The database management system, or DBMS, is a set of software routines that define the rules for creating, accessing and maintaining a database. The set of related fields that are physically stored together form a physical record. The set of related fields needed to complete one input/process/output cycle of a program is called a logical record. The database contents are defined in an overall schema and one or more subschema that include only those records and relationships needed by a particular user. Maintaining data integrity is difficult when several files are linked and a record on one of those files is updated or deleted.

All the data in a flat-file database are stored in a single table that is not linked with any other files. In a hierarchical database, the files are linked to form a hierarchy. The top record in a hierarchical database is called the root record. Database access flows from the top down, from a parent record to a child record. The relationships between files go in any direction in a network database. In a network database, a parent record is called an owner and a child record is called a member.

The files that form a relational database can be visualized as spreadsheet-like, two-dimensional tables. In a relational database, the data are organized to form tables (files) called relations. Each row (record) is called a tuple, and each cell holds a single attribute (or field). A domain is the range of values that can be assigned to a given attribute. The data in a relational database are accessed using three basic relational operators: join, select, and project.

An object is a thing about which data are stored and manipulated. Objects contain both data and methods. An object-oriented database holds objects.

Most database management systems include a data definition language (DDL) for specifying file structures, relationships, schemas, and subschemas. Once the database is created, its contents are accessed and maintained using a data manipulation language (DML) that might include a query language. Many database management systems support a common data manipulation language called Structured Query Language (SQL).

A query defines a view (or subset) of the database that includes only selected fields from the records that meet a set of conditions defined in a logical filter. Many query languages support a query-by-example (QBE) facility that allows a user to define a query by laying out an example on the screen. Report writers are another data manipulation language feature.

The database system manager uses the data control language (DCL) to monitor and control the system.

KEY TERMS

attribute
child
data control language (DCL)
data definition language (DDL)
data dependency
data dictionary
data element
data integrity
data manipulation language (DML)
data normalization
data redundancy
database management system (DBMS)
domain
entity

entity-relationship diagram
filter
flat-file database
hierarchical database
index
join
key
logical record
member
method
network database
object
object-oriented database
occurrence
owner
parent

physical record
project
query-by-example (QBE)
query language
redundant
relation
relational database
relationship
report writer
root record
schema
select
Structured Query Language (SQL)
subschema
tuple
view

CONCEPTS

1. What is data redundancy? Why is data redundancy a problem?
2. What is data dependency? Why is data dependency a problem?
3. Relate the terms *entity, occurrence,* and *attribute* to traditional fields, records, and files.
4. What is a record's key? What is a relationship? How are keys and relationships related?
5. Briefly explain how a data dictionary, entity-relationship models, and data normalization are used to help plan a database.
6. Explain how a database management system converts physical records to logical records. Why is that conversion necessary?
7. What is a schema? What is a subschema?
8. What is a flat-file?
9. Briefly describe the structure of a hierarchical database. Define the terms *root, parent,* and *child* in a hierarchical database.
10. Briefly describe the structure of a network database. How do you distinguish between an owner record and a member record in a network database?
11. Briefly describe the structure of a relational database. Relate the terms *relation, tuple, attribute,* and *domain* to traditional fields, records, and files.
12. Define the relational operators: join, select, and project.
13. What is an object-oriented database?
14. Identify several database software packages.
15. What is a data definition language? What is a data manipulation language? What is a query? What is query-by-example? What is a report writer?
16. What is a data control language? The use of a data control language is often restricted to the database system manager. Why?

PROJECT

1. Identify several files and databases maintained by your school that you know hold data about you. Request copies of your data. See if you can find any errors. You may find it difficult to obtain copies of some of your data. Is there any relationship between the form in which the data are stored (flat-file, database) and your ability to access the data?

INTERNET PROJECTS

1. *News and Notes.* Companies often post information about their very latest products on their World Wide Web home pages. Select a company such as Microsoft, IBM, Oracle, or Corel that markets database management software and access its home page. Try the address *http://www.xxx.com;* substitute the company name (for example, *microsoft*) for *xxx.* Once you find the home page, look for a button marked *Database products* (or something similar) and click on it. Identify and briefly describe at least two new products and submit your findings to your instructor in the form of a brief note or an e-mail message.

2. *Topic Searches.* Check the World Wide Web and/or other Internet resources for information on the following topics:

Key word	*Qualifiers*
software failure	2000
object-oriented database	application
Project Gutenberg	

Define the key word, identify at least two sources of information on the topic, and briefly summarize the nature of the information you find.

3. *Links to Other Sites.* After you access one or more of the following sites, write a brief note or send an e-mail message to your instructor outlining what you find.

   a. On the World Wide Web, check *http://www.ibm.com* for information on IBM products.

   b. On the World Wide Web, check *http://www.microsoft.com* for information on Microsoft products.

   c. On the World Wide Web, check *http://www.oracle.com* for information on Oracle products.

   d. On the World Wide Web, check *http://www.corel.com* for information on Corel products.

4. Access West Publishing Company's home page and find the Chapter 10 student activities for this book. See Internet Project 3 for the spotlight on *The Internet* following Chapter 1 (page 29) for more detailed instructions on accessing the home page. As appropriate, repeat projects 1, 2, and/or 3 using the more current references you find.

PART III

SYSTEMS

The chapters in this section show you how the components from Part II are assembled to form information systems. The chapters can be read in any order, but each chapter assumes that you have completed certain Part II chapters. Check the "before you begin" feature at the start of each chapter to be sure you have the appropriate background.

The *Spotlight* following Chapter 14 covers "Internet Technology." Social issues and ethics are examined in the *Spotlight* entitled "Computer Crime and System Security" following Chapter 15.

CHAPTER 11

Architectures

Before you start this chapter, you should be familiar with the following concepts:

▶ Computers (p. 6), hardware (p. 6), peripherals (p. 6), inside the computer (p. 7), and data (p. 10).

▶ Systems (p. 13) and computer classifications (p. 13).

▶ Main memory (p. 78), bits, bytes, and words (p. 78), and addressing memory (p. 82).

▶ How the processor works (p. 86), instructions (p. 86), machine cycles (p. 87), processor speed (p. 88), and processor hardware (p. 93).

When you finish reading this chapter, you should be able to:

▶ Explain how a computer's internal components are physically linked.

▶ Discuss the relationship between word size and architecture. Explain how processing speed, memory capacity, and precision are related to word size.

▶ Describe a single-bus architecture.

▶ Explain the relationship between the motherboard, expansion slots, and interface boards.

▶ Explain the purpose of a buffer and define the term *port*.

▶ Outline the process of loading and executing a program on a single-bus computer.

▶ Distinguish between single-bus and multiple-bus architectures.

▶ Explain how channels and I/O control units manage input and output operations on a multiple-bus computer.

▶ Define multiprocessing. Distinguish between symmetrical and asymmetrical multiprocessing.

▶ Briefly describe a fault-tolerant computer.

THE HARDWARE COMPONENTS

In this chapter, you will investigate how a computer's hardware components are assembled and linked electronically.

Chips and Boards

As you learned in Chapter 1, the basic building blocks of modern computers are tiny integrated circuit chips (Figure 11.1). To make the chips easier to handle they are usually mounted on boards (Figure 11.2), and the boards are then linked electronically to form the computer.

Inside a Computer

You can actually see the boards if you remove a microcomputer's cover (Figure 11.3). If you look closely (perhaps with a little help) you should be able to find the processor, the memory boards, the disk drives, and other boards that serve to connect peripheral devices to the system.

The Power Supply

Power supply
A device that conditions the power and feeds the appropriate voltage to a computer.

You should be able to see the **power supply,** too; it's a heavy metal box. A modern microcomputer consumes only about as much electrical power as a light bulb. The current that comes from your wall socket is enough to burn out all the chips on your computer's integrated circuit boards, so the power supply's job is to condition the power and feed the appropriate voltage to the computer. It works much like a transformer on an electric train, stepping down the voltage to a safe level.

▲ **FIGURE 11.1**

Integrated circuit chips.

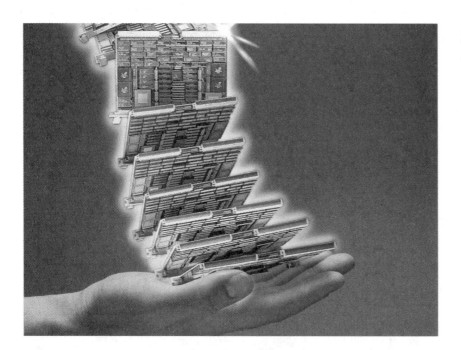

▲ FIGURE 11.2

A board.

Portable and laptop computers get their power from a wall outlet or from a battery pack. The batteries are rechargeable and hold enough power to keep the computer running for several hours.

▲ FIGURE 11.3

Inside a microcomputer.

PEOPLE

The Microcomputer Revolution

The November 15, 1971 issue of *Electronic News* featured a "computer on a chip," Intel's 4004, the very first microprocessor. The brainchild of Ted Hoff, the 4004 was followed (in 1974) by a more powerful microprocessor, the 8080.

Initially, Intel's microprocessors were used in such products as calculators and digital watches, but that was about to change. The January 1975 issue of *Popular Electronics* featured a cover photograph of a computer called the Altair 8800 that was created around an Intel 8080 chip by a hacker named Ed Roberts. Unlike the expensive mainframes that dominated the middle 1970s, the Altair 8800 was a true personal computer that sold (in kit form) for a mere $397! It would change forever the popular image of computers.

A few years later (1976), two young men named Steven Jobs and Steve Wozniak raised

$1,300 by selling an old car and a programmable calculator, bought some electronic equipment, and built a microcomputer they christened the Apple I. A more sophisticated version, the Apple II, reached the market in 1977. The revolution had begun.

Serial and Parallel Lines

Data, instructions, and control signals flow between a computer's hardware components in response to instructions executed by the processor. Internal components and high-speed peripherals are linked to the system by **parallel** lines; look for a ribbon-like set of wires or a wide plug (Figure 11.4). Slower peripherals are connected to the system by **serial** lines.

A serial line transmits one bit at a time. A parallel line, in contrast, transmits several bits at a time, in parallel. That makes parallel lines faster.

Parallel
Transmitting two or more bits simultaneously.
Serial
One at a time.

LINKING THE COMPONENTS

A computer system's **architecture** defines how its components are physically linked and how they communicate with each other.

Architecture
A description of how a computer's components are physically linked and how they communicate with each other.

▲ **FIGURE 11.4**

A parallel line transmits several bits at a time. A serial line transmits one bit at a time.

Open and Closed Architectures

An **open architecture** is a published, widely available computer design. The fact that the architecture is publicly available makes it possible for firms other than the original manufacturer to make compatible boards, peripherals, and even copies (called clones) of the computer. Additionally, a user can easily customize an open architecture computer by adding boards.

A **closed architecture,** in contrast, is a proprietary computer design that is not published or widely available. It is difficult for companies other than the original manufacturer to make products that are compatible with a closed architecture computer, and users find it difficult to customize such machines.

The original IBM PC had an open architecture, while early Macintosh computers were closed. A flood of PC-compatible products had a great deal to do with the early success of IBM's microcomputers, but the aggressive marketing of clones from such companies as Compaq negatively affected IBM's sales. On the other hand, many experts believe that Apple's decision to keep the Macintosh architecture closed meant fewer Mac-compatible products (particularly software) were developed and that, in turn, limited the Mac's market share.

Open architecture
A published, widely available computer design for which firms other than the original manufacturer can make compatible boards, peripherals, and even copies (called clones) of the computer.
Closed architecture
A proprietary computer design that is not published or widely available.

Buses

On most computers, the *internal* components are linked by high-speed parallel lines called **buses.** Binary data, instructions, and control signals move between the processor and memory over a bus. Input data are transferred from a peripheral device to the bus and from there into memory. Output data move from memory to the bus and then to the output device.

Bus
A set of electrical lines that link the computer's internal components.

Miniaturization

The very first computers were big enough to fill a room. Over the years, however, advances in integrated circuit technology and computer architecture have combined to shrink the size of these machines until today's (considerably more powerful) laptops are small enough to fit in a briefcase.

Clearly, modern computers are much more convenient and easier to use than their predecessors, but there are reasons for miniaturization that go beyond the obvious. One is reliability. Electrical devices are most likely to fail at the junction points where components are physically connected to each other. As circuit density (the number of transistors packed on a chip) has increased, computer engineers have been able to merge formerly autonomous components onto a single chip. That, in turn, has reduced the number of connections and improved reliability.

Speed is another reason for miniaturization. Electricity moves at the speed of light. Light travels roughly one foot per nanosecond (one billionth of a second), so each foot of wire is a built-in one nanosecond delay. Consequently, if you reduce the distance the electricity must travel, you increase the computer's processing speed.

For example, most computers are shaped like a rectangular box, but supercomputers (which are designed for speed) resemble cylinders. Why? Because the diameter of a cylinder is less than the diagonal distance across a rectangular box of equal volume. If you reduce the distance between components, you reduce the length of the wires that link them, and that means faster processing.

The limit to the linear distance versus volume ratio is a sphere. Perhaps future supercomputers will look like basketballs.

A data bus carries data and program instructions. A command bus carries control signals. On some computers, the data bus and the control bus are physically separate. On other machines, the same bus carries both data and control signals.

Word Size

On most computers, the processor, main memory, the bus, and the peripheral devices are all designed around a common word size. (A word is a unit of memory that consists of one or more bytes.) On a 32-bit computer, the processor manipulates 32-bit numbers, memory stores 32-bit words, and data and instructions move between components over a 32-bit bus. On a 16-bit computer the processor manipulates 16-bit numbers, memory stores 16-bit words, and the bus moves data and instructions 16 bits at a time.

Low-cost 4-bit and 8-bit microprocessors are used to perform specific tasks in a variety of consumer products, including automobiles, household appliances, and even children's toys. Some inexpensive microcomputers are designed around a 16-bit word, but the trend is toward more powerful, faster 32-bit machines. Most mainframes are constructed around a 32-bit word. Some expensive supercomputers have a 60- or 64-bit word.

PROCESSING SPEED AND WORD SIZE

A 32-bit computer transmits data and instructions between its components 32 bits at a time. A 16-bit computer transmits 16 bits at a time. Because it moves twice as much data in the same amount of time, the 32-bit machine is clearly faster.

A 16-bit computer is capable of adding two 32-bit numbers, but it must fetch the data from memory and perform the arithmetic 16 bits at a time. A 32-bit computer, in contrast, can fetch and add 32 bits at a time. Clearly, the 16-bit machine will need more machine cycles to execute a 32-bit add instruction. Generally, the bigger the word size, the faster (and more powerful) the computer.

Processing speed is measured in millions of instructions per second (MIPS). However, supercomputers are typically used to manipulate floating-point (scientific notation) numbers, so their speed is measured in floating-point operations (FLOPs) per second. A megaflop is one million, a gigaflop is one billion, and a teraflop is one trillion floating-point operations per second.

MEMORY CAPACITY

Memory capacity is also a function of word size. The processor fetches instructions and data by referencing a memory address. A 32-bit machine works with a 32-bit address, so the processor can directly access as many as 2^{32} memory locations (4,096 KB, or 4 MB). On the other hand, a 16-bit computer works with 16-bit addresses, limiting it to 2^{16} memory locations (64 KB). Generally, the bigger its word size, the more memory a computer can access.

There are 16-bit microcomputers that access considerably more than 64 KB of memory, but only if the addresses are broken into two or more parts and transmitted during successive machine cycles. Each cycle takes time, however, so memory capacity is gained at the expense of processing speed.

PRECISION

Precision refers to the number of significant digits in a value; for example, 1.97316 is more precise than 2, and 3.5 has the same precision as 3,500,000. A 16-bit computer works with 16-bit numbers, and a 32-bit machine works with 32-bit numbers. More digits makes it possible to have more significant digits and thus more precise answers.

Many 16-bit computers can work with 32-bit numbers, but they need two machine cycles to fetch the number from memory and at least two more to manipulate it. On a smaller machine, precision, like memory capacity, is achieved at the expense of processing speed.

SINGLE-BUS ARCHITECTURE

Most microcomputers are designed around a single bus. When all the computer's components are linked by a common bus, you have **single-bus architecture** (Figure 11.5). All communications between the components flow over the bus under control of the processor.

Single-bus architecture
A type of computer architecture in which all the components are linked by a common bus.

▲ FIGURE 11.5

Single-bus architecture.

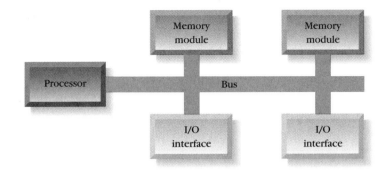

The Motherboard

Motherboard
The board that holds the processor.

A microcomputer is driven by a microprocessor, a complete processor on a single chip. The board that holds the microprocessor is called the **motherboard** (Figure 11.6).

If you look closely at a motherboard, you can usually see a set of parallel lines etched into the surface. That set of lines is the bus, and it serves to link the computer's *internal* components. Main or primary memory is directly connected to the processor over the bus.

Expansion Slots

Expansion slot or slot
A socket-like opening on a bus into which integrated circuit boards are plugged.

Components are added to a microcomputer by plugging boards into socket-like **expansion slots** arrayed along the bus (Figure 11.7). If you want to increase the computer's memory capacity you plug in additional memory boards. Other **slots** are used to link peripheral devices to the system.

▲ FIGURE 11.6

A motherboard.

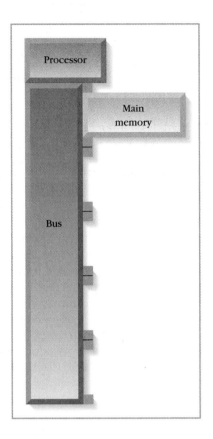

You add components to a computer by plugging boards into the expansion slots arrayed along the bus.

If you have an open slot on your microcomputer, you can add more memory, a modem, a sound card, or some other peripheral. Once all the slots are taken, however, you cannot add any more devices. The number of available slots limits the expandability of a microcomputer system.

Bus Standards

ADVANCED TOPICS

When IBM released its PS/2 microcomputers in 1987, the company also announced a proprietary bus design called Micro Channel Architecture (MCA). The new architecture defined a new standard for electronically communicating with the slots on the bus, and that, in turn, meant that many of the old PC's circuit boards would no longer work on a PS/2.

IBM's competitors were not pleased with the company's departure from the existing de facto standard and resented the fact that using the MCA bus meant paying a royalty to IBM, so a group of nine companies (AST, Compaq, Epson, Hewlett-Packard, NEC, Olivetti, Tandy, Wyse, and Zenith) banded together and defined a competitive bus architecture called EISA (extended industry standard architecture). The new bus configuration represented an open standard available to anyone, and it was compatible with the existing ISA (industry standard architecture) bus.

The open standard won. As a result, the cost of computers and components has declined due in part to the economies of scale that can be achieved by mass producing standardized parts.

Interface Boards

Data are stored in a computer as patterns of bits, and the patterns are consistent within a given machine. For example, if the code for the letter A is 1010 0001, that pattern and only that pattern can be used to represent an A inside the computer.

Peripherals are different. Each input or output device represents or interprets data in its own unique way. On a keyboard you press a key to generate a character. A color display screen forms characters and graphic images by controlling a pattern of red, green, and blue dots. A dot matrix printer extends and retracts metal pins to form a dot pattern. Optical devices read light intensity, and magnetic devices sense magnetic intensity. If a peripheral is to communicate with a computer, it is necessary to translate between its electrical signals and the signals used inside the computer.

The task of translating between internal and external data formats is performed by an **interface** board (Figure 11.8). On input, the interface board translates the signals generated by a peripheral device into a form acceptable to the computer. Output signals are electronically converted from the computer's internal code to a form acceptable to the peripheral device.

Because they are electronically different, every input or output device needs a unique interface board to translate its device-dependent signals to (or from) the computer's internal code. That is why there is normally one interface board per peripheral device.

Interface
An entity that links two or more components.

▲ FIGURE 11.8

Interface boards link peripherals to the computer.

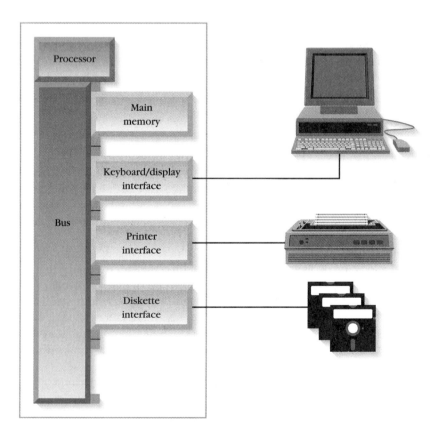

Secondary storage devices are also linked to the computer through an interface (Figure 11.8). The binary patterns stored on disk are the same patterns stored in memory, so no code translation is necessary, but the disk interface is needed to physically control the disk drive.

How a PC's Keyboard Works

Beneath each key on your keyboard is a tiny switch. When you press a key, you close its switch, and that generates a pulse of electrical current.

The switches (or keys) form a matrix of rows and columns. For example, on many keyboards the escape (Esc) key is located in the top row, leftmost column. Consequently, when you press the escape key you generate a current in two wires (row 1 and column 1), and no other key activates those two wires. That is how the system knows which key you pressed.

What if you press *two* keys? For example, what if you (for some unknown reason) press escape and control (Ctrl)? The escape key generates a current in row 1 and column 1. The control key affects row 6 and column 1. That pattern can only exist if you press escape and control. Once again the system (more accurately, the interface board) knows which keys you pressed.

PCMCIA Cards

A **PCMCIA** (PC Memory Card International Association) **card** (Figure 11.9) is a credit-card-size adapter that plugs into a standard slot on many portable

PCMCIA card
Acronym for PC Memory Card International Association. A credit-card-size adapter that plugs into a standard slot on many portable computers.

▲ **FIGURE 11.9**

A PCMCIA card.

computers. Additional memory, a modem, a portable hard disk, and many other peripherals can be linked to the computer through the PCMCIA card.

Buffers

Buffer
Temporary storage used to adjust for the speed disparity between two devices.

Many interface boards contain **buffers.** A buffer is temporary memory or storage used to adjust for the speed differential between two devices.

For example, if you have ever waited for a lengthy paper to print, you know that the printer is much slower than the computer. If waiting for the printer is a problem, you can add a buffer to your printer interface. Then, instead of sending the contents of memory directly to the printer, the computer can send the information to the buffer at computer speed (Figure 11.10). Subsequently, as the characters are dumped from the buffer to the printer at printer speed, you can use the computer for some other task.

Ports and Connectors

Port
A plug (and associated electronics) that allows a user to physically connect a terminal or a workstation to a network or a peripheral device to an interface board.

The plug through which you physically connect a cable to an interface is called a **port** (Figure 11.11); look on the back of a personal computer and you can probably see several. A serial port transmits data one bit at a time; a paral-

▲ **FIGURE 11.10**

The computer sends the contents of memory to a buffer (1). Later (2), the characters are dumped from the buffer to the printer at printer speed.

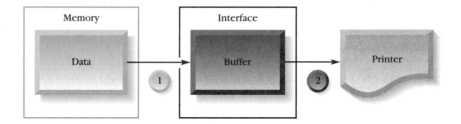

▲ **FIGURE 11.11**

You can see several ports on the back of a personal computer.

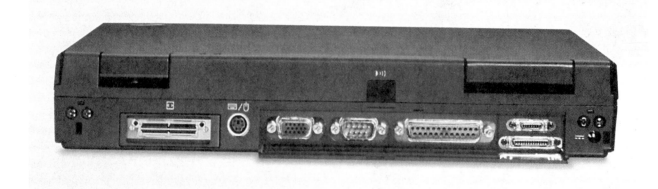

lel port transmits several bits in parallel. (Typically, the printer uses a parallel port and the mouse uses a serial port.) Inside the computer, the interface board links the port to the bus and thus to the computer's other components.

Loading and Executing a Program

Programs are typically stored on a secondary device, but because the processor is limited to accessing primary memory, programs must be copied into memory before they can be executed. Consider the process of loading and executing a program on a single-bus computer.

First, in response to a user command, the processor sends a control signal over the bus to the disk interface (Figure 11.12a). Responding to the signal, the interface activates the disk drive, and the program is transferred over the bus into memory (Figure 11.12b). Once the program is in memory, the

▲ **FIGURE 11.12**

Loading and executing a program on a single-bus computer.
a. A control signal is sent to the disk interface.
b. The program is transferred into memory.
c. The processor fetches and executes the instructions.
d. Data move over the bus.

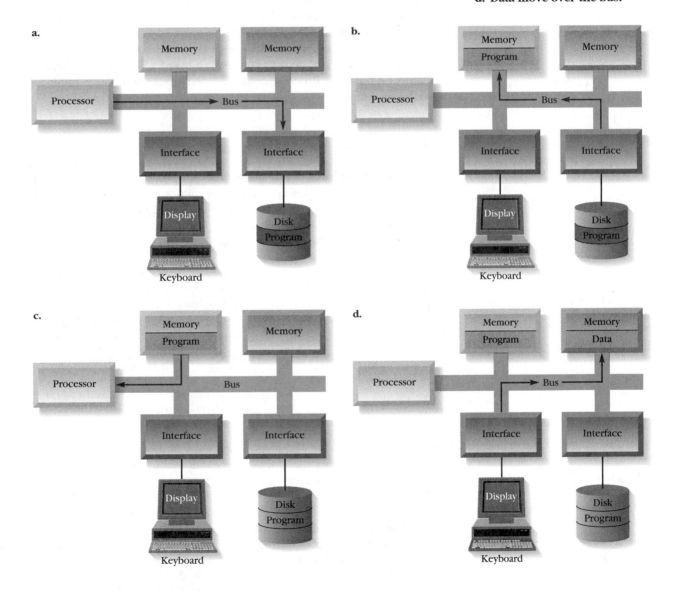

processor can execute it, fetching instructions over the bus, one by one (Figure 11.12c). As the program runs, input data move from the peripheral devices, over the bus, and into memory (Figure 11.12d), while output moves from memory, over the bus, to the output devices.

Note that the bus supports one task at a time. At any given instant, the computer might be transferring control signals, instructions, data, input, or output across the bus. There is only one electronic path, however. Consequently, the bus cannot support two or more simultaneous tasks because the signals would interfere with each other.

MULTIPLE-BUS ARCHITECTURE

The fact that all internal communications flow over the same bus limits the power of a single-bus system. That is rarely a problem on a personal computer designed for a single user, but mainframes are different. They are much more expensive, and they generally support scores (even hundreds) of concurrent users. Efficiency is crucial, so most mainframes have more than one bus. The way a peripheral device is linked to a mainframe computer through a channel and a control unit provides a good example of the advantages derived from using multiple buses.

Channels

Transferring data between peripheral devices and memory involves such logical functions as counting characters and computing memory addresses. The processor is a microcomputer's only source of logic, so the processor directly controls each input or output operation. While it is controlling I/O, the processor is not available to execute application program instructions, and that is inefficient.

One solution is to free the processor from responsibility for input and output. On most mainframe computers, that task is assigned to a **channel** (Figure 11.13). A channel is a built-in processor with (often) its own memory. Because it is a processor in its own right, a channel can perform logical functions in parallel with the computer's main processor, and that frees the main processor to do other things.

Channel
On a mainframe computer, a built-in processor with (often) its own memory that manages data transfers between memory and peripheral devices.

I/O Control Units

A channel handles such device-*independent* functions as counting characters and computing memory addresses. Device-dependent functions, such as interpreting magnetic patterns or generating dot patterns, are implemented through **I/O control units** or interface units (Figure 11.13).

Each physical device (or set of similar devices) has its own control unit. The channel communicates with the mainframe in the computer's language. The control unit communicates with the external device on the device's terms. The channel and the control unit, working together, translate between internal and external data form.

I/O control unit
A device attached to a channel that performs such device-dependent I/O functions, such as interpreting magnetic patterns or generating dot patterns.

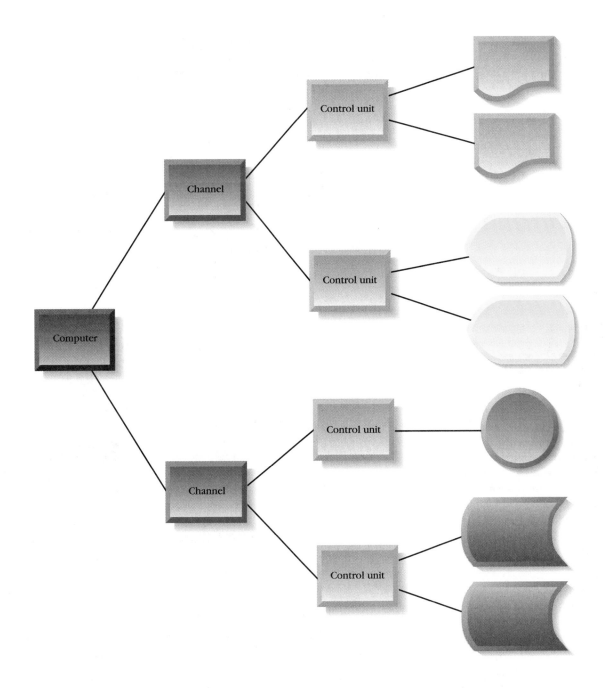

▲ FIGURE 11.13

On most large computer
systems, input and output operations are controlled by
channels and control units.

Multiple Buses

A channel moves data between memory and a control unit. The computer's
processor manipulates data in memory. Note that the processor and the
channel simultaneously access memory.

Allowing a channel and a processor to simultaneously access memory
will not work on a microcomputer because the single-bus architecture provides only one data path. Simultaneous operation requires independent data

paths, so mainframes use multiple buses (Figure 11.14). Given independent paths, the processor and the channels can operate in parallel.

As the name suggests, a **multiple-bus architecture** computer has more than one bus. For example, a mainframe might have separate buses to carry addresses, data, and control signals between the processor and memory and still more buses to link the processor and memory to each of the channels.

MULTIPROCESSING

The fact that a single processor can execute only one instruction at a time sets a limit on processing speed. To gain extra speed, many modern computers contain two or more processors. For example, some microcomputers have both a main processor and a math or graphics co-processor, and main-

Multiple-bus architecture
A computer with more than one bus.

▲ Figure 11.14

An I/O operation on a multiple-bus computer.
a. The processor sends a signal to the channel.
b. As program A's data move into memory over the channel's data bus, the processor, using its own data bus, can manipulate program B's data.
c. The channel notifies the processor when the I/O operation is finished.

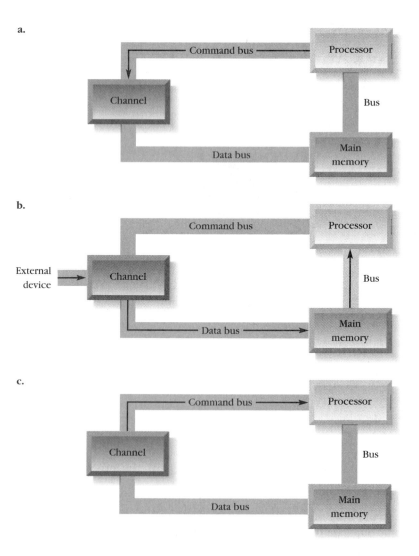

PEOPLE

Seymour Cray

Supercomputers are the fastest, most powerful computers available. They are used by governmental agencies, research centers, and commercial organizations to perform such number-crunching tasks as simulating nuclear reactions, tracing the implications of proposed changes in monetary policy, simulating the flight characteristics of a new airplane, animating dinosaurs in a movie, and predicting the weather.

One name is almost synonymous with supercomputers: Seymour Cray. Born in 1925 in Chippewa Falls, Wisconsin, Cray was one of the founders of Control Data Corporation (1957). His CDC 1604 (one of the first supercomputers), announced in 1958, helped make the new company profitable.

In most companies, designing a new computer is a group project that involves numerous specialists, but Seymour Cray is reclusive, preferring to work in almost total isolation. He creates his designs using paper and pencil and then gives his calculations to a development team that converts his ideas into integrated circuit chips. He is a generalist who deals with every aspect of the computer's architecture himself.

By 1962, Cray tired of administrative work and announced that he was leaving Control

Data to start his own company. Instead, Control Data Corporation agreed to build a laboratory in Cray's hometown of Chippewa Falls and give its star designer virtually free rein. The result, the CDC 6600, was clearly the best supercomputer of its time.

Cray finally left Control Data in 1972 and started a new company called Cray Research. The first CRAY-1 was delivered to Los Alamos National Laboratory in 1976, and although competition has increased, Cray Research continues to be an important player in the supercomputer marketplace.

frames often contain several parallel main processors plus additional secondary processors.

When two or more processors share the same memory and have the ability to execute instructions simultaneously, you have a **multiprocessing** system. Because each processor can independently execute instructions, a computer with multiple processors can execute multiple instructions simultaneously, and that increases processing speed.

Multiprocessing
Two or more processors sharing the same memory.

Parallel Processing

Parallel processing implies that several processors can be assigned to work on different aspects of the same program. By executing numerous

Parallel processing
Assigning several processors to work simultaneously on different aspects of the same program.

instructions simultaneously, a computer with multiple parallel processors can achieve remarkable speeds. For example, a Cray Research X-MP48 super-computer peaks at 1,000 million floating-point operations per second (1,000 MFLOP), and massively parallel hypercube systems (arrays of linked micro-processors) potentially can execute over 250 billion floating-point operations per second (250 GFLOP).

Symmetrical and Asymmetrical Multiprocessing

Symmetrical multiprocessing
An approach to multiprocessing in which the operating system dynamically assigns tasks to the next available main processor.

Asymmetrical multiprocessing
An approach to multiprocessing in which the programmer decides (at the time the program is written) which processor will be used to perform a given task.

Fault-tolerant computer
A computer that is designed to automatically sense and bypass a failed component.

With **symmetrical multiprocessing,** the operating system dynamically assigns tasks to the next available main processor. With **asymmetrical multiprocessing,** the programmer decides (at the time the program is written) which processor will be used to perform a given task. Note that writing software for an asymmetrical multiprocessing system is an extremely difficult task.

FAULT-TOLERANT COMPUTERS

Today's computers are remarkably reliable, but in some applications, such as controlling a space probe or monitoring air traffic, computer failure simply cannot be tolerated. Such applications call for **fault-tolerant computers** that are designed to automatically sense and bypass a failed component.

A fault-tolerant computer contains redundant components. For example, key chips and, in some cases, the processor, a disk, or even the complete computer system might be duplicated.

SUMMARY

Chips and boards are the basic building blocks of a computer. Inside every computer is a power supply that conditions the power and feeds a consistent voltage to the computer. A serial line transmits one bit at a time. A parallel line consists of numerous wires that transmit several bits at a time, in parallel.

A computer system's architecture defines how its components are physically linked and how they communicate with each other. An open architecture is published and widely known; a closed architecture is proprietary. On most computers, the *internal* components are linked by a high-speed parallel line called a bus. Most computers are designed around a standard word size. A computer's processing speed, memory capacity, and precision are functions of word size.

When all the computer's components are linked by a common bus, you have single-bus architecture. On a microcomputer, the board that holds the microprocessor is called the motherboard. You add components to a computer by plugging boards into socket-like expansion slots arrayed along the bus. The task of translating between internal and external data formats is performed by an interface board. A buffer is temporary memory or storage used to adjust for the speed differential between two devices. The plug through which you physically connect a cable to an interface is called a port.

On a mainframe, the responsibility for physically controlling input and output operations is assigned to a channel and an I/O control unit. Simultaneous operation requires independent data paths, so mainframes use multiple-bus architecture.

When two or more processors share the same memory and are capable of executing instructions simultaneously, you have a multiprocessing system. Parallel processing implies that several processors can be assigned to work on different aspects of the same program. With symmetrical multiprocessing, the operating system dynamically assigns tasks to the next available main processor. With asymmetrical multiprocessing, the programmer decides which processor will be used to perform a given task. A fault-tolerant computer contains redundant components.

KEY TERMS

architecture	interface	port
asymmetrical multi-processing	I/O control unit	power supply
buffer	motherboard	serial
bus	multiple-bus architecture	single-bus architecture
channel	multiprocessing	slot
closed architecture	open architecture	symmetrical multi-processing
expansion slot	parallel	
fault-tolerant computer	parallel processing	
	PCMCIA card	

CONCEPTS

1. Briefly describe what you see when you take the cover off a microcomputer.
2. What functions are performed by a computer's power supply? Why is the power supply necessary?
3. Distinguish between serial and parallel lines. What type of line is faster? Why?
4. Explain how a computer's internal components are physically linked. Explain the relationship between word size and architecture.
5. A computer's processing speed, memory capacity, and precision are all functions of its word size. Why?
6. What is single-bus architecture?
7. What is a motherboard? What is an expansion slot? Why does the number of available slots affect or limit the number of peripheral devices that can be attached to a computer?
8. What is a buffer? Why are buffers used? What is a port?
9. Outline the process of loading and executing a program on a single-bus architecture computer.
10. What is an interface? Why are interface boards necessary?
11. Explain how a channel and an I/O control unit work together to control input and output on a multiple-bus architecture computer.
12. Why do mainframe computers use multiple-bus architecture?

13. Define multiprocessing. What is parallel processing? Why does parallel processing help to increase processing speed?
14. What is the difference between symmetrical and asymmetrical multiprocessing?
15. What is a fault-tolerant computer? Why are fault-tolerant computers used?

PROJECTS

1. Make sure the power is turned off and the computer is unplugged; then take the cover off a microcomputer. Identify the function performed by each card or board. Trace the path characters follow from the keyboard into memory and from memory to the printer. Optional: Remove all the cards and then reassemble the computer.
2. Tracy Kidder's *The Soul of a New Machine* (Boston: Little, Brown and Company, 1981) is an fascinating case study of the daily lives of a team of computer designers. Read it.

 INTERNET PROJECTS

1. *News and Notes.* Companies often post information about their very latest products on their World Wide Web home pages. Select a company such as IBM, Dell, or Apple that manufactures personal computer systems and access its home page. Try the address *http://www.xxx.com;* substitute the company name (for example, *ibm*) for *xxx.* Once you find the home page, look for a button marked *New products* (or something similar) and click on it. Identify and briefly describe at least two new products and submit your findings to your instructor in the form of a brief note or an e-mail message.
2. *Topic Searches.* Check the World Wide Web and/or other Internet resources for information on the following topics:

Key word	Qualifiers
parallel processors	Cray
PCMCIA	modem
bus standard	personal computer

Define the key word, identify at least two sources of information on the topic, and briefly summarize the nature of the information you find.

3. *Links to Other Sites.* After you access one or more of the following sites, write a brief note or send an e-mail message to your instructor outlining what you find.

   a. On the World Wide Web, check *http://www.ibm.com* for information on IBM products.
   b. On the World Wide Web, check *http://www.apple.com* for information on Apple Corporation products.

   c. On the World Wide Web, check *http://www.dell.com* for information on Dell Corporation products.

4. Access West Publishing Company's home page and find the Chapter 11 student activities for this book. See Internet Project 3 for the spotlight on *The Internet* following Chapter 1 (page 29) for more detailed instructions on accessing the home page. As appropriate, repeat projects 1, 2, and/or 3 using the more current references you find.

CHAPTER 12

Multitasking

Before you start this chapter, you should be familiar with the following concepts:

▶ Hardware (p. 6), peripherals (p. 6), and inside the computer (p. 7).

▶ Machine cycles (p. 87).

▶ Operating system functions (p. 122), communicating with the operating system (p. 123), file management (p. 126), and hardware management (p. 130).

When you finish reading this chapter, you should be able to:

▶ Define the term *multitasking*. Distinguish between the words *concurrent* and *simultaneous*.

▶ Explain the relationship between concurrency and processor efficiency.

▶ Explain multiprogramming. List the basic functions of a multiprogramming operating system.

▶ Explain how a multiprogramming dispatcher manages the processor's time.

▶ Distinguish among fixed partition, dynamic, and virtual memory management.

▶ Explain scheduling and queuing. Distinguish between a program's internal and external priorities.

▶ Explain spooling.

▶ Distinguish between multiprogramming and time-sharing.

▶ Explain how a time-sharing system manages the processor's time and memory space.

▶ Briefly explain the virtual machine concept.

▶ Define the term *multiprocessing*.

CONCURRENCY

A modern computer is orders of magnitude faster than its peripheral devices. One way to take advantage of that speed economically is to allow numerous programs (or users) to occupy memory and share the processor. A single program or routine stored in memory and capable of being executed is called a **task.** The act of concurrently executing two or more tasks on a single processor is called **multitasking.**

Note that the tasks are executed concurrently, not simultaneously. As you learned in Chapter 4, a computer works by repetitively fetching and executing instructions one at a time. Simultaneous means *at the same instant.* Because a processor executes one instruction at a time, it cannot possibly execute two or more instructions simultaneously. Concurrent means *over the same time span.* Like a chess master playing multiple opponents, a processor can execute several programs concurrently by switching its attention from one to another and back again.

An example might help to clarify the distinction between simultaneous and concurrent. Perhaps, like many students, you like to study in front of the television set. It is impossible to *simultaneously* study and watch television. It is, however, possible to *concurrently* study and watch television by switching your attention from your work to the screen and back again.

For example, imagine that you are watching a football game and concurrently working on your math assignment. During commercial breaks and between plays your attention is focused on your homework. The commentator's voice tells you when to look at the screen. There is no instant during which you are watching the game *and* doing your homework, but by the time the game ends you have indeed done both.

A single processor executes two or more tasks concurrently by switching between them. This chapter explores two multitasking techniques: multiprogramming and time-sharing.

Task
A single program or routine stored in memory and capable of being executed.

Multitasking
The act of concurrently executing two or more tasks on a single processor.

NOTE

Multitasking in Windows 95

In the early 1960s, virtually all computers operated in serial-batch mode, executing one program at a time. In those days, a professional operator mounted the necessary tapes and disks, started a program, and then waited until all the output was generated before starting the next program. By the middle 1960s, however, improving technology made serial-batch mode uneconomical, and multitasking quickly became the mainframe standard.

Until recently, most personal computers ran in serial-batch mode, but today's microprocessors are powerful enough to support multitasking. To take advantage of that power, Windows 95 is specifically designed to support multitasking, allowing a personal computer user to launch multiple programs (perhaps a note pad, a calendar, an e-mail program, a spreadsheet, and a word processor), keep them all active in memory, and switch between them by issuing commands or clicking on icons.

MULTIPROGRAMMING

Imagine that there is only one program in memory and that it has just requested input data from the keyboard. Because it cannot process data it does not yet have, the processor can do nothing until the data are in memory.

Compare the speed of the processor to the speed of the input device. The processor can execute millions of instructions per second. How fast can *you* type? Granted, other peripherals are significantly faster than a keyboard, but the speed disparity still exists. Simply put, the processor is so much faster than any input or output device that it spends most of its time waiting for I/O (Figure 12.1), not processing data.

Now imagine that there are two programs in memory. If program A requests input data, the processor can switch its attention to program B (Figure 12.2). Store more programs in memory, and even more of that otherwise wasted input and output time can be utilized (Figure 12.3). Generally, as you increase the number of programs in memory you improve the utilization of the processor.

The act of concurrently executing two or more programs on a single processor by taking advantage of the speed disparity between the computer and its peripheral devices is called **multiprogramming.** The idea is to load several programs into memory and have the processor switch its attention from one to another every time an input or output operation begins or ends. The responsibility for switching from one program to another is normally assigned to the operating system. Using this technique, some large mainframes can concurrently execute hundreds of programs.

Multiprogramming
The act of concurrently executing two or more programs on a single processor by taking advantage of the speed disparity between the computer and its peripheral devices.

MULTIPROGRAMMING OPERATING SYSTEMS

Although a modern computer's resources are substantial, they are still finite. Whenever two or more users attempt to share a set of finite resources (such

▲ **Figure 12.1**

The processor spends most of its time waiting for I/O, not processing data.

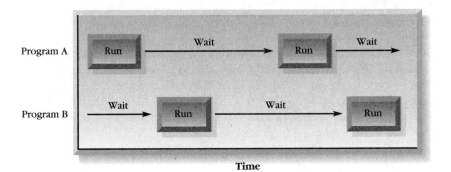

Time

▲ **FIGURE 12.2**

Multiprogramming.

▲ FIGURE 12.3

More programs means even
more efficient utilization of the
processor.

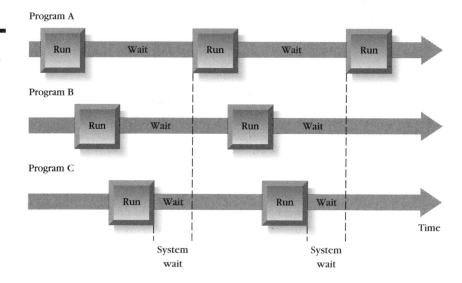

▲ FIGURE 12.3

More programs means even
more efficient utilization of the
processor.

as processor time, memory space, and peripheral devices), conflicts are
inevitable, and those conflicts must be resolved.

As you learned in Chapter 6, the operating system serves as a
hardware/software interface, making it the ideal place to implement resource
management. A multiprogramming operating system incorporates the basic
operating system elements introduced in Chapter 6 (a command processor or
shell, a file system, and an input/output control system), and adds modules to
manage processor time, main memory space, and peripheral device allocation.

Managing the Processor's Time

Processor management
A set of techniques for managing and
allocating the processor's time.

Processor management is concerned with resolving the conflicts that
occur when two or more tasks demand the processor's time. Imagine, for

PEOPLE

Frederick P. Brooks, Jr.

The 1964 announcement of
IBM's System/360 series was
a watershed event in the
history of computers. For the first time, a user
organization had access to a family of compatible computers, and migrating to a more
powerful machine no longer meant scrapping
and rewriting all your software.

A key element of the System/360 family
was a common multiprogramming operating

system called OS/360. At the time, the task of
writing OS/360 was the largest software
development project ever attempted,
consuming literally thousands of programmer
years. The man in charge of that massive
project was Frederick P. Brooks, Jr.

OS/360 taught Frederick Brooks a great
deal about managing large software projects,
and he wrote a book about his experiences.
His book, *The Mythical Man Month* (Reading,
Mass.: Addison-Wesley Publishing Company,
1975), is considered a classic.

example, that two programs, A and B, are in memory. Some time ago, program A requested data from disk (Figure 12.4), and the processor turned its attention to program B. Assume that the input operation has just been completed. *Both* programs are now ready to run. Which one goes first?

THE DISPATCHER

One way to select the next program is to display a message on the console and let the operator decide. While the operator is reading that message, however, the processor could easily execute instructions for *both* programs. A modern computer is so fast that a human operator cannot possibly make such real-time choices. Instead, the decision is made by an operating system routine called the **dispatcher.** The dispatcher's job is to decide which program is executed next.

Dispatcher
The operating system routine that decides which program is executed next.

INTERRUPTS

When a task starts an input or output operation, it must normally wait until that operation is completed before it can resume processing. The idea of multiprogramming is to take advantage of that wait time by starting another program. If the dispatcher is to start another program each time an input or output operation begins or ends, it must know when those events occur.

An **interrupt** is an electronic signal that causes the computer to stop what it is doing and activate one of the operating system's interrupt service routines. Interrupts can be generated by an application program, the computer's own hardware, a peripheral device, the computer operator, or by some external event that requires the computer's attention. Think of an interrupt as an electronic tap on the shoulder. The operating system "knows" when an input or output operation begins or ends because those two events are marked by interrupts.

Interrupt
An electronic signal that causes the computer to stop what it is doing and activate one of the operating system's interrupt service routines.

THE DISPATCHING PROCESS

The dispatching process is best illustrated through an example. When an application program needs data, it issues an interrupt (Figure 12.5a). In response, hardware starts the operating system's interrupt service routine, which drops the application program into a **wait state** (Figure 12.5b). A wait state implies that the program cannot continue until some event, in this case the input operation, is completed.

After the operating system starts the I/O operation, it calls the dispatcher. It is the dispatcher's job to start another application program (Figure 12.5c).

Wait state
The state of a program that is not ready to execute because it is waiting for the completion of some event, such as an input or output operation.

Program A — I/O — Run — Wait — Ready

Program B — Wait — Run — Ready

Time ⟶

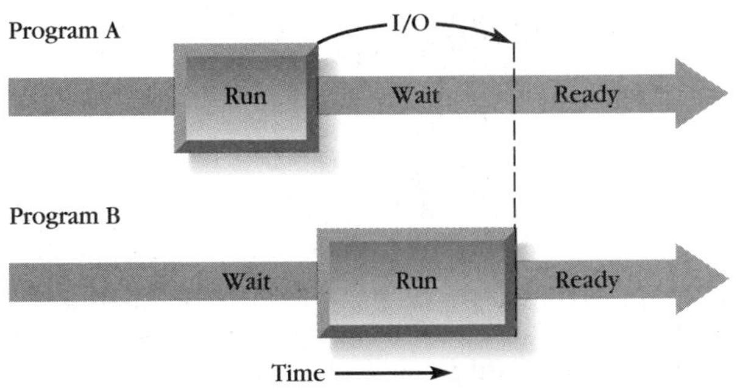

▲ **Figure 12.4**

If two programs are ready to run, which one goes first?

▲ **Figure 12.5**

The dispatching process.
a. An application program
   issues an interrupt.
b. The application program
   drops into a wait state.
c. The dispatcher starts another
   application program.
d. Later, another interrupt
   signals the end of the I/O
   operation.
e. The operating system marks
   the appropriate application
   program *ready*.
f. The dispatcher starts the
   highest priority program.

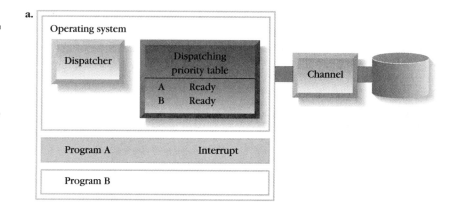

a.

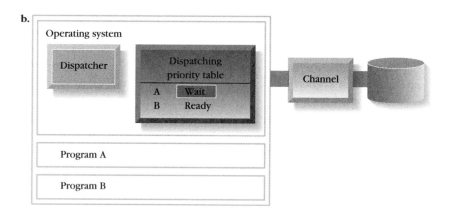

b.

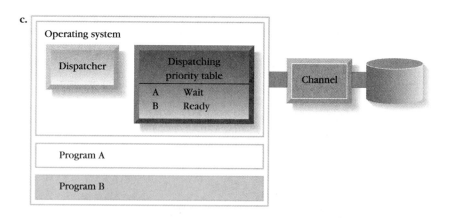

c.

Ready state
The state of a program that is ready to
be executed.

Eventually (a few microseconds later), another interrupt signals the end of
the I/O operation (Figure 12.5d). The operating system responds by resetting
the appropriate application program to a **ready state** (Figure 12.5e). (A ready
state implies that the program is ready to execute.) Then the dispatcher starts
the highest priority ready state application program (Figure 12.5f).

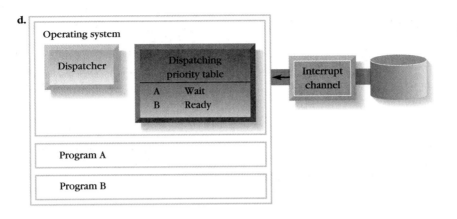

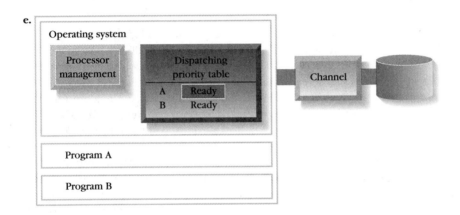

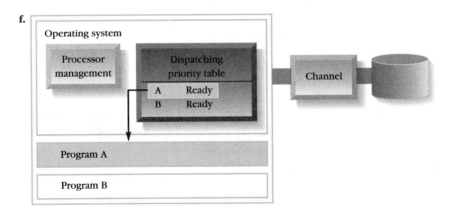

That process continues as long as the computer runs. An interrupt occurs. The operating system responds to the interrupt and then calls the dispatcher. The dispatcher starts a task. That task executes until the next interrupt occurs. And on and on.

DISPATCHING PRIORITY

Figure 12.5 shows a system with only two active application programs, but at any given time a real multiprogramming system can have dozens, even hundreds of programs in a ready state. The program to be executed next is generally selected based on its **dispatching priority.**

For example, all the active tasks might be listed in a table in priority order. A program's position on the table might be based on such criteria as its size, its location in memory, how much time it has spent in memory, or its significance. Following an interrupt, the dispatcher scans the table and selects the first (highest priority) ready task it encounters.

Dispatching priority
The order in which programs are executed.

ADVANCED TOPICS

Stacks and Queues

Imagine that you are taking telephone orders for a catalogue company. When the phone rings, you answer it immediately, fill out a form describing the customer's order, and drop the form on the top of your in-box. Between phone calls, you grab the top form, select and pack the appropriate merchandise, address the package, and place it in a bin for subsequent mailing. At peak times, the calls keep coming and the pile of forms keeps getting higher. During slow periods, you work the pile down, from the top to the bottom.

That pile of forms is a good visualization of a stack. Many operating systems set aside areas of memory to hold electronic stacks of the data associated with pending interrupts or the status of active programs.

Queues are similar to stacks, with one important difference. In a stack, the last message received is the first one processed. In a queue, the *first* message received is the first one processed.

Memory Management

Memory management is concerned with allocating memory space to application programs. Generally, as the number of programs in memory increases, so does the utilization of the processor.

FIXED AND DYNAMIC MEMORY MANAGEMENT

Fixed partition memory management (Figure 12.6) divides the available space into fixed-length **partitions** and loads one task into each partition. The amount of memory in a partition is determined when the system is started and remains fixed throughout the day.

More efficient memory utilization is achieved with **dynamic memory management.** Using this technique, the available memory is treated as a large pool of free space, and each program is dynamically assigned exactly as much memory as it needs. The space assigned to a task is called a **region,** and the size of a region can vary as the task runs.

Memory management
Allocating memory space to application programs.

Fixed partition memory management
A memory management technique that divides the available space into fixed-length partitions and loads one task into each partition.

Partition, memory
A fixed-length unit of memory that holds a single task.

Dynamic memory management
A memory management technique in which the available memory is treated as a large pool of free space, and each program is dynamically assigned exactly as much memory as it needs.

Region
A dynamically allocated, variable-length unit of memory that holds a single task.

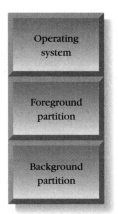

▲ **Figure 12.6**

Fixed partition memory management.

FOREGROUND AND BACKGROUND

On some multiprogramming systems, the decision to assign a given task to a particular partition or region reflects the task's dispatching priority. The highest priority task is loaded into the **foreground** partition (Figure 12.6). Other tasks are loaded into **background** partitions. Following any interrupt, the dispatcher attempts to start the foreground task. Only if that task is in a wait state does the dispatcher consider a background task.

For example, on most personal computer systems you can use a word processor, a spreadsheet, or some other application program while output is being printed. The application you are running is in the foreground. The printer routine is in the background. If both routines simultaneously request processor support, *you* get priority and the printer waits.

Foreground
In a multiprogramming system, the partition or region that holds the high priority program.
Background
On a multiprogramming system, the low priority partition or region.

MEMORY PROTECTION

When two or more programs share memory, there is always a danger that one task will attempt to utilize the space assigned to another task. If that happens, data and instructions can be destroyed. Consequently, a multitasking system must have a **memory protection** scheme that restricts each task to its own partition or region and prevents tasks from interfering with each other. Memory protection is usually implemented through a combination of hardware and system software techniques.

Memory protection
On a multitasking system, a scheme that restricts each task to its own partition or region and prevents tasks from interfering with each other.

OVERLAY STRUCTURES

A processor executes one instruction at a time. Consequently, it is not really necessary for the entire program to be in memory before execution can begin.

For example, imagine a program that contains three modules: one for input and output, one to process valid data, and one to process errors (Figure 12.7a). Clearly, if the data are valid the instructions in the third module are not needed, and if the data are not valid the *second* module's instructions are not needed.

▲ FIGURE 12.7

Overlay structures.
a. **The program in this example consists of three modules.**
b. **Initially, only the first two modules are loaded into memory.**
c. **When an error must be processed, module 3 overlays module 2.**

a.
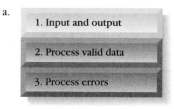

b.
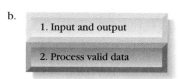

c.

Overlay
Storing a program module in the memory space previously occupied by another, no longer needed module of the same program.

Virtual memory
A technique for managing the space requirements of multiple concurrent tasks by dividing memory into a set of fixed-length pages and then swapping pages between memory and secondary storage.

Page
A fixed-length unit of memory.

Swapping
Moving pages between memory and secondary storage.

Because modules 2 and 3 are mutually exclusive, there is no need to load them both into memory. Initially, based on the assumption that most of the data are valid, modules 1 and 2 are loaded (Figure 12.7b). If module 1 encounters bad data, module 3 replaces or **overlays** module 2, and the errors are processed (Figure 12.7c). When the next set of valid data is input, module 2 overlays module 1. The advantage of using overlay structures is that no space is wasted on unnecessary program instructions.

VIRTUAL MEMORY

Overlay structures help to efficiently manage the memory space assigned to an individual program. **Virtual memory,** in contrast, is a technique for managing the space requirements of multiple concurrent tasks.

When virtual memory is used, each program is divided into a set of fixed-length pieces called **pages.** The pages are then stored on disk, and a few active pages from each program are loaded into memory.

As a given program executes, it eventually references one of the pages that is not yet in memory. At that point, an unneeded page is copied (swapped out) from memory to disk (Figure 12.8a), the referenced page is loaded (swapped in) from disk to memory (Figure 12.8b), and the program continues. Moving pages between memory and secondary storage is called **swapping.**

The disk space that holds the inactive pages is called virtual memory. The word virtual means *in essence though not in fact.* Virtual memory is not real memory because the processor cannot directly access anything stored

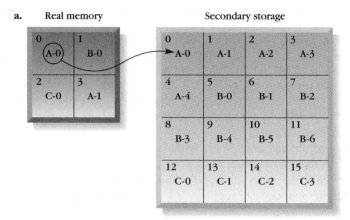

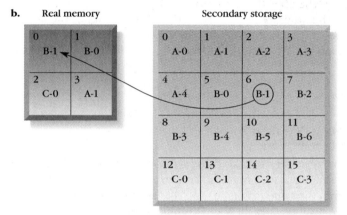

▲ **FIGURE 12.8**

With virtual memory, only the active pages are loaded into memory.
a. **An inactive page is swapped out.**
b. **An active page is swapped into real memory.**

on disk. To the programmer, however, virtual memory behaves just like real memory because swapping is transparent. (It is the responsibility of the hardware and the operating system.) For all practical purposes, a program stored in virtual memory acts just like a program stored in real memory.

Virtual memory allows more programs to be concurrently executed because only the active pages are physically loaded into memory. That means more efficient processor utilization.

Another advantage is that virtual memory frees the programmer from the need to worry about physical space limitations. For example, using virtual memory it might be possible to execute a 16 megabyte program on a computer with only 4 megabytes of RAM. Consequently, a programmer can use as much memory as the logic demands and still run the software on a small system.

There are problems with virtual memory, too. For example, as the ratio of virtual to real memory increases, the percentage of potentially active pages that are actually in real memory decreases. That, in turn, means more references to virtual memory and more swapping. At some point, the system begins **thrashing,** spending so much time swapping pages that it has little time left to do any processing. The solution is to add more real memory or reduce the number of active programs.

Thrashing
On a virtual memory system, spending so much time swapping pages that the processor has little time left to do any processing.

ADVANCED TOPICS

Memory Levels

Imagine a program that occupies a large amount of secondary storage. When that program is loaded into virtual memory, numerous specialized routines are left behind and loaded only if they are needed. As the program runs, selected pages move from virtual memory into real memory. From there, selected portions are copied to high-speed cache memory. Eventually, specific instructions are fetched from high-speed memory, copied into a register, and executed.

Review those memory levels: secondary storage, virtual memory, real memory, cache memory, and registers. As you move through those levels, speed increases, storage capacity declines, and the cost per byte goes up. At one extreme, the objective is to provide large amounts of low-cost mass storage. At the other extreme the objective is to maximize the utilization of the processor by allowing it to directly access the fastest memory possible. Staged memory levels help to bridge the gap between those two objectives.

Allocating Peripherals

If two programs were to take turns writing to the same printer, the output would be useless. If two programs were to take turns writing data to and reading data from the same magnetic tape, the data would be destroyed. Access to input and output devices must be carefully managed. The operating system is responsible for allocating peripheral devices to application programs.

Scheduling

Dispatching is concerned with deciding which of the programs already in memory will be allowed to execute next. **Scheduling** is concerned with deciding which program will be loaded into memory next. The scheduling decision typically involves two separate modules: a **queuing** routine and a **scheduler.**

As programs enter the system, they are placed in a queue (a waiting line) by the queuing routine (Figure 12.9). When space becomes available, the scheduler selects a program from the queue and loads it into memory (Figure 12.10). Often, the first program on the queue is the first one loaded, but more sophisticated priority rules can be used, too.

Once a program is in memory, it is no longer the scheduler's concern. Instead, that program's right to access the processor is determined by the dispatcher. The scheduler considers a program's *external* priority. The dispatcher determines its *internal* (dispatching) priority.

Spooling

The idea of multiprogramming is to improve the processor's efficiency by better utilizing its time. If the memory residency time of each program can be reduced, even greater efficiencies are possible.

Scheduling
The task performed by a scheduler.

Queuing
Placing pending programs in an electronic waiting line.

Scheduler
An operating system routine that determines the order in which application programs are loaded into memory.

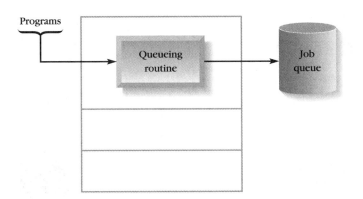

▲ **FIGURE 12.9**

As programs enter the system, they are placed in a queue.

For example, imagine that a system executes five concurrent programs and that each program occupies memory for exactly one minute. As soon as a program finishes executing, another one replaces it in memory, so the computer can run five programs a minute. If each program's residency time is reduced to thirty seconds, ten programs could run in that same minute.

One way to reduce a program's residency time is to limit its access to slow input and output devices. For example, instead of allowing a program to communicate directly with a printer, the data can be written to disk (Figure 12.11). Later, after the application program has finished executing, its output can be sent to the printer by an operating system routine.

The act of sending data to a high-speed device (such as a disk) for eventual output to a slow device (such as a printer) is called **spooling.** To spool input data, you copy them from a slow device (such as a keyboard or a scanner) to a fast device (such as a disk) before the application program is loaded. Later, because the application program gets its data from the high-speed device, it finishes processing more quickly, thus freeing space for another program.

Spooling
The act of sending data to a high-speed device (such as a disk) for eventual output to a slow device (such as a printer).

TIME-SHARING

If you have ever accessed a mainframe computer via a terminal, you have probably used a **time-sharing** system. Time-sharing is a technique that allows multiple users to share a single processor by, essentially, taking turns.

Time-sharing
A multitasking technique that works by dividing the processor's time into small slices and assigning the processor to application routines one time slice at a time.

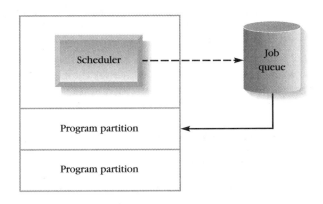

▲ **FIGURE 12.10**

Later, the scheduler selects a program from the queue and loads it into memory.

▲ FIGURE 12.11

Spooling.

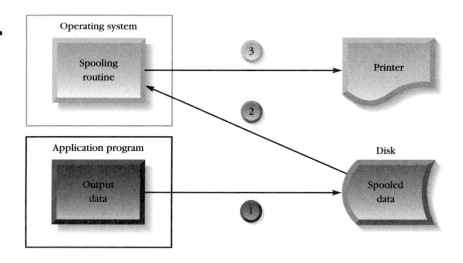

Time-Slicing

Time-slicing
Dividing the processor's time into tiny slices as a means of implementing multitasking.

The key to time-sharing is **time-slicing.** A time slice is a brief interval of time, perhaps 0.001 of a second. On a time-sharing system, an application program is allowed to control the processor for no more than a single time slice before ceding control to another program. A mainframe computer capable of executing millions of instructions per second can do a great deal of processing in a single time slice.

Most time-sharing applications are interactive. For example, imagine that you are entering data to perform a statistical analysis. You type a line of data, press the enter key, type the next line, and so on until all the data are entered. Each line represents one transaction. The task of formatting the data requires very little processor time, so a single time slice is more than enough to deal with each transaction.

At some point, all the data are entered and you issue a command to perform the statistical analysis. The necessary computations may take some time, so your program executes for a single time slice, waits while other programs take their turns, executes for a second time slice, waits again, and so on until the processing is finished. You may sense a delay of a few seconds, but that is better than forcing all the other users to wait while your lengthy transaction is processed.

To implement time-slicing, the operating system maintains a queue (or waiting line) of tasks (Figure 12.12). If the active task reaches a natural break point (such as a request for input or output) within a single time slice, the dispatcher starts the next task on the queue. If not, the long-running task is interrupted (by a clock signal), and the dispatcher starts the next task on the queue. After the dispatcher works through the entire queue, it goes back to the top and starts over again. Eventually, the interrupted program gets another turn.

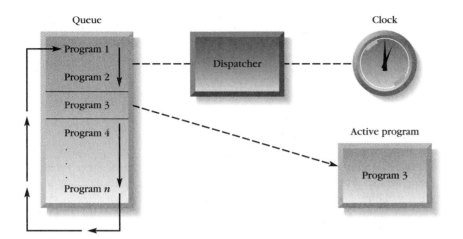

[▲] **Figure 12.12**

Time-sharing limits each program to a tiny slice of time.

Roll-In and Roll-Out

On most time-sharing systems, **roll-in** and **roll-out** techniques are used to manage memory. A typical time-sharing user spends a great deal of time thinking, typing, reading the screen, and moving the mouse. From the computer's perspective, very little processing is required to support that user. To the computer, each user represents a string of brief, widely spaced processing demands.

Once a transaction is processed, the system knows that considerable time will pass before that user's next transaction is received. Consequently, the user's work space can be rolled out to secondary storage, and that memory can be assigned to another user (Figure 12.13a). Later, when the first user's next transaction arrives, the associated work space is rolled back in (Figure 12.13b). By allowing multiple concurrent users to share memory space, roll-in and roll-out allows more users to be active, and that improves processor utilization.

Roll-in
On a time-sharing system, to copy a user's workspace from secondary storage into memory.
Roll-out
On a time-sharing system, to copy a user's workspace from memory to secondary storage.

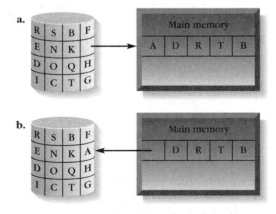

▲ **Figure 12.13**

Roll-in and roll-out.
a. **An inactive work space is rolled out to secondary storage.**
b. **Later, when the user resumes activity, the work space is rolled back into memory.**

VIRTUAL MACHINES

Virtual machine
A computing environment created by an operating system that allows a user to behave as though he or she has complete control over an independent computer with its own memory, peripheral devices, and other resources.

A **virtual machine** is a computing environment created by an operating system that allows a user to behave as though he or she has complete control over an independent *computer,* with its own memory, peripheral devices, and other resources. Virtual memory is concerned only with memory space. A virtual machine simulates a complete *system* running on a mainframe.

The operating system manages its virtual machines by automatically trapping the programs' references to virtual (imaginary) memory and virtual peripherals and activating the appropriate real components. Typically, time-sharing techniques are used to decide which one of the multiple, concurrent virtual machines is allowed to use the real processor. Within a given virtual machine, multiprogramming techniques might be used to manage concurrent programs.

MULTIPROCESSING

Multiprocessing
Two or more processors sharing the same memory.

Multiprogramming and time-sharing are techniques for concurrently sharing a single processor, but many modern computers contain two or more processors. When multiple processors share the same memory and have the ability to execute instructions simultaneously, you have a **multiprocessing** system. Because each processor can execute instructions independently, a computer with multiple processors can execute two or more instructions simultaneously.

SUMMARY

A single program or routine stored in memory and capable of being executed is called a task. The act of concurrently executing two or more tasks on a single processor is called multitasking.

The act of concurrently executing two or more programs on a single processor by taking advantage of the speed disparity between the computer and its peripheral devices is called multiprogramming. A multiprogramming operating system incorporates the basic operating system elements introduced in Chapter 6 and adds modules to manage processor time, main memory space, and peripheral device allocation.

The job of the operating system's processor management routine is to resolve the conflicts that occur when two or more tasks demand the processor's time. The dispatcher is the routine that decides which program is executed next.

An interrupt is an electronic signal that causes the computer to stop what it is doing and activate one of the operating system's interrupt service routines. The start and end of each input or output operation is marked by an interrupt. A wait state implies that the program cannot continue until some event, such as an input operation, is completed. A ready state implies that the program is ready to execute. The dispatcher selects the ready-state program with the highest dispatching priority.

Memory management is concerned with allocating memory space to application programs. Fixed partition memory management divides the available space into fixed-length partitions and loads one task into each partition. More efficient memory utilization is achieved with dynamic memory management; the space assigned to a task is called a region. The highest priority task is loaded into the foreground partition. Other tasks are loaded into background partitions. A multiprogramming system must have a memory protection scheme that restricts each task to its own partition and prevents tasks from interfering with each other.

Overlay structures can improve the utilization of the space assigned to a single program. Virtual memory is a technique for managing the memory space requirements of multiple concurrent tasks. Each program is divided into a set of fixed-length pieces called pages, which are swapped between real memory and virtual memory as necessary. Thrashing occurs when a virtual memory system spends so much time swapping pages that it has little time left to do any processing.

Scheduling involves a queuing routine and a scheduler. Scheduling and queuing are concerned with a program's external priority while the dispatcher deals with its internal (dispatching) priority. The act of sending data to a high-speed device (such as a disk) for eventual output to a slow device (such as a printer) is called spooling.

Time-sharing is a technique for managing the processor through time-slicing. Time-slicing is implemented by maintaining a queue of active programs, interrupting a program that exceeds its allocated time slice, and activating the next program on the queue. On most time-sharing systems, roll-in and roll-out techniques are used to manage memory.

A virtual machine is an operating environment created by an operating system that allows an application program to behave as though it has complete control over its own, independent virtual computer. When multiple processors share the same memory and have the ability to execute instructions simultaneously, you have a multiprocessing system.

KEY TERMS

background	multiprogramming	scheduler
dispatcher	multitasking	scheduling
dispatching priority	overlay	spooling
dynamic memory management	page	swapping
fixed partition memory management	partition, memory	task
	processor management	thrashing
foreground	queuing	time-sharing
interrupt	ready state	time-slicing
memory management	region	virtual machine
memory protection	roll-in	virtual memory
multiprocessing	roll-out	wait state

CONCEPTS

1. What is a task? What is multitasking?
2. Distinguish between the terms *concurrent* and *simultaneous*.

3. Placing more programs in memory and executing them concurrently improves the utilization of the processor. Why?

4. What is multiprogramming? Why is multiprogramming necessary (or desirable)?

5. List the basic functions of a multiprogramming operating system.

6. What is an interrupt? Why are interrupts important to a multiprogramming operating system?

7. Explain how a multiprogramming dispatcher manages the processor's time.

8. Distinguish between fixed partition and dynamic memory management. What is the difference between the foreground and the background? What is the relationship between a program's partition assignment and its dispatching priority? What is virtual memory?

9. Briefly explain how a multiprogramming operating system decides which program is loaded into memory next. Distinguish between a program's internal and external priorities.

10. What is spooling? Why is spooling used?

11. Distinguish between multiprogramming and time-sharing. How are they similar? How are they different?

12. Explain how a time-sharing system manages the processor's time. What is a time slice? How is time-slicing used to implement time-sharing?

13. Explain how a time-sharing system manages memory space.

14. Briefly explain the virtual machine concept.

15. Define the term *multiprocessing*.

PROJECT

1. Read *The Mythical Man Month* by Frederick P. Brooks, Jr. (Reading, Mass.: Addison-Wesley Publishing Company, 1975).

 ## INTERNET PROJECTS

1. *News and Notes.* Check the address *http://www.pulver.com* for current technology news and look for articles on multitasking and mainframe computers. Check through the *comp.* newsgroups for information on multitasking operating systems and parallel processing. Write a brief note or send an e-mail message to your instructor outlining what you find.

2. *Topic Searches.* Check the World Wide Web and/or other Internet resources for information on the following topics:

Key word	*Qualifiers*
parallel processors	Cray
multitasking	Windows 95
cache memory	personal computer

Define the key word, identify at least two sources of information on the topic, and briefly summarize the nature of the information you find.

3. *Links to Other Sites.* After you access one or more of the following sites, write a brief note or send an e-mail message to your instructor outlining what you find.

   a. On the World Wide Web, check *http://www.pulver.com* for current technology news.
   b. On the World Wide Web, check *http://www.ibm.com* for information on IBM products. Look for information on their mainframe computer systems.

4. Access West Publishing Company's home page and find the Chapter 12 student activities for this book. See Internet Project 3 for the spotlight on *The Internet* following Chapter 1 (page 29) for more detailed instructions on accessing the home page. As appropriate, repeat projects 1, 2, and/or 3 using the more current references you find.

CHAPTER 13

Data Communication

Before you start this chapter, you should be familiar with the following concepts:

▶ Hardware (p. 6), peripherals (p. 6), software (p. 9), and classifying computers (p. 14).

▶ Personal computer I/O (p. 56), display screens (p. 57), and terminals (p. 68).

▶ Bits, bytes, and words (p. 78), memory capacity (p. 78), and memory contents (p. 79).

▶ The operating system's input/output control system (p. 130).

▶ Communication software (p. 161).

When you finish reading this chapter, you should be able to:

▶ Identify the elements that are necessary for communication and briefly discuss the computer hardware and software that support data communication.

▶ Cite several examples of communication media.

▶ Explain how data communication speed is expressed.

▶ Distinguish between local and remote data communication. Distinguish between dedicated and switched lines.

▶ Briefly discuss several alternatives for increasing the utilization of a leased line. Explain data compression.

▶ Identify the three parts of a message. Explain the relationship between messages and signals.

▶ Explain why it is necessary to boost and filter a signal sent to a remote device. Explain modulation and demodulation.

▶ Distinguish between analog and digital data.

▶ Briefly discuss data communication protocols. Distinguish between asynchronous and synchronous data communication. Distinguish among simplex, half-duplex, and full-duplex.

▶ Briefly discuss how a communication protocol detects and corrects transmission errors.

COMMUNICATION

As a minimum, successful communication requires a message, a transmitter, a medium, and a receiver (Figure 13.1). The **message** is the data or the command being transmitted. The transmitter (or sender) is the source of the message. The medium is the physical link between the sender and the receiver. The receiver is the destination.

Message
The packet of information to be transmitted.

TRANSMITTERS AND RECEIVERS

Data communication is concerned with the transfer of data or information between two computers or between a computer and a terminal. Because computers are involved, the sender and the receiver consist of hardware and software.

Data communication
The act of transmitting data from one component to another.

Hardware

You learned about terminals in Chapter 3. A typical terminal (Figure 13.2) consists of a keyboard and a display linked by a communication line to (usually) a mainframe or a minicomputer. Personal computers and workstations can also serve as terminals.

A **modem** is a device that allows data to be transmitted between a terminal and a computer or between two computers over a telephone line. You will learn more about how a modem works later in this chapter. On some systems, a network interface card is used to link a microcomputer to a communication line.

Modem
A modulator/demodulator. A device that converts (or modulates) a signal from digital to analog and back again.

Communication lines are relatively slow compared to a computer's internal processing speed. To avoid wasting an expensive mainframe's time, a **front-end processor** (Figure 13.3) is sometimes placed between the computer and several communication lines. The front-end processor is a dedicated computer (often, a minicomputer) that takes care of the details of data communication, transferring data to and accepting data from the mainframe at the mainframe's convenience.

Front-end processor
A dedicated computer (often, a minicomputer) that takes care of the details of data communication, transferring data to and accepting data from the mainframe at the mainframe's convenience.

Software

A computer can do nothing without software to provide control. Communication software is needed to compose messages, send and receive messages, and route those messages to the appropriate application program. On some

▲ **Figure 13.1**

Communication requires a message, a transmitter, a medium, and a receiver.

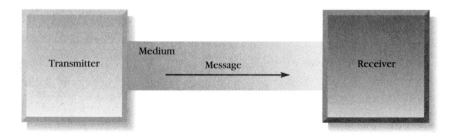

Transmitter   Medium   Message   Receiver

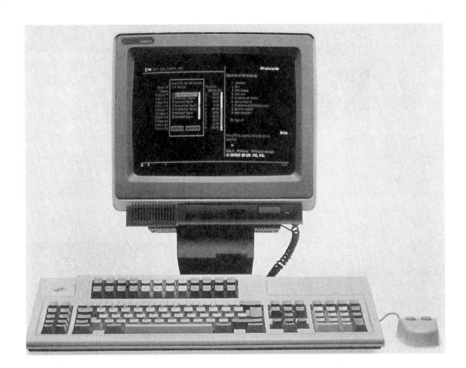

mainframes and minicomputers, the communication software is part of the operating system. Others use special system software routines or telecommunication monitors. A personal computer might run software that emulates (makes the computer act like) a terminal.

COMMUNICATION MEDIA

The communication medium, sometimes called a **line,** a **link,** or a **channel,** is the physical path over which the message flows.

Line, link, or channel
A general term for a data communication medium. The physical path over which the message flows.

Physical Links

A twisted pair (Figure 13.4) consists of two strands of wire twisted together; you probably use one to plug your telephone into a wall jack. A coaxial cable (Figure 13.5), such as the one that links your television set to a cable TV service, is more expensive but transmits a better quality signal. A **fiber-optic cable** (Figure 13.6) is a strand of glass fiber that can transmit impressive

Fiber-optic cable
A strand of glass fiber that can transmit impressive amounts of data at high speed with little or no distortion.

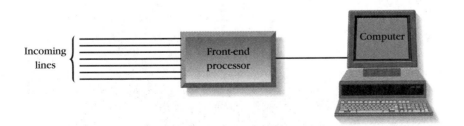

Incoming lines — Front-end processor — Computer

▲ **Figure 13.3**

A front-end processor sits between the computer and the communication lines.

▲ **Figure 13.4**

A twisted pair.

▲ **Figure 13.5**

A coaxial cable.

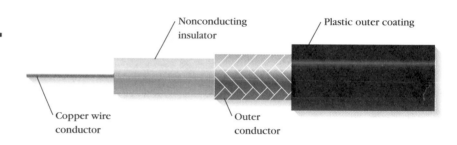

Nonconducting insulator

Plastic outer coating

Copper wire conductor

Outer conductor

amounts of data (in the form of light pulses) at very high rates with little or no distortion.

It is not necessary to run a physical line between the sender and the receiver; wireless communication via such media as radio, microwave, cellular telephone, or light beam is another option. Because the earth curves, wireless media require relay stations or satellites to transmit data over a significant distance (Figure 13.7).

Note that a single message might pass through several different media on its way from the sender to the receiver. For example, an e-mail message might

▲ **Figure 13.6**

Fiber-optic cables.

Global Satellite Communications

Early in 1994, two American billionaires, Bill Gates (of Microsoft Corporation) and Craig McCaw (the founder of McCaw Cellular Communications) announced the formation of Teledesic Corporation. The new company's mission is to develop a global communications network by launching more than 800 satellites into low-earth orbit.

One key to their proposal is the *global* nature of their network. High-speed cables already link major urban centers, but it will be many years before they reach the underdeveloped, rural, and isolated regions of the world. A satellite network, in contrast, can be accessed from virtually any spot on the planet as soon as the satellites are in place.

go from your computer to the local telephone company over a twisted pair. From there, it might be sent to the destination city via coaxial cable, fiber-optic cable, or even satellite before following another twisted pair from that city's telephone company to the target computer.

Transmission Speed

A message is transmitted over a communication line as a string of binary digits. The transmission speed (usually measured in bits per second) is called the **baud** rate. (The term *baud* is named after a French data communication pioneer named Emile Baudot.)

Today's most used data communication medium, the telephone, transmits thousands of bits (kilobits) per second. A standard **voice-grade** telephone line is rated at 2,400 baud, and a modem can transmit data over a voice grade line at integer multiples (2,400, 4,800, 9,600, 14,400, 19,200, 28,800 . . .) of that rated speed.

New technologies, such as fiber-optic cables and wireless media, support even faster speeds. Many of our intercity lines already use fiber-optic technology, and the process of wiring individual businesses and (eventually) homes with fiber-optic lines has already begun. In a few years, transmission rates of millions of bits (megabits) per second will be common.

Baud
A measure of data transmission speed (usually, bits per second).

Voice-grade line
A standard 2,400 baud telephone line.

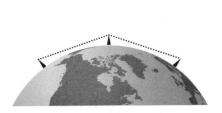

▲ **Figure 13.7**

Wireless media rely on relay stations or satellites.

Common Carriers

Some communication facilities are private; others are public. The companies that provide public communication services are called **common carriers.** Examples include AT&T, MCI, Sprint, GTE, and your local telephone company.

For years, the term "common carrier" has been almost synonymous with "telephone company," but that is beginning to change. Today, cable TV, cellular telephone, and direct satellite links are challenging the telephone company for dominance in the communication marketplace.

Local and Remote

Some communication lines are **local;** in other words, the sender and the receiver are relatively close to each other. In contrast, **remote** data communication implies widely separated devices linked (usually) by a line provided by a common carrier.

Dedicated and Switched Lines

Local communication is usually implemented through **dedicated,** point-to-point, hard-wired lines; a cable that stretches from a terminal in the registrar's office to the university's mainframe is a good example. A dedicated line is permanently assigned for a specific purpose; for example, the registrar's line is probably used only to access student records, and is not available for making telephone calls.

On a **switched line,** the connection is established at the time communication begins, maintained while communication is ongoing, and broken

Common carrier
A company that provides public communication services.

Local
Nearby. In close proximity to.
Remote
Distant.

Dedicated line
A line that is permanently assigned for a specific purpose.

Switched line
A connection that is established at the time communication begins, maintained while communication is ongoing, and broken when communication ends.

THE FUTURE

Mobile Communication

Today, doctors and other professionals carry pagers that allow them to stay in touch with their office no matter where they are. Mobile telephones allow you to place calls from your car, and you can even use a personal digital assistant to send a fax from the beach.

These modern communication devices all rely on a form of wireless radio transmission. Along with cable television, they represent very real competition to the telephone company. Even today, many organizations choose to bypass their local telephone company and rely on radio or cable technology to transmit their voice and data communications to their long-distance carrier.

We are on the verge of a communication revolution. Not too many years ago, Dick Tracy's wrist radio and Agent Maxwell Smart's shoe telephone seemed futuristic. Today, they seem quaint. Soon, if you choose to do so, you will be able to carry your telephone in your pocket and have your calls automatically forwarded to wherever you may be. You will have to decide if that is good or bad, however.

when communication ends. Dedicated lines are permanent. Switched lines are temporary.

For example, imagine that you have just dialed the telephone number of a friend who lives in another state. The number flows from your telephone over a local line to the telephone company's switching station, where a computer locates a free long-distance line and sends the number on to the next switching station (Figure 13.8). Eventually, perhaps after several jumps, the number reaches the local switching station in your friend's town. An instant later, your friend's telephone rings.

The switching process establishes a physical link between the sender and the receiver. Assuming your friend answers, that link is maintained while you communicate. As soon as you hang up, however, the link is terminated and the long-distance lines are freed for other users.

Line Utilization

Not all remote data communication uses switched lines, of course; dedicated, long-distance **leased** and **private lines** are available from the telephone company, and some organizations operate their own communication systems. High-speed lines are expensive, however, and data communication between any two devices tends to be sporadic, so it is sometimes necessary to share a leased line in order to get enough utilization to justify the cost.

Value-added carriers provide relatively low-cost access to high-speed lines by leasing a line from a common carrier and then subleasing the use of the line to their customers. In one technique, called **packet switching,** the carrier accepts a message, divides it into a series of small blocks (called packets), and then simultaneously transmits the packets from multiple sources over the line. At the other end of the line, the packets are reassembled to form the original messages and sent on to their destinations.

Leased line
A private communication line leased or rented from a common carrier.

Private line
A private communication line leased or rented from a common carrier.

Value-added carrier
A service that provides relatively low-cost access to high-speed lines by leasing a line from a common carrier and then subleasing the use of the line.

Packet switching
A network management technique in which the carrier accepts a message, divides it into a series of small blocks (called packets), and then simultaneously transmits the packets from multiple sources over the line.

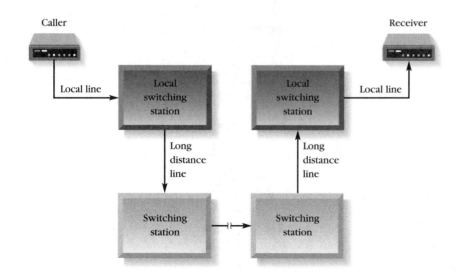

▲ **Figure 13.8**

A switched line is established at the time communication begins.

Multidrop line
A single line that links several terminals or workstations to a computer.
Multipoint line
A single line that links several terminals or workstations to a computer.
Multiplexor
A device that merges (or overlaps) messages from several low-speed lines and transmits the resulting single stream of data over a high-speed line.

A **multidrop** or **multipoint** line is used to link several terminals to a computer (Figure 13.9). A single terminal does not generate enough data volume to justify a leased line, but the combined data volumes of numerous terminals might be plenty.

A **multiplexor** (Figure 13.10) is a device that merges (or overlaps) messages from several low-speed lines and transmits the resulting single stream of data over a high-speed line. Another multiplexor at the other end of the line reverses the processes by recreating the original messages. Using slow, inexpensive lines to link individual terminals to the multiplexor and then

▲ **Figure 13.9**

A multidrop or multipoint line.

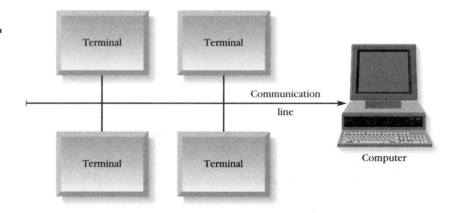

▲ **Figure 13.10**

A multiplexor combines messages from several lines.

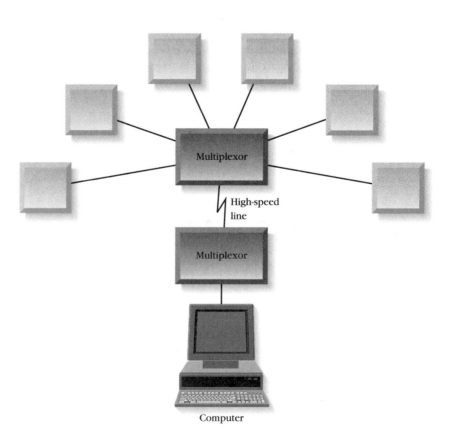

transferring the data to a high-speed line is much less expensive than running high-speed lines to each terminal.

Line Speed as a Bottleneck

A few decades ago, most remote applications transmitted data one line at a time over standard telephone lines. The ASCII code represents characters as 8-bit patterns. At 8 bits per character, the maximum data communication speed at 2,400 baud is 300 characters per second, and the actual rate is usually less than that.

A transmission speed of 300 characters per second is adequate for exchanging 80-character, 1-line messages, but as full-screen displays became the new standard, the communication link became a bottleneck (Figure 13.11). At 300 characters per second, it takes more than 6 seconds to transmit the contents of a single (80-character by 25-line) screen and more than 40 *minutes* to transmit all the pixels displayed on a high-resolution graphics screen. That is unacceptable.

Compression

The most obvious way to increase line speed is to use a faster medium, but the available technology sets a limit on pure speed. A second option is to transmit fewer data. For example, with an intelligent terminal (or a computer) at each end of the line, the sender can transmit raw, unformatted, highly compressed data and let the receiver do the formatting.

Data **compression** is particularly effective. Much of what you see displayed on a screen is background, single-color space, and every file contains blank characters and repetitive bit patterns. You can significantly reduce the size of the message if you replace all those null pixels, blank characters, and consecutive 0s or 1s with a code that tells the receiving computer how to reconstruct the message (Figure 13.12). No matter what the baud rate, short messages are transmitted faster than long messages.

MESSAGES AND SIGNALS

An electronic message consists of three parts: a header, a body, and a trailer (Figure 13.13). The header holds information for the system; think of it as

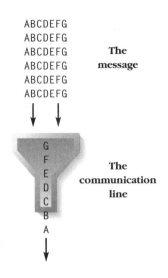

▲ **Figure 13.11**

The communication link can be a bottleneck.

Compression
Conserving memory, secondary storage space, and data transmission time by removing repetitive or unnecessary bits from data.

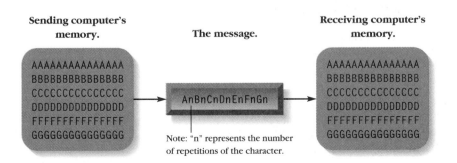

Sending computer's memory.

The message.

Receiving computer's memory.

AnBnCnDnEnFnGn

Note: "n" represents the number of repetitions of the character.

▲ **Figure 13.12**

Data compression.

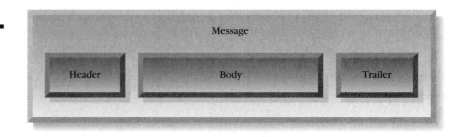

instructions for delivering the message. (For example, the header probably contains the receiver's address.) The actual information forms the body of the message. The final component is a trailer or end-of-message marker that tells the system the message is completed.

A message moves over a communication line in the form of a **signal;** for example, the signal might consist of a fluctuating electric current or a flashing light. Variations in the signal represent coded information. The sending device creates the signal variations. The receiving device interprets them.

Signal, communication
The form in which a message moves over a communication line.

Signal Degradation and Noise

When data are transmitted over a distance, the signal loses intensity and picks up electronic interference or **noise.** The farther it moves from its source, the weaker the signal becomes until, eventually, it is overwhelmed by the noise. To confirm that phenomenon, tune your car radio to a local FM station, drive away from town, and listen to what happens to the signal.

Because the signal degrades with distance, if you want to transmit a message between two devices that are separated by more than a mile or two, you must find a way to boost the signal, filter the noise, or both.

Noise
Electronic interference.

Analog Data

Inside a computer, data are represented as patterns of discrete binary digits, or bits. One way to transmit those bit patterns over a distance is to convert the message to **analog** form.

An analog signal is analogous to the real data; in other words, it varies with the real data. For example, the position of your car's speedometer needle is analogous to the car's speed and the height of a column of mercury in a thermometer is analogous to the temperature. Analog data are represented as a continuous signal that varies with the bit pattern. Continuous signals are much easier to boost and filter than discrete bit patterns.

Analog
A signal that is analogous to the real data or that varies with the real data.

Carrier Signals

To transmit data in analog form, you start with a continuous **carrier signal** such as the sine wave pictured in Figure 13.14. One complete S-on-its-side pattern is called a cycle. The height of the wave is its amplitude. The number of cycles per second (usually expressed in Hertz) is its frequency. Because the carrier signal's frequency and amplitude are known, equipment can be designed to filter and boost it.

Carrier signal
A continuous analog signal of known frequency and amplitude used to transmit data.

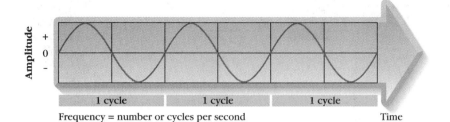

Amplitude
+
0
-

1 cycle   1 cycle   1 cycle

Frequency = number or cycles per second   Time

▲ **Figure 13.14**

Data are transmitted in the context of a carrier signal.

Baseband and Broadband

ADVANCED TOPICS

The transmission capacity of a communication line is a function of its bandwidth, the range of frequencies it can carry. With baseband technology, the entire bandwidth is used to transmit one high-speed signal at a time. With broadband technology, the available bandwidth is divided into distinct channels (separated by bands of unused frequencies) that act much like independent wires.

Baseband is faster than broadband, but it is limited to local data communication and can transmit only one signal at a time. Broadband is more flexible, supporting multiple, concurrent messages moving over the line at different frequencies.

Modulation and Demodulation

Computers store and manipulate discrete pulses, not continuous waves. Consequently, whenever data are transmitted between two computers over an analog line, the signal must be converted from pulse form to wave form and back again.

Converting to wave form is called **modulation;** converting back is **demodulation.** The task is performed by a device called a modem (modulator/demodulator) (Figure 13.15). Normally, there is one modem at each end of a communication line (Figure 13.16).

Modulation
Adding intelligence to a carrier signal.
Demodulation
Extracting information from a carrier signal.

▲ **Figure 13.15**

A typical modem.

▲ Figure 13.16

**There is a modem at each end
of the communication line.**

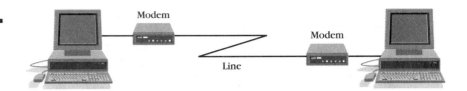

A modem transmits a continuous carrier signal of known frequency and amplitude over the line. (If you listen to the carrier signal, you hear a hum.) Intelligence (the message) is added by changing the signal's amplitude (amplitude modulation), frequency (frequency modulation), or some other measurable characteristic of the signal.

For example, imagine that the carrier signal is set at 1,000 cycles per second and that a single bit is transmitted during each cycle. The modem at the receiving end is tuned to the carrier signal; it expects one cycle every 0.001 seconds. A 1-bit might be represented by increasing the frequency for 0.001 seconds (Figure 13.17). A 0-bit might be transmitted by leaving the frequency alone. The receiving modem interprets a standard frequency cycle as a 0-bit and a high-frequency cycle as a 1-bit.

Note that it is possible to transmit more than one bit per cycle. For example, the telephone system uses a carrier frequency of 2,400 cycles per second, so one bit per cycle equates to 2,400 baud. If each cycle carries two bits, the effective data transmission speed over that same telephone line is 4,800 bits per second. Add more bits per cycle and you increases the effective speed to 9,600, 19,200, and even 28,800 baud.

Digital Data

Analog signals are boosted by amplifying them, but when you amplify the signal, you also amplify the noise. The background hiss you hear when you play a cassette tape is a good example; it gets louder when you turn up the

Radio Signals

A good way to visualize modulation and demodulation is to picture how radio works. A radio station broadcasts a continuous carrier signal with a frequency that matches the station's identifying number. For example, when you tune your receiver to 102.5, you pick up the station that broadcasts a 102.5 megaHertz carrier signal.

The station adds sound to the carrier signal by varying or modulating the frequency (FM) or the amplitude (AM). If you tune your radio to 102.5, you electronically subtract (or filter out) a 102.5 megaHertz carrier signal and what you have left is the sound that was added to that signal by the station. Change your tuner to 99.7, and you filter out a 99.7 megaHertz carrier signal, leaving the sound added by the station that broadcasts at 99.7 megaHertz.

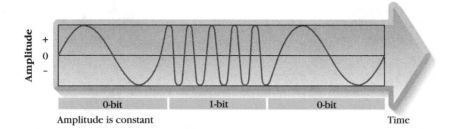

▲ **Figure 13.17**

Data are transmitted by selectively varying the carrier signal.

volume. In effect, an analog signal *accumulates* noise as it travels along a line, and that makes it difficult to maintain signal quality.

An option is to directly transmit the data in their pure binary form by using **digital** technology. Analog data are represented as a continuous signal that varies with the data. Digital data are represented as discrete pulses (Figure 13.18).

An analog signal is boosted by amplifying it. A digital signal, in contrast, is electronically captured, reconstructed, and retransmitted, so most of the noise is automatically filtered from the signal. Just as digital compact disks yield a clearer, sharper sound than analog cassettes and vinyl LPs, digital data transmission means better quality than analog data transmission.

Digital
A signal or data in the form of discrete digits. On a computer, digital usually implies binary.

Analog Lines

NOTE

Perhaps you have seen the advertisement in which one of the long-distance telephone companies demonstrates the clarity of its signal by dropping a pin. Other commercials talk about fiber-optic cables that promise a clear, distortion-free signal. Those advertisements feature digital technology.

Without question, the quality of digital data transmission is far superior to analog, so why do we continue to use analog lines? The answer has more to do with history and economics than technology.

Many existing telephone lines were installed decades ago. In those days, modern digital technology did not exist, and analog data transmission was the only practical alternative. The cost of replacing all those analog lines is prohibitive, so we continue to use them.

Although digital lines are much better for transmitting data, analog lines are fine for voice communication because people are very good at filtering out background noise and filling in an occasional lost syllable. In fact, some argue that those very background noises and pauses add a touch of personality and richness to the signal and thus enhance communication.

Unlike people, machines demand precision, however. There are real advantages to using digital lines for transmitting data, so as new facilities are constructed, most are digital. Eventually, the line that runs from your office or your home to the local telephone company is likely to be the only analog component involved in transmitting your message.

▲ Figure 13.18

Digital data are represented as discrete pulses.

PROTOCOLS

Data communication involves a message, a transmitter, a receiver, and a line. Generally, the transmitter and the receiver operate independently, so they must be electronically synchronized before they can exchange signals.

Establishing a link between two independent and perhaps incompatible devices is a complex task. The secret is to follow a **protocol,** a precise set of rules that governs data communication. For example, when you answer the telephone, you probably say "hello." You and the caller then identify yourselves, and the conversation begins. You exchange information by taking turns. Finally, you say "goodby" and hang up. That informal set of rules is a primitive protocol.

Electronic devices follow a similar (though much more formal) protocol to transmit data. First, the transmitter sends a signal to the receiver announcing that a message is coming. The receiver then returns a signal to the transmitter indicating that it is ready. The message itself comes next. Finally, the receiver acknowledges the message, and the transmission ends. The protocol defines such things as the structure of the message, the precise nature and the sequence of the control signals, the baud rate, the code to be used, and the rules that govern each step.

Transmission Modes

With **asynchronous** data transmission, the data are transmitted in short, irregular blocks, sometimes one byte at a time. With **synchronous** transmission, the sender collects a large block of data and sends the entire block at one time. In effect, the sender and the receiver must remain "in sync" while the entire block is transmitted because timing is used to distinguish the individual bytes.

On a **simplex** line, data flow in one direction only. A **half-duplex** line can transmit data in both directions, but in only one direction at a time. A **full-duplex** (or duplex) line can transmit in both directions at the same time.

Error Sensing

Although modern data communication seems highly reliable, electronic interference makes transmission errors common. The reason you rarely see the bad data is because most protocols incorporate effective error sensing and error correction routines.

Generally, an extra bit, called a **parity** bit, is transmitted with each byte. With odd parity, the total number of 1 bits (in the 9 bits that make up a byte plus its parity bit) must be an odd number. With even parity, the total number of 1 bits must be an even number. The sender and the receive must agree on

Protocol
A set of rules that governs data communication.

Asynchronous
Transmitting data in short, irregular blocks, sometimes one byte at a time.
Synchronous
Transmitting data in large blocks.

Simplex
A line that can transmit data in one direction only.
Half-duplex
A line that can transmit data in both directions, but in only one direction at a time.
Full-duplex
A line that can transmit in both directions at the same time.

Parity
An extra bit added to a byte to help reduce errors.

the type of parity to be used before data transmission can begin. Incorrect parity implies an error that can be detected by hardware or software.

In addition to adding a parity bit to each byte, parity-like bits and check digits can be attached to larger blocks of data, giving the data communication system the ability to screen for different types of errors. If the receiver detects an error, it sends a signal to the sender requesting retransmission of the bad data.

Summary

As a minimum, successful communication requires a message, a transmitter, a medium, and a receiver. Data communication is concerned with the transfer of data or information between two computers or between a computer and a terminal. A modem is a device that allows data to be transmitted over a telephone line. To avoid wasting an expensive mainframe's time, a front-end processor is sometimes placed between the computer and several communication lines. Communication software is needed to compose messages, send and receive messages, and route those messages to the appropriate application program.

The communication medium, sometimes called a line, a link, or a channel, is the path over which the message flows. Examples include a twisted pair of wires, a coaxial cable, a fiber-optic cable, radio, microwave, cellular telephone, and light beams. The transmission speed (usually measured in bits per second) is called the baud rate. A standard voice grade telephone line is rated at 2,400 baud. The companies that provide public communication services are called common carriers.

Some lines are local; others are remote. Local communication is usually implemented through dedicated lines. On a switched line, the connection is established at the time communication begins. Dedicated, long-distance leased and private lines are available from the telephone company.

A value-added carrier leases a high-capacity line from a common carrier and then subleases the use of the line. Packet switching involves dividing messages into small blocks (called packets) and then simultaneously transmitting the packets from multiple sources over the line. A multidrop or multipoint line links several terminals to a computer. A multiplexor merges messages from several low-speed lines and transmits the resulting single stream of data over a high-speed line. Data compression involves replacing repetitive patterns with codes that tell the receiving computer how to reconstruct the message.

A message moves over a communication line in the form of a signal. When data are transmitted over a distance, the signal loses intensity and picks up electronic interference or noise. One solution is to convert the message to analog form. To transmit analog data, you start with a continuous carrier signal. Converting a signal to wave form is called modulation; converting back is demodulation. Instead of transmitting an analog signal, you can directly transmit the data in their pure binary form by using digital technology.

A protocol is a precise set of rules that governs data communication. With asynchronous data transmission, the data are transmitted in short, irregular blocks. With synchronous transmission, the data are transmitted in long blocks. On a simplex line, data flow in one direction only. A half-duplex line can transmit data in both directions, but in only one direction at a time. A full-duplex line can transmit in both directions at the same time. Parity bits are used to help detect transmission errors.

KEY TERMS

analog	full-duplex	packet switching
asynchronous	half-duplex	parity
baud	leased line	private line
carrier signal	line	protocol
channel	link	remote
common carrier	local	signal, communication
compression	message	simplex
data communication	modem	switched line
dedicated line	modulation	synchronous
demodulation	multidrop line	value-added carrier
digital	multiplexor	voice grade line
fiber-optic cable	multipoint line	
front-end processor	noise	

CONCEPTS

1. Identify the elements that are necessary for communication. What is data communication?
2. List several examples of computer hardware that acts as a data communication sender and/or receiver. What is a modem? What is a front-end processor?
3. Identify several functions performed by data communication software.
4. Cite several examples of communication media.
5. How is data communication speed measured? What is a voice-grade line? How fast is a voice grade-line? What is a common carrier?
6. Distinguish between local and remote data communication.
7. What is a dedicated line? What is a switched line? What is a value-added carrier? What is packet switching?
8. What is a multidrop line? Why are multidrop lines used? What is a multiplexor? Why are multiplexors used?
9. Briefly explain data compression. Why are data compression techniques used?
10. Identify the three parts of a message and explain the purpose of each part.
11. What is a signal? What is the relationship between messages and signals? If you want to transmit data over a distance, you must boost and filter the signal. Why?
12. Briefly explain the modulation/demodulation process.
13. What are analog data? What are digital data? Why is analog used?
14. What is a protocol? Why are protocols necessary?
15. Distinguish between asynchronous and synchronous data communication. Distinguish among simplex, half-duplex, and full-duplex.

16. Briefly discuss how a communication protocol detects and corrects transmission errors.

PROJECTS

1. Ask your instructor or a data communication expert to allow you to listen as data are transmitted over a telephone line.

2. If you have access to an on-line service, make a connection at the highest available baud rate and access an electronic bulletin board or the World Wide Web. Then log off, reestablish your connection at a lower baud rate, and perform the same tasks. You will quickly learn why transmission speed is so important.

3. Tour a local radio station and find out how the station transmits its signal. Relate what you learn to modulation and demodulation.

4. Investigate how a cellular telephone works.

 ## INTERNET PROJECTS

1. *News and Notes.* Check one or more of the on-line newspapers listed in Appendix B and look for articles on the communication industry. Write a brief note or send an e-mail message to your instructor outlining what you find.

2. *Topic Searches.* Check the World Wide Web and/or other Internet resources for information on the following topics:

Key word	Qualifiers
fiber-optic	cable TV
Teledesic	
compression	data communication

Define the key word, identify at least two sources of information on the topic, and briefly summarize the nature of the information you find.

3. *Links to Other Sites.* After you access one or more of the following sites, write a brief note or send an e-mail message to your instructor outlining what you find.

   a. On the World Wide Web, check *http://www.att.com* for information about AT&T.

   b. On the World Wide Web, check *http://www.sprint.com* for information about Sprint.

   c. On the World Wide Web, check *http://www.mci.com* for information about MCI.

4. Access West Publishing Company's home page and find the Chapter 13 student activities for this book. See Internet Project 3 for the spotlight on *The Internet* following Chapter 1 (page 29) for more detailed instructions on accessing the home page. As appropriate, repeat projects 1, 2, and/or 3 using the more current references you find.

CHAPTER 14

Networks

Before you start this chapter, you should be familiar with the following concepts:

▶ Hardware (p. 6), peripherals (p. 6), software (p. 9), and data (p. 10).

▶ Classifying computers (14), networks (p. 17), and the Internet (p. 17).

▶ Operating system functions (p. 122).

▶ Commercial software (p. 146) and communication software (p. 161).

▶ Security (p. 206), accessing files (p. 207), and the database management system (p. 229).

Note: This chapter is related to, but not dependent on, Chapter 13. You can read Chapters 13 and 14 in any order, but it may be useful to read Chapter 13 first.

When you finish reading this chapter, you should be able to:

▶ Cite several reasons why networks are used.

▶ Briefly explain client/server computing.

▶ Distinguish among a local area network, a wide area network, and a metropolitan area network.

▶ Identify several common network topologies.

▶ Explain the purpose of bridges and gateways.

▶ Briefly explain network operating systems and agent processes.

▶ Trace the path of an internetwork message as it moves from node to node.

▶ Discuss network security.

▶ Briefly explain polling, collision detection, and token passing.

▶ Briefly describe the ISO/OSI model and the emerging ISDN network.

WHY NETWORKS?

As you learned in Chapter 1, a network consists of two or more computers linked by communication lines (Figure 14.1). There are many reasons for using networks, including:

- ▶ software sharing
- ▶ data sharing
- ▶ hardware sharing
- ▶ backup and workload sharing
- ▶ on-line services
- ▶ groupware
- ▶ electronic data interchange

Software Sharing

Software sharing involves storing a single copy of a program on a central computer and allowing multiple users to access it over the network. The network provides a means for maintaining the software, too. When a new release of a program is received, a master copy is stored on the network. Subsequently, because all users share the same copy, they all access the new version.

Data Sharing

The computers linked to a network can also share data. For example, all the students in your class might log onto the network at their convenience and access a single copy of a file your instructor created to support an assign-

▲ **Figure 14.1**

A network consists of two or more computers linked by communication lines.

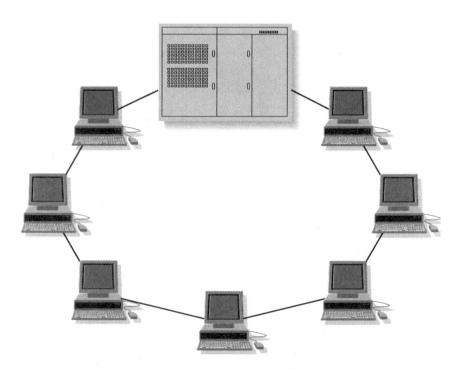

I S S U E S

Networks and the Copyright Law

Software sharing may be the reason your school implemented a network. The licensing agreements that accompany such programs as dBASE, WordPerfect, Word, and Excel limit their use to one user per copy, and a decade ago enforcing that limit was a serious problem on most campuses. The solution (at many schools) was (and still is) to create a network linking student PCs to a central computer with a high-capacity hard disk. A master copy of each program is stored on the hard disk and downloaded to student computers on request. Network software automatically tracks the number of copies in use and ensures that the school does not violate the copyright law.

ment. In many organizations, a central database is stored on one computer and accessed by many other computers over the network. Centralizing data simplifies data maintenance.

Hardware Sharing

Hardware can be shared, too. For example, the cost of attaching laser printers to each student computer is prohibitive, but you may be able to access a shared laser printer over your school's network. Even computational power can be shared; on some systems a computer facing a computational task that exceeds its capacity can shift the work to another machine.

Backup and Workload Sharing

Networks can also be used to provide backup. Because data and information move easily over the communication lines, key files and software can be copied from one computer and duplicated on another. Also, the ability to shift work between computers allows an organization to balance its workload during peak periods or even to pick up the work of a failed computer.

On-Line Services

Anyone with a properly equipped microcomputer, the right software, and a telephone can tap into stock quotations, library catalogs, gossip, electronic bulletin boards, e-mail, current news, weather reports, and similar information by accessing the Internet, the World Wide Web, or such commercial on-line services as America Online, CompuServe, Delphi, GEnie, the Microsoft Network, and Prodigy.

Groupware

The ability to share hardware, software, and data has literally changed the way people work. For example, picture the task of creating a newsletter. In the past, writers, copy editors, artists, and page designers did their work sequentially, with finished copy moving from the writer to the copy editor and only then to the page designer, where it was merged with the finished art.

Today, all those specialists can work together through a network (Figure 14.2). Because the data are shared, the copy editor can work in parallel with the writer, and the artist can access the current narrative to make sure the illustrations are consistent with the text. Meanwhile, the page designer can manipulate the narrative and the art and perhaps suggest changes to improve the page layout while the work is still in process. The software that supports cooperative group efforts over a network is called **groupware.**

Groupware
Software that supports cooperative group efforts over a network.

Electronic Data Interchange

A network can link an organization to other firms, too. For example, if such product manufacturers as Procter and Gamble, Kraft, and General Mills are electronically linked to computers in the supermarkets that sell their products, the suppliers can monitor stock at the store level and deliver new stock directly to the shelves, bypassing the supermarket chain's warehouse and saving both companies money. Such direct data communication between two organizations is called **electronic data interchange,** or **EDI,** and it has the potential to change the way companies do business.

Electronic data interchange (EDI)
Data communication between two companies.

Electronic data interchange implies the direct transfer of source data between the participating organizations' computers; for example, a customer might send a supplier an electronic purchase order, and a bank might electronically transfer funds to another bank. Note that there is no paperwork and no need for the receiving organization to enter the data into its computer. That saves both time and money.

▲ **Figure 14.2**

A network allows people to work together in a group.

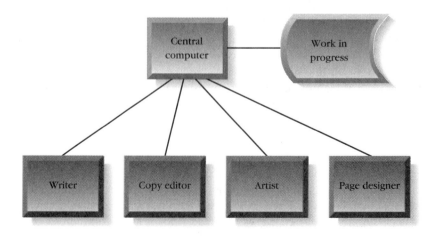

The Turnpike Effect

The Pennsylvania Turnpike was the first superhighway built in the United States. Its designers assumed that the road would be used primarily for long-distance travel because they could not imagine anyone paying a toll to drive across town. They were wrong. Shortly after the highway opened, traffic volume, particularly in metropolitan areas, regularly exceeded their worst case projections.

The reason why those projections were so inaccurate was that no one had ever experienced a modern, high-speed, limited access highway before. When people were asked if they would pay a toll to drive a few miles, they said, "Of course not." Then the turnpike opened. Suddenly, people discovered how convenient it was to bypass stoplights, stop signs, and intersections. Suddenly, it made sense to pay a toll to drive across town, and that is exactly what they did. They literally overwhelmed the system.

The tendency of people to discover new and unanticipated uses for technology after the technology is released has come to be called the Turnpike Effect. That phenomenon is particularly common in the computer field, and on-line network services could be the next example. Costs are dropping, the equipment is becoming easier to use, and the services are growing more and more interesting. One of these days, public network access is going to explode.

CLIENT/SERVER COMPUTING

Networks have led to a new approach to information processing called **client/server computing;** the topic was briefly introduced in Chapter 1. The idea is to assign common resources to the most appropriate computer (the server). The other computers on the network (the clients) then request the server's help to access one of those resources.

For example, imagine the simple two-computer network pictured in Figure 14.3. The mainframe controls access to the organization's database. Linked to the minicomputer is a high-speed laser printer.

When the minicomputer needs data from the database, it (the client) asks the mainframe (the server) for help. The mainframe responds by accessing the database and sending the requested data to the minicomputer. When a mainframe application wants to send some output to the laser printer, the mainframe assumes the role of client and asks the minicomputer (the server) for help. Note that a given computer might be the client or the server depending on the application.

Client/server computing makes key resources available to multiple users economically and efficiently. The alternative, duplicating resources on each user's system, is difficult to justify economically. Another advantage derived from client/server computing is control. For example, if the responsibility for accessing the database is assigned to one server, the necessary security procedures can be enforced by a single computer.

Client/server computing
A form of computing in which key tasks are assigned to different computers in a network. When a computer (the client) encounters a need to perform a task assigned to some other computer, it asks that computer (the server) for support.

▲ **Figure 14.3**

Client/server computing.

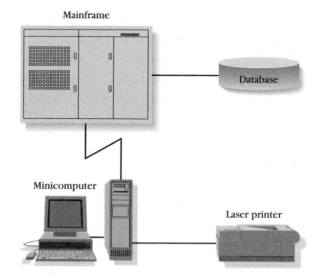

NETWORK STRUCTURES

The computers that form a network can be linked in several different ways.

Local Area Networks

Local area network (LAN)
A network composed of computers that are located in a limited area.
Workstation
A microcomputer used to access a network.

A group of computers located in close proximity (for example, within the same building) and linked by local communication lines (p. 292) form a **local area network,** or **LAN** (Figure 14.4). The end-user microcomputers through which people access a local area network are called **workstations.** (Note: The term *workstation* also refers to a high-performance, single-user graphic or scientific computer.)

▲ **Figure 14.4**

The computers in a local area network are geographically close to each other.

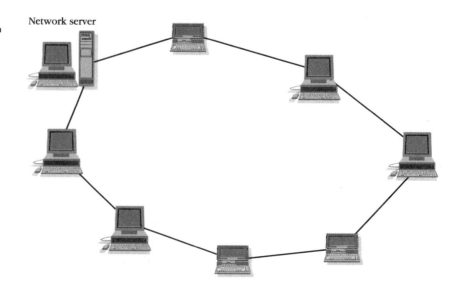

Most local area networks are controlled by a **network server,** a computer that provides the network's client computers with central access to files, peripherals, and other services. Normally, all communication is routed through the server. On a **peer-to-peer network,** in contrast, every computer can access the files and peripherals on every other network computer, so there is no need for an expensive server.

Wide Area Networks

A **wide area network,** or **WAN** (Figure 14.5) links computers that are geographically dispersed. Most wide area networks rely (at least in part) on public communication services such as the telephone company (p. 292). The computers that perform end-user tasks are called **hosts.** Other computers manage the network.

A **metropolitan area network,** or **MAN,** is a high-speed network that links computers separated by up to 50 miles. The area covered by a metropolitan area network lies in between a LAN and a WAN.

Network server
The computer that controls a local area network.

Peer-to-peer network
A network on which every computer can access the files and peripherals on every other network computer, thus eliminating the need for a server.

Wide area network (WAN)
A network that links geographically disbursed computers.

Host
A network computer that performs end-user tasks.

Metropolitan area network (MAN)
A high-speed network that links computers separated by up to 50 miles.

Private Branch Exchanges

ADVANCED TOPICS

When you make a long-distance call, you probably imagine the signal going from your telephone, over a line, directly to your friend's telephone, but the telephone company actually connects your call through a network. When the signal leaves your telephone, it flows over a local line to a local switching station. From there, it might pass through several additional switching stations before it finds its way to its destination.

Some organizations operate their own switching stations, called private branch exchanges (PBXs). Communications between two internal telephones

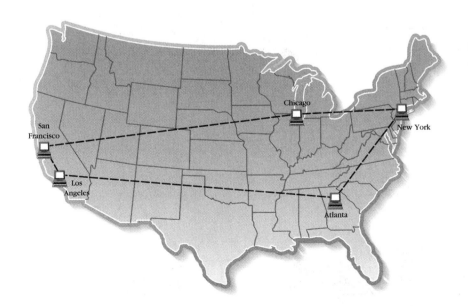

▲ **Figure 14.5**

A wide area network links computers that are geographically dispersed.

ADVANCED TOPICS

(or computers) pass through the PBX, bypassing the telephone company's public switches. A long-distance call goes from the user's telephone, through the PBX, to the telephone company's network.

Network Topology

Bus network
A network in which the server, the workstations, and various peripheral devices all share a common communication line, or bus.

Hierarchical network
A network in which the computers are linked to form a hierarchy.

Local area networks are sometimes configured as **bus networks** (Figure 14.6). In a bus network, the server, the workstations, and various peripheral devices all share a common communication line, or bus.

In a **hierarchical network** (Figure 14.7), the computers are linked to form a hierarchy. For example, a large corporation might link its sales associates' PCs to their office computers, several office computers to a regional computer, and the regional machines to the corporate mainframe. Data are typically collected at the bottom and analyzed at the top of the hierarchy.

▲ **Figure 14.6**

A bus network.

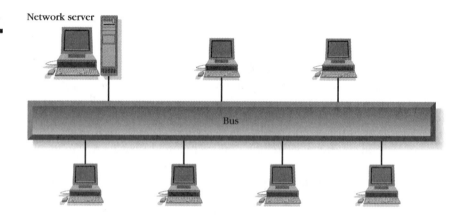

▲ **Figure 14.7**

A hierarchical network.

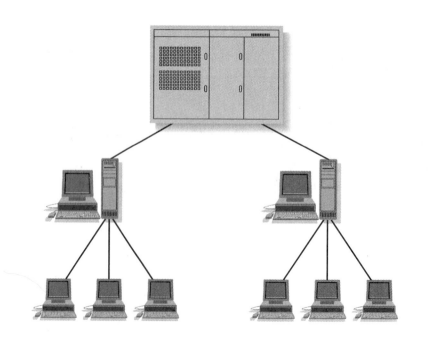

In a **star network** (Figure 14.8), each host is linked to a central "star" machine. A star network provides the same centralized control as a hierarchical network, but because there are fewer levels to traverse, the system can respond more quickly. If the star machine fails, however, the network ceases to function.

Another option is to link the host computers to form a **ring network** (Figure 14.9), with messages moving around the ring from machine to machine. A ring network lacks central control, but if one network computer fails, the others can continue to communicate. In fact, one of the advantages

Star network
A network in which each host is linked to a central machine in a star pattern.

Ring network
A network in which the host computers are linked to form a ring.

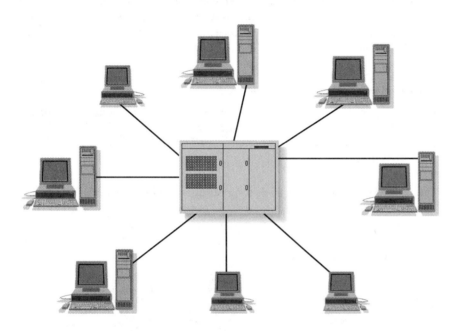

▲ **Figure 14.8**

A star network.

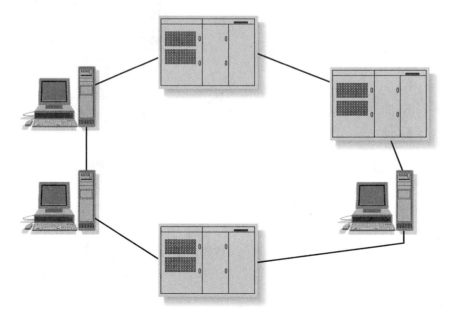

▲ **Figure 14.9**

A ring network.

of a ring network is that the computers can support each other, picking up work from a machine that fails or that faces an unusually heavy demand.

Bridges and Gateways

Bridge
A computer that links two similar networks.
Gateway
A computer that links dissimilar networks.

Networks are linked to other networks by bridges and gateways (Figure 14.10). A **bridge** is a computer that links two or more similar networks. A **gateway** links dissimilar networks; for example, a local area network might communicate with a wide area network over a gateway.

When you link two networks, you allow all the people and all the computers on both networks to communicate electronically with each other. Gateways and bridges support internetwork processing.

NETWORK MANAGEMENT

Simply transmitting messages across a network is not enough, of course. They must be routed to their correct destinations.

Network Software

Network operating system
The operating system that manages a network and controls network servers, network controllers, bridges, and gateways.
Agent process
A software routine stored in the memory of each host computer or workstation that handles communications between the computer's operating system and the network.

The task of managing a network requires special system software. Network servers, network controllers, bridges, and gateways run **network operating systems,** and stored in the memory of each host computer or workstation is an **agent process** (Figure 14.11) that handles communications between the

▲ **Figure 14.10**

Bridges and gateways link networks.

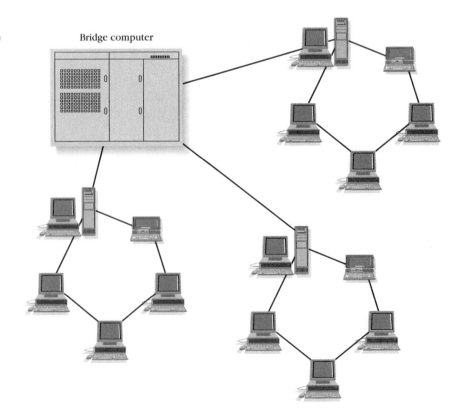

Bridge computer

computer's operating system and the network. An ideal agent process allows the user to access any available network service even if he or she has no idea what computer provides that service.

Nodes

Each computer (or terminal) on the network is a **node,** and each node has a unique address that distinguishes it from all other nodes. When data are transmitted across the network, they move from node to node.

Imagine, for example, that you have just sent an e-mail message to a friend (Figure 14.12). When you created the message, you specified your

Node
A single computer (or terminal) on a network. Generally, an addressable point on a network.

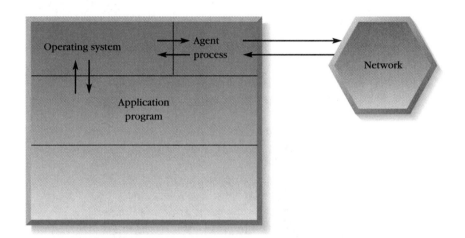

▲ **Figure 14.11**

Access to the network is managed by an agent process.

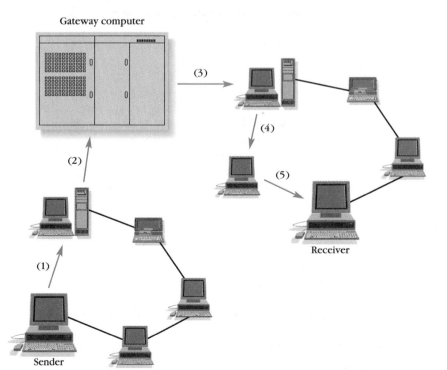

▲ **Figure 14.12**

Messages move from node to node.

I S S U E S

The Global Marketplace

During the second half of the twentieth century, we have experienced a revolution in communication. We expect up-to-the-second news coverage of events that occur halfway around the world. We think nothing of watching live coverage of sports events from other states and even other countries, and we take for granted the ability to communicate at any time with anyone virtually anywhere on the globe.

Modern global communication networks have changed the very nature of the marketplace. Once a business establishment could do quite well serving its local customers and battling its regional competitors. Today, however, because there is so little difference between communicating cross-town, cross-country, or cross-border, a company's customers and competitors can be almost anywhere. The global marketplace is a reality because communication technology and networks make it possible.

The global nature of the marketplace has implications for you, too. Once the competition for available jobs was limited to a relatively small geographic area, but that is changing. Today, a professional equipped with a networked computer can do his or her work literally anywhere in the world, and that spells both opportunity and risk.

friend's electronic address. That address identifies the node to which his or her terminal or workstation is attached.

When you transmit the message, you transfer it from your computer to the network (1). The network server (2) then sends the message to an intermediate node (in this example, to a gateway). The gateway computer reads the address and sends the message on toward its destination (3). Depending on the complexity of the network, the message might pass through several intermediate nodes (4) before it reaches your friend's computer (5).

Security

Information system security is concerned with protecting the organization's hardware, software, and data resources from unauthorized access, use, modification, or theft. Protecting a stand-alone personal computer against unauthorized access is relatively simple, but a network presents a much more serious problem because each of the computers linked to the network is a potential point of access.

Information system security is discussed in the Spotlight following Chapter 15.

Protocols

When two or more computers try to transmit data at the same time over the same line, their messages can interfere with each other. **Polling** is one solution (Figure 14.13).

The network controller starts the process by sending a polling signal to one workstation, literally asking if it is ready to transmit a message. If the workstation is ready, it sends the message. If not, the network controller polls the next workstation, and so on. Because messages can be transmitted only in response to a polling signal, simultaneous messages are impossible.

Polling
A network management technique. The terminals or workstations on the network are sent a polling signal in turn, and can transmit only in response to that signal.

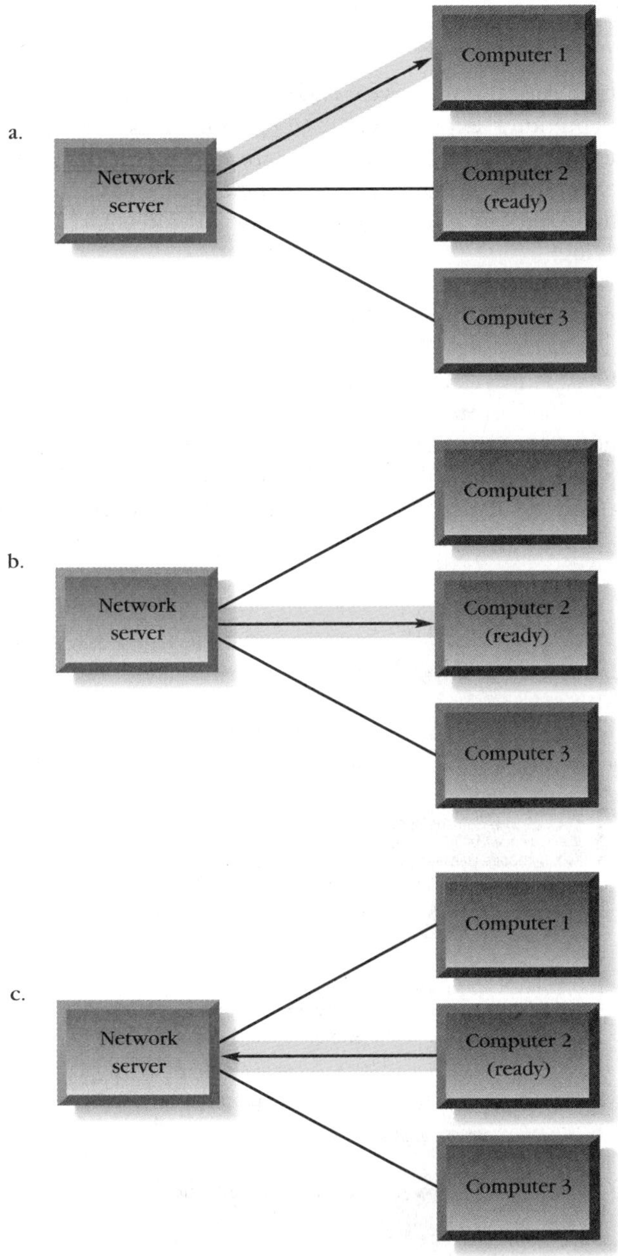

▲ **Figure 14.13**

Polling.
a. **A polling signal is sent to the first computer on the network.**
b. **The first computer has nothing to transmit, so a polling signal is sent to the second computer on the network.**
c. **The second computer transmits a message to the network server.**

Collision detection
A network management technique in which terminals and workstations are allowed to transmit at any time. If two messages collide, the collision is sensed and the messages are retransmitted.

Token passing
A network management technique in which an electronic token is passed continuously around the network and a terminal or workstation can transmit only when it holds the token.

An alternative, called **collision detection,** allows the workstations to send messages whenever the want. If two messages are transmitted at the same time, the signals interfere with each other and that "collision" is detected electronically. Following a collision, the messages are retransmitted.

On a **token passing** (or token ring) network, an electronic signal (the token) moves continuously around the network, and a computer is allowed to transmit a message only when it holds the token. Polling and token passing are similar in that both techniques force the workstations to take turns. The difference is that the token is passed from workstation to workstation, whereas the polling signals originate with the network controller.

NETWORK STANDARDS

There was a time (not too many years ago) when network standards were a joke. In fact, computer experts had a (tongue-in-cheek) saying: The good thing about network standards is that there are so many to choose from.

That is changing. De facto standards are emerging and, as the advantages of global networking become more and more obvious, international standards are evolving.

ISO/OSI

Open Systems Interconnection (OSI)
An International Standards Organization network model that specifies seven interconnection layers.

The International Standards Organization's **Open Systems Interconnection (OSI)** model specifies seven interconnection layers (Figure 14.14). At the bottom, level 1 defines the interface with the physical communication line. At the top, level 7 is the interface with the application program. In between are the primary tasks that must be performed to convert the message from the user's

▲ **Figure 14.14**

The OSI model defines seven interconnection layers.

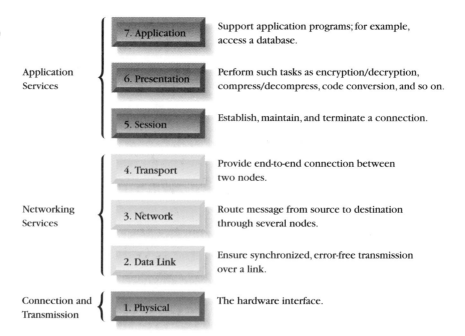

The National Information Infrastructure

Chapter 1 briefly introduced the information superhighway. The idea is to link everyone to a high-speed network that will replace existing data communication, telephone, and cable television services.

The information superhighway is not just a dream; in fact, the United States government is encouraging its development. The National Information Infrastructure (NII) is an official government plan that establishes guidelines, standards, and incentives to make sure everyone has access to the information superhighway at a reasonable cost.

view to the physical signals and back again. Note that all seven layers are present on each computer.

The reason the OSI model is important is because it defines the layers as independent functions. If, for example, a company in India discovers a new way to encrypt data, its technical specialists can focus on the presentation level, and as long as they maintain the proper interface with the application and session levels, they can ignore the rest of the layers. Likewise, a new data routing protocol affects only the network layer. The open architecture gives users and vendors a great deal of flexibility to change details without reinventing everything.

ISDN

ISDN is an acronym for **Integrated Services Digital Network.** It is emerging from the existing worldwide telephone network, and promises someday to replace the current system.

ISDN will be a digital network (p. 298) that will support voice, data, video, and other forms of communication. Once it is in place, you will be able to link your computer, your telephone, and other devices to it through a simple interface.

Integrated Services Digital Network (ISDN)
A network that is emerging from the existing worldwide telephone network and promises someday to replace the current system.

SUMMARY

A network makes it possible for several computers to share hardware, software, data, and workloads and provides backup, e-mail, and other on-line services. The software that supports cooperative group efforts over a network is called groupware. Electronic data interchange has the potential to change the way companies do business. Networks have led to a new approach to information processing called client/server computing.

A group of computers located in a limited area and linked by local communication lines forms a local area network. The end-user microcomputers through which people access the network are called workstations. Most local area networks are controlled by a network server. On a peer-to-peer network, every computer can access the files and peripherals on every other network computer, so there is no need for a server.

A wide area network links computers that are geographically dispersed. The computers that perform end-user tasks are called hosts. A metropolitan area network is a high-speed network that links computers separated by up to 50 miles. A bridge is a computer that links two similar networks. A gateway links dissimilar networks.

Local area networks are sometimes configured as bus networks. A hierarchical network links the computers to form a hierarchy. In a star network, each host is linked to a central "star" machine. On a ring network, the computers are linked to form a ring.

Network servers, network controllers, bridges, and gateways run network operating systems. Stored in the memory of each host computer or workstation is an agent process that handles communications between the computer's operating system and the network.

Each computer (or terminal) on the network is a node, and each node has a unique address that distinguishes it from all other nodes. Messages move across or between networks from node to node. Information system security is concerned with protecting the organization's hardware, software, and data resources from unauthorized access, use, modification, or theft.

On a polling network, the network controller literally asks each workstation, in turn, if it is ready to transmit a message. Collision detection allows the workstations to send messages whenever they want. If a collision is sensed, the affected messages are retransmitted. On a token passing network, an electronic signal moves continuously around the network, and a computer is allowed to transmit a message only when it holds the token.

The International Standards Organization's Open Systems Interconnection (OSI) model defines seven interconnection layers. ISDN (Integrated Services Digital Network) is emerging from the existing worldwide telephone network.

KEY TERMS

agent process	host	Open Systems
bridge	Integrated Services	Interconnection (OSI)
bus network	Digital Network (ISDN)	peer-to-peer network
client/server computing	local area network (LAN)	polling
collision detection	metropolitan area	ring network
electronic data inter-	network (MAN)	star network
change (EDI)	network operating system	token passing
gateway	network server	wide area network (WAN)
groupware	node	workstation
hierarchical network		

CONCEPTS

1. Why are networks used?
2. Identify several commercial on-line services.

3. What is groupware? Why is groupware important?
4. Briefly, what is electronic data interchange? Why do you suppose electronic data interchange is so important?
5. Briefly explain client/server computing.
6. Distinguish among a local area network, a wide area network, and a metropolitan area network.
7. Sketch or describe a bus network, a hierarchical network, a star network, and a ring network.
8. What is a bridge? What is a gateway?
9. What does a network operating system do? What is an agent process?
10. A message goes from node to node as it moves across a network or between networks. What does that mean?
11. What is the purpose of information system security? Why is network security a problem?
12. Briefly explain polling, collision detection, and token passing.
13. Why are network standards important?
14. List and describe the seven layers in the ISO/OSI model.
15. What is ISDN?

PROJECTS

1. Tour (or attend a presentation about) your school's or your employer's network. Identify the network server, the bridges and gateways, the network software, and the available services.
2. If your school (or your employer) has a network, identify the primary tasks performed by the network. What services does the network provide that would be impossible or impractical without the network?

INTERNET PROJECTS

1. *News and Notes.* Check the newsgroup *news.announce.important* for current news about USENET. Check *news.lists.ps-maps* for USENET traffic flows and statistics. Check World Wide Web site *http://www.white-house.gov* for the latest information posted by the White House. Write a brief note or send an e-mail message to your instructor outlining what you find.
2. *Topic Searches.* Check the World Wide Web and/or other Internet resources for information on the following topics:

Key word	*Qualifiers*
electronic data interchange	banking
ISO/OSI	implementation
NII	

Define the key word, identify at least two sources of information on the topic, and briefly summarize the nature of the information you find.

3. *Links to Other Sites*. After you access one or more of the following
   sites, write a brief note or send an e-mail message to your instructor
   outlining what you find.

   a. On the World Wide Web, check *http://www.att.com* for information
      about AT&T. Look for information on network services.
   b. On the World Wide Web, check *http://www.sprint.com* for informa-
      tion about Sprint. Look for information on network services.
   c. On the World Wide Web, check *http://www.mci.com* for information
      about MCI. Look for information on network services.

4. Access West Publishing Company's home page and find the Chapter 14
   student activities for this book. See Internet Project 3 for the spotlight
   on *The Internet* following Chapter 1 (page 29) for more detailed
   instructions on accessing the home page. As appropriate, repeat
   projects 1, 2, and/or 3 using the more current references you find.

INTERNET TECHNOLOGY

Before you start this feature, you should be familiar with the following concepts:

▶ Software (p. 9), networks (p. 17), and the Internet (p. 17).

▶ Internet addresses (p. 22) and the World Wide Web (p. 26).

▶ Display screens (p. 57) and terminals (p. 68).

▶ Files, file names (p. 126), and directories (p. 127).

▶ Gophers and browsers (p. 169).

▶ Hypertext and hypermedia (p. 170).

When you finish reading this feature, you should be able to:

▶ Briefly explain TCP/IP (Transmission Control Protocol/Internet Protocol).

▶ Briefly explain the purpose of Telnet and the file transfer protocol (FTP).

▶ Briefly explain http (hypertext transport protocol).

▶ Identify the components of a Uniform Resource Locator (URL).

THE INTERNET'S PROTOCOLS

A protocol is a set of rules for data communication. To a large extent the Internet is defined by its protocols.

TCP/IP

The standard Internet protocol is named **TCP/IP (Transmission Control Protocol/Internet Protocol).** It was created in the 1970s using public funds, so anyone can use TCP/IP without paying a royalty. The Internet can be defined as the set of continuously connected computers that use TCP/IP.

TCP/IP is hardware and software independent. It runs on virtually any computer under virtually any operating system. The protocol works by dividing a message into small packets and then sending the packets toward their destination through intermediate computers called routers or switches. The individual packets that make up a message might follow different paths, and they might arrive out of sequence. The TCP/IP routine in the receiving computer reconstructs the message.

Transmission Control Protocol/Internet Protocol (TCP/IP)
The standard Internet communication protocol.

SPOTLIGHT

323

Telnet

Telnet
An Internet application that uses TCP/IP to link to a remote computer.

Telnet is an Internet application that uses TCP/IP to link to a remote computer. When you issue the command

```
telnet name
```

(where *name* is the target computer's Internet address) you log onto the specified computer and your computer becomes a terminal. After you enter an acceptable log-on ID and password (often, something like *guest* or *newuser*), you can execute a program on that remote computer. A Telnet link might be used to access an electronic library catalog, a database, or an educational service.

File Transfer Protocol (FTP)

File transfer protocol (FTP)
An Internet protocol for copying files from one computer to another.

FTP, the **file transfer protocol,** is a routine that allows you to access files on a remote computer and copy them to your computer. An FTP link resembles a Telnet link. Typically, you log onto the remote computer as *anonymous* or *ftp* and use your Internet address as your password.

The original idea behind FTP was to save on-line time by allowing the recipient to study a file's contents off-line, but today FTP is also used to distribute data and software. If you read the *Spotlight* on *Internet Access Tools* following Chapter 7, you learned about Archie, gophers, Veronica, and WAIS. Those tools use FTP to transfer plain-text files, documents, graphic images, spreadsheets, sound files, program files, and virtually anything else you can store in a file.

Anonymous FTP archives
Storage space on the Internet where files can be left and subsequently retrieved by anyone.

The Internet's **anonymous FTP archives** represent storage space where files can be left and subsequently retrieved by anyone. The archives are used to distribute data or software to a wide audience. Users find the archives an excellent source of free programs.

Hypertext Transport Protocol (http)

Hypertext transport protocol (http)
A World Wide Web protocol that follows hypertext links to jump from computer to computer.

On the World Wide Web, you jump from page to page by following hypertext (or hypermedia) links that are managed by **http,** the **hypertext transport protocol.** When you click on a link on one home page, http automatically transfers you to the linked home page no matter where (on what computer) it might reside. The World Wide Web can be defined as a set of servers that allow users to access hyperbased information, and a reasonable way to visualize the Web is as a massive set of hypertext pages on the Internet.

Uniform Resource Locator (URL)
On the World Wide Web, an address that specifies the path from one home page to another.

The path from one home page to another is an address called a **URL (Uniform Resource Locator)** (Figure 14.15). In most cases the URL is hidden behind a highlighted key word or some other logical pointer, but if you know exactly where you want to go you can specify the appropriate URL yourself.

324

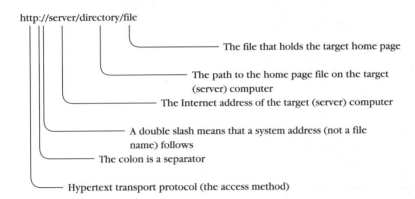

A Uniform Resource Locator (URL) is an address that leads to a home page.

S P O T L I G H T

The first part of a URL (*http* in Figure 14.15) specifies the access method. Most URLs start with http, but you can also link to another computer using FTP, Telnet, and several other protocols. The double slash indicates that the name of a computer system (rather than a file name) follows. The rest of the URL defines the path to the target home page. The URLs for several interesting World Wide Web sites are listed in Appendix B.

KEY TERMS

anonymous FTP archives

FTP (file transfer protocol)

http (hypertext transport protocol)

TCP/IP (Transmission Control Protocol/-Internet Protocol)

Telnet

URL (Uniform Resource Locator)

CONCEPTS

1. What is TCP/IP? Briefly, how does TCP/IP work?
2. What is Telnet? Why is it important?
3. What task is performed by FTP? What are the anonymous FTP archives? Why are they used?
4. What is http?
5. What is a Uniform Resource Locator (URL)? Briefly explain how http links home pages by following a URL.

PROJECTS

1. Appendix B lists some interesting World Wide Web URLs. Log onto the Internet, launch a Web browser, and investigate some of them.
2. If your school or your employer has a World Wide Web home page, identify its URL, log onto the Internet, launch a Web browser, and link to that page.

CHAPTER 15

System Development

Before you start this chapter, you should be familiar with the following concepts:

▶ The user (p. 6), hardware (p. 6), and classifying computers (p. 14).

▶ Data and information (p. 54), source data (p. 54), and reports (p. 54).

▶ The operating system (p. 122) and operating system functions (p. 122).

▶ Application software (p. 144) and the user interface (p. 144).

▶ Source data (p. 199), fields, records, and files (p. 202), and data maintenance (pp. 204–207).

▶ Entities, occurrences, and attributes (p. 225).

When you finish reading this chapter, you should be able to:

▶ Briefly explain what a systems analyst does.

▶ List the steps in the system development life cycle and explain the objectives of each step.

▶ Explain the purpose of a feasibility study.

▶ Identify the basic logical building blocks of an information system.

▶ Briefly describe such analysis tools as logical models, data flow diagrams, entity-relationship diagrams, data normalization, and prototypes.

▶ Briefly discuss computer-aided software engineering.

▶ Explain the purpose of the requirements specification.

▶ Explain why the interfaces must be designed before the other system components.

▶ Briefly discuss data design and user interface design.

▶ Discuss the tasks that must be performed after the system is developed.

INFORMATION SYSTEMS

A system is a set of components that work together to accomplish an objective. An *information* system is a set of hardware, software, data, people, and procedures that work together to make data and information available where, when, and to whom they are needed.

Examples abound. Your bank's information system tracks the status of your checking account. Your school's grade reporting system maintains your academic history and issues periodic grade reports. Another information system tracks inventory levels at the supermarket and reorders stock as necessary.

Information systems do not last forever. Technology changes. New problems emerge and new opportunities are recognized. Often, the best way to solve a problem or take advantage of an opportunity is to develop a new (or substantially modified) information system.

The Systems Analyst

The decision to create a new information system begins with a user who needs data or information. Most users lack technical expertise, so they must rely on technical experts to actually create the system. Unfortunately, many technical experts lack application expertise. In effect, the user and the technical experts do not understand each other's specialized languages, and that makes it difficult for them to communicate effectively.

Systems analyst
The person who defines the problem, expresses the user's needs in technical terms, and communicates resource requirements to management.

Bridging the gap between the user's understanding of the application and the experts' technical knowledge is the responsibility of the **systems analyst.** The analyst's job is to help the user define the problem and then translate the user's needs into technical terms (Figure 15.1). Additionally, the analyst communicates with management to obtain the resources needed to develop the system.

The System Development Life Cycle

System development life cycle (SDLC)
The systems analyst's methodology.

The process the analyst follows to create an information system is called the **system development life cycle,** or **SDLC** (Figure 15.2). The first step is

---

NOTE

Pick Any Two

You can have it fast, you can have it cheap, or you can have it right. Pick any two.

That old saying neatly summarizes the tradeoffs associated with developing information systems. You can have a high-quality, low-cost system, but only if you are willing to wait. You can have an inexpensive system in a short time, but only if you are willing to accept low quality. You can have a high-quality system in a short time, but only if you are willing to pay for extra analysts, designers, developers, and project managers. We tend to think of technology as black or white, but technical experts wrestle with such tradeoffs all the time.

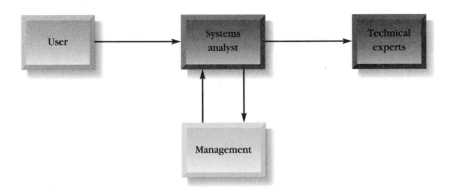

Problem definition
The first step in the system development life cycle.
Analysis
The phase that follows problem definition in the system development life cycle. During analysis the analyst determines what must be done to solve the problem.
Design
The phase that follows analysis in the system development life cycle. During design the analyst decides how to solve the problem.
Development
The phase in the system development life cycle during which the system is released to the user.
Implementation
The system development life cycle phase during which the new system is released to the user.
Maintenance
A system development life cycle phase that begins after the system is released to the user. The purpose of maintenance is to keep the system operating at an acceptable level.

problem definition. Once the problem is defined, **analysis** begins. The point of analysis is to determine *what* must be done to solve the problem. During the next stage, **design,** the analyst decides how to solve the problem.

The system is created during the **development** stage and then tested to ensure that it meets the user's needs. Once the system passes its final test, it is turned over (or released) to the user during the **implementation** stage. Following system release, **maintenance** begins. The point of maintenance is to keep the system functioning at an acceptable level.

Another way to visualize the system development life cycle is as a circle (Figure 15.3). A problem is defined and analyzed. A solution is designed, developed, and implemented. That solution is then maintained until wear and tear, obsolescence, or a new problem creates a need for a replacement system. At that point, another life cycle begins.

Some textbooks add another path to the life cycle to recognize the make or buy decision that often follows analysis (Figure 15.4). The development path is used when a new system is created internally. The acquisition path implies that the system is purchased from an outside supplier and then customized to fit the user's needs.

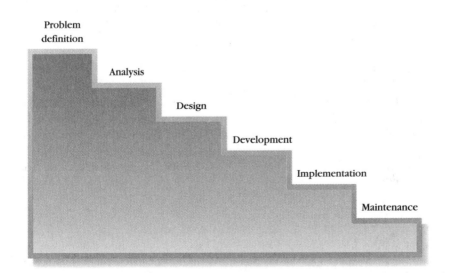

Problem definition
Analysis
Design
Development
Implementation
Maintenance

▲ **Figure 15.2**

The system development life cycle.

▲ **Figure 15.3**

▲ **Figure 15.3**

The system development life cycle can be visualized as a circle.

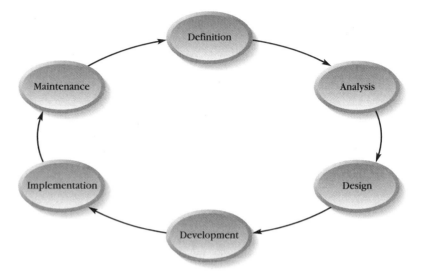

▲ **Figure 15.4**

The acquisitions path.

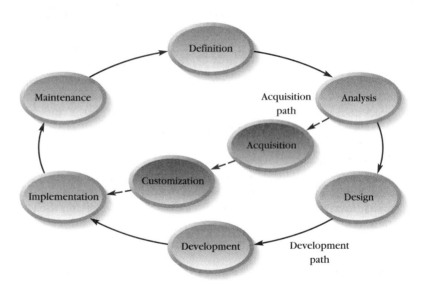

PROBLEM DEFINITION

The reason for creating a new system is the user's need for data or information. The user is the application expert. Thus the analyst's initial job is to observe, listen, and learn enough to understand the user's needs. You cannot solve a problem unless you know what caused it, so the underlying objective of the problem definition phase is to identify the problem's cause (or causes).

The Feasibility Study

Feasibility study
A preliminary system study intended to determine if the problem can be solved before significant resources are allocated.

Developing a new system is expensive. To avoid wasting time and money on impossible dreams, once the problem is defined the analyst often conducts a **feasibility study** to determine if it can be solved at a reasonable cost. A feasibility study is, in effect, a preliminary system study. The objective is to demonstrate that creating the proposed system is technically, economically, and operationally feasible (Figure 15.5).

The Steering Committee

In a large organization the number of problems to be solved usually exceeds the resources available to solve them. Consequently, choices must be made. Often, the responsibility for authorizing or rejecting information system development proposals is assigned to a **steering committee** composed of representatives from each of the major user departments.

The steering committee's job is to review all the active feasibility study reports, accept some, and reject the others (Figure 15.6). The approved

Steering committee
A committee composed of representatives from each of the major user departments that is responsible for authorizing or rejecting information system development proposals.

FEASIBILITY TYPE	KEY QUESTION	DEMONSTRATED BY
Technical	Can the problem be solved using current technology?	A comparable system.
Economic	Can the problem be solved at an acceptable cost?	Cost/benefit analysis.
Operational (or political)	Can the problem be solved in the user's environment?	The lack of significant intangible impediments.

▲ **Figure 15.5**

Feasibility study objectives.

▲ **Figure 15.6**

The steering committee decides which information system proposals will be developed.

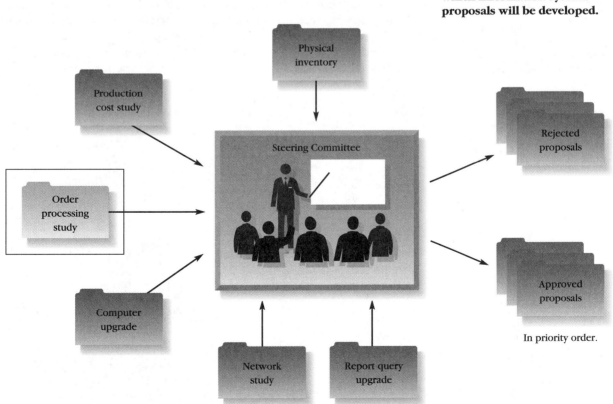

In priority order.

proposals are then assigned priorities. Subsequently, personnel and other resources are allocated to them in priority order.

ANALYSIS

Once the problem is defined, the analysis stage begins. To *analyze* something is to study it by breaking it down into its constituent parts. The point of analysis is to identify the system's basic components, improve them, and then reassemble them (perhaps in a different way) to create a new system.

Data, Processes, and Boundaries

The analyst begins by studying the present system. The problem is usually related to how the system works, not to what it does, so a key focus of this preliminary information gathering phase is to identify the system's essential functions. One way to do that is to focus on such basic building blocks as data, processes, and boundaries.

The data are a common starting point. Using the existing documents and screens as references, the analyst compiles lists of data elements and documents them in the **data dictionary** (Figure 15.7), a collection of data about the system's data.

A **process** is a set of steps for performing a task; in other words, the processes are the things that people and computers do. More formally, a process is an activity that transforms data in some way; for example, data can be collected, recorded, sorted, computed, summarized, and so on. Processes are identified by reading existing documentation and by observing and recording what the people and the equipment do.

An information system's **boundaries** are defined by people, activities, other organizations, and other systems that lie outside the system but com-

Data dictionary
A collection of data about a system's data.
Process
A set of steps for performing a task. An activity that transforms data in some way.
Boundary
A limit to a system defined by a person, activity, other organization, or other system that lies outside the target system but communicates directly with it.

▲ **Figure 15.7**

The data dictionary.

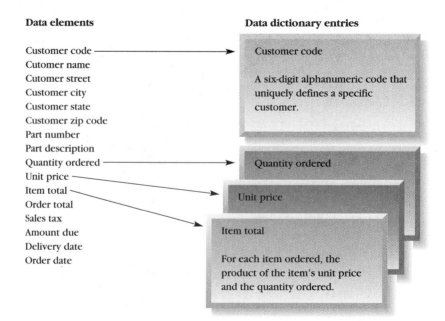

Data elements	Data dictionary entries

Customer code
Cutomer name
Cutomer street
Customer city
Customer state
Customer zip code
Part number
Part description
Quantity ordered
Unit price
Item total
Order total
Sales tax
Amount due
Delivery date
Order date

Customer code

A six-digit alphanumeric code that uniquely defines a specific customer.

Quantity ordered

Unit price

Item total

For each item ordered, the product of the item's unit price and the quantity ordered.

municate directly with it. By definition, any entity that lies outside the system's boundaries can act independently and thus is not subject to the system's control.

Consider a supermarket, for example. Customers are essential if the store is to stay in business, but the store has little control over its customers' actions. (They can, after all, choose to go to a different store.) Because customers communicate with the system but are not controlled by the system, they represent a boundary.

Logical Models

One problem with decomposing a system into its basic elements is that most systems have so many processes, data elements, and boundaries that the analyst quickly becomes swamped by details. To help make sense of all that detail, logical models are constructed.

A **logical model** emphasizes what the system does, not how it works. It exists on paper, in a computer, or in the analyst's mind. Because it contains no physical components, the model can be manipulated and modified quickly and inexpensively.

Logical model
A model that exists on paper, in a computer, or in the analyst's imagination.

DATA FLOW DIAGRAMS

A **data flow diagram** is a logical model that shows how data flow through a system. The model uses four symbols to represent the system's logical elements (Figure 15.8). Boundaries (called sources and destinations) are represented by squares or rectangles. Processes (activities that change or move data) are shown as round-cornered rectangles or circles. A data store (data at rest) is depicted as an open-ended rectangle, and data flows (data in motion) are represented by arrows. For example, Figure 15.9 shows a data flow diagram for an inventory/order processing system.

Data flow diagram
A logical model that shows the relationships between a system's processes, data, and boundaries.

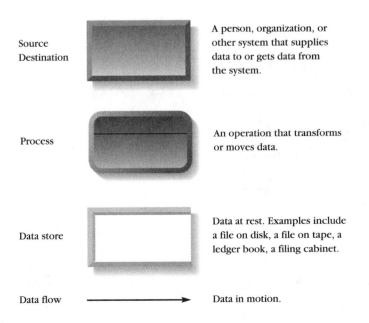

Source Destination	A person, organization, or other system that supplies data to or gets data from the system.
Process	An operation that transforms or moves data.
Data store	Data at rest. Examples include a file on disk, a file on tape, a ledger book, a filing cabinet.
Data flow	Data in motion.

▲ **Figure 15.8**

A data flow diagram uses these four symbols.

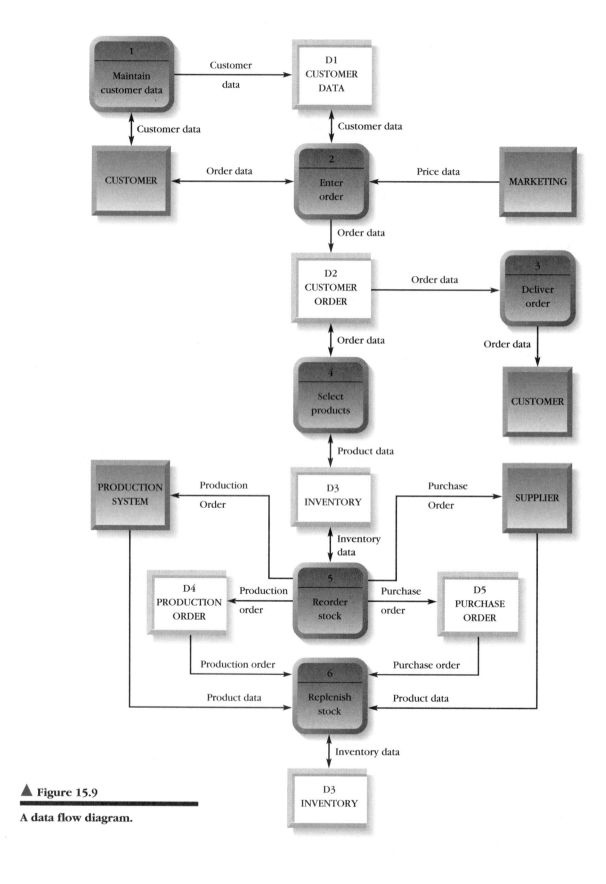

▲ **Figure 15.9**

A data flow diagram.

The Existing System

T he analyst's objective is not simply to automate the present system because (almost by definition) there is something wrong with it. (Were that not true, there would be no need to fix it.) When you automate a defective system you continue to make the same mistakes, only faster.

The existing system is far from useless, however. It must be performing a useful function. (Were *that* not true, there would be no need to fix it.)

The point of studying the present system is to determine what it does. Once the analyst knows what the present system does, he or she can distinguish the things it does well from the things it does poorly and then fix the right things. That, in a nutshell, is the point of analysis.

It is important to remember that a data flow diagram's symbols stand for logical, not physical entities. A process might be a manual procedure or a computer program. A data store might be a notebook, a filing cabinet, or an electronic file on disk. A data flow might be an electronic link between two computers, a telephone call, or a letter. When you represent a component as a data flow diagram symbol, you strip away its physical characteristics.

The key to creating a data flow diagram is the link between a system's data and its processes (Figure 15.10). Data flow into a process, those data are manipulated in some way, and the results flow out from the process. In other words, data imply processes and processes imply data. By showing how the data flow from the system's sources, through its processes and data stores, to its destinations, the data flow diagram helps the analyst visualize the essential relationships between the system's basic elements.

DATA MODELS

A data flow diagram emphasizes processes, not data. Consequently, to help ensure that no key data are overlooked, the analyst often prepares data models as well. An **entity-relationship diagram** is a logical model that shows how the system's data are related.

As you learned in Chapter 10, an entity is an object (a person, group, place, thing, or activity) about which data are stored. In an entity-relationship model, the data entities are linked by relationships that can usually be stated in the form of short sentences (Figure 15.11). For example, Figure 15.12 is an entity-relationship diagram that shows how the inventory/order processing system's primary entities are related.

Entity-relationship diagram
A logical model of the relationships between the system's primary data entities.

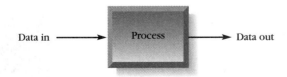

Data in → Process → Data out

▲ **Figure 15.10**

Data and processes are related.

▲ Figure 15.11

Entities are linked by relationships.

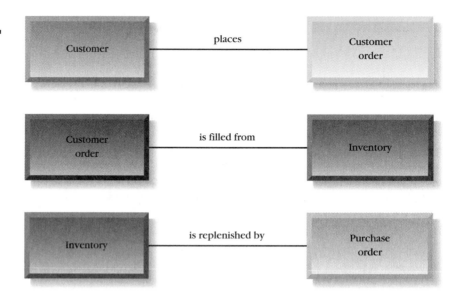

▲ **Figure 15.11**

Entities are linked by relationships.

Cardinality
A measure of the relative number of occurrences of the two related entities.

The strength and stability of the relationship between two data entities is a function of **cardinality,** a measure of their relative numbers of occurrences. For example, consider an examination. Each student submits one answer sheet and each answer sheet is associated with one student, so the relationship between students and exams is one-to-one. At the end of the term, each student has several exams, but each discrete exam is associated with only one student, so the relationship between students and exams is one-to-many. You might be enrolled in several courses, and each of those courses enrolls numerous students, so the relationship between students and courses is many-to-many.

For a variety of reasons, one-to-many relationships tend to be the most stable and the easiest to maintain. Analysts often prepare an entity-relationship

▲ **Figure 15.12**

An entity-relationship diagram.

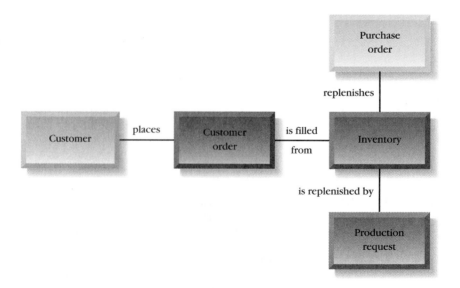

model to help them document the cardinality of each relationship and to test alternative ways of converting one-to-one and many-to-many relationships into one-to-many relationships.

An entity/relationship model starts with the entities and works down to the attributes. **Data normalization** is a formal procedure that starts with the attributes and shows the analyst how to group them to define efficient, easy-to-maintain data structures.

The data flow diagram and the data models complement each other. When you create a data flow diagram, you focus on the processes and you identify the key data entities those processes suggest. The data models start with the data and often reveal previously overlooked details about the data *and* the processes. By using both tools, you get a better system.

Computer-Aided Software Engineering

Although it is possible to create data flow diagrams, entity-relationship diagrams, and other logical models by hand, many analysts use **CASE** (Computer-Aided Software Engineering) tools to do at least some of the work. A CASE product is a set of software routines designed to automate all or part of the system development life cycle.

At the heart of most CASE products is a **repository** that holds descriptions of the system's data, processes, and boundaries (Figure 15.13). A graphic interface simplifies the task of creating models. When you change a

Data normalization
A formal technique for organizing entities and attributes into efficient, easy to maintain fields, records, and files.

CASE
Acronym for Computer-Aided Software Engineering. A set of software routines designed to automate all or part of the system development life cycle.
Repository
A CASE component that holds descriptions of the system's data and processes.

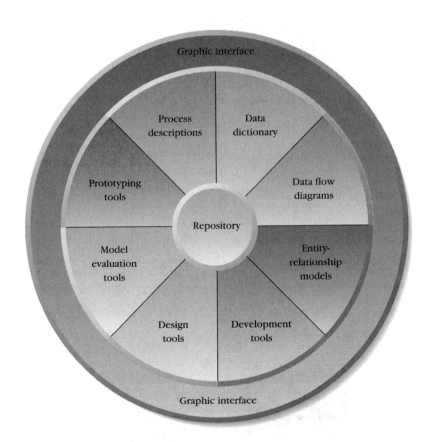

▲ **Figure 15.13**

The repository forms the core of a CASE product.

model, the CASE software uses the information in the repository to adjust for ripple effects. Still other CASE tools support the design and development stages and even generate ready-to-execute program code.

ADVANCED TOPICS

The CASE Workbench

An integrated set of CASE tools is called a CASE workbench. Upper CASE tools support problem definition and the feasibility study. Middle CASE tools support the analysis and design stages. On some CASE products, the upper CASE and middle CASE tools are integrated to form the front-end CASE workbench. Lower CASE (or back-end CASE) tools support system development, implementation, and maintenance.

Prototyping

Prototyping
An alternative to logical modeling in which a working, physical model of the system is created.

Prototyping is an alternative to logical modeling. The idea is to build a working, *physical model* (or prototype) of the system. In some cases, the user actually writes the prototype using an application software tool such as dBASE or Lotus 1-2-3.

Think of the prototyping process as a loop (Figure 15.14). Based on preliminary analysis, a first draft of the prototype is created. The user then tests the prototype. Based on the user's suggestions, the prototype is quickly mod-

▲ **Figure 15.14**

The prototyping process.

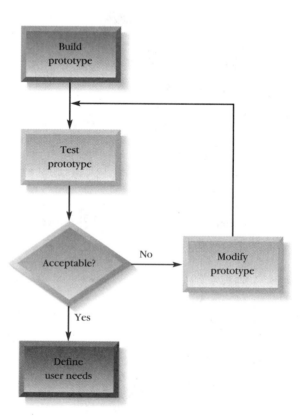

ified and tested again until, usually after several iterations, an acceptable prototype emerges. In effect, the prototype is a first draft of the system that serves as a mechanism for defining the user's needs.

A variation of prototyping, **rapid prototyping,** calls for developing nonoperational mockups of the system's input and output interfaces (screen layouts, printed reports, and so on). Because the underlying logic need not be defined, such prototypes can be created, tested, and modified quickly, and that helps the user get involved.

The Requirements Specification

The last step in the analysis process is to prepare a formal **requirements specification** to document exactly what must be done to solve the problem. Where the logical models and prototypes are unclear, ambiguous, difficult to test, or inconsistent, requirements are written to precisely define the analyst's intent. A clear requirements specification is particularly important when subsequent design and development work is subcontracted because the requirements define the terms of the contract.

Requirements are logical. They document the application needs, not the technical specifications. The physical details are planned during the design stage.

DESIGN

The point of analysis is to make sure you are doing the right thing. The key question to be answered during analysis is *what*.

The point of design is to make sure you are doing the thing right; in other words, the key question is *how*. During the design stage, the analyst (or the designer) translates the requirements into technical terms by specifying the hardware components, computer programs, databases, files, manual procedures, and other entities that will constitute the new physical system.

Alternatives

The requirements define exactly what the new system must do, but there are usually several ways to achieve those objectives. Thus, the first step in the design stage is to identify a number of realistic **alternative** high-level system designs and then to select one.

One way to document an alternative is to draw a **system flowchart** that shows how the physical components are related. System flowcharts use symbols such as the ones pictured in Figure 15.15; note that each symbol visually suggests a physical component, such as a program, a printer, or a file on disk.

Figure 15.16 shows a high-level system flowchart for one inventory/order processing system alternative. The system flowchart acts like a map of the system, identifying the primary components and the links between them.

The System Environment

Before any computer-related components can be designed, the analyst must first define the system environment. Mainframes, minicomputers,

Rapid prototyping
Developing nonoperational mockups of a system's input and output interfaces (screen layouts, printed reports, and so on) rather than a full, working prototype.

Requirements specification
A document, prepared during the analysis stage of the system development life cycle, that defines exactly what the system must do.

Alternative
A choice.

System flowchart
A diagram that shows how a system's physical components are related.

▲ **Figure 15.15**

System flowcharting symbols.

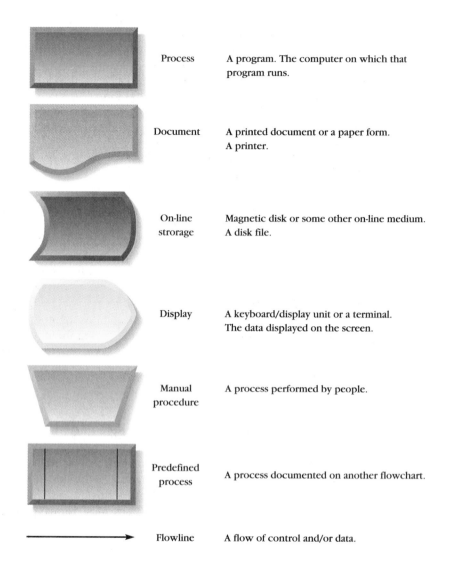

	Process	A program. The computer on which that program runs.
	Document	A printed document or a paper form. A printer.
	On-line strorage	Magnetic disk or some other on-line medium. A disk file.
	Display	A keyboard/display unit or a terminal. The data displayed on the screen.
	Manual procedure	A process performed by people.
	Predefined process	A process documented on another flowchart.
⟶	Flowline	A flow of control and/or data.

microcomputers, and networks are fundamentally different. At the microcomputer level, PCs and Macintosh computers are incompatible, and such operating systems as MS-DOS, Windows 95, and UNIX define different platforms.

The decision to select a particular system environment constrains all subsequent design decisions. That is why the platform must be selected first.

Designing the Interfaces

Once a specific alternative and a system environment are selected, work can begin on the individual components. Although some design and development activities can be performed in parallel, task sequence is important because early design decisions constrain all the decisions that follow.

Typically, the **interfaces** that link two or more system components are designed first. For example, consider two programs that share the same file. If the file (an interface) is defined first, both programs can be designed to fit

Interface
An entity that links two or more components.

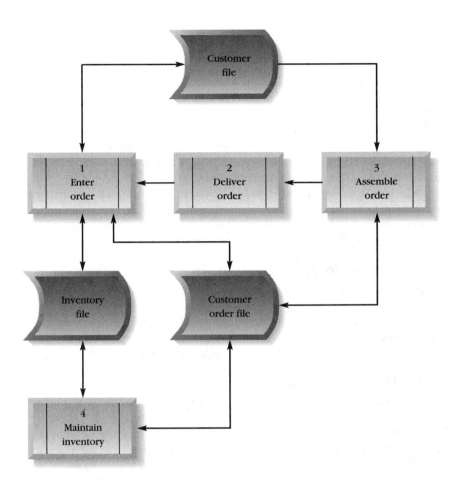

the common data structure. On the other hand, if the programs are done first, it is likely that one or both will have to be redesigned to fit the subsequent file design.

DATA DESIGN

In most information systems, the files and the databases are accessed by several programs; in other words, the data represent an important interface. Data design starts with the data elements and data structures identified during analysis. Next, a file organization or a database management system is selected for each data entity. Given the data dictionary, the file organizations, and the database management system, the analyst then creates the system's physical data structures.

See Chapters 9 and 10 for more on file and database design.

USER INTERFACE DESIGN

The user interface consists of screens, reports, forms, peripheral devices, and other components that allow the user to enter data to the system, obtain information from the system, or both. On an interactive system, the set of screens and the rules for using them define a dialogue that allows the computer and the user to exchange information. During the design stage, the elements that comprise the user interface are documented in the **user manual.**

User manual
The documentation for the user interface.

Component Design

Once the interfaces are defined, the design team turns to the individual hardware, software, and procedural components.

PROCEDURES

Procedure
Guidelines, rules, and instructions that tell people how to perform a task.

In information system terms, a **procedure** is a process that is performed by a human being. Procedures define the rules for communication with the system, and they must be carefully designed. An outstanding system does little good if the user cannot figure out how to use it.

In addition to defining the rules for system access, a well-designed system also includes security, system control, auditing, backup, and recovery procedures. We tend not to see the procedures when we visualize an information system, but they are there and they are crucial.

SELECTING HARDWARE

Given the incredible array of commercially available computer equipment and peripheral devices, very few organizations create their own hardware these days. Instead, they select components and configure a system. Because most hardware is designed to work with a specific platform, the environment defined earlier in the design stage constrains the design team.

PROGRAM DESIGN

Not too long ago, virtually all application software was custom designed and developed by information system professionals who worked for the user's own company. That is changing. Given today's high-quality, inexpensive commercial software, it is often difficult to justify writing original programs

ISSUES

Downsizing and Computer Programmers

In the face of increasing, often international competition, more and more companies are downsizing (or right-sizing) their work forces. Given the fact that computers make downsizing possible, it might surprise you to learn that computer programmers have been affected by downsizing, too.

Except in companies that sell hardware or software, programming is a support task, and it sometimes makes economic sense to dismiss those expensive employees and outsource the technical work. To some programmers that means opportunity. To others, however, it may mean unemployment.

Beta Testing

Have you ever missed an obvious spelling error when you proofread a term paper? It is difficult to evaluate your own work because you tend to see what you thought you wrote, not what you really wrote. Technical people have the same problem, so before they are released, programs and systems are almost always tested by people who were not involved in designing or developing them.

One option is to bring in technical experts from other projects (or even from outside the firm) and challenge them to break the system. Another option is to give beta test copies of a program to outside experts and ask them to use the software. The beta testers (consultants, academics, users of a previous version of the program, application developers who might use the software, and so on) can often identify problems that would not have occurred to the creators, and those problems can be corrected before the program is formally released.

unless the application is truly unique. If software that meets your needs can be purchased for a fraction of the cost of writing it, why reinvent the wheel?

Some applications still call for custom software, however. See Chapter 8 for an overview of the software design and development process.

THE DEVELOPMENT STAGE

The system is created during the development stage. New software is written. Purchased software and hardware are selected and installed. Files and databases are created and initialized, and procedures are refined. At the end of the development stage, all the system's components are assembled and tested.

AFTER DEVELOPMENT

After the system is designed and developed, it is tested, implemented, and turned over to the user.

The System Test

The purpose of the **system test** (Figure 15.17) is to ensure that the system actually meets the user's needs. The test criteria and the test data are derived from the requirements specifications and a set of expected test results is generated. When the system is completed, it is tested and actual outputs are obtained. If the actual outputs match the expected results, the system passes

System test
A test that follows system development. Its purpose is to ensure that the system meets the user's needs.

344

PART III SYSTEMS

▲ **Figure 15.17**

The system test.

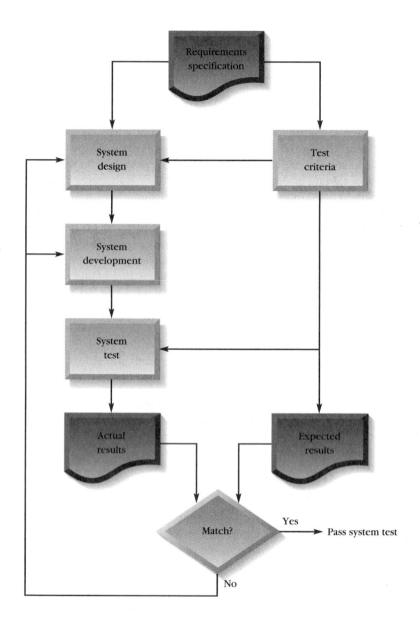

the test. If the results do not match expectations, corrections are made and the system is retested.

Implementation

After the system is tested, the users are trained and the system is formally turned over or **released** to the user. Sometimes, support for the old system is discontinued and the entire organization switches directly over to the new one. In other cases, the old and the new systems run in parallel for a time. The new system might be released in stages (a phased implementation) or introduced to a subset of the organization first (a pilot implementation). The process of releasing an information system is sometimes called cut-over.

Release
The act of turning a system over to the user.

The Postrelease Review

After the system is released, the users, the analysts, and the managers who were involved in the project conduct a **postrelease review** to discuss any remaining problems and determine how well the project's objectives were achieved. During the review, actual system performance is compared to the objectives, cost estimates and schedules are compared to the actual outcomes, and significant differences are studied and explained. The idea is to learn from any mistakes and improve performance on future projects.

Postrelease review
A review of the system development process conducted after the system is released.

Maintenance

Maintenance is a continuing cost. The objective is to keep the system running at an acceptable level. Errors that slip through the system test must be corrected. Hardware components fail and must be replaced or repaired. Data must be added, deleted, and modified. Technology and the application both change over time, and portions of the system will eventually need revision. Over a period of years, the cost of maintaining a system can easily exceed the cost of creating it.

SUMMARY

An information system is a set of hardware, software, data, people, and procedures that work together to make data and information available where, when, and to whom they are needed. The systems analyst helps the user define the problem, translates the user's needs into technical terms, and works with management to obtain the resources needed to develop the system.

The first step in the system development life cycle is problem definition. The point of analysis is to determine what must be done to solve the problem. During design the analyst decides how to solve the problem. The system is created during the development stage and released to the user during the implementation stage. Following system release, maintenance begins.

Before starting the analysis stage, the analyst might conduct a feasibility study to determine if the problem can be solved at a reasonable cost. In many organizations, the responsibility for authorizing or rejecting information system proposals is assigned to a steering committee composed of representatives from each of the major user departments.

The data dictionary is a collection of data about the system's data. A process is a set of steps for performing a task. An information system's boundaries are defined by people, activities, other organizations, and other systems that lie outside the system but communicate directly with it.

A logical model exists on paper, in a computer, or in the analyst's mind. A data flow diagram is a logical model that shows how data flow through a system. An entity-relationship diagram is a logical model that shows how the system's data are related. Data normalization is a formal procedure for grouping attributes to define efficient, easy to maintain data structures. A CASE product is a set of software routines designed to automate all or part of the system development life cycle. At the heart of most CASE products is a repository that holds descriptions of the system's data and processes.

Prototyping is an alternative to logical modeling. Rapid prototyping, calls for developing nonoperational mockups of the system's input and output interfaces. The last step in the analysis process is to prepare a formal requirements specification to document exactly what must be done to solve the problem.

The first step in the design stage is to identify several realistic alternatives and then to select one. Alternatives are documented by drawing system flowcharts that show how the physical components are related. Typically, the interfaces that link two or more system components are designed first. Such interfaces as data structures, files, and databases are among the first components to be designed. On an interactive system, the set of screens and the rules for using them define a dialogue that allows the computer and the user to exchange information. During the design stage, the elements that comprise the user interface are documented in the user manual.

A procedure is a process that is performed by a human being. Few organizations create their own hardware. Given today's commercial software, it is often difficult to justify writing original programs, but some applications still call for custom software.

The system is created during the development stage. The purpose of the system test is to ensure that the system actually meets the user's needs. After the system is tested, the users are trained and the system is formally released to the user. Later, a postrelease review is conducted to determine how well the project's objectives were achieved.

KEY TERMS

alternative

analysis

boundary

cardinality

CASE (computer-aided software engineering)

data dictionary

data flow diagram

data normalization

design

development

entity-relationship diagram

feasibility study

implementation

interface

logical model

maintenance

postrelease review

problem definition

procedure

process

prototyping

rapid prototyping

release

repository

requirements specification

steering committee

systems analyst

system development life cycle (SDLC)

system flowchart

system test

user manual

CONCEPTS

1. What does a systems analyst do? Why is someone like a systems analyst necessary?
2. List the steps in the system development life cycle and explain the objectives of each step.
3. What is the purpose of a feasibility study?

4. What is the purpose of a steering committee? A typical steering committee is composed of representatives from each of the major user departments. Why?

5. List and define the three basic logical building blocks of an information system.

6. The point of studying the present system is to determine what it does. What does that statement mean? Why is it important? How does the analyst go about accomplishing that objective?

7. What is a logical model? What is a prototype? Why does the analyst use such tools as logical models and prototypes?

8. Identify the four symbols used in a data flow diagram and briefly explain what each symbol means. The key to creating a data flow diagram is the relationship between processes and data. Briefly explain that relationship. Why is it important?

9. What is the purpose of an entity-relationship diagram? What is the purpose of data normalization?

10. What advantages are derived from using computer-aided software engineering?

11. What is a requirements specification? Why is the requirements specification necessary?

12. A system's interfaces are typically designed before the other system components. Why?

13. A system's data structures, files, and databases are among the first components to be designed. Why? A system's user interface is among the first components to be designed. Why?

14. What is the purpose of the system test?

15. Briefly describe several alternative techniques for releasing a system to the user.

PROJECTS

1. Often, the best way to grasp a system is to follow the flow of paperwork through it. For example, see if you can find answers to the following questions:

   a. What happens to your grades between the time you finish your final exams and you receive your end-of-term grade report?

   b. How does your school convert your course registration requests into your final course schedule?

 ## INTERNET PROJECTS

1. *News and Notes.* Use the World Wide Web to search for consulting organizations and opportunities for project (or outsourcing) work. Write a brief note or send an e-mail message to your instructor outlining what you find.

2. *Topic Searches.* Check the World Wide Web and/or other Internet resources for information on the following topics:

Key word	*Qualifiers*
downsize	programmer
requirements	competitive bidding
beta test	a current software product

Define the key word, identify at least two sources of information on the topic, and briefly summarize the nature of the information you find.

3. *Links to Other Sites.* After you access one or more of the following sites, write a brief note or send an e-mail message to your instructor outlining what you find.

   a. On the World Wide Web, check *http://www.arthurandersen.com* for information about Arthur Andersen, an auditing and consulting firm. Once you reach the home page, click on *Contract Services.*
   b. Check *http://www.dcsys.com/dcscorp/* for information about DCS Corporation, a consulting firm.
   c. On the World Wide Web, check *http://www.wall-street-news.com* for information about Internet Media Services, a company that specializes in developing web sites for its clients.

4. Access West Publishing Company's home page and find the Chapter 15 student activities for this book. See Internet Project 3 for the spotlight on *The Internet* following Chapter 1 (page 29) for more detailed instructions on accessing the home page. As appropriate, repeat projects 1, 2, and/or 3 using the more current references you find.

COMPUTER CRIME AND SYSTEM SECURITY

Before you start this feature, you should be familiar with the following concepts:

▶ Data and information (p. 4).

▶ The user (p. 6), hardware (p. 6), inside the computer (p. 7), software (p. 9), and data (p. 10).

▶ Computer systems (p. 13), classifying computers (p. 14), networks (p. 17), and the Internet (p. 17).

▶ The boot (p. 133), data integrity (p. 206), and security (p. 206).

When you finish reading this feature, you should be able to:

▶ Define the term *computer crime* and briefly explain why outdated laws complicate the problem.

▶ Distinguish among hackers, crackers, and insider computer criminals.

▶ Briefly describe time bombs, Trojan horses, logic bombs, rabbits, viruses, and worms.

▶ Distinguish between logical and physical security.

▶ Briefly explain data encryption.

COMPUTER CRIME

Computer crime is any criminal activity in which a computer is a target, a tool, or both. The theft of hardware, software, data, and information are obvious examples. Unauthorized access and use are more difficult to prove, but potentially more damaging.

Computer crime
Any criminal activity in which a computer is a target, a tool, or both.

Outdated Laws

Computer crime is particularly difficult to fight because, when it comes to modern technology, many of our laws are outdated. The U.S. copyright laws provide a good example. They were written with traditional literary, musical, dramatic, and artistic works in mind, and they simply do not fit the new electronic media very well. We need new copyright laws.

Transborder data flows add another variable. When data or software created in one country flow electronically across an international border before they are copied, which country's copyright laws are in effect? Computer crime is an international problem that transcends national borders and national laws.

Hackers and Crackers

Hacker
Originally, an expert program-mer with a knack for creating elegant solutions to difficult problems. Today the term is more commonly applied to someone who illegally breaks into computer systems.

Cracker
A person who breaks into a computer with malicious intent. A person who breaks into a computer over a com-munication line.

Back in the 1970s, to be called a **hacker** was a compliment. In those days, a hacker was an expert programmer with a knack for creating elegant solu-tions to difficult problems. Today, however, the term is more commonly applied to someone who illegally breaks into computer systems.

Within the programming community, hackers are viewed as relatively harmless pests. In contrast, **crackers,** people who break into computers with malicious intent, are viewed as criminals. In popular usage, however, hacker (the more common term) is applied to both benign and malicious intruders, and some sources use cracker to refer to a hacker who gains access to a computer over a communication line.

True hackers (in the original sense) have an unwritten code of ethics. They believe that software and data are intellectual property that should be shared. To a hacker, secrecy is the ultimate sin because it retards intellectual growth and forces us to rediscover what is already known. Some people believe that the hackers have a point and consider them modern-day Robin Hoods. There have been numerous cases, however, where hackers have unin-tentionally erased or damaged sensitive data and software, and industrial spies sometimes masquerade as benign hackers.

NOTE

The Internet Virus

On November 2, 1988, an unknown virus struck the Internet. From Berkeley, to Santa Monica, to MIT, Internet computers all over the country were inundated by a rabbit-like routine. For a time, things were so bad that the Ballistic Research Lab in Maryland suspected a foreign invasion.

The virus (or worm) was traced to a Cornell University graduate student named Robert Tappan Morris. (Ironically, the young Mr. Morris was the son of Bob Morris, chief scientist at the National Computer Security Center.) Taking advantage of a little-known flaw in a popular e-mail program, Morris wrote a routine that masqueraded as a harmless message and essentially tricked the target computer into executing it. Unfortunately, his program contained a flaw of its own: It reproduced much too quickly. As a result, the virus spread out of control and actually threatened to shut down the Internet for a time.

Fortunately, the virus was quickly contained and little or no permanent damage was done. Some people actually credited Morris with identifying the e-mail program flaw, but in spite of their support he was tried, convicted, and sentenced to three years' probation, a $10,000 fine, and 400 hours of community service.

Insider Crime

Given all the publicity about hackers and crackers, it might surprise you to learn that most computer crimes are committed by such insiders as employees, former employees, consultants, clients, and customers. Unlike hackers, they have relatively free access to the computer system, and they generally know exactly what they want and how to find it.

Industrial spies have been known to approach insiders with offers of money in exchange for sensitive information or software. Disgruntled information system employees (both current and former) are particularly dangerous. For example, angry programmers have been known to intentionally execute a program with the intent of damaging a computer system.

Bombs and Rabbits

A **time bomb** is a program that executes on a particular date or when a particular condition is met. A **Trojan horse** is a seemingly harmless program that invites an unsuspecting user to try it. Sometimes, time bombs and Trojan horses set off **logic bombs,** programs that (symbolically) blow up in memory, often taking the contents of a hard disk with them.

A **rabbit** is a program that replicates itself until no memory is left and no other programs can run. For example, one well-known rabbit creates two copies of itself and then starts them. A few microseconds later there are four rabbits running. Then eight, then sixteen, then. . . . By the time the operator realizes what is happening, the rabbit is out of control.

Viruses and Worms

A **virus** is a program that is capable of replicating itself and spreading between computers. Like its biological namesake, a virus is a parasite that must attach itself to another program if it is to survive and propagate. (The boot routine found on every diskette is a common target.) Viruses typically spread to other computers through infected diskettes or downloaded copies of infected programs. Figure 15.18 lists and briefly describes several common viruses.

A virus needs a host, but a **worm** is a program that is capable of spreading under its own power. One common technique is to send out small, virus-like scout programs from a source computer. Once the scout is established on the target computer, it sends a message back to the source requesting transmission of the body of the worm routine.

At best viruses and worms are an annoyance. At worst they can do real damage. In addition to the logic needed to replicate and establish themselves on a new computer, they can also carry a payload that holds a logic bomb, a time bomb, a rabbit, or some other type of destructive code. They have been known to erase disks, crash programs, and modify data.

Time bomb
A destructive program that executes at a predetermined time or when a certain predetermined conditions are met.

Trojan horse
A seemingly harmless program that invites an unsuspecting user to try it.

Logic bomb
A program that (symbolically) blows up in memory and damages software or data.

Rabbit
A program that replicates itself until no memory is left and no other programs can run.

Virus
A program that is capable of replicating itself, attaching itself to a host program, and spreading between computers.

Worm
A program that is capable of spreading under its own power.

351

S P O T L I G H T

Antivirus software
Software that detects and removes viruses.

Viruses can be difficult to detect or remove, so the best defense is prevention. Be careful about borrowing disks or accepting "free" software unless you know the source is clean. Also, be sure to use **antivirus software** to screen foreign disks and downloaded programs. Such software is designed to recognize certain code patterns (called virus signatures) and sound an alarm when a virus is detected.

SYSTEM SECURITY

Security is the first line of defense against computer crime. The objective of security is to protect the hardware, software, data, and other system resources from unauthorized access, use, modification, or theft.

▲ **Figure 15.18**

Some common viruses.

VIRUS	DESCRIPTION
Ambulance	Displays an ambulance moving across the screen accompanied by the sound of a siren.
B1	A potentially nasty virus that can physically damage a floppy drive's read/write head.
Casino	Displays a slot machine and insists that you play. If you lose, the virus renders your hard disk unusable.
Christmas Tree	Also known as Tannenbaum. Activates on December 21 and stays active until the end of the year. Displays a Christmas tree.
Colors	Infects Microsoft Word documents and changes your screen color settings.
Flame	Displays a row of red flames on a blue background.
Girafe	Displays a bright green marijuana leaf and the words "Legalize Cannabis."
Happy Birthday	On November 13, plays "Happy Birthday" until you press a key. Not really a virus.
Jerusalem	Draws black boxes at lower left of screen. If the virus is in memory on any Friday the 13th, it deletes from the hard disk every program that is executed.
Joshi	Insists that you type the words "Happy Birthday Joshi!"
Michelangelo	Activates on March 6, Michelangelo's birthday. Destroys much of the information on your hard disk.
Monkey	Difficult to detect. Makes your hard disk inaccessible if you boot from diskette.
Parity Boot	Displays "PARITY CHECK" and crashes your computer. Initially spread in late 1994 via an infected disk distributed by a large circulation German computer magazine.
Rescue	Displays an elaborate message insisting that we stop killing defenseless viruses. A tasteless satire of anti-abortion literature.
Stoned	Displays "Your computer is now stoned." Designed to be harmless, but can damage a disk directory.
Walker	Displays a figure walking across the screen.

Source: http://datafellows.fi/vir-desc.html

To an expert, an item is considered secure if the cost of breaking security (including the risk of getting caught) exceeds the item's value. It is easy to estimate the value of such tangible items as jewelry and money and thus determine the appropriate level of security, but to some people such things as military secrets or a corporation's strategic data are priceless. That is one reason why information system security is so difficult to ensure.

Physical Security

Physical security is concerned with denying physical access to a system. For example, mainframe computers are often located in controlled-access rooms, personal computers are sometimes cabled to work tables or placed in locked cabinets when they are not in use, and a network connection might be deactivated when the office is closed.

Access to a secure area is typically controlled by issuing identification cards, badges, keys, or personal identification numbers (PINs) to authorized personnel. Even better are **biometric devices** (Figure 15.19) that identify an individual via retinal scan, fingerprint analysis, voice print, or signature analysis.

Biometric device
An authentication device that verifies a person's identity by using such biological factors as fingerprints, retinal patterns, or voice prints.

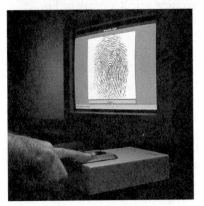

▲ Figure 15.19

Biometric security devices.
a. A retinal scanner.
b. A fingerprint scanner.
c. A signature analysis device.

Password
A secret code used to log onto a computer or a network.

Authentication
The process of verifying a user's identity.

Firewall
A software routine that screens all communication between the network and the system and allows only authorized transactions to get through.

Logical Security

Logical security is provided by the computer itself. Typically, each authorized user is assigned a unique identification code and a **password** that must be entered each time he or she logs onto the system. On some systems, additional passwords are required to access more secure data or to execute sensitive programs. Additionally, a transaction log might be maintained. Although logs cannot prevent unauthorized access, they can provide legal proof that a security breach has occurred.

Just having a valid user code and password does not necessarily prove that a given user really is the person he or she claims to be. **Authentication,** the process of verifying the user's identity, often relies on remembered information (such as a PIN or your mother's maiden name) or variations of the biometric devices described earlier.

Callback is another authentication tool. After a user logs on from a remote workstation, the host computer verifies the user code and password, breaks the connection (hangs up), and then redials the workstation. If a user with a valid password logs on through an approved, physically secure workstation, it is reasonable to assume that the user is authorized.

Many networks (particularly Internet-accessible networks) are designed to allow virtually anyone to log on. One way to protect the system from hackers, crackers, and other potentially destructive visitors is to construct a **firewall** between the network access routine and the rest of the system (Figure 15.20). A firewall is a software routine that screens all communication between the network and the system and allows only authorized transactions to get through.

NOTE

Selecting Good Passwords

A good password is easy to remember and difficult to guess. The most common mistake people make when they select a password is forgetting the second part of that objective. Your nickname, your initials, your birthdate, and your telephone number may be easy to remember, but they are also easy to guess.

Discard any password that appears on or can be deduced from the documents you carry in your wallet. Avoid using any word that appears in the dictionary because hackers have been known to use dictionaries to crack passwords. Intentional misspellings are good, and combinations of two or more words separated by digits are even better. For example, if your name is Pat and you own two bicycles, *pat2bykes* is both easy for you to remember and difficult for someone who does not know you to guess.

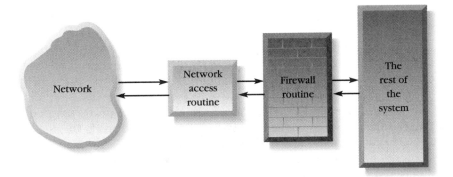

▲ **Figure 15.20**

A firewall offers protection from unauthorized or malicious intruders.

I S S U E S

The Clipper Chip

Traditional wiretapping is almost useless when you combine data encryption with high data volume, and law enforcement agencies fear that they will lose one of their most effective crime detection tools when sophisticated criminals begin using the information super-highway. One proposed solution is the Clipper chip.

If the government has its way, all future computers will contain a Clipper chip that incorporates an efficient, state-of-the-art encryption/decryption algorithm called SkipJack. Data to be encrypted will pass through the Clipper chip before entering the information super-highway. To ensure law enforcement access, the government will maintain a set of decryption keys (the keys to the "back door") that will allow the authorities, given the appropriate court orders, to wiretap and decode targeted messages.

Opponents offer many counterarguments. They fear the potential for increased electronic surveillance by "Big Brother," and doubt that the government can guarantee the integrity of the keys to the back door. They suggest that people with something to hide will find ways to bypass or thwart the Clipper chip. They argue that requiring domestic computer manufacturers to incorporate in their products a chip that is superfluous to the rest of the world will hurt sales of computers made in the U.S.A. or force American firms to move their manufacturing facilities to foreign countries.

Both sides have compelling cases. What do you think?

355

Encrypt
To convert data to a secret code.
Decrypt
To translate an encrypted message to plain text.
Data Encryption Standard (DES)
A national standard data encryption standard.
PGP
Acronym for Pretty Good Privacy. A public domain data encryption standard.

Encryption

Communication lines can be tapped. To make sensitive information difficult to read even if a message is intercepted, the data can be **encrypted** (converted to a secret code), transmitted, and then **decrypted** at the other end of the line.

The U.S. National Bureau of Standards' **Data Encryption Standard (DES)** is considered very difficult (perhaps impossible) to break. DES is used for secure government transmissions and for most electronic funds transfers. Another popular encryption algorithm called **PGP** (for Pretty Good Privacy) was created without government support and is available on the Internet.

SUMMARY

Computer crime is any criminal activity in which a computer is a target, a tool, or both. The fact that many of our laws are outdated makes computer crime difficult to fight.

At one time, a hacker was a technical expert, but today the term is more commonly applied to someone who illegally breaks into computer systems. People who break into computers with malicious intent are called crackers. Most computer crimes are committed by insiders. Examples of malicious programs include time bombs, Trojan horses, logic bombs, rabbits, viruses, and worms. Antivirus software is designed to sound an alarm when a virus is detected.

The objective of security is to prevent computer crime by protecting the hardware, software, data, and other system resources from unauthorized access, use, modification, or theft. Physical security is concerned with denying physical access to a system. Biometric devices can identify an individual via retinal scan, fingerprint analysis, voice print, or signature analysis.

Logical security precautions include user identification codes and passwords. Authentication is the process of verifying a user's identity. One way to protect a system from intruders is to construct a firewall between the network access routine and the rest of the system.

To make sensitive information difficult to read even if a message is intercepted, the data can be encrypted, transmitted, and then decrypted. The U.S. Data Encryption Standard and PGP are two well-known encryption standards.

KEY TERMS

antivirus software	decrypt	rabbit
authentication	encrypt	time bomb
biometric device	firewall	Trojan horse
computer crime	hacker	virus
cracker	logic bomb	worm
Data Encryption Standard (DES)	password	
	PGP	

CONCEPTS

1. What is computer crime? Cite several examples.
2. Briefly explain why outdated laws complicate the computer crime problem.
3. What is a hacker? What is a cracker?
4. Most computer crimes are committed by insiders. Why do you suppose that is true?
5. Briefly describe time bombs, Trojan horses, logic bombs, rabbits, viruses, and worms.
6. Distinguish between logical and physical security. Identify several techniques for implementing both types of security.
7. Why is data encryption/decryption necessary? Identify two data encryption standards.

PROJECTS

1. Log onto the Internet, activate a World Wide Web browser, and check the descriptions of common viruses maintained at http://datafellows. fi/vir-desc.html. The screen simulations of actual viruses are particularly interesting.
2. One of the more interesting books about hackers and crackers is *Masters of Deception, The Gang That Ruled Cyberspace* by Michelle Slatalla and Joshua Quittner (New York: HarperCollins Publishers, 1995). Get a copy and read it. For a more pro-hacker point of view, try Bruce Sterling, *The Hacker Crackdown* (New York: Bantam, 1992).

S P O T L I G H T

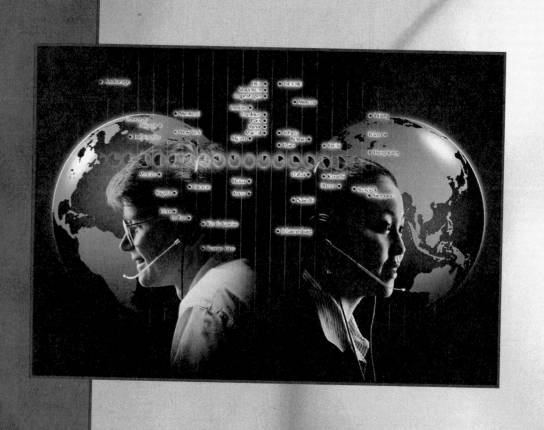

CHAPTER 16

Applications

Before you start this chapter, you should be familiar with the following concepts:

▶ Data and information (p. 4).

▶ The user (p. 6), software (p. 9), and data (p. 10).

▶ Computer systems (p. 13), classifying computers (p. 14), networks (p. 17), and the Internet (p. 17).

▶ Source data (p. 54), documents, images, and multimedia (p. 55), and terminals (p. 68).

▶ Commercial software (p. 146).

▶ Hypertext and hypermedia (p. 170).

When you finish reading this chapter, you should be able to:

▶ Briefly discuss process-bound and real-time applications.

▶ Distinguish among a transaction processing system, a decision support system, and an executive information system.

▶ Briefly discuss personal information management and groupware.

▶ Define the term *multimedia* and identify several common multimedia tools.

▶ Define the term *virtual reality,* briefly describe several applications of virtual reality, and identify several virtual reality tools.

▶ Define the term *artificial intelligence* and identify several areas of artificial intelligence research.

▶ Define the term *expert system,* briefly describe several expert system applications, and identify and briefly describe the primary components of an expert system.

▶ Discuss the intent of natural language processing.

▶ Briefly explain how natural language processing works and discuss the use of a natural language processing shell.

▶ Discuss the relationship between natural language processing and speech recognition.

PROCESS-BOUND AND REAL-TIME APPLICATIONS

Process bound
An application in which so many computations are performed that the computer spends most of its time actually processing data and relatively little time on input or output.

Such tasks as solving complex equations, analyzing weather data, and simulating natural phenomena are considered **process bound** because there are so many computations to be performed that the computer spends most of its time actually processing data and relatively little time on input or output. The fastest supercomputers (Figure 16.1) are specifically designed with such applications in mind.

Until recently, supercomputers were almost exclusively used to support scientific and military computation, but that is changing. For example, computer-generated animation is a highly process-bound application, and supercomputers were used to generate the dinosaurs in Jurassic Park and the animated characters featured in Toy Story (Figure 16.2).

Real-time
An application in which the computer responds immediately to events as they occur and (typically) provides feedback to influence or control those events.

In a **real-time** application, the computer responds immediately to events as they occur and (typically) provides feedback to influence or control those events. Examples include automatic pilots on airplanes, air traffic control systems, manufacturing process control systems, hospital patient monitoring systems (Figure 16.3), defense early-warning systems, and even the telephone company's call-forwarding feature.

BUSINESS INFORMATION SYSTEMS

In a business organization (Figure 16.4), authority and responsibility flow from the top, down. Executives make long-range strategic decisions that affect the entire organization. Under them come the middle managers who make tactical decisions that affect a single division or group. Below them are the supervisors who make day-by-day operational decisions and directly con-

▲ **Figure 16.1**

A supercomputer.

▲ **Figure 16.2**

The characters in *Toy Story* were animated on a supercomputer.

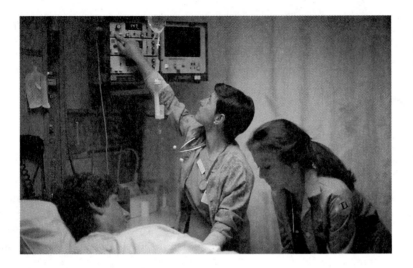

▲ **Figure 16.3**

A real-time patient monitoring system.

trol the employees who create, sell, maintain, and monitor the company's products and services.

An individual's information needs vary with his or her position in the organization. Consequently, a business information system must meet a variety of needs, providing employees and supervisors with detailed, current data, middle managers with summaries and near-future projections, and top management with highly summarized information and long-term projections.

Transaction Processing Systems

The summaries and projections required by middle and top-level management are derived from detailed current data; in other words, the detailed data

▲ **Figure 16.4**

The management pyramid.

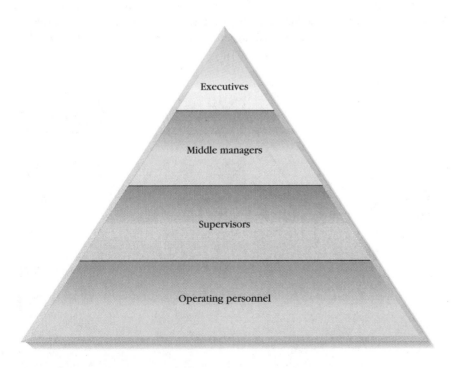

Transaction processing system (TPS)
A system that accepts and processes operational-level transactions.

must come first. Consequently, the earliest commercial computers supported **transaction processing systems (TPS).** A transaction is one occurrence of a business activity; a single customer order and a single shipment from a supplier are good examples. The purpose of a transaction processing system is to process and maintain data on the organization's day-to-day business transactions.

Management Information Systems

Early transaction processing applications were designed to support a single task, such as payroll, accounts receivable, or inventory. The problem is that business applications are not independent; they are related. For example, the data recorded on a sales invoice (Figure 16.5) might be used to compute the sales associate's commission, update the stock on hand for the item sold, update the customer's billing account, and provide input to the accounting system.

By the middle 1960s, integrated databases made it possible to develop integrated applications. For example, given a database, a single program can accept a sales transaction and automatically update the customer's account, inventory stock levels, the appropriate accounting records, and the sales associate's payroll data.

At about the same time, data communication systems that linked user terminals to a computer began to evolve. All of a sudden, it was no longer necessary for a user to visit the computer center to drop off data or pick up reports. Instead, data communication brought the information directly to the user and managers were able to generate demand reports and exception reports (for example, a list of overdue bills) in response to unscheduled queries or questions.

The ability to obtain on demand such focused feedback changed the very nature of business computing. Instead of merely tracking and summarizing paperwork, a computer in the hands of a clever manager could be used to actively support the decision-making process. When you add centralized data

▲ **Figure 16.5**

Business applications are related.

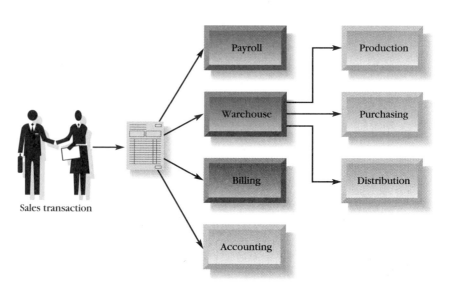

Sales transaction

management, integrated applications, distributed access, and interactive processing to the base created by a transaction processing system, you have the framework for a **management information system (MIS).**

Decision Support Systems

Following the development of inexpensive microcomputers in the late 1970s and early 1980s, the nature of business information systems changed once again. Intelligent workstations support **end-user computing,** and that makes it possible for a user to download and then *process* corporate data without the direct support of a computer professional and without affecting the original data.

An information system that supports operational and tactical decision making by providing interactive end-user computing, database access, and network support is called a **decision support system (DSS).** A typical decision support system incorporates an easy-to-use interface, data access routines, a model base of accounting, budgeting, financial, quantitative, statistical, market analysis, simulation, queuing, and optimization models, and other management tools (Figure 16.6).

Executive Information Systems

The point of an **executive information system (EIS)** is to help high-level managers spot problems, opportunities, and trends that might create, enhance, or threaten their company's competitive position. An executive information system adds to the MIS/DSS base features to support strategic decision making. Typically, the executive uses the EIS to identify a problem or a need for action and then delegates responsibility to lower level management. Consequently, in an EIS, tools to recognize problems are more important than tools to solve them.

Office Automation

Business information systems are not just for managers; they support day-to-day operations, too. For example, **office automation** is concerned with automating and/or electronically supporting such office tasks as preparing,

---

Management information system (MIS)
An information system that combines such attributes as centralized data management, integrated applications, distributed access, and interactive processing to provide the information needed to support operational (and some tactical) decision making.

End-user computing
Processing activities performed under the direct control of an end user.

Decision support system (DSS)
An information system that adds the local processing needed by tactical management to a management information system base.

Executive information system (EIS)
An information system that adds strategic information and executive tools to a decision support system base.

Office automation
Automating and/or electronically supporting such office tasks as preparing, storing, and retrieving documents, managing time, managing voice mail and e-mail, coordinating meetings, making presentations, monitoring a budget, and so on.

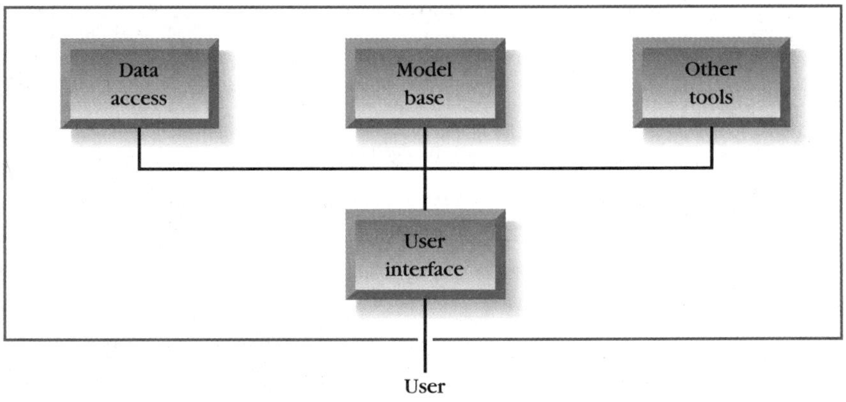

▲ **Figure 16.6**

The elements of a decision support system.

THE FUTURE

Telecommuting

Atelecommuter works at home and communicates with the office through a personal computer linked by telephone to the office network. Office automation makes telecommuting possible because if much of the work is done on electronic devices that are linked to the network, there is little need for the employee to be physically in the office.

In addition to the obvious savings in commuting time and expense, telecommuting saves the company the cost of providing office space for its work-at-home employees. Also, reducing the number of people who drive to work can only be good for the environment. Many professionals already telecommute, and the number is sure to grow.

storing, and retrieving documents, managing time, managing voice mail and e-mail, coordinating meetings, making presentations, monitoring a budget, and so on. The objective is to transfer much of the busy work to computers, facsimile machines, telephone networks, and similar electronic devices and thus make the employees more efficient.

PERSONAL INFORMATION MANAGEMENT

Personal information management (or personal productivity) tools are electronic forms of such traditional, paper-based business tools as pocket calendars, appointment calendars (Figure 16.7), contact lists, name and address books, business card files, to-do lists, and note pads. Maintaining such per-

Personal information management (PIM)
Such software as an electronic calendar, a note pad, and a card file that supports an individual's daily activities.

▲ **Figure 16.7**

An electronic appointment calendar.

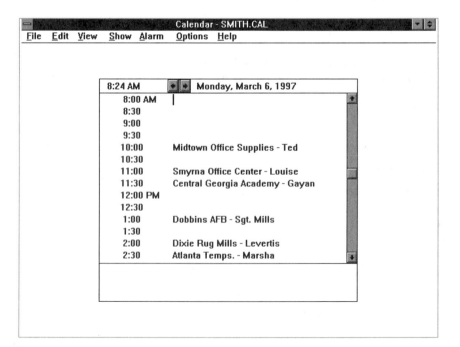

The Electronic Open Door

NOTE

Many managers pride themselves on maintaining an open-door policy. The idea is to encourage employees to stop into the manager's office at any time, even without an appointment, to discuss a problem.

The nature of business is changing, however. These days, employees are expected to work with very little direct management supervision; for example, a sales associate might spend most of his or her time on the road, visiting the office perhaps once or twice a week. An open-door policy is meaningless if the manager is not available during the limited block of time when a given employee is in the office.

On-line personal information management provides a solution. The manager starts the process by posting his or her electronic appointment calendar on the office network. The employees (even those who are on the road) have access to the boss's calendar via the network and can, on their own initiative, schedule personal meetings in open blocks. As a result, an employee can plan to be in the office at a time when the manager is available.

sonal data on the computer simplifies maintenance and allows the data from one application to be shared with others. For example, the data in an electronic name and address book might be linked to a business contacts list and used by a word processing program to prepare a customer mailing. Later, the same data might allow the user to select a contact by name and automatically dial his or her telephone number.

GROUPWARE

Groupware is software that supports work group computing by allowing people who are working together on a common project to share data and information over a network. An electronic meeting system is a good example. Finding an acceptable time for several people to meet can be difficult, but if the participants' individual appointment calendars are electronically linked, the groupware routine can scan the individual calendars, find a time when everyone is free, and automatically add the meeting to everyone's calendar.

In fact, given the right equipment and a network, it is no longer necessary to assemble a group of people in the same physical room in order to hold a meeting. Instead, they can use their equipment to meet and exchange information interactively and electronically, a process called teleconferencing (Figure 16.8).

Groupware
Software that supports cooperative group efforts over a network.

MULTIMEDIA

The term **multimedia** suggests the combined use of several media (such as text, graphics, animation, video, pictures, music, sound, and speech) in a single integrated application. For example, Figure 16.9 shows a screen from a

Multimedia
The combined use of several media, including text, graphics, animation, moving pictures, slides, music, sound, and lighting, in a single application.

▲ **Figure 16.8**

Teleconferencing.

popular CD-ROM called *BodyWorks,* a multimedia tour of the human body. Each medium delivers information in its own way, but the impact is enhanced by their interaction.

Multimedia Tools

A multimedia platform is a computer equipped with a sound card, a color monitor, a set of speakers, a CD-ROM drive, a microphone (for audio input),

▲ **Figure 16.9**

A multimedia presentation combines text, graphics, animation, video, sound, and other elements.

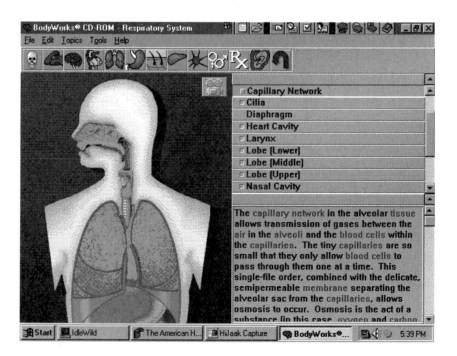

perhaps a scanner, and other equipment for capturing, storing, retrieving, and presenting multimedia information. Key software tools include a word processor, a desktop publishing program, hypertext and hypermedia, a video editor, audio capture software, image processing tools, and synchronization tools.

NAVIGATING A MULTIMEDIA PRESENTATION

When you read a traditional printed book, you normally follow a linear path through the material. A multimedia presentation removes that constraint and allows you to navigate the material in almost any order. The process is similar to "surfing" an encyclopedia by looking up one topic, noting a few points of interest in its entry, looking up those topics, and so on. It can be a very effective way to learn.

A multimedia presentation consists of a set of nodes and hyperlinks. Clicking on a link in one node activates the linked node. Sometimes the links are embedded in the text and highlighted in some way; for example, in Figure 16.10 the word *hardware* might be displayed in blue or reverse video. Clicking on a highlighted word might open a window containing the definition of that term. Links can also be represented as buttons or icons; for example, Figure 16.10 shows hyperlinks to a photograph of a hardware component, a film clip, and an animation.

Most multimedia presentations start with a set of default navigation rules such as pointers to the presentation's next node, previous node, and first node. Some systems maintain a stack of backward navigation links (called history lists), and many allow the user to define **bookmarks** that make it easy to return to particularly interesting or useful nodes.

Bookmark
A hypertext or hypermedia marker that makes it easy to return to interesting or useful nodes.

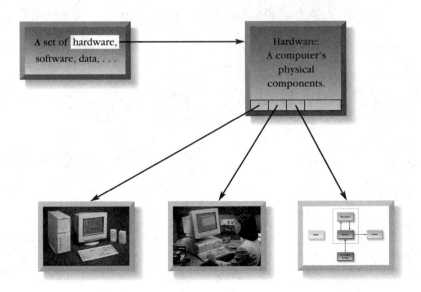

▲ **Figure 16.10**

Navigating a multimedia presentation.

VIRTUAL REALITY

Virtual reality is a step beyond multimedia. A virtual reality application combines sound, motion, and images in such a way that you literally feel you are part of the action. Virtual reality is interactive and multisensual. The user not only sees and hears his or her surroundings, but actually manipulates them with natural body movements. The word *virtual* means in essence but not in fact. Virtual reality is a simulation of reality that looks, feels, sounds, behaves, and (someday) tastes and smells just like reality.

Virtual Reality Applications

If you have ever visited a major theme park, you may have experienced virtual reality. The "Back to the Future" attraction at Universal Studios in Orlando, Florida, is a good example (Figure 16.11). Your experience begins when you enter a small room and climb into a simulated automobile. Suddenly, a fog-like cloud engulfs the vehicle. You feel motion. You see colored lights. Then the fog clears, and you would swear you were flying through space and time. You never leave the room, but your senses tell you otherwise.

During the Persian Gulf war, American pilots used virtual reality flight simulators to practice their bombing runs. By the time the actual missions took place, the pilots were so well trained and had "experienced" so many possible scenarios that there were no surprises. In fact, some pilots claimed that the virtual reality runs were tougher than the real thing. The wider application of similar virtual reality techniques could revolutionize education and training.

In the medical field, virtual reality is used to improve learning by allowing medical students and interns to simulate surgery. Experienced surgeons use virtual reality models of patients as diagnostic aids. Architects use virtual reality models to walk through a design that exists only in the computer. If

▲ **Figure 16.11**

You might be able to experience virtual reality at your favorite theme park.

ISSUES

Virtual Reality in Fiction

In a classic story called "The Machine Stops," E. M. Forster describes an imaginary future in which everyone lives in his or her own private universe and direct human contact is rare. Then one day the machine that controls all those virtual realities (Forster did not use that term) fails, and society collapses. In spite of its age (it was written in 1928), the story seems particularly relevant today.

The danger associated with what we now call virtual reality is a common science fiction theme. Ray Bradbury touched on it in a short story entitled "The Veldt" and again in *The Martian Chronicles*. More recently, William Gibson described a place called cyberspace in such books as *Neuromancer* and *Mona Lisa Overdrive*.

Virtual reality is moving from the realm of fiction into the real world. Is that good or bad? The answer is probably a little of both. How would you react if someone gave you the opportunity to literally live in your own fantasy world? What will happen to society if significant numbers of people decide to do exactly that?

the design fails to work, the architect simply makes the appropriate changes on the computer and then tries again.

On the Internet, it is possible to send your virtual persona to a virtual chat room and conduct a virtual conversation with other virtual personae. That may sound silly, but if you talk to the (real) participants, they will tell you that it can be a rewarding experience.

Virtual Reality Tools

The ultimate objective of virtual reality is to convince the user that the virtual world is real. Generally, the more senses you involve, the more effective the simulation.

Head-mounted displays that resemble helmets, goggles, or glasses (Figure 16.12) are the most recognizable virtual reality devices. Often, they are designed to transmit a slightly different image to each eye so the user sees a stereoscopic view of the scene. Most include devices to track and report head movement. The system responds by changing the image to correspond to the user's changing viewpoint.

Sounds are important, too. Although earphones can be effective, the best virtual reality systems incorporate stereoscopic surround sound that gives the user directional cues. Note that sound and vision are related; in the real world, we tend to look toward sounds.

▲ **Figure 16.12**

A head-mounted display.

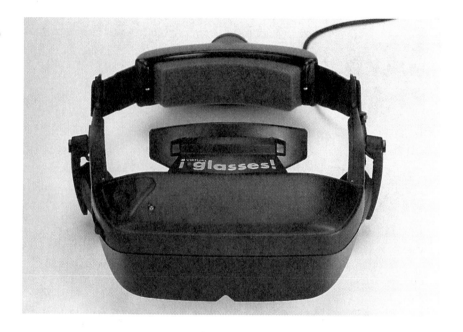

▲ **Figure 16.12**

A head-mounted display.

Today's state of the art systems add tactile sensations to the simulation. Specially designed gloves sense hand movement, finger movement, the yaw and pitch of the wrist, and the arch of the palm, and transmit that information to the computer. Tiny bladders in the glove (like "the pump" in some athletic shoes) are inflated and deflated to simulate the pressure you feel when you grasp something (a doorknob, for example) and then let go. Thermodes are used to convey hot and cold sensations. A body suit, such as the one pictured in Figure 16.13, is essentially a data glove for the body.

There are several ways to simulate motion. Treadmills convey a sense of walking through a virtual reality, and a stationary bicycle is an effective metaphor for riding through. Other models simulate flying through the virtual reality.

Smell and taste are the two most difficult senses to simulate, but research is ongoing. Using this new technology, you will soon be able to create incredibly realistic artificial worlds. Virtual reality could literally change the way we live.

Augmented Reality

Augmented reality
To superimpose information on a real scene.

Augmented reality is similar to virtual reality. The idea is to superimpose information on a real scene. For example, a repair technician might wear special goggles that superimpose a wiring diagram onto an electronic component to be repaired, and an warplane might display weapon sights and key status information on the windshield so the pilot does not have to look away from the target.

ARTIFICIAL INTELLIGENCE

Artificial intelligence
A branch of computer science concerned with developing machines to perform activities normally thought to require intelligence.

Artificial intelligence is a subdivision of computer science devoted to creating hardware and software that allow a computer to perform activities that

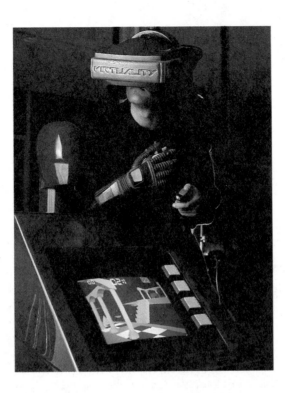

▲ **Figure 16.13**

A virtual reality body suit.

are normally thought to require intelligence. Currently, artificial intelligence research is concerned with such topics as natural language processing, speech recognition, machine learning, computer vision, robotics, and expert systems.

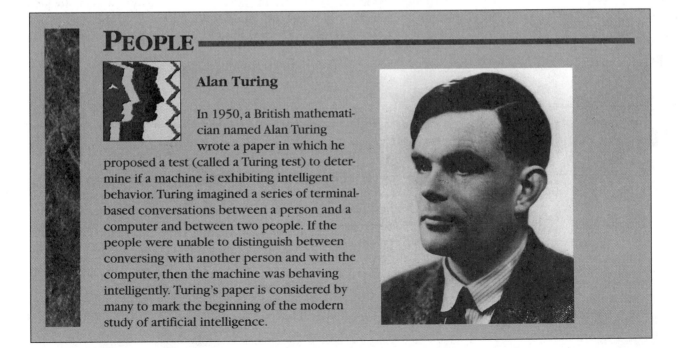

PEOPLE

Alan Turing

In 1950, a British mathematician named Alan Turing wrote a paper in which he proposed a test (called a Turing test) to determine if a machine is exhibiting intelligent behavior. Turing imagined a series of terminal-based conversations between a person and a computer and between two people. If the people were unable to distinguish between conversing with another person and with the computer, then the machine was behaving intelligently. Turing's paper is considered by many to mark the beginning of the modern study of artificial intelligence.

Expert Systems

Expert system
A computer program that simulates (or emulates) the thought processes of a human expert.
Knowledge
Understanding.

An **expert system** (or knowledge-based system) is a computer program that emulates the thought process of a human expert. Data are facts. Information has meaning. **Knowledge** implies understanding. Expert systems deal with knowledge.

EXPERT SYSTEM APPLICATIONS

In the medical field, expert systems show great promise as diagnostic aids. They are used to inexpensively screen patients, provide second opinions, and check the accuracy of a diagnosis, and they even serve as primary sources of medical expertise in situations where no doctor is available.

For example, MYCIN, developed in the mid-1970s, is used to diagnose bacterial infections of the blood, and the program can arrive at a reasonable conclusion even given incomplete information. In a 1979 trial, MYCIN performed as well as a group of experts and better than inexperienced physicians. PUFF, a lung infection diagnosis program similar to MYCIN, is in routine use today.

Geologists use expert systems to analyze satellite photographs and other survey data and help pinpoint oil and mineral deposits. One example, Prospector, is a geological expert system developed in 1982.

Business expert systems support such tasks as training, capital resource planning, loan application analysis, and strategic planning. Expert systems are particularly good at extracting the handful of best alternatives from a long list of choices. People are most comfortable when the list of choices is reduced to perhaps three or four, so the combination of a skilled manager and an expert system can enhance the effectiveness of both.

Telephone companies use expert systems to reroute telephone traffic during peak hours and to suggest the best type of phone service for their business customers. Computer manufacturers use expert systems to help configure computer systems. For example, XCON was developed in 1984 by Digital Equipment Corporation to configure VAX computer systems for customer orders.

NOTE

Chess-Playing Computers

Most people consider chess a challenging game and regard those who play it well as highly intelligent. Consequently, creating a chess-playing computer was an early objective of artificial intelligence pioneers. They succeeded.

On February 18, 1996, world chess champion Garry Kasparov defeated an IBM supercomputer named Deep Blue in a historic six-game match. The match was historic because the computer, actually a supercomputer with 32 parallel processors, won the first game and forced a draw in two others. For the first time ever, a machine demonstrated an ability to play chess at the very highest level.

In the military, "smart" bombs are guided by expert systems that match navigational data against preprogrammed maps, make appropriate route changes, and precisely deliver the payload to a specific target. Battlefield control is another military application. For example, on a naval warship an expert system backs up the ship's tactical officer and actually takes control of certain weapons systems if the tactical officer is killed or incapacitated.

Some information systems incorporate expert system routines called **agents.** An agent is a process that performs a function on behalf of a client. For example, the information superhighway makes so much information available that it is often difficult to find the material you want. Instead of personally monitoring the information superhighway, it is possible to assign that job to an expert-system agent that filters the information flow and gathers only the information that fits your personal interest profile.

THE COMPONENTS OF AN EXPERT SYSTEM

Conventional computer programs are algorithm based; essentially, a programmer tells the computer exactly how to solve the problem. Human experts use algorithms, too, but they also rely (at least in part) on **heuristics** (general rules derived from experience, common sense, inferences, and intelligent trial and error) to help them make decisions. Consequently, an expert system is built around a **knowledge base** (Figure 16.14) that incorporates data, algorithms, and heuristic rules.

The process of creating a knowledge base begins with a human expert whose expertise is captured and encoded by a **knowledge engineer** and entered through a **knowledge acquisition facility.** Once the knowledge base is established, a user accesses the system through a user interface called the **expert system shell** and enters the parameters of a problem into another software component called an **inference engine.** The inference engine uses the input parameters to access the knowledge base, reach a conclusion, and offer expert advice. Most expert systems also contain an **explanation facility** that reproduces the logic the inference engine followed to reach its conclusion.

Agent
A process that performs a function on behalf of a client.

Heuristic
A general decision-making rule derived from experience, common sense, inferences, and intelligent trial and error.

Knowledge base
The set of data, information, and decision-making rules around which an expert system is constructed.

Knowledge engineer
The person who creates a knowledge base.

Knowledge acquisition facility
An expert system feature used to create a knowledge base.

Expert system shell
An expert system's user interface.

Inference engine
An expert system routine that analyzes a knowledge base and arrives at a conclusion.

Explanation facility
An expert system feature that explains the logic the expert system followed to reach a conclusion.

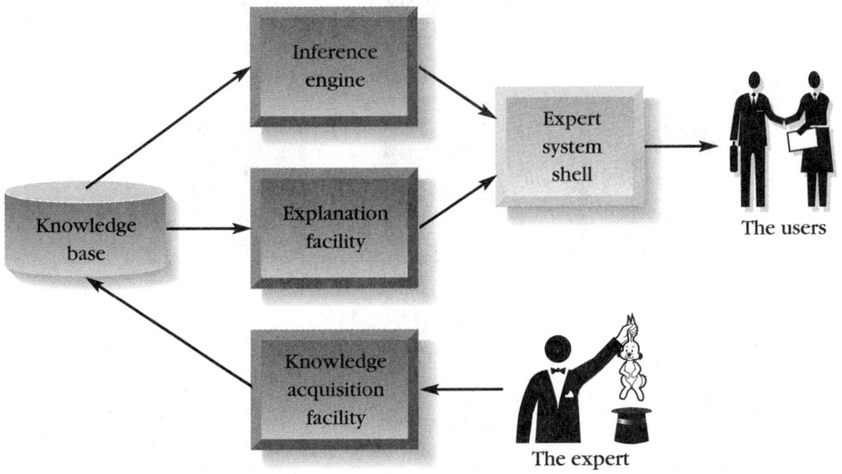

▲ **Figure 16.14**

The elements of an expert system.

Many expert systems are able to "learn" from experience. Each time a user exercises the system, he or she asks questions, defines parameters, and makes choices. Over time, the expert system senses patterns in those interactions, adds the new knowledge to its knowledge base, and, in effect, learns to anticipate the user. In fact, the study of **machine learning** is itself a significant area of artificial intelligence research.

Natural Language Processing

As the name implies, the ultimate objective of **natural language processing** is to allow people to communicate with computers in much the same way they communicate with each other. (Picture Spock speaking to the computer on the starship *Enterprise*.) If we are able to develop inexpensive natural language interfaces, many of the impediments that keep some people from using computers will disappear.

SYNTACTIC AND SEMANTIC ANALYSIS

Natural language processing starts with the input of a string of plain English words, such as a question or a statement (Figure 16.15). During the first phase, syntactic analysis, a **parser** routine separates (or parses) the string into individual words and, essentially, diagrams the sentence. The result, called a parse tree, resembles the sentence diagrams you once prepared in English class.

Next, during the semantic analysis stage, the system determines the meaning of each word by looking it up in a dictionary. If necessary, an expert system is consulted to deduce the meanings of ambiguous terms and expressions based on context, questions asked earlier in the session, organization-specific rules, and other factors stored in the knowledge base.

Machine learning
An area of artificial intelligence research.

Natural language processing
A subfield of artificial intelligence that focuses on developing hardware and software to allow people to communicate with computers in much the same way they communicate with each other.

Parser
A routine that separates (or parses) an input string into individual words and, essentially, diagrams the sentence.

▲ **Figure 16.15**

Natural language processing.

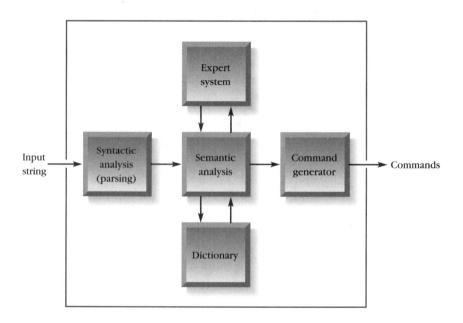

A natural language processing shell.

Once the semantic analysis routine understands the user's meaning, the results are sent to a command generator and output as one or more commands that the computer can execute. For example, a plain English query might be converted to a set of SQL commands.

THE NATURAL LANGUAGE SHELL

Most experts envision the natural language processing routine as a shell (Figure 16.16). The user communicates with the shell by entering plain English character strings. The shell translates the plain English strings into the appropriate commands and passes the commands to an application program.

Using a common shell makes more sense than duplicating the same complex logic in multiple application programs. Perhaps someday you will be able to purchase a natural language processing chip for your personal computer and use it to provide input to virtually all your application programs.

SPEECH RECOGNITION

Speech recognition is a special field related to natural language processing. The idea is to use a speech recognition routine (or a chip) to create a string of words, input the string to a natural language processing routine, and then pass the resulting commands to an application program (Figure 16.17).

One problem with speech recognition is that human language is imprecise and loaded with subtle shades of meaning. Add an incredible variety of

Speech recognition
Using hardware and software to recognize and interpret human speech.

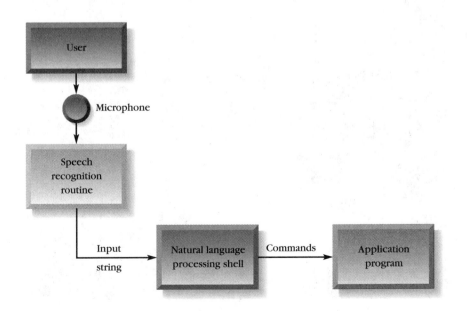

▲ **Figure 16.17**

Speech recognition.

languages, dialects, and accents, and you have a very complex problem. Additionally, few people are skilled at issuing orders or precisely specifying their needs. For example, when things get serious on board the starship *Enterprise,* it is always Spock who talks to the computer. He is precise, but then he is only half human.

Robotics

Robot
A machine that (sometimes) resembles a human being and is capable of performing a variety of often complex, human-like tasks without direct human control.

A **robot** is a machine that (sometimes) resembles a human being and is capable of performing a variety of often complex, human-like tasks without direct human control. Television, the movies, and science fiction have given us popular images of robots, but hand-like grasp-and-place devices, such as the robot pictured in Figure 16.18, are more realistic.

The first robots were not very intelligent. For example, on an assembly line parts had to be precisely positioned for the robots to work with them, and if the operator's hand just happened to be where the robot was programmed to drive a staple, it drove the staple into the operator's hand.

A great deal of current research is aimed at making robots more intelligent so they can adjust to changing conditions. For example, because it takes so long to send control signals from Earth to Mars, a robot designed to roam the Martian surface and send back pictures must be able to sense changes in topography and make its own decisions to stop, back up, or change directions if it is to avoid falling off a cliff.

One key to flexible self-control is providing real-time feedback. Computer vision systems apply searching algorithms, pattern recognition logic, and pattern matching rules to a digital image, and modern grasp-and-control devices can sense tactile stimuli. Consequently, today's robots can "see" and "feel" the objects they are programmed to manipulate and thus make whatever adjustments are necessary.

▲ **Figure 16.18**

Typical robots.

SUMMARY

On a process-bound application, the computer spends most of its time processing data and relatively little time on input or output. In a real-time application, the computer responds immediately to events as they occur and provides feedback to influence or control those events.

The purpose of a transaction processing system is to process and maintain data on the organization's day-to-day business activities. When you add centralized data management, integrated applications, distributed access, and interactive processing to the base created by a transaction processing system, you have the framework for a management information system. An information system that supports operational and tactical decision making by providing interactive end-user computing, database access, and network support is called a decision support system. An executive information system is designed with strategic decision making in mind.

Office automation is concerned with automating and/or electronically supporting common office tasks. Personal information management tools are electronic forms of such traditional paper-based business tools as to-do lists and appointment calendars. Groupware is software that supports work group computing by allowing people who are working together to share data and information over a network.

Multimedia suggests the combined use of text, graphics, animation, video, pictures, music, sound, and speech in a single integrated application. Some multimedia systems allow the user to define bookmarks that make it easy to return to particularly interesting or useful nodes. A virtual reality application combines sound, motion, and images in such a way that you literally feel you are part of the action. Virtual reality applications use such tools as head-mounted displays, earphones, surround sound systems, special gloves, body suits, and motion simulators. Augmented reality superimposes information on a real scene.

Artificial intelligence is a subdivision of computer science devoted to the study of ways of making machines behave intelligently. An expert system is a computer program that emulates the thought process of a human expert. Expert systems deal with knowledge. An agent is a process that performs a function on behalf of a client.

An expert system is built around a knowledge base that incorporates heuristic rules. The knowledge base is created through a knowledge acquisition facility by a knowledge engineer. A user accesses the system through an expert system shell. The inference engine uses input parameters to access the knowledge base, reach a conclusion, and offer expert advice. Most expert systems also contain an explanation facility that reproduces the logic the inference engine followed to reach its conclusion. Machine learning is an area of artificial intelligence research.

With natural language processing, a string is input to a parser that diagrams the sentence. During the semantic analysis stage, the system looks up each word in a dictionary and consults an expert system to deduce the meanings of ambiguous terms. Once the meaning is known, the results are sent to a command generator and output as one or more commands.

The idea of speech recognition is to convert sounds into a string of words and then input the string to a natural language processing shell. The ultimate objective of natural language processing is to allow people to communicate with computers in much the same way they communicate with each other.

A robot is a machine that resembles a human being and is capable of performing a variety of often complex, human-like tasks without direct human control.

KEY TERMS

agent	heuristic	office automation
augmented reality	inference engine	parser
artificial intelligence	knowledge	personal information
bookmark	knowledge acquisition	management
decision support system	facility	process bound
(DSS)	knowledge base	real-time
end-user computing	knowledge engineer	robot
executive information	machine learning	speech recognition
system (EIS)	management information	transaction processing
expert system	system (MIS)	system (TPS)
expert system shell	multimedia	virtual reality
explanation facility	natural language	
groupware	processing	

CONCEPTS

1. What is a process-bound application? Cite some examples.
2. What does real-time mean?
3. What is the difference between a transaction processing system, a decision support system, and an executive information system? Transaction processing systems evolved first, followed by decision support systems and then executive information systems. Why?
4. What is the objective of office automation? Identify several personal information management tools and briefly explain why they are useful.
5. What is groupware? Why is groupware valuable?
6. What is multimedia? Identify several common multimedia tools. Briefly explain how a user navigates a multimedia presentation.
7. What is virtual reality? Briefly describe several applications of virtual reality. Briefly identify several tools you would expect to use in a virtual reality application.
8. What is augmented reality? How does it differ from virtual reality?
9. What is artificial intelligence? List several areas of artificial intelligence research.
10. What is an expert system? Briefly describe several expert system applications.
11. Briefly explain how an expert system works. What are the primary components? What is the purpose of each component? How are the components linked?
12. What is the intent of natural language processing? Briefly explain how natural language processing works.

13. What is a natural language processing shell? Why does it make sense to implement natural language processing as a shell?
14. Briefly explain how natural language processing and speech recognition are related.
15. What is a robot?

PROJECTS

1. Tour a local business information center.
2. Interview some business people, both managers and employees, and ask them how and why they use computers. Write a short paper contrasting the way managers and operational-level personnel see and use computers.
3. Science fiction is particularly good at envisioning possible futures. The following short stories and novels consider how some of the topics introduced in this chapter are likely to affect society. Read one or more of them.

   ▶ Asimov, Isaac. *Robot Visions.* New York: Roc Books, (1990). This collection of short stories includes several Asimov classics.
   ▶ Bradbury, Ray. "The Veldt," in *The Vintage Bradbury.* New York: Vintage Books, (1965).
   ▶ E. M. Forster. "The Machine Stops," 1928. Forster's classic novella is found in numerous collections including: *The Science Fiction Hall of Fame,* Vol. IIB. Edited by Ben Bova. New York: Avon Books, 1973.
   ▶ Gibson, William. *Neuromancer.* New York: Ace Science Fiction Books, (1984).

4. If you have access to a computer with a CD-ROM drive, spend some time navigating a multimedia presentation such as *Bodyworks* or *Microsoft Bookshelf.*
5. If you have never experienced virtual reality, visit a major theme park and ride one of the virtual reality attractions. If that is not possible, schedule some time on your school's flight simulator or driving simulator.

 ## INTERNET PROJECTS

1. *News and Notes.* Use the World Wide Web to search for new virtual reality rides and attractions at various theme parks. Write a brief note or send an e-mail message to your instructor outlining what you find.
2. *Topic Searches.* Check the World Wide Web and/or other Internet resources for information on the following topics:

Key word	Qualifiers
chess	computer
telecommute	home office
virtual reality	game

Define the key word, identify at least two sources of information on the topic, and briefly summarize the nature of the information you find.

3. *Links to Other Sites*. After you access one or more of the following sites, write a brief note or send an e-mail message to your instructor outlining what you find.

   a. On the World Wide Web, check *http://www.rockhall.com* for a virtual tour of the Rock and Roll Hall of Fame.
   b. Check *http://mistral.enst.fr/~pioch/louvre/* for a virtual tour of the Louvre in Paris, France.
   c. On the World Wide Web, check *http://www.disney.com* for information about Mickey and his friends. Look for new rides and attractions at the Disney theme parks.

4. Access West Publishing Company's home page and find the Chapter 16 student activities for this book. See Internet Project 3 for the spotlight on *The Internet* following Chapter 1 (page 29) for more detailed instructions on accessing the home page. As appropriate, repeat projects 1, 2, and/or 3 using the more current references you find.

APPENDIX A

A Brief History of the Computer

BEFORE COMPUTERS

Although computers are a relatively recent innovation, the need for data and information processing is at least as old as recorded history.

▲ FIGURE A.1

The first real aid to computation, the abacus, was developed in China as early as 2600 B.C.

▲ FIGURE A.2

In 1617 John Napier invented a primitive slide rule called Napier's bones (below).

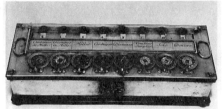

▲ FIGURE A.3

Blaise Pascal's Machine Arithmetique (1647) was the first mechanical adding machine.

▲ FIGURE A.4

Charles Babbage's analytical engine (1843) incorporated virtually every component and function of a modern computer.

▲ FIGURE A.5

Were it not for the writings of Ada Augusta, Countess of Lovelace, Babbage's contribution to the evolution of computing technology might have been lost to history.

The Dawning of the Computer Age

Throughout the first half of the twentieth century, punched card equipment represented the state of the data processing art, but the computing needs of World War II led to the development of the first real computers.

▲ FIGURE A.6

As the data for the 1890 census began to come in, Herman Hollerith had them punched into cards and tabulated electronically. Using his system, the 1890 census was completed within two years.

▲ FIGURE A.7

By the late 1920s, card-tabulating equipment had become the data processing standard.

▲ **FIGURE A.8**

In 1939, Howard Aiken of Harvard University started work on a machine to help solve polynomials. His Mark I, the first electromechanical computer, was finished in 1944. One of his assistants, a U.S. Navy lieutenant named Grace Hopper, would later lay the groundwork for COBOL, a popular business programming language.

▲ **FIGURE A.9**

The ENIAC (1945), developed at the University of Pennsylvania by a team headed by John W. Mauchly and J. Presper Eckert, was the first significant electronic computer. It launched the computer age.

THE FIRST, SECOND, AND THIRD GENERATIONS

Between 1950 and 1965, electronic-tube-based first-generation computers were supplanted by a second generation which was, in turn, rendered obsolete by third-generation, integrated circuit computers.

▲ FIGURE A.10

During the 1952 presidential election, CBS arranged to have a first-generation UNIVAC computer programmed to accept partial voting returns and predict the outcome. The political experts expected a close race, but the UNIVAC projected an Eisenhower land-slide well before the polls had closed. The computer was right and, as a result of that television exposure, computing machines, for the very first time, became a part of popular culture.

▲ FIGURE A.11

Second-generation computers like this one replaced the first generation's electronic tubes with transistors.

▲ FIGURE A.12

Third-generation computers used integrated circuit technology.

THE MICROCOMPUTER REVOLUTION

The January, 1975, issue of *Popular Electronics* marked a significant milestone in computer history. On the cover was a photograph of a computer called the Altair 8800, the first personal computer. Compared to today's personal computer systems, the Altair 8800 was incredibly primitive, but it started a revolution.

A year later, two young men named Steven Jobs and Steve Wozniak raised $1,300 by selling an old car and a programmable calculator, bought some electronic equipment, and built a microcomputer they christened the Apple I. A more sophisticated version, the Apple II, reached the market in 1977. The revolution had begun.

▲ FIGURE A.13

The Altair 8800, the first personal computer.

a.

b.

▲ FIGURE A.14

a. The Apple I.
b. The Apple II.

▲ FIGURE A.15

Following the release of the IBM PC, personal computer sales soared.

▲ FIGURE A.16

The Apple Macintosh set a new standard for ease of use.

APPENDIX B

Some Interesting USENET Newsgroups and World Wide Web Home Pages

Disclaimer: *Given the rate at which the Internet changes, it is likely that at least some of the entries on these lists will have changed or disappeared by the time this book is published. View the list as a starting point.*

USENET

Getting Started: These newsgroups are designed for first-time visitors. They contain tips, pointers on "netiquette," and the answers to frequently asked questions (called FAQs). Start here.

alt.newbies	An *alt.* newsgroup can be about almost anything, so be careful.
comp.answers	The *comp.* newsgroups discuss computer-related topics.
misc.answers	An *misc.* newsgroup can be about almost anything, but the discussions and topics tend to be more focused and less controversial than what you find in *alt.*
news.announce.newusers	Announcements and discussions aimed at new users
news.answers	The *news.* newsgroup contains news about USENET.
rec.answers	The *rec.* newsgroups discuss recreational topics.
sci.answers	The *sci.* newsgroups discuss scientific issues.
soc.answers	The *soc.* newsgroups discuss social issues.
talk.answers	The *talk.* newsgroups feature debates on controversial issues. Stay away if you are easily offended by strong opinions.

Computers: Discussions of computer-related topics.

alt.best.of.internet	Opinions regarding the best things happening on the Internet
alt.folklore.computers	Yes, the computer field does have its own folklore.

alt.hackers	About and for hackers and crackers
alt.hackers.malicious	Bad hackers
alt.security.pgp	The PGP encryption program
alt.wais	The Internet WAIS search tool
comp.human-factors	Ergonomics and human-computer interaction
comp.society.folklore	More computer folklore
comp.society.privacy	Computers and privacy
comp.virus	Computer viruses

Different Perspectives: These newsgroups are a little different.

alt.angst	For the anxious?
alt.flame.___	A place to let off steam. Add the name of your favorite target.
alt.whine	A place to whine

Employment: Job opportunities. Organizations looking for people with Internet skills often advertise on the Internet because simply finding the job listing demonstrates Internet skills.

bionet.jobs.wanted	Biologists looking for jobs
biz.jobs.offered	Jobs in business
misc.jobs.contract	Part-time or short-term contract or consulting opportunities
misc.jobs.misc	Discussions about employment
misc.jobs.offered	Job postings
misc.jobs.offered.entry	Entry-level positions
misc.jobs.resumes	Résumés of people looking for jobs
news.announce.conferences	Conferences are excellent places to look for a job
us.jobs.contract	Consulting opportunities in the United States
us.jobs.misc	Miscellaneous job postings in the United States
us.jobs.offered	Job postings in the United States
us.jobs.resumes	Résumés of people looking for jobs in the United States

Entertainment:

alt.fan.elvis-presley	For Elvis fans
rec.food.cooking	Cooking-related topics
rec.food.restaurants	For people who like to dine out
rec.sport.golf	For golfers
rec.sport.soccer	For soccer players and fans
rec.travel.europe	For the European traveler

For Sale: On-line classified advertisements.

| alt.forsale | Stuff for sale |
| misc.forsale.non-computer | Miscellaneous noncomputer stuff for sale |

misc.forsale.computers.___	Computer equipment for sale. Add the component you need.
us.forsale.computers	Computers for sale in the United States
us.forsale.misc	Miscellaneous stuff for sale in the United States

Humor: Warning! Many Internet users have strange senses of humor.

alt.comedy.british	British comedy
alt.fan.monty.python	The classic British comedy troupe
rec.humor.funny	The jokes of the day

Politics: Political forums and political information.

alt.politics.democrats.d	The Democratic Party
alt.politics.usa.republican	The Republican Party
soc.feminism	Feminism
talk.politics	Lively discussions of politics

Reviews: Book reviews, movie reviews, and the like.

alt.books.reviews	Book reviews
alt.books.technical	Technical books
rec.arts.movies.current-films	The latest releases
misc.books.technical	Technical books

Social Issues: A very broad category.

alt.missing-kids	Pictures and descriptions
soc.culture.italian	About Italy. Substitute the name of the country that interests you, and you might find a discussion group.
soc.men	About men
soc.women	About women

Television: What is happening on the tube?

alt.fan.letterman	About the guy on *Late Night*
alt.fan.letterman.top-ten	Dave's top ten list
rec.arts.tv.soaps.___	Your favorite soap opera. Add the appropriate network.
us.arts.tv.soaps	More about soap operas

Writing: Interesting stuff for authors and potential authors.

alt.authorware	Software for writers
bionet.journals.contents	For academic writers in the field of biology, the contents of current biological journals
misc.writing	A discussion group for writers

THE WORLD WIDE WEB

Getting Started: These indexes and directories are excellent places to begin navigating the World Wide Web.

http://www.yahoo.com	Yahoo is probably the best known, most popular Web directory.
http://home.netscape.com/ home/whats-cool.html	What's cool on the net?

Art Galleries and Museums: Virtual tours.

http://mistral.enst.fr/ ~pioch/louvre/	The Louvre in Paris
http://www.rockhall.com/	The Rock and Roll Hall of Fame
http://www.si.edu/start.htm	The Smithsonian Institution
http://www.sptimes.com/ treasures/default.html	The "Treasures of the Czars" exhibit from the Florida International Museum in St. Petersburg, Florida

Corporations: Many of our best-known corporations have their own home pages. Note the pattern and try substituting the name of the company you want to visit.

http://www.aol.com	America OnLine
http://www.att.com	AT&T
http://www.bankamerica. com	BankAmerica
http://www.cocacola.com	The soft drink maker
http://www.corel.com	Corel Corporation, the software maker
http://www.disney.com	Mickey and his friends
http://www.hp.com	Hewlett-Packard
http://www.ibm.com	IBM
http://www.microsoft.com	Microsoft
http://www.toyota.com	The Japanese auto maker
http://www.wal-mart.com	The discount store
http://www.westpub.com	The publisher of this book

Employment: Job opportunities. Organizations looking for people with Internet skills often advertise on the Internet because simply finding the job listing demonstrates Internet skills. Note that many corporations post job opportunities that can be accessed through their home pages.

http://collegegrad.com	Tips for landing that first job
http://www.careerpath.com	Newspaper employment ads from seventeen major cities
http://www.cweb.com	The Career WEB
http://www.espan.com	E-Span online employment connection
http://www.occ.com/occ	The Internet's online career center

http://www.studentcenter.com   Career planning assistance for students and recent
                               graduates

Financial Information: Stock quotes, financial advice, financial news, and
the like.

http://pawws.secapl.com   Financial quotes and other information from the
                               PAWWS Financial Network

http://www.amex.com   The American Stock Exchange

Government: Various government agencies.

http://thomas.loc.gov   Congressional news

http://www.census.gov   The Census Bureau

http://www.gsa.gov   The General Services Administration. Consumer
                               information, publications, education and training,
                               and so on

http://www.house.gov   The U.S. House of Representatives

http://www.sec.gov   The Securities and Exchange Commission

http://www.ssa.gov   The Social Security Administration

http://www.ustreas.gov   The Treasury Department, including the Internal
                               Revenue Service

http://www.whitehouse.gov   The president's house at 1600 Pennsylvania Avenue

News: Newspapers and other sources.

http://www.globe.com   The *Boston Globe*

http://www.chicago.   The *Chicago Tribune*
   tribune.com

http://www.nnic.noaa.gov   The National Oceanic and Atmospheric Administra-
                               tion. Weather information

http://www.nytimes.com   The *New York Times*

http://www.pulver.com   Technology news

http://www.sfgate.com   The *San Francisco Examiner* and the *San
                               Francisco Chronicle*

http://www.usatoday.com   *USA Today*

http://www.wsj.com   The *Wall Street Journal*

http://www.zdnet.com   Computer news

Politics: Political news and views.

http://www.democrats.org   The Democratic National Committee

http://www.gop.org   The Republican WEB Central

Shopping: On-line catalogue shopping. Be careful about giving these sites
your credit card number.

http://shop.internet.net   The Internet Shopping Network. Computer-related
                               products

http://www.cdnow.com   Compact disks, magazines, and T-shirts

http://www.clbooks.com	The Computer Literacy Bookshop
http://www.dealernet.com	New car information and a virtual showroom
http://www.homeshop.com	Cybershop, "a paradise for shoppers who enjoy shopping"
http://www.sharperimage.com	The Sharper Image catalog
http://www.software.net	The Software Net home page Software reviews and some free samples

Sports and Entertainment: News and information.

http://www.casino.org	The Internet casinos
http://www.nbctonightshow.com	The *Tonight Show* with Jay Leno
http://www.sony.com	Sony and its entertainment subsidiaries
http://www.sportsline.com	Sportsline USA

Television Networks: News and entertainment.

http://abctelevision.com	The ABC Television Network
http://www.cbs.com	The CBS Television Network
http://www.cnn.com	The Cable News Network
http://www.foxnetwork.com	The Fox Television Network
http://www.nbc.com	The NBC Television Network

Travel: Reservations, travel information, and the like.

http://io.com:8001/	The Internet travel mall
http://travel.epicurious.com	From Condé Nast
http://www.city.net	A link to the home pages of cities around the world
http://www.iflyswa.com	Southwest Airlines
http://www.mediabridge.com/nyc	A paperless guide to New York City
http://www.pctravel.com	Airline tickets and reservations from PC Travel

APPENDIX C

Computer Arithmetic

THE DECIMAL NUMBER SYSTEM

A decimal number consists of a series of digits—0, 1, 2, 3, 4, 5, 6, 7, 8, 9—written in precise relative positions. The value of a given number is found by multiplying each digit by its place or positional value and adding the products (Figure C.1).

Take a close look at the decimal place values: 1, 10, 100, 1,000, 10,000, and so on. Rather than writing all those zeros, you can use scientific notation. For example, 10,000 is 10^4. Because any number raised to the zero power is (by definition) 1, you can write the decimal place values as the base (10) raised to a series of integer powers:

$$\ldots 10^8 \ \ 10^7 \ \ 10^6 \ \ 10^5 \ \ 10^4 \ \ 10^3 \ \ 10^2 \ \ 10^1 \ \ 10^0$$

A few general rules can be derived from this discussion of decimal numbers. First is the idea of place or positional value represented by the base (10) raised to a series of integer powers. The second is the use of the digit zero (0) to represent "nothing" in a given position. (How else could you distinguish 3 from 30?) Finally, only values less than the base (in this case, 10) can be represented as a single digit. That is why you need ten different digits (0 through 9) to write decimal numbers.

THE BINARY NUMBER SYSTEM

There is nothing to restrict the application of those rules to a base-10 number system. If the positional values are powers of 2, you have the framework of a binary or base-2 number system:

$$\ldots 2^8 \ \ 2^7 \ \ 2^6 \ \ 2^5 \ \ 2^4 \ \ 2^3 \ \ 2^2 \ \ 2^1 \ \ 2^0$$

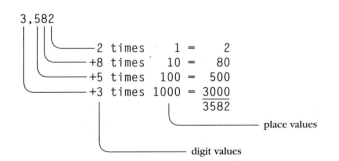

```
3,582
        ┌─ 2 times       1 =      2
        ├─+8 times       10 =     80
        ├─+5 times      100 =    500
        └─+3 times     1000 =   3000
                                ─────
                                 3582
                                       └── place values
               └── digit values
```

▲ FIGURE C.1

The value of any number is the sum of the products of its digit and place values.

As in any number system, the digit zero (0) is needed to represent "nothing" in a given position. Additionally, the binary number system needs only one other digit, 1. Given this structure, you can find the value of any binary number by multiplying each digit by its place value and adding the products (Figure C.2).

The decimal number 2 is 10 in binary; the decimal number 4 is 100. Decimal 5 is 101 (1 four, 0 twos, and 1 one). Figure C.3 shows you how to count from 0 to 15 in binary.

OCTAL AND HEXADECIMAL

Other number systems, notably octal (base 8) and hexadecimal (base 16) are commonly used with computers. The octal number system uses powers of 8 to represent positional values and the digit values 0, 1, 2, 3, 4, 5, 6, and 7. The hexadecimal number system uses powers of 16 and the digits 0, 1, 2, 3, 4, 5, 6, 7, 8, 9, A, B, C, D, E, and F. The hexadecimal number FF is:

$$
\begin{aligned}
15 \text{ times } 16^1 &= 240 \\
+ 15 \text{ times } 16^0 &= \underline{15} \\
& \ 255
\end{aligned}
$$

There are *no* computers that work directly with octal or hex; a computer is a *binary* machine. These two number systems are used because it is easy to convert between them and binary. Each octal digit is exactly equivalent to three binary digits, and each hexadecimal digit is exactly equivalent to four binary digits. Thus, octal and hex can be used as shorthand for displaying binary values.

BINARY ADDITION AND MULTIPLICATION

The rules for adding binary numbers are identical to the rules for adding decimal numbers. Adding two decimal digits yields values ranging from 0 (0 + 0) to 18 (9 + 9). Adding two bits produces four possible results ranging from 0 to 10 (Figure C.4). Just as in decimal addition, the high-order digit is carried to the next column (the next positional value).

Inside a computer are electronic circuits that add binary numbers at very high speed. Multiplication is repetitive addition, so (although they use shortcuts) computers rely on their addition circuitry to multiply binary numbers.

▲ FIGURE C.2

Converting the binary number 1100011 to decimal.

```
1100011
      └─── + 1 times 2⁰ = 1 times  1 =  1
     └──── + 1 times 2¹ = 1 times  2 =  2
    └───── + 0 times 2² = 0 times  4 =  0
   └────── + 0 times 2³ = 0 times  8 =  0
  └─────── + 0 times 2⁴ = 0 times 16 =  0
 └──────── + 1 times 2⁵ = 1 times 32 = 32
└───────────1 times 2⁶ = 1 times 64 = 64
                                       ──
                                       99
```

DECIMAL	BINARY	DECIMAL	BINARY
0	0	8	1000
1	1	9	1001
2	10	10	1010
3	11	11	1011
4	100	12	1100
5	101	13	1101
6	110	14	1110
7	111	15	1111

▲ FIGURE C.3

Counting to 15 in binary.

COMPLEMENTARY ARITHMETIC

A computer subtracts and divides by adding, too. How is that possible?

Subtraction and division are performed electronically by using complementary arithmetic. For example, consider the range of two-digit decimal numbers 00 through 99. The complement of 01 is 99, the complement of 02 is 98, the complement of 97 is 03, and so on; just subtract the number from 100. Note (in this example) that all values are expressed as two-digit numbers, so the complement of 00 is 00, not 100.

You can use complements to subtract by adding. For example, 98 minus 17 is 81. The complement of 17 is 83. Repeat the subtraction operation using complementary arithmetic: 98 plus 83 is 181. Throw away the high-order 1 (in this example you can only keep two digits) and you get 81, the same answer.

The complement of a binary number is very easy to find; just change every 0 to 1 and every 1 to 0. A computer might work with 32-bit numbers rather than 2-digit numbers, but the principle is the same. Given a complement, it is possible to subtract by adding. Division is repetitive subtraction, so it is also possible to divide by adding.

```
0 + 0 = 00
0 + 1 = 01
1 + 0 = 01
1 + 1 = 10
        └── carry bit
```

▲ FIGURE C.4

Possible results of adding two bits.

GLOSSARY

Access arm
The mechanism that carries a disk's read/write heads.

Accounting software
Application programs that perform such accounting tasks as accounts payable, accounts receivable, general ledger, and payroll.

Accumulator
On many computers, a work register used to add or accumulate values.

Activity
A measure of the percentage of a file's records that are accessed each time the relevant application program is run.

Add, record
To add a record to a file or a database.

Address
The location of a byte or word in memory.

Agent
A process that performs a function on behalf of a client.

Agent process
A software routine stored in the memory of each host computer or work-station that handles communications between the computer's operating system and the network.

Algorithm
A rule for arriving at an answer in a finite number of steps.

Alternative
A choice.

Analog
A signal that is analogous to the real data or that varies with the real data.

Analysis
The phase that follows problem definition in the system development life cycle. During analysis the analyst

determines what must be done to solve the problem.

Anonymous FTP archives
Storage space on the Internet where files can be left and subsequently retrieved by anyone.

Antivirus software
Software that detects and removes viruses.

Application programmer
A person who writes application software.

Application software
Software that performs end-user tasks.

Archie
An Internet program that allows a user to access and search (by file name) an index of files that reside on roughly 1,500 host computers around the world.

Architecture
A description of how a computer's components are physically linked and how they communicate with each other.

Arithmetic and logic unit
The processor component that executes instructions.

Array
A data structure that resembles a table or a spreadsheet.

Artificial intelligence
A branch of computer science concerned with developing machines to perform activities normally thought to require intelligence.

ASCII
Acronym for American Standard Code for Information Interchange. A common computer code.

Assembler
A program that translates assembly language instruction to machine level.

Assembly language
A programming language in which the programmer writes one source statement for each machine-language instruction.

Associative link
A hypertext or hypermedia link that connects two nodes.

Assumption
A number that is treated as a constant but that might subsequently be assigned a different value.

Asymmetrical multiprocessing
An approach to multiprocessing in which the programmer decides (at the time the program is written) which processor will be used to perform a given task.

Asynchronous
Transmitting data in short, irregular blocks, sometimes one byte at a time.

Attribute
A single fact that describes, qualifies, or is otherwise associated with an entity.

Audit
A review of financial and other documents intended to ensure that the established procedures and controls are followed.

Augmented reality
To superimpose information on a real scene.

Authentication
The process of verifying a user's identity.

Background
On a multiprogramming system, the low priority partition or region.

Back up
To copy the contents of a secondary storage device to another secondary medium.

Backup file
A copy of a master file or a transaction file that is used to recover data if disaster strikes.

Bar code
A code defined by variable-width bars that can be read optically.

Batch
A set of source data records collected over a period of time and processed together.

Batch data entry
Entering source data in a batch.

Baud
A measure of data transmission speed (usually, bits per second).

BBS
See Bulletin Board Service.

Benchmark
A standard program used to estimate a computer's processing speed.

Beta test
A software test in which real users who are unfamiliar with the technical details exercise a preliminary, prerelease version of the software.

Beta version
A preliminary, prerelease version of a program used in a beta test.

Binary
A number system that uses two digits, 0 and 1.

Biometric device
An authentication device that verifies a person's identity by using such biological factors as fingerprints, retinal patterns, or voice prints.

Bit
A binary digit.

Bit-map
An image that is stored as a pattern of pixels or dots.

Black box testing
A technique for identifying bugs.

Block
A set of logical records that are physically stored together.

Board
A hardware component that holds numerous related chips.

Boolean logic
A system of logic developed in the middle 1800s by George Boole, based on manipulating true and false conditions, or two states.

Bookmark
A hypertext or hypermedia marker that makes it easy to return to interesting or useful nodes.

Boot
A program that loads the operating system into memory.

Boundary
A limit to a system defined by a person, activity, other organization, or other system that lies outside the target system but communicates directly with it.

Bridge
A computer that links two similar networks.

Bridge routine
A program that provides a link to a commercial software routine.

Browser
A program used to navigate the World Wide Web.

Buffer
Temporary storage used to adjust for the speed disparity between two devices.

Bug
A logical error in a program.

Bulletin board service (BBS)
A service that allows users to post and read electronic messages.

Bus
A set of electrical lines that link the computer's internal components.

Bus network
A network in which the server, the workstations, and various peripheral devices all share a common communication line, or bus.

Byte
A group of eight bits that can hold a single character.

Cache memory
High-speed memory that is used as a staging area for the processor.

CAD/CAM
Acronym for computer-aided design/computer-aided manufacturing.

Cardinality
A measure of the relative number of occurrences of the two related entities.

Carrier signal
A continuous analog signal of known frequency and amplitude used to transmit data.

CASE
Acronym for Computer-Aided Software Engineering. A set of software routines designed to automate all or part of the system development life cycle.

Case structure
A form of selection block that provides more than two logical paths.

CD-ROM
A type of secondary storage that resembles a compact disk.

Cell
The intersection of a row and a column.

Central processing unit (CPU)
Another term for the processor.

Channel
On a mainframe computer, a built-in processor with (often) its own memory that manages data transfers between memory and peripheral devices.

Channel, communication
A general term for a communication medium. The physical path over which the message flows.

Chief Information Officer (CIO)
The person who is responsible for an organization's management information system.

Child
A lower-level record in a hierarchical database.

Chip
The basic electronic component of a modern computer.

CISC
Acronym for Complex Instruction Set Computer.

Class
A set of similar objects. *See also* object class, object type.

Client/server computing
A form of computing in which key tasks are assigned to different computers in a network. When a computer (the client) encounters a need to perform a task assigned to some other computer, it asks that computer (the server) for support.

Clip art
Predrawn electronic images that can be inserted into a document.

Clock
A device that drives a processor by emitting carefully timed electronic pulses.

Close
To break the link between a program and a data file. To make a data file unavailable for use.

Closed architecture
A proprietary computer design that is not published or widely available.

Cluster
The file system's basic disk space allocation unit.

Coding
The phase during which the programmer writes the source statements in a programming language.

Cohesion
A measure of a module's completeness.

Collision detection
A network management technique in which terminals and workstations are allowed to transmit at any time. If two messages collide, the collision is sensed and the messages are retransmitted.

Column
A vertical set of cells in a spreadsheet or a table.

Command
A cryptic message, usually typed on a single line, that tells the system to carry out a specific task.

COMMAND.COM
The MS-DOS command processor.

Command interface
A user interface that allows the user to communicate with the computer by issuing commands.

Command language
A programming language for issuing commands to an operating system.

Command processor
The operating system module that accepts, interprets, and carries out commands.

Comment
A brief written note in a program that explains the code.

Common carrier
A company that provides public communication services.

Communication software
Application programs that support data communication.

Compiler
A program that reads source code written in a human-like language, translates those instructions to machine language, and produces an object module.

Compression
Conserving memory, secondary storage space, and data transmission time by removing repetitive or unnecessary bits from data.

Computer
An information processing machine that works under the control of a program.

Computer-Aided Software Engineering
See CASE.

Computer crime
Any criminal activity in which a computer is a target, a tool, or both.

Computer engineer
A technical expert who plans, designs, and builds computer hardware.

Computer engineering
An academic discipline that trains computer engineers.

Computer information systems (CIS)
An academic program that is more technical than MIS but more applied than computer science.

Computer operator
A person who operates a computer.

Computer science (CS)
An academic program that studies the basic principles and theories that underlie computer hardware and software.

Computer scientist
A technical expert who plans, designs, and implements computer hardware and/or software.

Computer system
See information system.

Consultant
A person who provides advice and/or expertise on a temporary or project basis.

Control structure
Program logic that determines the order in which the computational modules are executed.

Control unit, I/O
A device attached to a channel that performs such device-dependent I/O functions as interpreting magnetic patterns or generating dot patterns.

Coprocessor
A second processor that works with the main processor.

Coupling
A measure of a module's independence.

CPU
An acronym for central processing unit.

Cracker
A person who breaks into a computer with malicious intent. A person who

breaks into a computer over a communication line.

Cursor
A blinking bar or a small box displayed on the screen that helps you communicate with the computer.

Cylinder
On a disk, one position of the read/write heads that defines a family of tracks, one on each surface.

Data
Facts.

Data capture
The process of recording data.

Data communication
The act of transmitting data from one component to another.

Data Control Language (DCL)
A database tool used to perform such activities as backing up files, keeping track of user names and passwords, and monitoring system performance.

Data Definition Language (DDL)
A database language that is used to specify file structures, relationships, schema, and subschema.

Data dependency
The state of a program whose logic is so tightly linked to the data that changing the structure of the data will almost certainly require changing the program.

Data dictionary
A collection of data about a system's data.

Data element
The smallest unit of data that has logical meaning. A unit of data that cannot be logically subdivided.

Data Encryption Standard (DES)
A national standard data encryption standard.

Data entry
The process of converting data to electronic form.

Data flow diagram
A logical model that shows the relationships between a system's processes, data, and boundaries.

Data integrity
The state of a database that is protected against loss or contamination. Data integrity is ensured by carefully controlling and managing data entry, data maintenance, and data access from the time the data first enter the system until they are of no further use.

Data management
Capturing, entering, storing, maintaining, and retrieving data.

Data Manipulation Language (DML)
A database language that is used to access and maintain the database.

Data normalization
A formal technique for organizing entities and attributes into efficient, easy to maintain fields, records, and files.

Data processing
Performing calculations, selecting, filtering, summarizing, and otherwise manipulating data in an attempt to clarify underlying patterns.

Data redundancy
A state that occurs when the same data are stored in two or more different files.

Data structure
A rule (or set of rules) for organizing data. A set of data elements that are stored, manipulated, or moved together.

Data transfer time
Following seek time and rotational delay, the time required to physically transfer data between memory and a disk's surface.

Database
A set of related files.

Database administrator (DBA)
The person in an organization who is responsible for the data.

Database management system (DBMS)
A system software routine that defines the rules for accessing the database.

Database software
Application software that allows a user to create, access, manage, and maintain a database.

DCL
Acronym for data control language.

DDE
Acronym for dynamic data exchange.

Debug
To remove errors from program code.

Decision block
A block of program logic in which the result of a logical comparison determines which instructions are executed.

Decision support system (DSS)
An information system that adds the local processing needed by tactical management to a management information system base.

Decrypt
To translate an encrypted message to plain text.

Dedicated line
A line that is permanently assigned for a specific purpose.

Delete, record
To delete a record from a file or a database.

Demand report
A one-time report that summarizes selected data in response to an unscheduled query.

Demodulation
Extracting information from a carrier signal.

DES
Acronym for Data Encryption Standard.

Design
The phase that follows analysis in the system development life cycle. During design the analyst decides how to solve the problem.

Desktop publishing
Application software that allows you to lay out a page that combines text and graphic images.

Detail report
A report that includes one line for each source transaction.

Development
The phase in the system development life cycle during which the system is created.

Device driver
A routine that holds the control instructions that are unique to a given peripheral device.

Dialogue
A set of screens and the rules for using them that together allow the computer and the user to exchange information.

Digital
A signal or data in the form of discrete digits. On a computer, digital usually implies binary.

Digitize
To convert data to a pattern of (often binary) digits.

Direct access
Selecting a specific record from the database.

Directory
A list of the addresses of every program and every set of data stored on a disk.

Disk
The most common type of secondary storage. A thin, disk-shaped platter coated with a magnetic material on which data can be stored.

Disk address
A track, a side, and a sector.

Disk cache
Pronounced "disk cash." A portion of main memory set aside to simulate a disk.

Disk drive
A device that reads and writes a disk.

Diskette
A disk-shaped secondary storage medium that can be inserted into and removed from a disk drive by a user.

Dispatcher
The operating system routine that decides which program is executed next.

Dispatching priority
The order in which programs are executed.

Display screen
An output device that resembles a television screen. Also know as a monitor.

Document
A logically complete unit of data, such as a term paper, that does not follow the traditional field/record/file data hierarchy.

Documentation
Flow diagrams, charts, comments, and other materials that explain a program's logic.

Domain
The range of values that can be assigned to a given attribute.

Domain name
An Internet address.

Dot-matrix printer
A printer that uses pins to form characters and graphic images as patterns of dots.

Dots-per-inch (DPI)
A common measure of print quality.

Dot pitch
On a display screen, the space between adjacent pixels.

DRAM
Acronym for Dynamic Random Access Memory.

DSS
Acronym for decision support system.

Dumb terminal
A terminal that contains no processor and thus operates only in response to commands from a computer.

Dynamic data exchange (DDE)
A technique for combining in a single document information (text, charts, graphic images, sound clips, spreadsheets) created by several different applications.

Dynamic memory management
A memory management technique in which the available memory is treated as a large pool of free space, and each program is dynamically assigned exactly as much memory as it needs.

EBCDIC
Acronym for Expanded Binary Coded Decimal Interchange Code. A common computer code.

EIS
Acronym for executive information system.

Electronic data interchange (EDI)
Data communication between two companies.

Electronic data processing (EDP)
An early computer system that processed applications primarily in batch mode.

Electronic spreadsheet
An application program that simulates a spreadsheet on the screen.

E-mail
Electronic messages input to one computer and transmitted to another computer.

Encapsulation
Hiding implementation details by enclosing data and methods inside an object.

Encrypt
To convert data to a secret code.

End user
A person who needs the output generated by application software. A person who actually uses all or part of the system at an operational level.

End-user computing
Processing activities performed under the direct control of an end user.

Entity
A person, place, activity, or thing about which data are stored.

Entity-relationship diagram
A logical model of the relationships between the system's primary data entities.

EPROM
Acronym for erasable programmable read-only memory.

Ethics
The study of the general nature of morals and of the specific moral choices to be made by a person.

Exception report
A report that shows only exceptions.

Execution time (E-time)
The phase of a machine cycle during which a single instruction is executed by the arithmetic and logic unit.

Executive information system (EIS)
An information system that adds strategic information and executive tools to a decision support system base.

Expansion slot
A socket-like opening on a bus into which integrated circuit boards are plugged. The physical mechanism for adding peripherals and other components to a microcomputer.

Expert system
A computer program that simulates (or emulates) the thought processes of a human expert.

Expert system shell
An expert system's user interface.

Explanation facility
An expert system feature that explains the logic the expert system followed to reach a conclusion.

Extension
A three-character addition to a DOS file name.

Facsimile transmission (FAX)
A facsimile or copy (similar to a photocopy) of a document that is transmitted over telephone lines.

FAT
Acronym for file allocation table.

Fault-tolerant computer
A computer that is designed to automatically sense and bypass a failed component.

Feasibility study
A preliminary system study intended to determine if the problem can be solved before significant resources are allocated. The purpose of a feasibility study is to demonstrate technical, economic, and operational feasibility.

Fetch
To transfer a copy of an instruction or data from memory to the processor.

Fiber-optic cable
A strand of glass fiber that can transmit impressive amounts of data at high speed with little or no distortion.

Field
A group of related characters.

File
A group of related records.

File allocation table (FAT)
An index to the disk's sectors used by the operating system to keep track of which sectors are allocated to which files.

File name
A logical name assigned by a user to a file.

File system
An operating system routine that helps the user keep track of files.

File transfer protocol (FTP)
An Internet protocol for copying files from one computer to another.

Filter
A set of logical conditions defined in a database query.

Firewall
A software routine that screens all communication between the network and the system and allows only authorized transactions to get through.

Firmware
Permanent software implemented in ROM.

Fixed partition memory management
A memory management technique that divides the available space into fixed-length partitions and loads one task into each partition.

Flash memory
A type of EPROM that can be erased and reprogrammed by a personal computer without using special equipment.

Flat-file database
A single, spreadsheet-like table that is not linked with any other files.

Flat-panel display
A thin display screen, such as the screen found on a laptop computer.

Floating-point
A type of numeric data that emulates scientific notation on a computer.

Floppy disk
A 5.25-inch diskette.

Folder
A directory.

Font
A complete set of characters in one typeface and size.

Foreground
In a multiprogramming system, the partition or region that holds the high priority program.

Format
To prepare a disk for use. The process (usually performed by the operating system) of electronically recording a track/sector pattern and necessary control tables on a disk's surface.

Formula
In a spreadsheet, an algebra-like expression for computing the value of a cell.

Front-end processor
A dedicated computer (often, a minicomputer) that takes care of the details of data communication, transferring data to and accepting data from the mainframe at the mainframe's convenience.

FTP
Acronym for file transfer protocol.

Full-duplex
A line that can transmit in both directions at the same time.

Functional decomposition
To break down (or decompose) a program into small, independent units

called modules based on the processes or tasks they perform.

Gateway
A computer that links dissimilar networks.

Gigabyte (GB)
Approximately one billion bytes.

Gopher
An improved, menu-based version of Archie that allows a user to locate a file and transfer a copy to his or her computer.

Grammar checker
A common word processing feature that checks a document's syntax, punctuation, and so on.

Graphic image
Computer data in such forms as art, a photograph, or an animation.

Graphic user interface (GUI)
An interface that utilizes windows, boxes, icons, and other graphical elements to provide the user with visual cues. Generally, the user chooses an option by pointing and clicking with a mouse.

Groupware
Software that supports cooperative group efforts over a network.

Hacker
Originally, an expert programmer with a knack for creating elegant solutions to difficult problems. Today the term is more commonly applied to someone who illegally breaks into computer systems.

Half-duplex
A line that can transmit data in both directions, but in only one direction at a time.

Hard copy
A printed copy.

Hard disk
A high capacity disk that is often located inside the computer cabinet. A hard disk is faster and has greater storage capacity than a diskette.

Hardware
A general term for a computer's physical components.

Heuristic
A general decision-making rule derived from experience, common sense, inferences, and intelligent trial and error.

Hierarchical database
A database in which the files are linked to form a hierarchy.

Hierarchical network
A network in which the computers are linked to form a hierarchy.

History file
A file of already processed transactions.

Home page
The starting point for browsing (or surfing) the World Wide Web. The first page you see when you link to a Web site.

Host
A network computer that performs end-user tasks.

html
Acronym for hypertext markup language.

http
Acronym for hypertext transport protocol.

Hypermedia
The multimedia version of hypertext that links text, graphics, sounds, videos, and so on.

Hypertext
A method for defining logical pointers that link one text passage to another.

Hypertext markup language (html)
A programming language for creating and maintaining home pages and hypertext/hypermedia links.

Hypertext transport protocol (http)
A World Wide Web protocol that follows hypertext links to jump from computer to computer.

Icon
A picture or symbol that represents a program or a file.

If-then-else
Another name for a selection block.

Impact printer
A printer that forms characters and images by physically striking the paper.

Implementation
The system development life cycle phase during which the new system is created.

Index
A list of the keys and locations of each record in a file.

Indexed sequential file
A file in which the records are physically stored in sequential order and indexed. Consequently, the records can be accessed sequentially or directly.

Inference engine
An expert system routine that analyzes a knowledge base and arrives at a conclusion.

Information
The meaning that human beings assign to or extract from data.

Information superhighway
A merger of today's computing, television, and communication technologies that promises to dwarf existing information services.

Information system
A set of hardware, software, data, human, and procedural components intended to provide the right data and information to the right person at the right time.

Initial program load (IPL)
The process of starting a mainframe computer.

Ink-jet printer
A printer that forms characters and images by spraying tiny droplets of ink onto the paper.

Input
The act of entering data into a computer.

Input device
A hardware component used to input data to a computer.

Input/output control system (IOCS)
The operating system routine that bridges the gap between the user's request for data and the specific hardware operations needed to physically access them.

Input/process/output cycle
The standard cycle of an application program in which data are input and processed and the results are output.

Instruction
One step in a program.

Instruction control unit
The processor component that fetches an instruction from memory.

Instruction counter
A special register that holds the address of the next instruction to be executed.

Instruction register
A special register that holds the next instruction to be executed.

Instruction set
The complete set of instructions a computer is capable of executing.

Instruction time (I-time)
The phase of a machine cycle during which the instruction control unit fetches and decodes a single instruction.

Integer
A whole number with no fractional part.

Integrated program
A program that incorporates several applications, for example, word processing, spreadsheet, database, and presentation graphics.

Integrated Services Digital Network (ISDN)
A network that is emerging from the existing worldwide telephone network and promises someday to replace the current system.

Intelligent terminal
A terminal that contains its own processor and thus can perform certain functions on its own.

Interactive processing
A form of information processing in which a user exchanges information with the computer interactively.

Interface
An entity that links two or more components.

Interface board
A board used to attach a peripheral device to a computer.

Internet
A well-known, widely accessed, world-wide network of networks. The set of continuously connected computers that use TCP/IP.

Interpreter
A program that reads a single source statement, translates it to machine level, executes the resulting instructions, and then moves on to the next source statement.

Interrupt
An electronic signal that causes the computer to stop what it is doing and activate one of the operating system's interrupt service routines.

I/O
An acronym for input/output.

I/O control unit
A device attached to a channel that performs such device-dependent I/O functions, such as interpreting magnetic patterns or generating dot patterns.

IOCS
Acronym for input/output control system.

IO.SYS
The MS-DOS routine that communicates directly with hardware.

IPL
Acronym for initial program load.

ISDN
Acronym for Integrated Services Digital Network.

ISO/OSI
Acronym for International Standards Organization/Open Systems Interconnection. A network model that specifies seven interconnection layers.

Iteration
A logic block in which the instructions are executed repetitively as long as an initial condition holds (DO WHILE) or until a terminal condition is met (DO UNTIL).

Join
To merge or combine data from two or more relations (tables or files).

Kernel
An operating system routine that holds the instructions that deal directly with the hardware.

Kerning
On a printed or displayed document, considering the relationship between adjacent characters to yield optically even letter spacing.

Key
A field that uniquely defines a single occurrence of an entity.

Keyboard
A device for entering input data in character form.

Kilobyte (KB)
Approximately 1000 bytes. Because a computer is an electronic machine, the term kilobyte actually refers to 1024 bytes.

Knowledge
Understanding.

Knowledge acquisition facility
An expert system feature used to create a knowledge base.

Knowledge base
The set of data, information, and decision-making rules around which an expert system is constructed.

Knowledge engineer
The person who creates a knowledge base.

Label
A character (non-numeric) value in a spreadsheet cell.

Laser printer
A nonimpact printer that works much like a photocopier.

Latency
The time that elapses between the processor's initial request for data and the actual start of data transfer. The sum of seek time and rotational delay.

Leased line
A private communication line leased or rented from a common carrier.

Letter-quality printer
A printer that forms complete, solid characters and produces a clean, sharp impression with typewriter-like quality.

Line
A general term for a communication medium. The physical path over which the message flows.

Link
A general term for a communication medium. The physical path over which the message flows.

List
The most basic data structure.

Local
Nearby. In close proximity to.

Local area network (LAN)
A network composed of computers that are located in a limited area.

Lock
To make a file or record unavailable for use.

Logic bomb
A program that (symbolically) blows up in memory and damages software or data.

Logical drive (or Logical disk)
A partition on a hard disk that appears to the programmer or the user to be a different disk drive.

Logical I/O
The input or output of a logical record.

Logical model
A model that exists on paper, in a computer, or in the analyst's imagination. A logical model can be manipulated and modified quickly and inexpensively.

Logical record
The set of related fields needed to complete one input, process, output cycle of a program.

Loop
Another name for an iteration block.

Machine cycle
The process of fetching and executing a single instruction.

Machine language
The binary instructions that are stored in memory and actually control a computer.

Machine learning
An area of artificial intelligence research.

Machine-level instruction
A program instruction that is actually executed by the computer's hardware.

Macintosh
A popular microcomputer operating environment developed by Apple Corporation.

Macro
A routine, often written by a user, that performs an application-specific task in the context of a more general program.

Macro instruction
An assembly language instruction that generates more than one machine-level instruction.

Magnetic ink character recognition (MICR)
The magnetic characters printed on the bottom of a check.

Magnetic medium
An input medium that relies on magnetic properties.

Magnetic strip card
A credit-card size card with a strip of magnetic tape on the back. A common banking medium.

Magnetic tape
A type of secondary storage that is often used as a backup medium.

Mail merge
A software routine used to prepare letters by merging the data from a name and address file with a template.

Main memory
The memory that is directly connected to the processor via the internal bus.

Main processor
The central processing unit.

Mainframe
A large, relatively expensive computer used to support information processing at the corporate level.

Maintenance
A system development life cycle phase that begins after the system is released to the user. The purpose of maintenance is to keep the system operating at an acceptable level.

Maintenance programmer
A programmer who maintains existing software.

MAN
Acronym for metropolitan area network.

Management information system (MIS)
An information system that combines such attributes as centralized data management, integrated applications, distributed access, and interactive processing to provide the information needed to support operational (and some tactical) decision making.

Management information systems (MIS)
An academic discipline that studies computers and information management in a business environment.

Master file
A permanent data file.

Megabyte (MB)
Approximately one million bytes.

MegaHertz
One million cycles per second. A common measure of clock speed.

Member
A child record in a network database.

Memory
The hardware component on which data and results are held or stored inside a computer.

Memory management
Allocating memory space to application programs.

Memory protection
On a multitasking system, a scheme that restricts each task to its own partition or region and prevents tasks from interfering with each other.

Menu
A list of available commands or other options.

Message
The packet of information to be transmitted.

Method
A procedure associated with an object.

Metropolitan area network (MAN)
A high-speed network that links computers separated by up to 50 miles.

MICR
Acronym for magnetic ink character recognition.

Microcode
A layer of integrated circuits that translate machine- level instructions into the appropriate Boolean operations.

Microcomputer
A computer built around a single-chip microprocessor.

Microprocessor
A complete processor on a single chip.

Minicomputer
A mid-size computer that is often used to support the computing needs of a department or an office.

MIPS
An acronym for one million instructions per second. A common measure of processor speed.

MIS
Acronym for management information system.

Modem
A modulator/demodulator. A device that converts (or modulates) a signal from digital to analog and back again.

Modulation
Adding intelligence to a carrier signal.

Module
A portion of a larger program that performs a specific task. *See also* routine.

Monitor
An output device that resembles a television screen. Also, known as a display screen.

Monospacing
In a printed or displayed document, assigning the same amount of space to each character without regard for the character's size.

Motherboard
The board that holds the processor.

Mouse
A pointing device used to select objects or menu choices on a computer screen.

MS-DOS
A popular microcomputer operating system developed by Microsoft Corporation.

MSDOS.SYS
The MS-DOS routine that deals with logical input and output operations.

Multidrop line
A single line that links several terminals or workstations to a computer.

Multimedia
The combined use of several media, including text, graphics, animation, moving pictures, slides, music, sound, and lighting, in a single application.

Multiple-bus architecture
A computer with more than one bus.

Multiplexor
A device that merges (or overlaps) messages from several low-speed lines and transmits the resulting single stream of data over a high-speed line.

Multipoint line
A single line that links several terminals or workstations to a computer.

Multiprocessing
Two or more processors sharing the same memory.

Multiprogramming
The act of concurrently executing two or more programs on a single processor by taking advantage of the speed disparity between the computer and its peripheral devices.

Multitasking
The act of concurrently executing two or more tasks on a single processor.

Natural language processing
A subfield of artificial intelligence that focuses on developing hardware and software to allow people to communicate with computers in much the same way they communicate with each other.

Network
Two or more computers linked by communication lines.

Network database
A database in which links or pointers can be defined to describe relationships between any two files in any direction.

Network operating system
The operating system that manages a network and controls network servers, network controllers, bridges, and gateways.

Network server
The computer that controls a local area network.

Newsgroup
A USENET discussion group devoted to a single topic.

Node
A single computer (or terminal) on a network. Generally, an addressable point on a network.

Node (hypertext/hypermedia)
The basic unit of hyperinformation (analogous to a single index card). A given node can hold text, a graphic

image, a video clip, a sound clip, a window, the name of a program on a remote computer, and so on.

Noise
Electronic interference.

Nonimpact printer
A printer that forms characters and images without physically striking the paper.

Nonprocedural language
A programming language that allows the programmer to simply define the logical operation and let the language translator decide how to perform it. Sometimes called a fourth-generation or declarative language.

Object
A thing about which data are stored and manipulated.

Object class
A set of similar objects. *See also* class, object type.

Object linking and embedding (OLE)
A technique for combining in a single document information (text, charts, graphic images, sound clips, spreadsheets) created by several different applications.

Object module
A binary, machine-language translation of a set of source code that can be loaded into memory and executed.

Object-oriented
An approach to programming that focuses on objects.

Object-oriented database
A database of objects.

Object type
A set of similar objects. *See also* class, object class.

Occurrence
A single instance of an entity.

OCR
Acronym for optical character recognition.

OEM
Acronym for original equipment manufacturer.

Office automation
Automating and/or electronically supporting such office tasks as preparing, storing, and retrieving documents, managing time, managing voice mail and e-mail, coordinating meetings, making presentations, monitoring a budget, and so on.

OLE
Acronym for object linking and embedding.

On-line
Directly linked to a computer.

Open
To prepare a file for use.

Open architecture
A published, widely available computer design for which firms other than the original manufacturer can make compatible boards, peripherals, and even copies (called clones) of the computer.

Open Systems Interconnection (OSI)
An International Standards Organization network model that specifies seven interconnection layers.

Operand
The portion of a machine-level instruction that specifies the address of data to be processed by the instruction.

Operating environment
A particular operating system running on a particular computer. Also known as a platform.

Operating system
System software that defines a platform or operating environment for writing and executing application programs.

Operation
An external view of an object that can be accessed by other objects.

Operation code
The portion of a machine-level instruction that specifies the operation to be performed.

Optical character recognition (OCR)
A technique for reading printed characters optically.

Optical medium
A data medium that is read optically.

Original equipment manufacturer (OEM)
The manufacturer of a hardware component.

OS/2
A microcomputer operating system developed by IBM Corporation.

OSI
An acronym for Open Systems Interconnection.

Output
The act of obtaining data or results from a computer.

Output device
A hardware component used to output data and results from a computer.

Overlay
Storing a program module in the memory space previously occupied by another, no longer needed module of the same program.

Owner
A parent record in a network database.

Packet switching
A network management technique in which the carrier accepts a message, divides it into a series of small blocks (called packets), and then simultaneously transmits the packets from multiple sources over the line. At the other end of the line, the packets are reassembled to form the original messages and sent on to their destinations.

Page
A fixed-length unit of memory.

Page description language
A programming language that defines text, graphic images, fonts, and other elements in a form that makes sense to the printer.

Parallel
Transmitting two or more bits simultaneously.

Parallel processing
Assigning several processors to work simultaneously on different aspects of the same program.

Parent
A high-level record in a hierarchical database.

Parity
An extra bit added to a byte to help reduce errors.

Parser
A routine that separates (or parses) an input string into individual words and, essentially, diagrams the sentence.

Partition, memory
A fixed-length unit of memory that holds a single task.

Password
A secret code used to log onto a computer or a network.

PCMCIA card
Acronym for PC Memory Card International Association. A credit-card-size adapter that plugs into a standard slot on many portable computers.

Peer-to-peer network
A network on which every computer can access the files and peripherals on every other network computer, thus eliminating the need for a server.

Pen-based computer
A computer that supports handwritten or hand-marked input.

Peripheral
A hardware component that is external to the computer.

Personal computer
A microcomputer system that is designed to be used by one person at a time.

Personal digital assistant (PDA)
A hand-held electronic device that integrates several personal productivity tools.

Personal finance software
Application programs that perform such tasks as managing a checking account, tracking a stock portfolio, or computing income tax.

Personal information management software (PIM)
Such software as an electronic calendar, a note pad, and a card file that supports an individual's daily activities.

PGP
Acronym for Pretty Good Privacy. A public domain data encryption standard.

Physical I/O
The physical transfer of data between memory and a peripheral device.

Physical record
The set of related fields that are physically stored together in the same file.

Physical system
A working system with real, physical components.

Picture element (pixel)
A single dot on a graphic display.

PIM
Acronym for personal information management.

Pitch
The number of characters printed or displayed per inch.

Pixel
A picture element.

Platform
A particular operating system running on a particular computer. Also known as an operating environment.

Plotter
A device for creating hard copy graphic output.

Point size
The size of a character measured in points. A point is roughly $1/72$ of an inch.

Polling
A network management technique. The terminals or workstations on the network are sent a polling signal in turn, and can transmit only in response to that signal.

Port
A plug (and associated electronics) that allows a user to physically connect a terminal or a workstation to a network or a peripheral device to an interface board.

Postrelease review
A review of the system development process conducted after the system is released.

Power supply
A device that conditions the power and feeds the appropriate voltage to a computer.

Presentation graphics
Application software that allows a user to create graphic images.

Pretty Good Privacy (PGP)
A public domain data encryption standard.

Primitive command
A command that tells a peripheral device to perform one of its basic operations.

Print preview
A feature of many application programs that allows the user to see a document on the screen exactly as it will appear when printed.

Printer
An output device that prints data and results on paper.

Privacy
The state of being free from unsanctioned intrusion.

Private line
A private communication line leased or rented from a common carrier.

Problem definition
The first step in the system development life cycle.

Procedural language
A programming language that requires the programmer to write a step-by-step procedure to tell the computer exactly how to perform a logical operation.

Procedure
Guidelines, rules, and instructions that tell people how to perform a task.

Process
A set of steps for performing a task. An activity that transforms data in some way.

Process bound
An application in which so many computations are performed that the computer spends most of its time actually processing data and relatively little time on input or output.

Process flowchart
A graphic depiction of the flow of logic through a process.

Processor
The component that manipulates the data.

Processor management
A set of techniques for managing and allocating the processor's time.

Program
A set of instructions that guides a computer through a process.

Program generator
A program that starts with information in graphical, narrative, list, or some other logical form and outputs the appropriate source code.

Programmer
A person who writes computer programs.

Project
To extract the requested attributes from a set of selected tuples.

Project leader
The person in charge of a temporary project team.

Project management software
Application software for organizing and managing a project team.

PROM
Acronym for programmable read-only memory.

Prompt
A message from the operating system that tells the user that the command processor is ready to accept a command.

Proportional spacing
Allocating space to characters in proportion to character size.

Protocol
A set of rules that governs data communication.

Prototype
A working, physical model of a system.

Prototyping
An alternative to logical modeling in which a working, physical model of the system is created.

Pseudocode
A rough approximation of a programming language that ignores many syntax details. Used to plan program logic.

Public domain software
Software that is available free to anyone who wants to use it.

QBE
Acronym for query-by-example.

Query
A question. Usually, a request for data or information.

Query-by-example (QBE)
A common database feature that allows a user to define a query by, essentially, outlining an example of the desired output.

Query language
A language for specifying queries.

Queuing
Placing pending programs in an electronic waiting line.

Rabbit
A program that replicates itself until no memory is left and no other programs can run.

RAID
An acronym for Redundant Array of Inexpensive Disks.

RAM
See random access memory.

RAM disk
A disk cache.

Random access
Selecting a specific record from the database.

Random access memory (RAM)
The type of main memory used on most computers.

Rapid prototyping
Developing nonoperational mockups of a system's input and output interfaces (screen layouts, printed reports, and so on) rather than a full, working prototype.

Read
To extract the contents of one or more bytes or words from memory without changing them.

Read-only memory (ROM)
A type of memory that can be read but not modified.

Ready state
The state of a program that is ready to be executed.

Real-time
An application in which the computer responds immediately to events as they occur and (typically) provides feedback to influence or control those events.

Record
A group of related fields.

Recovery
Restoring a computer system and/or a set of data files after a disaster.

Redundant
Stored repetitively in two or more places.

Region
A dynamically allocated, variable-length unit of memory that holds a single task.

Register
A temporary storage device in the processor that holds control information, current data, and intermediate results.

Relation
A table (analogous to a file) in a relational database.

Relational database
A database in which the files can be visualized as two-dimensional tables or spreadsheets.

Relationship
A logical link between two files.

Relative record
A record's location relative to the beginning of a file.

Release
The act of turning a system over to the user.

Remote
Distant.

Report
A listing of data or information. *See* demand report, exception report, summary report.

Report writer
A common database feature that allows a user to quickly generate a report by specifying the contents.

Repository
A CASE component that holds descriptions of the system's data and processes.

Requirements specification
A document, prepared during the analysis stage of the system development life cycle, that defines exactly what the system must do.

Resident
A routine that stays in memory as long as the computer is running.

Resolution
The level of detail a screen can show, a function of the number of pixels on the screen.

Ring network
A network in which the host computers are linked to form a ring.

RISC
Acronym for Reduced Instruction Set Computer. A computer processor that contains a limited number of very efficient instructions.

Robot
A machine that (sometimes) resembles a human being and is capable of performing a variety of often complex, human-like tasks without direct human control.

Roll-in
On a time-sharing system, to copy a user's workspace from secondary storage into memory.

Roll-out
On a time-sharing system, to copy a user's workspace from memory to secondary storage.

ROM
See read-only memory.

Root directory
A disk's primary directory.

Root record
The top record in a hierarchical database.

Rotational delay
On a disk, after the access mechanism is positioned over the proper track, the time required for the target sector to rotate to the read/write head.

Routine
A set of instructions that performs a specific, limited task. *See also* module.

Row
A horizontal set of cells in a spreadsheet or a table.

Scanner
A device for electronically capturing data and images from paper.

Scheduler
An operating system routine that determines the order in which application programs are loaded into memory.

Scheduling
The task performed by a scheduler.

Schema
A general description of the entire database that shows all the record types and their relationships.

Secondary storage
A nonvolatile form of supplemental memory.

Sector
A sequentially numbered subdivision of a track. Data move between a disk and memory a sector at a time.

Security
Procedures and safeguards designed to protect hardware, software, data, and other system resources from unauthorized access, use, modification, and theft.

Seek time
On a disk, the time required to position the access mechanism over the target track.

Select
To extract specific tuples (rows, or records) from a relation.

Selection
A block of program logic in which the instructions to be executed depend on a condition that cannot be known until execution time.

Sequence
A block of program logic in which the instructions are executed in a fixed order.

Sequential access
A data access technique in which a series of records is processed in sequence.

Serial
One at a time.

Server
A computer that provides a service on a network.

Shareware
A copyright-protected program you can try free of charge. If you decide to keep a shareware program, you are expected to register your copy and pay a small fee.

Shell
Another name for the command processor.

Signal
The means by which two objects communicate.

Signal, communication
The form in which a message moves over a communication line.

Simplex
A line that can transmit data in one direction only.

Single-bus architecture
A type of computer architecture in which all the components are linked by a common bus.

Site license
A legal agreement that allows an organization to distribute numerous copies of the program (on disk or over a network) for a fixed fee.

Slot
A socket-like opening on a bus into which integrated circuit boards are plugged. The physical mechanism for adding peripherals and other components to a microcomputer.

Smart card
A credit card with an embedded integrated circuit chip.

Software
A general term for programs.

Software engineer
A technical expert who plans and designs software, usually system software.

Software license
A legal agreement that gives a user the right to use a given program on a single computer.

Sound board
An integrated circuit board that generates audio output.

Source code
Instructions written by the programmer in an assembler or a compiler language.

Source data automation
Capturing data electronically and entering them immediately to a computer.

Spanned record
A logical record on a disk that is physically stored in two or more sectors.

Speech recognition
Using hardware and software to recognize and interpret human speech.

Spelling checker
A common word processing feature that checks spelling.

Spooling
The act of sending data to a high-speed device (such as a disk) for eventual output to a slow device (such as a printer).

Spreadsheet
See electronic spreadsheet.

SQL
Acronym for structured query language.

SRAM
Acronym for static random access memory.

Star network
A network in which each host is linked to a central machine in a "star" pattern.

Statistical package
A set of application programs that allow a user to perform statistical analysis.

Steering committee
A committee composed of representatives from each of the major user departments that is responsible for authorizing or rejecting information system development proposals.

Stored program
A program that is physically stored in the memory of the computer it controls.

Strategic decision
A decision that affects the entire organization.

String
Data values stored as sets of individual coded characters, generally one character per byte.

Structured English
A tight, highly constrained version of English used to plan program logic.

Structured programming
An approach to programming that calls for decomposing the program into small, independent units called modules based on the processes or tasks they perform.

Structured Query Language (SQL)
A data manipulation language that is common to many database management systems.

Subdirectory
A directory that is stored as a file in another directory.

Subschema
A partial schema that includes only those records and relationships needed by a particular user or class of users.

Suite, software
A set of application programs that are designed to work together.

Summary report
A report that shows counts and totals for groups of transactions.

Supercomputer
The most powerful class of computers.

Swapping
Moving pages between memory and secondary storage.

Switched line
A connection that is established at the time communication begins, maintained while communication is ongoing, and broken when communication ends.

Symbolic address
A variable-like source code reference that is later converted by a compiler or an assembler into a specific memory location.

Symmetrical multiprocessing
An approach to multiprocessing in which the operating system dynamically assigns tasks to the next available main processor.

Synchronous
Transmitting data in large blocks.

System
A set of components that work together to accomplish an objective.

System 7
The Macintosh operating system.

System development life cycle (SDLC)
The systems analyst's methodology.

System flowchart
A diagram that shows how a system's physical components are related.

System integrator
A business that combines hardware, software, and (often) maintenance services to create a complete package.

System programmer
A programmer who specializes in installing and maintaining operating system and other system software.

System software
Software that directly controls and manages the computer's hardware.

System test
A test that follows system development. Its purpose is to ensure that the system meets the user's needs.

Systems analyst
The person who defines the problem, expresses the user's needs in technical terms, and communicates resource requirements to management.

Task
A single program or routine stored in memory and capable of being executed.

TCP/IP
Acronym for Transmission Control Protocol/Internet Protocol.

Telecommuting
Working at home and communicating electronically with your office.

Telnet
An Internet application that uses TCP/IP to link to a remote computer.

Terminal
A keyboard/display unit that allows a user to access a multiple-user computer system or a network.

Thesaurus
An electronic version of a book of synonyms.

Thrashing
On a virtual memory system, spending so much time swapping pages that the processor has little time left to do any processing.

Time bomb
A destructive program that executes at a predetermined time or when certain predetermined conditions are met.

Time-sharing
A multitasking technique that works by dividing the processor's time into small slices and assigning the processor to application routines one time slice at a time.

Time-slicing
Dividing the processor's time into tiny slices as a means of implementing multitasking.

Token passing
A network management technique in which an electronic token is passed continuously around the network and a terminal or workstation can transmit only when it holds the token.

Top-down testing
A software testing technique in which modules are added to a control structure one by one and then tested.

TPS
Acronym for transaction processing system.

Track
A concentric circle around which data are recorded on a disk surface.

Transaction
One occurrence of a business activity; for example, a single customer order or a single shipment from a supplier.

Transaction file
A file of records that describe current transactions.

Transaction processing system (TPS)
A system that accepts and processes operational-level transactions.

Transient
A program that is stored on disk and read into memory when needed. Normally applied to system software routines.

Transient area
A region of memory where application programs and less

essential operating system routines are loaded.

Transmission Control Protocol/Internet Protocol (TCP/IP)
The standard Internet communication protocol.

Tree structure
A directory structure that resembles a tree growing from the root.

Trojan horse
A seemingly harmless program that invites an unsuspecting user to try it.

Tuple
One row in a relational database table (or relation). Analogous to a record.

Typeface
A complete set of characters in a particular design or style.

Uniform Resource Locator (URL)
On the World Wide Web, an address that specifies the path from one home page to another.

UNIX
An operating system developed by AT&T. The de facto Internet standard operating system.

Update, record
To modify the contents of a record.

USENET
The Internet's electronic bulletin board service.

User
The person who needs data or information.

User interface
A set of hardware and software components that define how a user accesses the system.

User manual
The documentation for the user interface.

Utility program
A program that performs a single system function.

Value
A number in a spreadsheet cell.

Value-added carrier
A service that provides relatively low-cost access to high-speed lines by leasing a line from a common carrier and then subleasing the use of the line.

Verification
Obtaining the same data from two different sources, at two different times, or in two different forms and then comparing them.

Veronica
An Internet program that searches (by key word) menus at gopher sites around the world, in effect giving the user access to numerous gophers. An acronym for Very Easy Rodent-Oriented Netwide Index to Computerized Archives.

Version number
A number that tells you when a particular copy of an operating system or an application program was released and what features it contains.

View
A subset of a database that includes only selected fields from the records that meet a set of conditions defined in a logical filter.

Virtual machine
A computing environment created by an operating system that allows a user to behave as though he or she has complete control over an independent computer with its own memory, peripheral devices, and other resources.

Virtual memory
A technique for managing the space requirements of multiple concurrent tasks by dividing memory into a set of fixed-length pages and then swapping pages between memory and secondary storage.

Virtual reality
An application that combines sound, motion, and images in such a way that you feel you are part of the action.

Virus
A program that is capable of replicating itself, attaching itself to a host program, and spreading between computers.

Voice-grade line
A standard 2,400 baud telephone line.

Voice input
The act of directly entering spoken data and commands to a computer.

Voice synthesizer
A device that generates spoken output.

Volatile
Easily changed. A computer's main memory is considered volatile because it loses its contents when power is cut.

WAIS
Acronym for Wide-Area Information Servers. An Internet service that allows a user to search the contents of files based on search criteria that are defined by asking natural language questions.

Wait state
The state of a program that is not ready to execute because it is waiting for the completion of some event, such as an input or output operation.

Walkthrough
A peer review.

WAN
Acronym for wide area network.

What-if analysis
A form of numerical analysis in which you determine the likely outcomes of each alternative and select the option that yields the best outcome.

Wide area network (WAN)
A network that links geographically disbursed computers.

Window
A screen box that holds a message, a menu, or some other unit of information.

Windows
A popular microcomputer operating environment developed by Microsoft Corporation.

Windows 95
An operating system developed by Microsoft Corporation that features a graphic user interface.

Word
A unit of memory composed of two or more bytes.

Word processing
Application software that supports writing text.

Word wrap
A word processing feature that senses when the text has moved beyond the right margin and automatically advances to the next line, thus eliminating the need to press the return key at the end of each line.

Workstation
A microcomputer used to access a network.

World Wide Web
A segment of the Internet that features a simple, graphic, point-and-click navigational system that allows a user to quickly jump from computer to computer all over the world.

Worm
A program that is capable of spreading under its own power.

WORM
Acronym for write once, read many. A type of CD-ROM.

Write
To record new values in memory, thus destroying the old contents.

Write-protect
To set a disk so that data can be read from but not written to it.

WYSIWYG
Acronym for what-you-see-is-what-you-get.

INDEX

Figure credits

35 (Figure 2.1) Reprinted from Forecast 1996 issue of *Money* by special permission, © 1995, Time, Inc., 64 (Figure 3.15) Courtesy of Deluxe Corporation, 170 (Figure 7.24) photos courtesy of Dell Computer Corporation, 367 (Figure 16.10) photos courtesy of Dell Computer Corporation

Photo credits

2 FPG International/The Telegraph Colour Library, 6 photo courtesy of Apple Computer, Inc./John Greenleigh, 8 (top) photo courtesy of Tiger Direct, 8 (bottom right) The Telegraph Colour Library/FPG International, 8 (bottom left) photo courtesy of Intel Corporation, 14 (both) photos courtesy of Dell Computer Corporation, 15 (top left) photo courtesy of International Business Machines Corporation, 15 (top right) photo courtesy of Apple Computer, Inc., 15 (bottom) photo courtesy of International Business Machines Corporation, 16 photo courtesy of International Business Machines Corporation, 20 Courtesy of NCSA/University of Illinois at Urbana-Champaign, 32 FPG International/Peter Beavis, 36 Westlight/Chuck O'Rear, 37 (top left) FPG International/The Telegraph Colour Library, 37 (top right) photo courtesy of Intel Corporation, 37 (bottom) Tony Stone Images/Andy Sacks, 38 (top) Tony Stone Images/Tim Brown, 38 (bottom) photo courtesy of International Business Machines Corporation, 39 photo courtesy of COMPUSA, 40 photo courtesy of Apple Computer, Inc., 41 (both) photos courtesy of International Business Machines Corporation, 42 Tony Stone Images/Jon Riley, 43 AP/Wide World Photos, 52 Tony Stone Images/Phil Jason, 56 (top) photo courtesy of International Business Machines Corporation, 56 (bottom) photo courtesy of Microsoft Corporation, 57 photo courtesy of International Business Machines Corporation, 59 photo courtesy of International Business Machines Corporation, 60 (top) photo courtesy of Microsoft Corporation, 60 (bottom) photo courtesy of Dell Computer Corporation, 61 photo courtesy of Hewlett-Packard Company, 62 photo courtesy of Hewlett-Packard Company, 66 (top) photo courtesy of Norand Corporation, 66 (bottom left) photo courtesy of Hewlett-Packard Company, 66 (bottom right) photo courtesy of Hewlett-Packard Company, 67 photo courtesy of Communication Intelligence Corporation, 68 photo courtesy of International Business Machines Corporation, 69 (top) PhotoEdit/Tom McCarthy, 69 (bottom) photo courtesy of Catalina Marketing Corporation, 76 FPG International/The Telegraph Colour Library, 83 PhotoEdit/Tony Freeman, 89 The Computer Museum, Inc., 93 photo courtesy of Intel Corporation, 95 photo courtesy of Intel Corporation, 100 FPG International/The Telegraph Colour Library, 103 (left) Comstock, Inc., 103 (right) photo courtesy of Quantum Corporation, 104 photo courtesy of International Business Machines Corporation, 105 (top) photo courtesy of Iomega, 105 (bottom) photo courtesy of Pioneer, 120 Tony Stone Images, 124 photo courtesy of Microsoft Corporation, 142 FPG International/Tom Wilson, 156 The Computer Museum, Inc., 172 FPG International/The Telegraph Colour Library, 176 AP/Wide World Photos, 185 Smithsonian Institution, 196 FPG International/The Telegraph Colour Library, 201 photo courtesy of NCR, 204 photo courtesy of International Business Machines Corporation, 220 Tony Stone/J. W. Burkey, 244 FPG International/The Telegraph Colour Library, 246 FPG International/The Telegraph Colour Library, 247 (top) The Stock Market/Clayton J. Price, 247 (bottom) photo courtesy of Tiger Direct, 248 photo courtesy of Apple Computer, Inc., 249 Paul Hansen, 252 photo courtesy of Intel Corporation, 255 photo courtesy of International Business Machines Corporation, 257 photo courtesy of International Business Machines Corporation, 261 The Computer Museum, Inc., 266 Tony Stone Images/Ray Massey, 286 FPG International/The Telegraph Colour Library, 289 photo courtesy of International Business Machines Corporation, 290 The Stock Market/John Feingersh, 297 photo courtesy of U.S. Robotics, 304 FPG International/The Telegraph Colour Library, 326 Tony Stone Images/John Lund, 353 (top) photo courtesy of IriScan, Inc., 353 (bottom left) photo courtesy of Cadix International, Inc., 353 (bottom right) photo courtesy of National Registry, Inc., 358 FPG International/The Telegraph Colour Library, 360 (left) photo courtesy of Cray Research, Inc., 360 (right) photo © Disney Enterprises, Inc., 361 Custom Medical Stock Photo/K. Glasser and Associates, 366 photo courtesy of PictureTel Corporation, 368 photo courtesy of Universal Studios, 370 photo courtesy of Virtual i.O Inc., 371 (top) Photo Researchers, Inc./James King-Holmes, 371 (bottom) The Computer Museum, Inc., 376 Tony Stone Images/Mark Segal, 381 (top) Bettmann Archive, 381 (middle left) Bettmann Archive, 381 (middle center) photo courtesy of International Business Machines Corporation, 381 (bottom left) photo courtesy of The Babbage Institute, 381 (bottom right) Culver Pictures, 382 (both) photos courtesy of International Business Machines Corporation, 383 (top) photo courtesy of International Business Machines Corporation, 383 (bottom) Reprinted with permission of Unisys Corporation, 384 (top) photo courtesy of Unisys Corporation, 384 (bottom left) photo courtesy of International Business Machines Corporation, 384 (bottom right) photo courtesy of International Business Machines Corporation, 385 (top) The Computer Museum, Inc., 385 (center) The Computer Museum, Inc., 385 (bottom) photo courtesy of Apple Computer, Inc., 386 (top) photo courtesy of International Business Machines Corporation, 386 (bottom) photo courtesy of Apple Computer, Inc.,